D1570441

HOLMAN
New
Testament
Commentary

HOLMAN *New Testament* Commentary

I & II *Thessalonians* I & II *Timothy, Titus, Philemon*

GENERAL EDITOR

Max Anders

AUTHOR

Knute Larson

HOLMAN
REFERENCE

Nashville, Tennessee

Holman New Testament Commentary
© 2000 Broadman & Holman Publishers
Nashville, Tennessee

ISBN 0-8054-0209-28

Dewey Decimal Classification: 226.6
Subject Heading: BIBLE. NT. Thessalonians, Titus, Philemon
Library of Congress Card Catalog Number: 98-39365

Larson, Knute.
    1, 2 Thessalonians, 1, 2 Timothy, Titus, Philemon by Knute Larson
      p.   cm. — (Holman New Testament commentary)
    Includes bibliographical references.
    ISBN 0–8054-0209–8 (alk. paper)
  BS2625.3G36   2000   98–39365
  226.6'07—dc21   CIP

5 6 03
D

Contents

Contents

Editorial Preface

Today's church hungers for Bible teaching, and Bible teachers hunger for resources to guide them in teaching God's Word. The Holman New Testament Commentary provides the church with the food to feed the spiritually hungry in an easily digestible format. The result: new spiritual vitality that the church can readily use.

Bible teaching should result in new interest in the Scriptures, expanded Bible knowledge, discovery of specific scriptural principles, relevant applications, and exciting living. The unique format of the Holman New Testament Commentary includes sections to achieve these results for every New Testament book.

Opening quotations from some of the church's best writers lead to an introductory illustration and discussion that draw individuals and study groups into the Word of God. "In a Nutshell" summarizes the content and teaching of the chapter. Verse-by-verse commentary answers the church's questions rather than raising issues scholars usually admit they cannot adequately solve. Bible principles and specific contemporary applications encourage students to move from Bible to contemporary times. A specific modern illustration then ties application vividly to present life. A brief prayer aids the student to commit his or her daily life to the principles and applications found in the Bible chapter being studied. For those still hungry for more, "Deeper Discoveries" take the student into a more personal, deeper study of the words, phrases, and themes of God's Word. Finally, a teaching outline provides transitional statements and conclusions along with an outline to assist the teacher in group Bible studies.

It is the editors' prayer that this new resource for local church Bible teaching will enrich the ministry of group, as well as individual, Bible study, and that it will lead God's people to truly be people of the Book, living out what God calls us to be.

Holman Old Testament
Commentary Contributors

Vol. 1, Genesis
ISBN 0-8054-9461-8
Kenneth O. Gangel and Stephen Bramer

Vol. 2, Exodus, Leviticus, Numbers
ISBN 0-8054-9462-6
Glen Martin

Vol. 3, Deuteronomy
ISBN 0-8054-9463-4
Doug McIntosh

Vol. 4, Joshua
ISBN 0-8054-9464-2
Kenneth O. Gangel

Vol. 5, Judges, Ruth
ISBN 0-8054-9465-0
W. Gary Phillips

Vol. 6, 1 & 2 Samuel
ISBN 0-8054-9466-9
Stephen Andrews

Vol. 7, 1 & 2 Kings
ISBN 0-8054-9467-7
Gary Inrig

Vol. 8, 1 & 2 Chronicles
ISBN 0-8054-9468-5
Winfried Corduan

Vol. 9, Ezra, Nehemiah, Esther
ISBN 0-8054-9469-3
Knute Larson and Kathy Dahlen

Vol. 10, Job
ISBN 0-8054-9470-7
Steven J. Lawson and Kenneth O. Gangel

Vol. 11, Psalms 1-72
ISBN 0-8054-9471-5
Steven J. Lawson

Vol. 12, Psalms 73-150
ISBN 0-8054-9481-2
Steven J. Lawson

Vol. 13, Proverbs
ISBN 0-8054-9472-3
Max Anders

Vol. 14, Ecclesiastes, Song of Songs
ISBN 0-8054-9482-0
David George Moore and Daniel L. Akin

Vol. 15, Isaiah
ISBN 0-8054-9473-1
Trent C. Butler

Vol. 16, Jeremiah, Lamentations
ISBN 0-8054-9474-X
Fred M. Wood and Ross McLaren

Vol. 17, Ezekiel
ISBN 0-8054-9475-8
Mark F. Rooker

Vol. 18, Daniel
ISBN 0-8054-9476-6
Kenneth O. Gangel

Vol. 19, Hosea, Joel, Amos, Obadiah, Jonah, Micah
ISBN 0-8054-9477-4
Trent C. Butler

Vol. 20, Nahum, Habakkuk, Zephaniah, Haggai, Zechariah, Malachi
ISBN 0-8054-9478-2
Stephen R. Miller

Holman New Testament Commentary Contributors

Holman New Testament Commentary

Twelve volumes designed for Bible study and teaching to enrich the local church and God's people.

Series Editor	Max Anders
Managing Editors	Trent C. Butler & Steve Bond
Project Editor	Lloyd W. Mullens
Marketing Manager	Greg Webster
Product Manager	David Shepherd
Page Composition	TF Designs, Mt. Juliet, TN

Introduction to

1 Thessalonians

LETTER PROFILE: FIRST THESSALONIANS

- While in Corinth, Paul, Silas, and Timothy jointly authored a letter to the Christians in Thessalonica around A.D. 51.
- Sent to a young, inexperienced assembly of believers in the city of Thessalonica, many of whom were Gentiles.
- Letter written by Paul, but with the greeting and support of Silas and Timothy who had been with Paul when he first traveled to Thessalonica. The three men were jailed, then run out of town. Timothy was later sent back to encourage the believers.
- Paul praised the Thessalonians' faith; defended his ministry against outsiders' attacks; and laid down basic theology about righteous living in a decaying culture, and the final hope of all believers, both living and dead—eternity with God.

AUTHOR PROFILE: PAUL

- Jewish-born in Tarsus, near the Lebanese border in modern Turkey.
- Roman citizen.
- Prominent, Jewish religious leader, highly educated as a Pharisee.
- Persecuted Christians before his own dramatic conversion in A.D. 35.
- Visited Thessalonica on his second missionary journey about A.D. 51 (see Acts 17). There he witnessed instant conversions followed by strong persecution.
- Known for his tireless pioneer work to Gentiles.
- Imprisoned by Nero's regime in A.D. 67 in Rome (see 2 Tim. 4), where he was executed the next year.

CITY PROFILE: THESSALONICA

- An urban center of the Roman Empire, the city of Thessalonica had strong Greek culture; it was built in 315 B.C. by Cassander, a general under Alexander the Great.
- Located in European Macedonia, present-day Balkans; the city's population in the first century was about two hundred thousand.
- Thessalonica, the capital of Macedonia, was a booming commercial center located at the crossroads of the great road from the north and the main east-west trade route.
- Many foreign merchants lived in the city, making Thessalonica an ethnically and culturally diverse city.

1 Thessalonians 1

A Working Model of a Church

I. INTRODUCTION
Where and Why God Grows Vegetables

II. COMMENTARY
A verse-by-verse explanation of the chapter.

III. CONCLUSION
A Divinely Charged Ability

An overview of the principles and applications from the chapter.

IV. LIFE APPLICATION
In Step with God

Melding the chapter to life.

V. PRAYER
Tying the chapter to life with God.

VI. DEEPER DISCOVERIES
Historical, geographical, and grammatical enrichment of the commentary.

VII. TEACHING OUTLINE
Suggested step-by-step group study of the chapter.

VIII. ISSUES FOR DISCUSSION
Zeroing the chapter in on daily life.

Quote

It is "impossible to separate works from faith—yea, just as impossible as to separate burning and shining from fire."

Martin Luther

1 Thessalonians 1

IN A NUTSHELL

In summary, this is what Paul said to the Thessalonian Christians in chapter 1.

Greetings to the church in the city of Thessalonica, but especially to a group of people connected with our God, who is our constant help. I am so grateful for the loving way you are serving our Lord and each other. His strength has helped you receive his message and model it. People everywhere are talking about the way God has changed you for now and eternity.

A Working Model
of a Church

I. INTRODUCTION

Where and Why God Grows Vegetables

*O*ur next-door neighbor always grows a beautiful garden. With its carrots, beans, peas, squash, and other vegetables, it would be the envy of any neighborhood. Little green shoots poke out of the soil in early spring and continue to grow through the summer. Often I will see our neighbor just standing in the garden munching a green bean; sometimes she is carrying baskets of carrots and tomatoes into her house. It is not that I mind, of course. It is just that our backyard is right next to this burgeoning bit of horticulture. And despite our proximity, our plot has nothing of such vegetables.

Now why would God do that?

Everyone knows that only God can grow vegetables. So why would he favor our neighbor and go barren with us? I own a shovel and spade. I even brought home a free packet of seeds from the gas station once (cannot remember where I put it). Still, it does not seem fair. I keep hoping that a few seeds from next door will blow our way and take root. But, so far, nothing.

Of course it is God who gives the increase. Without the miracle of life which resides in the seed, nothing can happen. Without the grace of God's rain and sun, the seed shrivels. But, as any farmer knows, we have a part to play as well. No one expects a garden to appear spontaneously without some preparation and work. We must plant and water, weed and care.

And so it is with our spirits. God works in the hearts of those who work with him.

The old cliché, "God helps those who help themselves," is horrible theology when it comes to receiving justification. This is a work of God which needs no added effort from us—only our trust. But it teaches a measure of truth when related to abiding in Christ with our faithful obedience.

God gives growth and spiritual strength and results (the fruits of righteousness) to everyone who works on the garden of his heart. And it is no easy task! It requires "work . . . labor . . . and endurance" (1 Thess. 1:3).

The Thessalonians clearly modeled the principle of cooperation with God in living the Christian life as defined in Philippians 2:12–14: "Work out your salvation with fear and trembling, for it is God who works in you to will and to act according to his good purpose. Do everything without complaining or arguing."

The Thessalonians received the message of grace as a call to action and loving service to others. Paul saw this, so he spent his first chapter of 1 Thessalonians applauding them. Then, like the good teacher he was, he reminded them how it all happened.

We can study Paul's insights for help in working on our own hearts. And, like our next-door neighbors, the evidence of this cooperative effort will be in the harvesting.

II. COMMENTARY

MAIN IDEA: *People who receive God's call of grace are changed and strengthened by him to discipline their lives and become effective examples of the grace of Christ. Such Christians form God's idea of a healthy, productive church.*

A Greeting (1:1)

SUPPORTING IDEA: *The church exists only in God the Father and his Son Jesus.*

1:1. First Thessalonians reads like many of Paul's letters, but authorship of the book is attributed equally to Paul, Silas, and Timothy. The reason, most likely, is that all three men were well known to the Thessalonian Christians—Paul and Silas having started the church (Acts 17:1–9), and Timothy later being sent back to instruct and encourage the new believers (it was his report which inspired the letter). Paul was the recognized leader, but the respect and enormous help given by Silas and Timothy prompted the co-authorship; the three men spoke with a single voice.

Their letter was addressed to a gathering of people in a particular city—Thessalonica. Paul, Silas, and Timothy undoubtedly recalled names and faces as they wrote the letter. But, by adding the descriptive phrase "in God the Father and the Lord Jesus Christ," the authors made more precise identity of this group and emphasized its spiritual nature. They wanted the believers to realize that the local church has a spiritual location just as real and even more important than Thessalonica.

This is also true today. God sees the church as specific gatherings of believers, varied in cultural expression and diverse in need and ministry. He also sees the church as the redeemed of all ages. Both realities are important.

Paul's standard greeting, "grace and peace to you," was loaded with reminders that our best health and riches are the personal, relational gifts from God himself. To this greeting, some early manuscripts add the phrase "from God our Father and the Lord Jesus Christ. "Grace" and "peace" are gifts bestowed from the throne room of heaven. Grace is the unmerited favor of God upon which we are so dependent. Peace is a judicial statement related to our daily fellowship with God as well as our eternal standing. The conflict created through sin has been resolved through Jesus Christ, restoring the broken relationship between humankind and God, thereby granting peace and harmony. *Shalom* is the Hebrew counterpart of "peace," meaning wholeness. Peace is a condition of completeness, a work totally finished through Christ, yet progressively realized.

𝔅 What Church People Are Meant to Look Like (1:2–3)

SUPPORTING IDEA: *The discipline of the Christian's heart and life shows in hard work that is long-lasting and based on love.*

1:2. Do not miss the example of love and appreciation expressed for the believers in Thessalonica: **We always thank God for all of you.** Paul was known for his keen awareness of the goodness and graciousness of God. Thankfulness was his constant response. And, as he explained in verse 3, his great joy was the changed lives of people who trusted and followed Jesus Christ. These believers kindled his continual praise of thanksgiving.

Paul not only thanked *God* for these brothers and sisters in the faith, he also was not afraid to tell them personally how much he appreciated them. It is a good reminder to all of us to express our "thanks" out loud.

1:3. Paul often made parallel statements, re-emphasizing particular feelings or thoughts. So when he wrote that **We continually remember,** he was underscoring the fact that Paul, Silas, and Timothy constantly prayed for the Thessalonians. They were a source of delight. In this section the authors listed what they found so admirable in these believers.

The people's **work produced by faith** was commended first. Faith always leads to works. According to the apostle James, "faith without deeds is dead" (Jas. 2:26). But rather than debating the nuances of the lordship/salvation issue—whether a person can belong to Christ and do little, or how much believers should work for Christ—we should first be sure of our own hearts.

Second, their "labor" was **prompted by love.** Labor involves cost, fatigue, and exhaustion. Love here is the Greek word *agape,* meaning unselfish, sacrificial living for others. Love, along with faith, drives us in our faith.

Believers would do well to check their lives and schedules and notice what they do for others out of pure love. The church is not a club we join, a retirement plan we subscribe to, or a competition we enter to win a trophy. It is a family of love where we serve one another. This is possible only because of our relationship with God.

The third commendation given to the Thessalonians was for their **endurance inspired by hope**. This is not passive endurance, but heroic constancy, no matter what the obstacles. Hope always looks forward, beyond now, to a future. For the Thessalonians, as for all believers, hope rests in God's promised eternity. And this assured future makes faith, work, suffering, and love possible. Hope looks to something that is sure, but just not here yet. It is coming.

Our greatest joys and hopes are future. This is a marathon race, not a quick sprint. If we serve because we feel that God has promised good things only in this life, we will be disappointed and may even give up.

All of this is clearly connected with our **Lord Jesus Christ**. Faith, love, and hope are eternal qualities which find their source in God. As Paul later expressed so beautifully in 1 Corinthians 13, they are the way of excellence which can withstand the fires of judgment.

The Gospel Is a Powerful Part of God's Eternal Plan (1:4–5)

SUPPORTING IDEA: *The gospel is more than facts. It is part of an effective, life-stirring energy that God uses to change our lives for his glory and to spread the gospel to others.*

The good news about God's love and Christ's transforming power through his death and resurrection is not a last-minute plan or knee-jerk reaction by God. It is part of a comprehensive strategy conceived before the earth's creation (Eph. 1:4). It is worldwide and eternal (Isa. 49:6). It is from the center of God's heart.

1:4. The credit and gratitude for belonging eternally to God should be given to our Lord. His mercy and love come to us not because of who we are, but because of the kind of person *he* is. Love and election always go together. He rescues those who will respond to his initiations of love and revelation (Eph. 1:4–5; 2 Thess. 2:13).

1:5. The gospel is "the power of God for . . . salvation" (Rom. 1:16). It comes from embracing Jesus, the centerpiece of the gospel. One evidence that salvation is entirely God's work is the way in which it enters our lives. It comes **not simply with words, but also with power.**

The word *power* means the ability to do something. The gospel always comes with inherent power (Heb. 4:12; 1 Cor. 1:18), but its effect depends upon the hearer. There are those for whom the gospel is "simply words"—interesting, perhaps even disturbing—but that is all. The power of the gospel explodes, however, when the hearer allows its truth to penetrate the heart. The Holy Spirit empowers the message so that it comes alive; it stirs the spirit within; it brings conviction and change. God wants us to be his children.

The church is challenged to announce and model the good news for everyone. The rest of the paragraph shows that the Thessalonians were doing this.

This Powerful Gospel Produces Model Lives (1:6–9)

SUPPORTING IDEA: *The church works most effectively when it follows the "imitation model" and the "reputation model," as the Thessalonian church demonstrated.*

1. Imitation Model

1:6. Jesus showed Paul how to live, and even personally instructed him (Gal. 1:12). Paul lived, led, and taught by the example he had received from Christ. In the same manner, the people Paul taught along the way—those in the churches he planted—got their signals from him. He became the model to others, just as Christ was the model to him.

In their letter to the Thessalonians Paul, Silas, and Timothy appealed to the Thessalonians' memory, drawing them back to the lifestyle of the three men when they lived in Thessalonica: **You know how we lived among you for your sake. You became imitators of us and of the Lord.** This pattern forms a great circle of discipleship and leadership which still applies today.

Leaders and teachers in the church are to follow Christ; those in the leaders' care follow after his example; they, in turn, become models of Christlikeness to people outside the church. It was the manner of Christ in Paul, Silas, and Timothy which helped inspire the Thessalonians to follow Christ.

It is a reminder to all of us that it is the image of Jesus in us—the way we model him—that attracts people to become like Christ.

Furthermore, the Thessalonians followed Paul and Christ with determination, **in spite of severe suffering.** Paul and Silas's stay in Thessalonica was shorter than planned due to a riot which the Jews staged (Acts 17:5–10). Friends were arrested, the community shouted accusations, government officials became uneasy, and Paul and Silas escaped to the neighboring town of Berea under cover of darkness. With this background, the church in Thessalonica undoubtedly suffered under suspicion and community unrest. But the Holy Spirit gave them the joy and ability to receive the full message of Christ and to follow him.

Suffering and joy are almost always linked. It is the confirmation of John 15:18–21, that those who follow Christ will suffer as Christ did. As Paul later wrote in his letter to the Philippians, there is fellowship in suffering for Christ, a fellowship with Christ himself (Phil. 3:10). This brings a joy sustained by the Holy Spirit.

1:7. In the first century, the word *model* referred to the mark left by a hammer or die as in the making of a coin, leaving an impression like the original. Thus, the Thessalonian church became a "model" of believers banded together, a prototype of what a church should be.

After commending the local gathering and the way it was living and responding in a hostile culture, Paul, Silas, and Timothy opened the eyes of the Thessalonians to the influence they were having beyond their city. They were connected to a great network of God's kingdom. Their adherence to the faith had become an encouragement and example to other churches. The authors knew that understanding their place in the broader context of God's church would encourage the Thessalonians to continue in faithfulness.

Many believers care about the ways of Christ, and even seek to grow and serve—but primarily as individuals. As good and necessary as our personal efforts are, in the process we can easily forget that there is a distinct model for the local church's actions and reputation. To model Christ is not only a call to each church member, but to the church as a whole. Many involved in church skirmishes need to read and apply this truth.

2. Reputation Model

1:8. Paul next described the "reputation model" for the church—**your faith in God has become known everywhere.** The northern and southern provinces (Macedonia and Achaia) heard about the changes brought about by God in the hearts and actions of the believers in Thessalonica. Reports about their faith were being heard, often carried by unbelievers. As a result, the Lord's message **rang out**, was trumpeted throughout the region. It is a reminder that we have reputations that influence how others respond to our Lord. The vibrancy of our faith can spread the gospel and influence the reception which it receives beyond our area and region.

🄴 This Life-Changing Gospel Is Defined (1:9–10)

SUPPORTING IDEA: *The gospel based on the resurrection of Jesus Christ from the dead brings conversion, hope for the future, and the certainty of judgment.*

1:9–10. By simple observation of the Thessalonian believers, the authors brought out some of the main components of the gospel message as given and activated by our Lord. We see at least these themes:

- Conversion. They **turned to God from idols to serve the living and true God.**
- Future. We **wait for his Son from heaven.**
- Basis. The Son **whom he raised from the dead,** and his work for us.
- Judgment. There is a **coming wrath** to be avoided.

Those who want to avoid the wrath to come should consider that nothing in Paul's succinct rehearsal of the Thessalonians' conversion makes much sense without the reality of judgment.

Why turn from idols to the Lord? Why the need for heaven if there is no hell? Why did Christ die and need to be raised? Why? Because God wanted to save us from the wrath ahead—a wrath exercised in holy justice against a rebellion which lies at the center of our sins.

The only way to avoid **the coming wrath** is by believing that only God is true and rules with authority. Through Jesus Christ the judgment for our sins has been satisfied, and our future belongs with Christ.

MAIN IDEA REVIEW: *People who receive God's call of grace are changed and strengthened by him to discipline their lives and become effective examples of the grace of Christ. Such Christians form God's idea of a healthy, productive church.*

III. CONCLUSION

A Divinely Charged Ability

God does not hand us a book and leave us on our own. The words of his message are filled with power; they are truth, energized by the Holy Spirit. By his divine power he convicts and enlightens those who honestly seek and listen. This applies equally to the questioning unbeliever and to the Christian who desires a closer relationship with God.

It is easy to become so absorbed in strategies for evangelism, methods of discipleship, and programs for effective prayer that we forget the real agent for convincing people of the needs of the heart is the Holy Spirit. He alone can bring change.

Once we become Christians, trusting Christ's ability to restore us to God, we are helped along the way with a divinely charged ability to do what God desires. Even so, the Christian must work hard and have a determined will. Following Christ is built on firm commitment and a resolve to serve God because of the certainty of a future in heaven with him. Sometimes this means great suffering; it always means sacrificial love.

As believers working alongside Christ, we also have the fellowship, love, companionship, and encouragement which comes from participating in a local church. It is God's design. As struggling but faithful followers, we are to bind ourselves to one another in a community of worship and service. As we share our lives together, the church becomes an example of God's kingdom before a watching world. We also encourage other Christian gatherings beyond our neighborhood.

PRINCIPLES

- The message of God, and the Holy Spirit, convict people and change lives.
- Christians are known by hard work, hope, and love.
- The church displays to the world a new community ruled by God and patterned on love.
- Faithfulness to God is rewarded by greater effectiveness and influence.
- The Christian's future is certain, and it includes life with Christ and rescue from God's coming judgment.

APPLICATIONS

- Take the long view of life, looking ahead to a certain eternity with God. This gives proper perspective to your work and produces endurance when setbacks or difficulties come.
- Be a responsible member of a local church, caring for other believers and growing in faith and service.
- Work with God as you commit yourself to spiritual growth and a close relationship with Christ.
- When telling others about Christ, depend upon the power of Scripture and the Holy Spirit.
- Above all, be known by your love—to God, and to others.

IV. LIFE APPLICATION

In Step with God

In our Christian journey we can become confused as we wonder about our part in the process of Christian development. What does God expect me to do?

We can sit back and do nothing, expecting change and growth to occur automatically; we can work at our Christian growth as if everything depended on us; or we can vacillate between the two, holding back with uncertainty at times, taking the task in hand at others.

But there is a better way. In writing to the believers in Thessalonica, Paul commended a spiritual growth based on relationship. We see God initiating an action and the Thessalonians responding in faith and love.

All of us long for a close bond with others; we desire intimacy and acceptance. And while we realize that we can know God personally, we often find ourselves confused in the day-by-day interchange between ourselves and the Lord.

The solution to our uncertainty is to focus less on tasks and more on our responses. This turns our attention away from trying to figure out what God is doing. We learn to take the biblical principles which God has given and turn them to our daily circumstances as well as the unconquered territory of our hearts and wills. Rather than following a simple checklist of how to behave, God wants us to live through the continual development of a relationship with him. We can do this by developing a sensitivity to his Spirit, a greater knowledge of his revelation, and a stronger commitment to obedience. Then we will continue to change and deepen within ourselves. This strengthens the bond of love between ourselves and God, accomplishing what rules and duty never could.

God made the first move by choosing the Thessalonians, empowering the words of Paul, and convicting the listeners. The Thessalonians responded to the initiations of God, turning from idols and imitating Paul and Christ. Their exemplary reaction was evidenced by their hard work of love and their perseverance in the face of hardship. God responded to their faithfulness by implanting within these believers a supernatural joy. God and the Thessalonians interacted with each other—they lived in relationship.

In a relationship there is often such beautiful harmony between two people that they seem to move as one. But the truth is that someone does direct the movements, just as one person must take the lead in a dance.

So it is in our Christian life. The beauty of our faith is most apparent when Christ is our lead and we follow in intimate closeness, keeping "in step with the Spirit" (Gal. 5:25). We live in relationship with a living God who initiates, empowers, and responds to us. We must respond to his leading, his movements, his designs. We must respond to the graces of his Spirit by allowing *him* to captivate our hearts day by day.

V. PRAYER

God, give us the determination to follow you in a close and intimate relationship. Keep us from looking for quick formulas and give us the courage to follow the promptings of your Spirit. Keep our hearts and minds open to change. Help us to value your will as revealed in the Bible, so that we respond in holiness to all of life. Amen.

VI. DEEPER DISCOVERIES

A. Church (v. 1)

Paul addressed his letter "to the church of the Thessalonians." The Greek term *ekklesia*, which is translated into English as "church," has decidedly religious references in most cultures today. In the Roman society of Paul's day, however, *ekklesia* had no such religious connotations. It can just as easily be translated as "meeting" or "gathering." In the first century, it described political meetings, fraternal gatherings, and social get-togethers. At this point in the Greco-Roman world, small group gatherings, voluntary organizations, fraternal and cult associations were quite popular. The early church fit easily into this milieu.

So, it was not the fact of gathering which was unique. What distinguished the meeting of Christian believers was that they met "in God the Father and the Lord Jesus Christ." That, more than the fact of meeting together, is what differentiated this group from all others. If we could rephrase it, we might say, "Who called this meeting?" And the reply would be, "God the Father and the Lord Jesus Christ." Because the meeting was called by God, the practices of the community of believers, as well as the words given to them, carried divine power. In turn, such a meeting carried with it serious responsibilities that each believer would feel toward one another and the community at large.

B. Chosen (v. 4)

The "brothers [and sisters] loved by God" at Thessalonica were "chosen," as Paul reminded them—chosen by God, as a gift of mercy and an act of sovereignty.

Over the centuries, Calvinist and Armenian theologians have debated the issue of man's free will and God's sovereignty. Unfortunately, both viewpoints have been defended in exclusive terms, as though believing in God's sovereignty negates a person's will; or that admitting to an active will in people destroys God's sovereignty. And as long as human beings try to comprehend the mysteries of an infinite God, the debate is certain to continue.

We can be certain that our Lord drew us to himself (John 6:44), and that he also extends an invitation to choose: "Come to me, all you who are weary and burdened" (Matt. 11:28). He did not say, "all you who are chosen." Paul echoed this double-sided grace when he declared the Thessalonian believers to be "chosen by God," and then went on to commend their efforts—their welcome of the message (1:6), their strength of will and purpose, and their work and efforts to obey the gospel, live it, and share it (1:3,7,9).

God's sovereign purposes and individual choice exist together. But the important thing is to focus our attention on God. No one in his right mind debates whether we deserve to belong to God as his children. He is the God of love. He is the sovereign Lord who chooses to dwell among us, who makes it possible for us to live with him forever.

When we realize what God has done, we will stand in awe. We will give thanks, worship him and enjoy being his.

C. The Wrath of God (1:10)

In most English versions of the Bible, *wrath* is the last word of chapter 1, though it is not the chapter's main point. But its obvious themes of faith, salvation, spiritual growth, and service mean little if there is no such thing as the "coming wrath" of God.

When we think of "wrath," we often envision people with selfish tempers displaying their anger, or someone who "felt the wrath" of a coworker or boss. God's wrath, though extreme, is holy and just, and will be vented against all unbelief and disobedience toward our Lord.

When we understand what we deserve and the implications of God's holiness and judgment, then we can begin to appreciate the grace of forgiveness for all who believe. Actually, the most loving act ever planned, Christ's death at Calvary, is also a portrait of the wrath of God poured out on him as he bore the curse for our sins.

"The wrath of God is being revealed from heaven against all the godlessness and wickedness of men who suppress the truth by their wickedness" (Rom. 1:18)—that is present tense. But there will also be a future climactic day when he will "punish those who do not know God and do not obey the gospel of our Lord Jesus" (2 Thess. 1:8). This is "in blazing fire" (2 Thess. 1:7) and "everlasting destruction . . . shut out from the presence of the Lord" (2 Thess. 1:9).

This portrait of God's wrath makes even more beautiful and significant the message of joy and power so clearly described in 1 Thessalonians 1.

VII. TEACHING OUTLINE

A. INTRODUCTION

1. Lead Story: Where and Why God Grows Vegetables

2. Context: In the first chapter of 1 Thessalonians, Paul, Silas, and Timothy reviewed the beginnings of the church in Thessalonica and its continued development. They wished also to encourage these believers to continue in the way they had chosen: to work because of faith, to labor in love, to remain steadfast because of the reality of seeing Jesus Christ some day. But the authors did not want these believers to think it was all struggle and effort. They reminded them of God's saving grace, the Holy Spirit's enabling power, the divine gift of joy.

3. Transition: We can gain the same encouragement today. It may be that in our daily efforts to follow Christ we feel alone, as if it is all up to us to grow and serve and pray and . . . the list goes on and on. But by looking closely at the interaction between God and these believers in Thessalonica—real people, in a real time, in a real city—we can be assured that we are never alone. God works tirelessly on our behalf, giving us power and strength to do what he calls us to do. He is faithful when we trust him—for salvation, for strength, for godliness . . . the list goes on and on. And as part of a church, we are surrounded by people who demonstrate obedience and friendship with God—people who can help us along the way, and others whom we can help as well.

B. COMMENTARY

1. Greeting (1:1)
   a. Authors—Paul, Silas, and Timothy (1:1)
   b. Recipients—the church of the Thessalonians (1:1)
   c. Greetings—grace and peace (1:1)
2. What Church People Are Meant to Look Like (1:2–3)
   a. Thankful and prayerful (1:2)
   b. Workers of the faith (1:3)
   c. Laborers in love (1:3)
   d. Steadfast because of hope (1:3)
3. What the Gospel Is and Does (1:4–5)
   a. We are chosen by God (1:4)
   b. The gospel comes with power (1:5)
   c. The gospel comes with the Holy Spirit (1:5)
   d. The Holy Spirit brings conviction (1:5)
4. This Powerful Gospel Produces Model Lives (1:5–9)
   a. Imitators of Paul and the Lord (1:6)
   b. They welcomed the message with joy (1:6)
   c. The Thessalonians became models to others (1:7)
   d. Their faith became known everywhere (1:8)
5. This Life-Changing Gospel Is Defined (1:9–10)
   a. Conversion—turning to God (1:9)
   b. Future—waiting for Jesus from heaven (1:10)
   c. Basis—Christ's death and resurrection (1:10)
   d. Judgment—the coming wrath of God (1:10)

C. CONCLUSION: IN STEP WITH GOD

VIII. ISSUES FOR DISCUSSION

1. What is the church? What roles does the church play in our society? How does your church function as an imitation model? a reputation model? How far is the influence and reputation of your church reaching?
2. For what do you thank God as you pray for your church?
3. What occurs in conversion?
4. What does it mean to you that God has chosen you? How can you explain this to a person who does not believe in Christ? What part does your free will play in conversion?
5. What experiences have you had with the Holy Spirit? What effects does the indwelling Spirit have on your daily life?
6. For whom are you a model of Jesus Christ? What kind of model are they seeing?

1 Thessalonians 2

A Model for Christian Leadership

I. **INTRODUCTION**
Finding Our Way in the Media Maze

II. **COMMENTARY**
A verse-by-verse explanation of the chapter.

III. **CONCLUSION**
"I Am Just a Layman"
An overview of the principles and applications from the chapter.

IV. **LIFE APPLICATION**
Wolf Prints: In Step with God
Melding the chapter to life.

V. **PRAYER**
Tying the chapter to life with God.

VI. **DEEPER DISCOVERIES**
Historical, geographical, and grammatical enrichment of the commentary.

VII. **TEACHING OUTLINE**
Suggested step-by-step group study of the chapter.

VIII. **ISSUES FOR DISCUSSION**
Zeroing the chapter in on daily life.

Quote

"*N*ow orthodoxy, that is, right and sound doctrine, is important. Yet we can have the truth in a purely intellectual sense without the truth having us. And Christian truth, let it never be forgotten, is personal truth; it centers in a person and it must possess the lives of the persons who in the fullest sense become servants of the Truth. Christian truth must not only be believed, it must be obeyed. Men must do the truth."

John A. Mackay

1 Thessalonians 2

IN A NUTSHELL

Paul wants us to understand how he served the people. His ethics and his love were very strong, and the response the people gave was extremely gratifying—so Paul was eager to see them again.

A Model for Christian Leadership

I. INTRODUCTION

Finding Our Way in the Media Maze

*M*ost Americans spend their off hours in worlds of fantasy. We relax in realms built by imagination and inhabited by characters paper-thin or celluloid-slick. Night after night we live through intense moments with these fabricated people, identifying with their emotions and responses, straining to overcome the same obstacles. In the process, their ideas and attitudes mold our own. Whether in books, movies, or television shows, these fictional stories and people influence our thinking as well as mirror our outlook on life. The reason, perhaps, is because we approach our fantasies with much less reserve and personal caution than we do real-life relationships.

Occasionally in our fiction, a priest or minister has found his way into the spotlight. Though some authors and producers have drawn their ministers in positive strokes, most have been critical.

Tennessee Williams's minister in *Cat on a Hot Tin Roof* is insensitive and crass; Sinclair Lewis holds up the evangelist to cynical review in his novel, *Elmer Gantry*. In what seems a caricature, Lewis defines Gantry as a mercenary of the gospel—manipulating emotion, entertaining for souls, and using sensational storytelling. Gantry is uncompassionate, pompous, and ambitious. He has no depth as a person, nor has he a heart for God or his people. And though we might like to dismiss the story as exaggeration, there are elements that remind us of real-life personalities we may have seen or heard.

Popular, too, is the minister or priest who fails morally. From Nathaniel Hawthorn's *The Scarlet Letter* to the more modern *Thornbirds*, impurity among those aspiring to a holy calling finds instant fascination and recognition.

Less scathing, but still harmful, is the portrait of the pastor or priest as a nice but unimportant person. Such was the case of Father Mulcahy in the classic television show *M*A*S*H*. This quiet, unassuming man was kind, gentle . . . and marginal. He never managed to influence others or persuade the viewers as did the outspoken, unconventional, carousing Hawkeye. Many today view the church in just this way—nice but unimportant, good but disconnected from life.

Pastors and ministers of the gospel face confusing and often demanding expectations from their congregations and society; they are surrounded by misunderstandings and often by antagonism; they are not always respected, nor is their work appreciated. That is why it is so crucial for ministers to find their job descriptions and values in God.

In 1 Thessalonians 2, Paul describes, through personal illustration, what a minister of the gospel is to be. And though we are not all called to the office of pastor, all believers are called to maintain the same mindset. Paul's description of a church leader in Philippians is applicable to everyone, calling us all back to order our lives: "Your attitude should be the same as that of Christ Jesus: Who, being in very nature God, did not consider equality with God something to be grasped, but made himself nothing, taking the very nature of a servant" (Phil. 2:5–7).

II. COMMENTARY

MAIN IDEA: *Effective church leaders and pastors seek God's approval in what they do. Shepherding is not just a "job"; it is a commitment to serving God which envelopes one's entire lifestyle. In the church community, the emphasis is on relationships more than roles.*

A Spreading the Gospel (2:1–2)

SUPPORTING IDEA: *Telling others about Christ often involves perseverance in the face of resistance, opposition, and persecution.*

2:1. The second chapter of Thessalonians begins with Paul's reassurance that **our visit to you was not a failure.** Considering the tumult which erupted shortly after their arrival, such a statement could be made only by a person who measured success differently than society's standards. Acts 17:1–9 describes his brief and dramatic stay in the city.

On Paul and Silas's swing through Macedonia, they headed west out of Philippi, passing through the towns of Amphipolis and Apollonia. These towns were bypassed, and they were mentioned only as progress markers on their journey. But in the next city, Thessalonica, there was a synagogue, so Paul and Silas halted their travels. As was their habit, the two men spent time in the synagogue and "reasoned with [the Jews] from the Scriptures, explaining and proving that the Christ had to suffer and rise from the dead" (Acts 17:2–3).

Through these discussions and teachings came the conversion of some Jews and, perhaps more alarming, the embrace of Christianity by a "large number of God-fearing Greeks and not a few prominent women" (Acts 17:4). These Greeks, though uncircumcised, followed Jewish ceremonies and theology, and they were favorable toward Jewish ambitions. Their responses threatened Jewish tradition and thinking and the power of the religious rulers. As a result, a riot was instigated by the Jewish leaders; they gathered a mercenary mob eager for violence. With accusations of subversion and anti-Roman activity, Paul and Silas were eventually ordered out of town by nervous city officials.

But the success was fixed. Despite the tumult which surrounded their visit, despite the misunderstandings and rumors, despite the mob violence and threats, Paul stated that their visit **was not a failure.** Jews and Greeks had turned to Christ.

2:2. As he did at the beginning of the letter, Paul again looked back to the time he spent with these new Thessalonian believers—the fledgling church. He recalled his visit in the wider context of his missionary travels, mentioning his stay in Philippi: **We had previously suffered and been insulted in Philippi.** Again, we must turn to Acts to fill in the context for these statements.

After being arrested and beaten, Paul and Silas spent the night in a Philippian jail. In the morning the magistrates of the town sent their underlings to tell Paul and Silas they were free to go as though nothing had happened. Paul felt the sting of injustice. He wanted it established that he and Silas had been mistreated. He declared his Roman citizenship, underlining the outrage of being publicly beaten and thrown in prison without a trial.

Even so, as Paul rubbed his sores, he reminded his friends that, despite everything, he still did not alter the message: **we dared to tell you his gospel.** How easy to adopt the cultural attitudes of the time, tweaking the message to make it more palatable. How safe to sound less threatening by presenting Jesus as just another possibility. But Paul did not.

Do not miss the qualifying statement that explains, in part, why he did not buckle to social pressure, bad experiences, or others' opinions. The reason was because of **the help of our God.** It is the partnership between God and his servants that enables success. Paul did not just suck up his courage and march on; God did not magically dissolve all fear or concern. But with Paul's unwavering conviction of who Jesus is, together with God's enabling power, the Thessalonian church was established.

Ⓑ Motive as Paul Went to the Thessalonians (2:3–6a)

SUPPORTING IDEA: *Telling others about Christ or aspiring to church leadership should not be seen as a means to financial advancement or personal popularity. It is all for Christ.*

2:3. The reasons for their courage are continued in this verse. These men had no hidden agenda. They were not peddling opinion or theory. Their appeal did not **spring from error**. They knew deep within their souls that what they were saying was absolute truth.

Everything which is true can be traced back to the person of God. "In the beginning was the Word, and the Word was with God, and the Word was God. He was with God in the beginning. Through him all things were made; without him nothing was made that has been made" (John 1:1–3). Nothing can be true and exist outside his counsel and nature.

This is not simply a spiritual statement; it is a declaration that invades every part of life—every thought, action, plan, and intention. Anything else that makes claims on us is false, tainted, an illusion that cannot withstand experience, examination, or time.

Paul, Silas, and Timothy knew their appeal did not spring from **impure motives**. They had examined their motives; the people had observed their actions (v. 5); it was clear that their intentions were pure. They were not trying to con anyone.

Impurity can destroy. Drinking water cannot be labeled safe if one person out of a thousand dies from it. Truth cannot be right 98 percent of the time. Impurities are weaknesses around which everything else will fail. These men possessed purity of content (their message) and purity of heart (their motives).

2:4. They were **approved by God to be entrusted with the gospel.** The word *approve* is translated from the Greek word *dokimazo,* a word which was used in reference to metal purifying. It was a testing of the metals to prove their genuineness. The implication is that Paul, Silas, and Timothy bore the approval and commission of God because they had been proved through divine testing. God had stamped their lives as trustworthy because their faith had been proved genuine.

We are not trying to please men. Their entire focus was on pleasing God. They believed in God's existence, his judgment, his rewards, his presence, his empowerment, his attentiveness, his love. Why should they be concerned about popularity polls?

If there is ineffectiveness within the church or the individual, it has little to do with methodology, persecution, leadership vacuums, or ecclesiastical structures. Instead, it comes from being less than convinced that we deal with truth (the message). It comes from trying to please anyone or anything other than God (the motive).

In the early 1990s when President George Bush had fiery John Sununu as his chief of staff in the White House, Sununu was once asked by a reporter if his job was difficult. He answered a quick and deliberate "No." The reporter thought that Sununu had misunderstood the question, so he asked again. And got the same reply.

The chief of staff explained, "I have only one constituent." He knew his job was to please the President.

Paul and all who follow Christ have a similar goal when it comes to life's message and methods—to honor one person, Jesus Christ. When writing to the Corinthians, Paul summed up what our commitment should be: "whatever you do, *do it all for the glory of God*" (1 Cor. 10:31, emphasis added). That is the way to live because God tests the heart.

The word translated "test" is the same word, *dokimazo,* used previously. It is a probing which is done with the full expectation that whatever is under scrutiny will be approved. This is not a sweaty-palm event, wondering whether God will be pleased or angry. Paul was content and certain of God's approval. It did not matter what others might think.

2:5. Flattery uses words in the service of self interest. Flattery never has the well-being of others in mind. It is a case of heaping nice-sounding phrases and compliments upon a person in order to obtain some personal gain—personal advancement, admiration, or favors. Paul never trafficked in such deceit.

But deceit can come in many disguises. One which was popular in Paul's day, as well as our own, was preaching for financial benefit—saying attractive words, stirring up religious zeal, then pocketing the cash and moving on. Paul denied using such tactics and called God as his witness.

2:6a. Paul emphasized again that they were **not looking for praise from men.** The charge to all believers, and to the church, is to be vigilant in examining what we truly believe (message), and in exposing our actions and thoughts (motives) to the scrutiny of God's Spirit.

The Manner in Which Paul Helped Them (2:6b-12)

SUPPORTING IDEA: *Church leaders should serve as examples of righteous living and dedication to God and his people.*

2:6b. Paul first made it clear that leadership—those with authority (apostleship in his case)—can make some claims upon those they lead. **We could have been a burden to you,** he declared.

The "burden" he referred to was the demands that power can make. The missionaries could have pressed this congregation to do certain things, putting upon them the obligations of obedience out of the sheer weight of apostolic authority.

2:7. Instead, Paul and Silas chose to be **gentle.** There is no tenderness quite like a mother's, and Paul dared to identify with maternal love and care. Greek writers used the term *gentleness* to describe those who dealt patiently and with a mild manner toward those who were difficult—obstinate children, unmanageable students, those who had not reached maturity and were experiencing the inconsistencies and struggles of development. Whatever difficulties the Thessalonians may have presented, Paul and Silas recognized that these new Christians were not yet "grown up." So rather than dealing with these people in an authoritarian manner, they chose to be patient—like a mother.

It is a great lesson for the church today, because we have not always been patient with new or young believers. Sometimes we have cut a mold and demanded that they fit it—now. Instead of this approach, we need to see each individual's need for help and encouragement as he or she struggles to conform to the image of Christ.

2:8. Here is a classic understanding of biblical love. To Paul, love is always a verb, it is doing. Feelings may accompany love, but they do not define it. Instead, the commitment of acting in the best interest of another opens the way for feelings: **We loved you so much that we were delighted to share . . . our lives.**

It is easier to teach theology than to love, easier to share lists than time. Paul gave not only the message of the gospel, but the example of it as well. He spent time. He shared joys and headaches. Parents and teachers, coaches and mentors, pastors and leaders know what it means to give part of their heart away to others. Love is not just a job. It is a way of life.

But note that Paul did *share* the gospel of God. He was balanced. He gave his life and love. He gave content as well. It is not enough to visit people in the hospital or prison, or to show compassion to the poor or those new in the faith. Somewhere, carefully and candidly, they must also hear the truth of the cross and what it means to trust and follow Christ.

Arguing whether the church should meet people's physical needs, or whether it should limit itself to preaching the gospel is like debating which wing of an airplane is more important. Both are essential!

2:9. As an apostle, Paul could have expected, perhaps insisted, that he and Silas be paid or cared for while in Thessalonica. At that time, when philosophers traveled from place to place teaching, they were usually paid by their followers. Paul could have taken advantage of that cultural practice.

The interesting point is that the choice of "non-payment," or to go without a salary, was not the vote of the congregation but the decision of the leaders. Paul's intention was to provide an example of what this particular church needed, not to establish a precedent for how churches in general should limit their provisions for their pastors. To this church, which had a problem with laziness (1 Thess. 3:7–13), these men were examples of hard work—**toil and hardship.** They worked **night and day**—these were long and tedious hours. They modeled sacrificial love and giving for the sake of this new church.

2:10. Paul also speaks candidly and positively of his own heart. He knew people watched him; they had that right. Those who lead will be examined to see if their words match their lives. So Paul called these Thessalonian believers as witnesses to what he was about to say. If anyone could dispute his assertions, it would be these people. Paul had lived with them shoulder to shoulder. You cannot hide much when you live day in and day out with the same people. But Paul then went further and called God as his witness. He knew that, above all, he was answerable to God, who is always able to see deep within the heart.

Backed by these expert witnesses, Paul went on to make some strong claims, characterizing himself as **holy, righteous and blameless. Holy** has to do with being devout, separate from selfishness and sin. **Righteousness** is moral correctness, doing what God defines as just and good. **Blameless** does not mean perfection but a life characterized by godly habits; it is being up-to-date on confession before God and apologies with others.

2:11–12. Paul declared, **We dealt with each of you as a father deals with his own children.** Not only did Paul express the nurturing tenderness of a mother; he also demonstrated the strength of a father's love by encouraging, comforting, and urging these people toward godly living.

Encouraging is a heart-felt term, not a one-time shot in the arm just to make a person feel better. It is the strong support and trust that imparts courage to others. Paul wrote it in the present tense, implying that it was continual in his leadership style. People need to be infused with courage again and again, as a matter of practice, to be emboldened in what they know is right.

Comforting is the gentle empathy which comes and stays alongside someone as they experience failures and distresses in life. **Urging** comes from a solemn and earnest view of a situation, asking someone to do or be something for the highest good. Urging has a clear view of what is right, leading a person through the maze of emotions and conflicts which can confuse an issue.

Why did Paul live among them as a father, inspiring them to be courageous, standing with them in difficulty, addressing serious issues? So that they might live **worthy of God, who calls you into his kingdom and glory.** What does it mean to live worthy of God? To gain a fuller understanding of this, we must view God and ourselves accurately.

God determined to create for himself a people who bear his character and nature. It was his intention even before he created Adam. Despite the dark rebellion of Satan and his subversion which penetrated all the created order, God has constantly pursued mankind, revealing his personhood, justice, love, and mercy. He involved himself with his world in order to demonstrate his glory and, after man's rebellion, to bring back to himself what was rightfully his.

Jesus Christ is the extreme effort God went to—God himself planting his feet upon the dirt in the face of injustice, misunderstanding, weariness, and hatred.

As followers of Christ, are we living lives worthy of him? God has put this call upon our lives—to make us like Christ. We are the presence of Christ in this age—here and now, in this time, at this place. Are we living in a way that matches the worthiness of that call?

God has promised us **his kingdom and glory.** Those who have chosen to follow Christ will be welcomed by him into heaven. But in the meantime, before that glory is realized, we are to be like him, to bear his character and nature. He gives us his Spirit, enabling us to live as he did. But the choice is always ours. Are we living lives worthy of his plan, his promise, his provision?

D Thessalonians as Receivers of the Gospel (2:13–16)

SUPPORTING IDEA: *When we trust God's Word, we accept it into the depths of our hearts and minds. This gives us the desire and power to live it.*

2:13. Paul applauded the Thessalonians again by expressing thanks to God for their spiritual development. He was concerned, perhaps, that his forced and abrupt departure from Thessalonica might have left them weak and floundering, making the church unstable. But after Timothy's report, Paul gave thanks because these young believers were proving to be genuine followers of Christ. They received the word preached to them as the **word of God.** The proof was in their changed lives, **which is at work in you.** The power of God is released through faith in his Word; it becomes an active, spiritual energy, cutting like a scalpel to the depths of the soul (Heb. 4:12).

2:14. The Thessalonians identified with Christ and the Judean church through their suffering. They became **imitators of God's churches in Judea . . . in Christ Jesus.**

No one sets out to suffer, but when suffering comes it reveals those with whom we identify. As the Thessalonians began feeling the anger and suspicions of their countrymen, they stood firm in their faith. They sided with all others who remain faithful . . . just like the Christians had done in Judea.

2:15–16. All persecutors are of the same mentality; they are part of the war between good and evil which fills every page of history. Those who were persecuting the Thessalonians were following in the path of those who had previously killed the prophets as well as the Lord Jesus. The Thessalonians were receiving from their own countrymen the same treatment the Judean Christians had received from the Jews.

Obviously the antagonism of persecutors toward Christ and his message displeases God, but how can this be seen as hostility to **all men?** By trying to suppress the truth, they are agents of destruction to all human-kind. By trying to prevent the spread of God's saving grace, they become enemies of all people.

Those who attack the gospel and Christ's church **always heap up their sins to the limit.** They fill up the cup of God's wrath. Their guilt results in God's wrath—his just vengeance. It is not an angry outburst, but the settled nature of God's judgment. Those who reject the grace of God suffer his righteous indignation and punishment.

The good news is that it does not have to be that way. Those who rely upon Christ's death and resurrection to remove their sin are transformed from enemies of God to children of God. The accusations against those who believe are removed by faith in Jesus Christ. The charges are nailed to the cross and canceled (Col. 2:14).

Paul Describes His Love for the Thessalonians (2:17–20)

> **SUPPORTING IDEA:** *People are to remain the priority of our lives and efforts.*

2:17. Paul was not a subtle man. He was bold in his instruction. He was equally bold in his affection. He wrote of his **intense longing** to see the Thessalonians, of making **every effort** to see them.

It is not clear what "every effort" is, but we can be assured that Paul was vigorous in his attempts to return to the fledgling church. Despite false accusations, riots, and being run out of Thessalonica (**we were torn away**), Paul did not forget about the new believers. Despite the current persecutions he was experiencing in Corinth, the Thessalonians were not pushed from his thoughts and prayers. Paul was not content to remain at a distance. Knowing the hostile environment in Thessalonica to himself and all believers, he, Silas, and Timothy still made "every effort" to return to Thessalonica.

2:18. Paul wanted to see them again, **but Satan stopped us.** This does not refer to some strange vision or doing battle with demons. Paul viewed anything which opposed the work of Christ as spiritual warfare.

On the matter of evil and demons, we can go about life nonchalantly without prayer or without trusting Christ in his strength, not recognizing the spiritual battle which rages around us. We can also become obsessed about fighting spirits and become influenced by extra-biblical books which promote specific formulas to battle the unseen.

The more balanced view is to see that all of life is an issue of the spirit and spiritual warfare—that we are called to walk in Christ day by day, moment by moment. Then we can give God credit for all that is good, knowing that he can work to bring glory to himself through us. We can see obstacles as something which Satan throws at us, calling us to greater faith and reliance upon Christ. This is the biblical pattern.

2:19. Here Paul gives a glimpse into why he was so persistent. These people were his **hope, joy,** and **crown.** Paul understood life today in the light of the eternity to come. He built the present upon the certainty of the future. Everything pointed toward that day when he would stand in the presence of Christ. He knew that people were the treasure and glory for which God worked and suffered. Paul's vision of life centered upon people because he knew that all of God's revelation—from creation through the prophets to Christ himself—was intended to redeem people.

2:20. To Paul, the Thessalonian believers were **our glory and joy.** God is interested in people. The heavens are his, the mountains are the work of his hand, the oceans are his handiwork—but people are his pride and treasure. Like Paul, we should express our love to others, treasuring the moments when people come to faith in Christ.

> **MAIN IDEA REVIEW:** *Effective church leaders and pastors seek God's approval in what they do. Shepherding is not just a "job"; it is a commitment to serving God which envelopes one's entire lifestyle. In the church community, the emphasis is on relationships more than roles.*

III. CONCLUSION

"I Am Just a Layman"

People still say it: "I am just a layman." Sometimes it is said to avoid a ministry challenge—an opportunity to teach a Bible study, help someone in trouble, or lead in a public prayer. Sometimes it is said in admiration and contrast to someone "in the work of the Lord." But more often, it is said to excuse our weaknesses or inadequacies.

Those who feel they are "just a layman" can read Paul and easily assume the apostle had greater strength than "we" do, that he lived in a different world and faced different tests than we do.

Let us get it straight. Paul certainly had the daily help of God's Spirit in his life, and he did accomplish amazing things. But he would be the first to remind us that he was a sinner just like the rest of us. He needed to obey his Lord, walk in the ways of the Spirit, and love people, just as we do.

This chapter is a careful description of Paul's ways with people—commendable and loving ways, but also ways we can all adopt. He stood up under great stress and endured. He tried to please God instead of all the people around him. Paul loved people tenderly, like a mother, and he tried to guide and encourage them like a father. He worked hard—"night and day."

We can also choose to relate to people in the name of Christ. What Paul did was not uniquely apostolic or restricted to New Testament times. We must adopt similar values—the kingdom of our Lord Jesus, the worth of people, the high call of serving and loving others in his name.

When you live like that, you are just exactly what God looks for in his children. And you are a great deal more than "just a layman."

PRINCIPLES

- Leaders of God's cause on earth put what God thinks ahead of the opinion polls.
- Both gentleness and firmness are needed at times.
- Purity and holiness are not just things to be talked about. We should show them in our actions.
- Obedient submission to the Word of God is the mark of a follower of Christ.
- God will judge all sins.
- Christians often have their plans thwarted.

APPLICATIONS

- Learn what God thinks by knowing his Word and then resting in his sovereignty as you obey it.
- Love the people you serve by doing and saying what is best for them, no matter how you feel.
- Express your love and appreciation for others.
- Expect some opposition, tests, and persecution when you are faithful to the Lord.

IV. LIFE APPLICATION

Wolf Prints: In Step with God

In the far north, the wolf pack spends the summer around the den or beside the ponds or lakes. Long grasses waver in the heat, camouflaging the flickering tail of a pup as he waits to ambush his sibling; rustling bushes and snapping twigs betray the calculations of youth.

The parents lead and tend. They are the organizing authorities and the protectors. As the pups grow they learn through imitation, caring for the younger ones, helping to feed, play with, and watch them just as much as the parents.

Paul—apostle, recognized leader, and authority—wrote with affection to the young church at Thessalonica. He presented himself not as the prototype of the modern CEO/manager, the isolated individualist, or strategizing committee man, but as a tender mother and an encouraging father. These metaphors placed the Christian leader in the center of community. It is a portrait of leadership delineated by love and sacrifice, bonded to others with the same ties of affection that hold families together.

These parental images elicit strong connotations of sacrifice: "We loved you so much that we were delighted to share with you not only the gospel of God but our lives as well" (2:8). A mother is a mother whether she is sleeping or awake, whether the child is at home or away, whether the child is two or seventeen. The same is true of the father. We can say the same of a Christian pastor or leader. Location and time do not determine who we are.

Paul's metaphor of a mother and father, his defense of his blameless character, and his example of "working night and day" were not written so others would slavishly follow his exact lifestyle. He was not suggesting that pastors work non-stop. He wrote these words to help us examine our hearts. The questions we need to ask are: How much does culture or personal pleasure determine my workload, my dedication to Christ and his church, the time I give? Are my struggles concerned with personal ambition or the welfare of God's people? Do I love people with the same devotion as a mother? Do I guide them with the tenderness of a father? Am I willing to sacrifice for the sake of others if that is called for?

All Christians need to invest their lives in others. We need to examine and measure ourselves against this profile of self-giving and vigorous self-discipline.

The adult wolf, having invested in its children, sees the results of its love and labor. The wolf pups imitate the hunt in snapping forays. They enjoy the tender nuzzle of belonging and understand the demands of the pack.

Sun and leaves ignite the forest with oranges, reds, and yellows. Then, seemingly the next day, only skeletal branches, a dusting of snow, and the harsh tingle of a Canadian gust. Ponds turn from blue to gray to white. Now, paths stretch along the edge of winter's silence, tight and narrow, tamped firm beneath the gentle paws of the wolves. One behind another, all following one leader, they break through the snow, creating a path for those behind. Each wolf follows step upon step as the pack assumes the intention; deep cut and compressed, a trail emerges complete and certain in its definition. The heritage is secure.

The giving of our lives in tenderness, nurturing, listening, and encouragement—the time spent disciplining ourselves in purity, right choices, and good actions—are investments which will insure the health of the church. By devoting ourselves to others and training them in godliness, we will help those who follow, making the path clear and trackable, the faith secure. For always there comes the time of testing, of winter—for the church, the pastor, the leader, and all who claim Christ as Lord.

V. PRAYER

Lord, head of the church, servant-master, shine the light of your life upon our hearts. As you have promised, cut cleanly with your Word and expose our motives, lay our spirits bare before our eyes so that we may purify our purposes. Then, following you, we will serve each other, love each other, and so bring glory to you, who deserves all praise. Amen.

VI. DEEPER DISCOVERIES

A. Background Experiences in Philippi (v. 2)

While in Philippi, Paul commanded an evil spirit to come out of a demon-possessed slave girl. This deprived her owners of their profitable fortune-telling business. A mob scene developed with angry shouts and accusations of political rebellion and anti-Roman practices. To the crowd it was not a religious issue, but a social issue. To the slave-owners it was purely economical. But the government officials, always frightened by hysterical crowds, took no chances and had Paul and Silas beaten. It was a brutal concession to a mob, and Paul and Silas were then thrown into prison.

These were bruised and bloodied men, uncertain of what would happen next. Stuck in the dark inner chamber of the prison, their feet fastened to stocks, they began to sing hymns. Then came an earthquake.

These men held a faith firm in the conviction that "God is our refuge and strength, an ever-present help in trouble. Therefore we will not fear, though the earth give way and the mountains fall into the heart of the sea . . . The LORD Almighty is with us; the God of Jacob is our fortress" (Ps. 46:1–2,7).

B. The Word of God (v. 13)

Most of us are acquainted with the playground rhyme, "Sticks and stones may break my bones, but words can never hurt me." It is patently wrong. Words do have power.

Bruises and broken bones will heal, but words sink deep within our minds and souls. We carry their joy or poison with us wherever we go, and they can affect us for a lifetime. They can heal or wound, inspire or devastate.

Perhaps that is why Jesus warned that "men will have to give account on the day of judgment for every careless word they have spoken. For by your words you will be acquitted, and by your words you will be condemned" (Matt. 12:36–37). Why? Because "out of the overflow of the heart the mouth speaks" (Matt. 12:34).

If our words hold that kind of power, carrying our hearts upon their breath, what about God's words? God's revealed words also come from the overflow of his heart: "the word of the LORD is flawless" (2 Sam. 22:31). God is perfect, complete, the source of all truth and reality. His Word carries the dynamic of his nature; it speaks with the power of eternal reality. That is why he could speak the world into existence.

The Word of God, the Bible, is more than an interesting book to study, more than good ideas, beautiful prose or poetry. The Thessalonians recognized the implication of hearing the speech of God. We need to recapture that same awe and reverential dread at being given the thoughts of the eternal God.

God's Word has inherent power because it is the carrier of undisputed truth. Nothing can withstand it, succeed against it, overcome it, or disprove it. In fact, God's Word "is living and active. Sharper than any double-edged sword, it penetrates even to dividing soul and spirit, joints and marrow; it judges the thoughts and attitudes of the heart" (Heb. 4:12).

Because God is timeless, living in the continual present, his Word is always immediate. These are not mere ideas we read and study in the Bible; they are the contemporary thoughts and expressions of the boundless God who is always now. That is why they are living, used by the Holy Spirit to penetrate and effect change where mere words or ideas could not.

Even so, for the power of God's Word to explode in regenerative change it must be connected to faith. As James writes, "Do not merely listen to the word, and so deceive yourselves. Do what it says" (Jas. 1:22). That is faith—believing and then acting on that belief. It is then that the energy of God is unleashed within us.

Weymouth's translation says the Thessalonians "embraced and welcomed" the Word of God. They brought it into their hearts recognizing it as truth. Anyone who trivializes, ignores, or mishandles God's Word is in danger of God's wrath. As Paul wrote to the Galatians, "Even if we or an angel from heaven should preach a gospel other than the one we preached to you, let him be eternally condemned" (Gal. 1:8).

This should cause us to take seriously the words of God, revealed by his mercy, to us who depend upon his grace.

VII. TEACHING OUTLINE

A. INTRODUCTION

1. Lead Story: Finding Our Way in the Media Maze
2. Context: Many of the false teachers who tried to get listeners to deviate from what Paul taught attacked his theology as well as his

personal motives and manner. This chapter is one of Paul's finest explanations of his purposes and integrity.

B. COMMENTARY

1. Spreading the Gospel (2:1–2)
2. Motive as Paul Went to the Thessalonians (2:3–6)
   a. Approval from God (2:3–4)
   b. No approval by men (2:5–6)
3. The Manner in Which Paul Helped Them (2:6–12)
   a. His tenderness yet hard work (2:6–9)
   b. His holiness and encouragement (2:10–12)
4. Thessalonians as Receivers of the Gospel (2:13–16)
   a. Their reception of the Word (2:13)
   b. Their obedience and suffering (2:14)
   c. The opposite response (2:15–16)
5. Paul Describes His Love for the Thessalonians (2:17–20)
   a. His desire to see them (2:17–18)
   b. His love for them (2:19–20)

C. CONCLUSION: WOLF PRINTS: IN STEP WITH GOD

VIII. ISSUES FOR DISCUSSION

1. Have you used unethical or selfish approaches to avoid ministry involvement? What were they? Discuss the issues which should be considered before responding to a ministry opportunity or personal commitment.
2. What essentials must be remembered if a person wants to be a pleaser of God rather than of people?
3. Name some people who love others the way Paul did. What stands out about them? What beliefs must we hold if we want to live like this?
4. All of us will be judged on how we respond to the Word of God, by whether we let it influence us. Can you describe some situations in which you had to choose whether to follow the authority of Scripture?
5. What are some practical ways you can express your love for others the way Paul did to the Thessalonians?

1 Thessalonians 3

Responding to Life's Pressures

Quote

"*Occasions make not a man fail,*

but they show what the man is."

T h o m a s   à   K e m p i s

1 Thessalonians 3

 I N   A   N U T S H E L L

Paul desperately wanted to go back and visit the Thessalonians to see how they were doing. He was overjoyed when he found out his prayers for their growth and love were being answered.

Responding to Life's Pressures

I. INTRODUCTION

A Matter of the Heart

Among the archipelagos of the South Seas is a small, secluded island only recently discovered. Bone-white beaches stretch along part of its curving shoreline, palms wave gently in the tropical breezes, grasses sway in the salty air.

No one is certain how it came about, whether through shipwreck or adventure, but a man landed upon this island about fifty years ago. Since that time he has lived alone, both monarch and slave of this Pacific paradise.

When a scientific expedition sailed through the island's tranquil blue waters, they laid anchor and went ashore. They wished only to rest a bit, take in the sun, and poke about the beach until lunch. It was not long before each one of the crew felt as though he were being watched. It was quite unnerving. Eventually, one of the scientists spotted a bearded man peering through the bushes.

In time, through gestures and a bit of patience, each came to understand that neither wished ill to the other. The hermit became excited and began to show the scientists and crew around the island. He showed them a nine-hole golf course which he had constructed (it was a small island) with fairways curving around waterfalls, and greens pitched over cliffs. To occupy himself on Saturday nights he had built a drive-in restaurant just a short distance from a movie theater. And to assure that he would not spend his days in spoiled leisure and frivolity, he had erected a library.

He also took the crew past a beautiful church. It was simple yet graceful in style with curved lines reaching skyward; its stained-glass windows glistened against the turquoise and greens of the tropics.

As the visitors stood gaping at the wonders around them, all created by this one man, one of the crewmen asked, "But if this is the church you worship in, what church is that?"

Everyone looked down the street toward another church building. It was also beautiful, a little more ornate.

"Oh, that? Why that is my former church," the man replied.

So it is with many disputes within the church and with most disagreements between people—they are rooted in self-centeredness. We feel the tug-of-war within ourselves as we combat our own egocentric tendencies. But Christ calls us to a new dynamic which bursts forth in love.

Chapter 3 of 1 Thessalonians is a beautiful model of love—the love of the Thessalonians for each other, and the love of Paul for these new believers. The love described and demonstrated through the narrative of this chapter is strong, active, unwavering. It persists through persecution and hardship. This love gives selflessly to others. It never fades but strengthens through time.

II. COMMENTARY

MAIN IDEA: *Faithful obedience to Christ will always result in misunderstandings and persecutions from those outside the faith. Thus, encouragement becomes a source of strength in our relationships with one another and in our ability to persevere.*

The Inevitability of Persecution and Hardship (3:1–5)

SUPPORTING IDEA: *The Christian life will not be easy. In fact, since it is guaranteed to be difficult, it is crucial for Christians to encourage each other in the faith.*

3:1. Paul declared, **We could stand it no longer.** This is a good reminder that these men of the first century were not cut from flannel graph. They had strong emotions and inner turmoils.

Having abruptly left Thessalonica, the missionaries had traveled to Berea, and from there to Athens. In the intervening time there had been little contact or correspondence between them and the Thessalonian church. Leaving a young, inexperienced church would have been difficult for any leader, but Paul and the others knew that these Christians were under great stress from the unbelieving Jews and even the Roman authorities. Paul had experienced the hatred of the Jews in Philippi and Thessalonica as riots, accusations, and arrests swirled around the missionaries and Christian followers. Paul was anxious and worried about how these Thessalonians were being treated and how they were holding up.

His concern became so great that he had to do something. He could wait no longer: **we thought it best to be left by ourselves in Athens.** A plan was put together that would (1) strengthen the Thessalonian church and, (2) get Paul information as to how the believers were doing.

Paul felt he could not return, but must stay in Athens. His love for the Thessalonians was so great, however, that he was willing to remain alone, literally "abandoned." Evidently Paul felt great loneliness when Timothy departed.

3:2. Paul's words, **We sent Timothy**, is a statement of fact, followed by a brief description of Timothy which underscored the high regard Paul held for him. He called Timothy **our brother and God's fellow worker in spreading the gospel.**

Brother carries the feeling of warm, family relationship. This is how workers in the gospel and members of a local church often felt toward one another. There was a strong tie of community and family.

God's fellow worker is an amazing and gracious title. It is given to Timothy, and all those who work hard and faithfully in the service of Christ. We work alongside the Lord; we are partners with him: "We are God's fellow workers" (1 Cor. 3:9). This is the highest, most important position anyone can choose—to work together with the Lord in caring about people, to spread the gospel, to love and encourage. Every day we have many opportunities to demonstrate this kind of lifestyle.

Paul then stated the purpose of Timothy's visit: **to strengthen and encourage you in your faith.** The word strengthen has the literal meaning of supplying a buttress for a wall or building. One of the purposes of Timothy's visit was to provide strengthening support for their faith.

To **encourage** is to impart courage to another. Timothy was to build their faith so they could withstand the battles around them, the persecutions, the temptations. Courage is needed when facing a battle, and Timothy was to cultivate their faith for this.

3:3. Strength and courage are needed in the life of faith because the world is hostile. Paul was concerned that the trials, difficulties, and pains in life would not **unsettle** the believers, making them waver in their faith.

These trials could mean many things. Undoubtedly it referred to the accusations of political subversion which were thrown at the Christians. It could represent all the misunderstandings of their faith that circulated in the city. There may have been those who were trying to deceive the believers, drawing them into Judaism. In all practicality, these "trials" are anything which causes Christians to suffer because of their faith.

Even so, Paul declared rather boldly, **we were destined for them.** Paul was not surprised by pain. Christ had said it first: "In this world you will have trouble. But take heart! I have overcome the world" (John 16:33). Paul knew trouble and trials were part of life, and he had warned the Thessalonians about it.

Today we generally ask, "Why?" when problems hit us. While it is O.K. to ask hard questions, one of the answers is simply "because." Because we live in a fallen world where evil and Satan reign at the present moment. Because the rain falls on the just and the unjust. Because the world system and its values are against Christ and all who follow him. Because this world is groaning until the day of its redemption. Because Christ is not Lord in totality yet.

In the meantime, we find our strength in Christ and know that difficulties and attacks to our faith will come.

3:4. Paul reminded the Thessalonians that he had warned them about the coming trials when he was with them. Time and again he had told them that hard times lay ahead. These difficulties should not have taken anyone by surprise.

Paul had done the Thessalonian believers a great service by this warning, and we do well to warn new believers as well. To let people think that Christ will usher them into a life of ease and unending happiness is not only untrue, but also very harmful. Christ warned us, Paul warned us, and we should make it clear to new believers that difficulties lie ahead in life.

3:5. Paul declared, **For this reason . . . I sent to find out about your faith.** Paul had some fears about the faith of the new believers in Thessalonica. He knew these Christians had faith. That had been proven. But was it strong enough to stand in the assault of persecution and the tempter?

The tempter was Satan, and Paul always understood Satan as an enemy of the gospel. He described him as the tempter because Satan's aim in regard to Christians is always to make them fall into sin and error. It is well to remember that Satan still tries to devour our faith through difficulties.

Having been tempted to abandon the faith, Paul was not certain of the result and whether **our efforts might have been useless.** The maturity of the believer is dependent on his commitment and determination to follow after Christ. There is no guarantee that having once begun well, every believer will finish the Christian faith and life well. That is why we are to encourage one another, to be diligent in our obedience, and relentless in our desire for righteousness.

I remember visiting in a hospital once with two men who were dying of cancer. In fact, both died on the same day the following week. In rooms beside each other, they showed such opposite reactions. One was bitter and angry with God. He died with that forsaken attitude.

The man in the next room held my hand as we prayed and cried tears of thanksgiving to God for the benefits of his life. He thanked God for his grace and for what Christ had done for him. He rejoiced in the thought of meeting God.

Two men in the same situations. One was abiding in Christ and his sovereign grace, and the other's faith could not stand the test. This doubled his pain in the face of death.

B The People's Strength in Pain (3:6–10)

SUPPORTING IDEA: *Not only must we sympathize with and pray for those in difficulty; we must also tell them that we stand with them in love.*

3:6. The little word *but* signals relief. After cataloging all his concerns and the anxiety it had caused, Paul wrote, **But**. His excitement can almost be felt as he continued, **Timothy has just now come to us from you and has brought good news about your faith and love.** The description of the Thessalonian church caused Paul to write with warmth and enthusiasm as his fears found relief in what Timothy had to say.

Faith refers to the Thessalonians' attitude toward God and their relationship with him. **Love**, though connected to faith, is more the demonstration of it as expressed toward other people. On both counts, the Thessalonians were doing well. These were the important matters of life. Paul found his greatest joy in people who lived out their faith and love.

Then followed other news that was also encouraging to Paul. The Thessalonians must have sat around with Timothy and talked. In their discussions Paul's visit to them was mentioned again and again: **He has told us that you always have pleasant memories of us**. It is good to compliment, to recall good times and voice them. It strengthens the bond of love, giving encouragement to others. It became apparent that the Thessalonians felt toward Paul the same way he felt toward them: **you long to see us, just as we also long to see you**.

3:7. Paul was having a difficult time of it, too. He was always under intense persecution by those who opposed Christ. His life was not easy, and he never pretended it was. Even so, the Thessalonians had brought the missionaries strength and encouragement because of the way they were living—specifically their faith. It had been their faith which had caused Paul such anxiety, and now it was the certainty of their faith that gave Paul the greatest reason for rejoicing.

3:8. It is as though Paul could not find enough words to describe the uplifting and positive effect of their steadfast faith: **Now we really live, since you are standing firm**. Timothy's conversations about the Thessalonians' genuine faith had been like a shot of life, a new injection of purpose. Our faith can have such an effect on those around us.

3:9. Paul's words, **How can we thank God enough . . . ?** showed his great joy at seeing progress and strength in the lives of those he loved.

The apostle James once wrote that we should count it a joy when we "face trials of many kinds" (Jas. 1:2–4), because they produce long-lasting, persistent faith and maturity. While we should not go searching or praying for pain, neither should we feel that pain is outside our Lord's sovereign plan for us any more than it was outside the Father's will for the Son. He was complete or "made perfect" (Heb. 5:9) through suffering.

3:10. Although Paul was thrilled with the strength of the Thessalonians' faith, he prayed throughout the day and night, on various occasions and day after day. He literally "begged" God to allow him to see these Christians again in order to **supply what is lacking in [their] faith.** Paul recognized that, despite the wonderful news of their tenacious faith, these Christians were not fully developed in knowledge and understanding. They lacked many things for which teaching, warning, and instruction were still needed. Spiritual progress is always to be commended, but it is never to be considered complete.

Ⓒ Prayer for Increasing Strength (3:11–13)

SUPPORTING IDEA: *It is imperative that we go to God on one another's behalf so we will be blameless and holy before God.*

3:11. Paul became a bit more explicit about the nature of his praying (v. 10). He addressed **our God and Father,** clearly an inclusive term that God is sovereign and relates to all believers as Father. Though eternal, he is still our Father. Paul also addressed **our Lord Jesus.** The deity of the earthly Jesus is exalted to the same position and authority as God the Father.

Paul desired that God himself would direct the missionaries back to Thessalonica. He wanted nothing other than divine intervention: **clear the way for us to come to you.** The decision, of course, is up to the all-knowing and all-powerful God, who sees the beginning and the end. But Paul was not passive about this. He asked for God to step in and make possible a return trip to this church.

3:12–13. Whatever the outcome, the desire of Paul's heart follows: **may . . . your love increase and overflow,** may you be **blameless and holy in the presence of our God** when Christ returns.

Paul acknowledged that the Thessalonians did have love. But as the great proof of the Christ-life in us, love must always be on the increase. It must increase to flood-like proportions. It was to spill over to the other believers in the local church and to **everyone else.** The love of God through us extends to all, even our enemies.

3:13. Love, and every other virtue, springs from the heart. It is not a matter of following rules, but of the inner life that makes Christianity vibrant. Paul's prayer was that the believers' **hearts** would be **strengthened.** He realized that unless the heart is firmly established, there will be no growth and development. Changing methods or habits sometimes lasts for a short time, but lasting change begins with the heart. This change can come only from the Lord.

The reason our hearts need to be strengthened is so that we **will be blameless and holy in the presence of our God and Father.** But how can we be blameless before God on that great day of judgment?

First, we must share the judicial position with Christ. Paul told the Corinthian believers, "You are in Christ Jesus, who has become for us wisdom from God—that is, our righteousness, holiness and redemption" (1 Cor. 1:30). He gives us, at salvation, the "gift of righteousness" (Rom. 5:17), so that God sees us through the new creation of his Son, forgiven by the death of Christ, and covered by the righteousness which belongs to him.

With this gift we are to draw on the strength of Christ to "live a life worthy of the calling you have received" (Eph. 4:1). This means we seek to make righteous decisions and to choose righteous, holy motives and actions. Blamelessness is possible if we deal with sin whenever it enters our heart. When we sin, we should deal with it immediately through confession. With this additional grace, we stand blameless before our Lord, now and when **Jesus comes with all his holy ones.**

MAIN IDEA REVIEW: *Faithful obedience to Christ will always result in misunderstandings and persecutions from those outside the faith. Thus, encouragement becomes a source of strength in our relationships with one another and in our ability to persevere.*

III. CONCLUSION

The One-Minute Manager

Ken Blanchard, consultant and writer about business and leadership methods, made popular the idea that leaders and managers should do a better job of communicating, encouraging, and warning those for whom they were responsible. He emphasized the need to express feelings of encouragement or criticism. He found that these positive messages reduced tensions and problems.

Other leadership experts recommend that negative concerns be communicated in person, not on paper. Positive feedback, however, should be written. Words on paper, they say, make thoughts much stronger. Commending, approving, loving words are more powerful when they are written.

Paul was a master at expressing his strong love and deep concern for the people of the churches. He was not hesitant to tell them of his desire to be with them and to reveal how much he hoped they were doing well. He seemed to know how important it is to God to see strong love in the lives of his children. People in a church should be constantly encouraging and building one another up.

PRINCIPLES

- Pain and temptations are regular components in a Christian's life.
- Faith is a growing, daily commitment to believe God, no matter what happens to us.
- Only God can help us grow in his kind of holiness and love.

APPLICATIONS

- We should let others know that we care about their faith and growth.
- Prayer for one another's character should come before concerns for the physical aspects of life.
- Our Christian relationships will be characterized by love and care for the good of others.

IV. LIFE APPLICATION

Houston, We Have a Problem

Do you ever worry? This is a very human tendency that arises from our inability to know what the future holds. It stems from our limited knowledge and experience—and at times, our limited faith.

Paul, the same person who wrote "Do not be anxious about anything" (Phil. 4:6), writes to the Thessalonian Christians, "When I could stand it no longer . . . I was afraid" (1 Thess. 3:5). Is there a contradiction here? He sounds a bit anxious.

There seem to be two different kinds of worry or anxiety. One type of worry is a fretting over situations we cannot control or influence; the other concerns real dangers or possibilities. Paul's anxiety grew out of this second type of worry.

Paul understood the hazards that these new believers faced. They were not grounded in their faith; they had no one who could instruct and encourage them in the face of persecution; and they were the targets of Satan. These Thessalonian believers were so young in their faith that they were at high risk for failure.

On April 11, 1970, Apollo 13 blasted away from earth. While most of the nation yawned at another moon shot, the men at Mission Control in Houston and the three astronauts on board knew that every space flight was full of risk. Then, on April 13, an explosion rocked the command module. Mystery and curiosity gave way to the realization that the spacecraft was losing fuel and oxygen. The situation was critical. Heading toward the moon, their fears changed from *I wonder what this is going to do to the lunar landing,* to *I wonder if we are going to get back.* Anxiety was just as real in Houston where scientists were scrambling to solve all the problems which were occurring on Apollo 13. This was not empty fretting; the dangers were real.

The calm, problem-solving approach of the ground crew and the astronauts allowed them to think through solutions to their problems. It did not take all the anxiety away, nor was the worry unfounded. But choosing to respond creatively rather than simply fret about the problem saved their lives.

In the same way, Paul knew that sitting around worrying would not solve anything and would be counterproductive. Worry without action, however justified, ruins our health and well-being and offers no solution. So Paul, fearful and concerned as he was, took steps: He "sent Timothy" (v. 2), and he prayed "night and day" (v. 10).

Prayer is not an empty exercise; it is the power of God brought to bear upon a dilemma. Paul recommended it in the same place he advised: "Do not be anxious about anything, *but in everything, by prayer and petition, with thanksgiving,* present your requests to God" (Phil. 4:6, emphasis added).

Paul also did all he could to defuse the worrisome situation: he sent Timothy. It was a practical and useful action that accomplished two goals. Timothy was able to provide the encouragement and instruction which the new believers needed, thereby reducing the risk of spiritual ruin. Timothy was also able to bring back news of how the Thessalonians were doing, thereby giving an accurate picture of their spiritual condition.

Some anxiety or worry is natural if the perils are real. But it should never stop there. Prayer is always called for, and then we should take the responsibility to act upon the situation in whatever way is necessary or possible.

V. PRAYER

Sovereign Lord, life is full of difficulties, pain, and situations which test our strength and faith. So often we cannot see beyond the moment, the press of agonizing uncertainty. By your Spirit, by your Word, remind us to pray, resting in your loving authority. Then, release your wisdom to us so that we may act with courage and grace. Amen.

VI. DEEPER DISCOVERIES

A. Trials (v. 3)

Trials can be unsettling. They can plunge us into doubts, fears, compromise. But it does not need to be so. Trials can also forge trust, confidence, and commitment. What makes the difference? Probably several factors, but a couple surface in this section of 1 Thessalonians 3.

Paul had sent Timothy "so that no one would be unsettled by these trials." Timothy was to support and encourage, instruct and guide so these believers would gain hope and courage. God uses other believers to assure and keep us on course spiritually. Throughout this letter Paul exhorted several times: "encourage each other." As part of a community with a common Lord and common purpose, we have the responsibility to help one another along the way, to hold one another accountable, to inspire when needed, to comfort, to keep one another focused on the true purpose of life.

As the author of Hebrews wrote, "But encourage one another daily, as long as it is called Today, so that none of you may be hardened by sin's deceitfulness" (Heb. 3:13). Again he wrote, "And let us consider how we may spur one another on toward love and good deeds. Let us not give up meeting together . . . but let us encourage one another—and all the more as you see the Day approaching" (Heb. 10:24–25).

Paul also reminded the Thesssalonians that "we were destined for [trials]." There is help and strength in knowing that everything is going according to plan. No matter how the situation looks, God is still sovereign; life has not taken a wrong turn. We have all been told ahead of time. Paul must have told the Thessalonians when he was with them, he wrote it again, and Jesus spoke of it several times: "In this world you will have trouble" (John 16:33).

So perhaps when difficulties arise, or when we are hurting or suffering in any way, the question is not so much, "Why?" but, "What did I expect?" This world system and Satan are set against us.

B. Overflowing Love (v. 12)

Agape (love) is a word used by New Testament writers to describe a new kind of love. Its peculiar definition is found exclusively within the pages of the New Testament.

Paul told the Thessalonians to *agape* "each other" and "everyone else." He left no escape clause. For those who try to find excuses, or exceptions, there simply are none. This command applies not only to fellow believers, but to all outside the community of faith. Perhaps Paul was even thinking of Christ's startling command in his Sermon on the Mount to love our enemies (Matt. 5:44). The Christian is to love. This love should be constantly increasing and overflowing. It cannot be hidden.

Love is more than an emotional stirring of the heart, although it often involves this. The kind of love that Christians are to express can be given to other persons, in spite of their treatment or abuse. This is a love that looks beyond self. Consequently, it is a love which comes from the Spirit of God.

VII. TEACHING OUTLINE

A. INTRODUCTION

1. Lead Story: A Matter of the Heart
2. Context: Paul was more than an apostolic CEO. He was a friend and mentor to people who came into the church by faith. He seemed to identify with the heart of the Lord, who loves us in such a pure and strong manner. In this chapter, Paul expressed that love candidly.

B. COMMENTARY

1. The Inevitability of Persecution and Hardship (3:1–5)
   a. Paul's desire to know their status (3:1–2)
   b. Paul's warnings about persecution (3:3–4)
   c. Paul's fears about how they were doing (3:5)
2. The People's Strength in Pain (3:6–10)
   a. The good news about the Thessalonians (3:6)
   b. Paul's joy about their growth (3:7–8)
   c. Paul's prayers for them (3:9–10)
3. Prayer for Increasing Strength (3:11–13)
   a. Hopes for seeing the people (3:11)
   b. Prayer for their love (3:12)
   c. Hopes for their future (3:13)

C. CONCLUSION: HOUSTON, WE HAVE A PROBLEM

VIII. ISSUES FOR DISCUSSION

1. Do you find it hard to share your emotions of love with others? If so, what can you do to overcome this problem?
2. What was Paul's main concern for his friends and fellow Christians? Looking back over your week, what were *your* main concerns for friends and fellow Christians? How could you approach the coming week differently?
3. How do prayers help people who are going through pain or persecution? Discuss personal examples. What motivates or encourages you to pray for others?
4. What desires and hopes highlight Paul's beautiful statement of best wishes for his friends in the last paragraph of this chapter?

1 Thessalonians 4

The Difference Christ Makes

I. **INTRODUCTION**
Where Are We Headed?

II. **COMMENTARY**
A verse-by-verse explanation of the chapter.

III. **CONCLUSION**
Timely Advice

An overview of the principles and applications from the chapter.

IV. **LIFE APPLICATION**
Under Construction

Melding the chapter to life.

V. **PRAYER**
Tying the chapter to life with God.

VI. **DEEPER DISCOVERIES**
Historical, geographical, and grammatical enrichment of the commentary.

VII. **TEACHING OUTLINE**
Suggested step-by-step group study of the chapter.

VIII. **ISSUES FOR DISCUSSION**
Zeroing the chapter in on daily life.

"*D*espair is not the loss of the beloved, that is misfortune, pain, suffering; but despair is the lack of the eternal."

Soren Kierkegaard

1 Thessalonians 4

IN A NUTSHELL

*P*aul calls all Christians to holy lives, emphasizing sexual purity and a growing agape-love for each other. He reminds us to live our own lives with care, in view of the assured return of Christ to earth and in view of the coming resurrection.

The Difference Christ Makes

I. INTRODUCTION

Where Are We Headed?

*T*he sky over Germany in 1941 was as blue as it had ever been. Dark green shoots struggled through the soil, then spring awakened in bursts of color. The sun cast its rays among the birch and alder leaves, lighting them to electric green. Spiders spun webs in filigree while finches scavenged sticks and grass for nests.

The heavens seemed unaware, even mocking in the routine march of the seasons while the long winter of hardship saw no end for the Jews who were laboring and dying in Nazi concentration camps. They scratched for survival. They died alone, frozen behind a hut, shot in a ditch, gassed in an underground chamber. Still the sun shined on and the rain fell, predictably, as it always had.

Yet within the human heart stirs a tenacious determination to find meaning, to discover purpose even in the midst of meaninglessness. And in the darkened hole of suffering, when the universe seems out of control, the human soul searches desperately for even the smallest pebble with which to build an altar of hope.

Under the gaze of Nazi guards, a group of Jewish men were assigned to carry stones from one end of the camp to the other. It was rumored that they were going to construct a building. Others whispered that the stones were part of a road project. Day after day the men hauled stones, their backs aching, their bodies groaning against the load. Then, finally, they completed the task. The stones were piled in an enormous mass, ready for use. The men stretched upon their bunks that night with a slight flutter of accomplishment.

The next day the men were ordered into the camp yard as usual. Their new assignment was to carry the same stones to the other side of the camp—back to where they had been in the beginning. With dampened spirits they began.

It became apparent that the task was meaningless. The stones were moved back and forth, without purpose. And as the men realized that they were acting in futility—that they and their work were meaningless—they began to waver and then to die.

There is a divine grace within us which urges us to believe that life is not pointless, that we are not superfluous. That is why when hope dies, we die. Our God-given sensibilities will not allow such nonsense.

Paul wrote to the Thessalonians, urging them to live by God's standards. His constant plea was for Christians to live a holy life, worthy of God's name. Yet Paul was aware of the hostile atmosphere and the persecutions faced by all believers. He was aware that evil seems to prosper and righteousness seems to suffer. So he was quick to link the present with the future. Today makes sense only when eternity is kept in our sights. Live in holiness and obedience now, for "the Lord himself will come down from heaven, with a loud command, with the voice of the archangel and with the trumpet call of God . . . And so we will be with the Lord forever" (1 Thess. 4:16–17).

II. COMMENTARY

MAIN IDEA: *The point of life is to please God, to learn what brings him honor and delight. By living a worthy life today, we will then be prepared for that great day when Christ returns and ushers us into the eternal Now.*

A Our Call to Holiness (4:1–8)

SUPPORTING IDEA: *The call to godliness never stops. There is always something else we can learn, one more habit we can conquer, another practice we can adopt. One of the most important areas of holiness is our sexuality.*

4:1. The little word **Finally** does not signal a conclusion. It is a transition to the rest of what Paul had to say.

He was ready to give the Thessalonian Christians another reminder—that they already knew how to live in a way that pleased God. Paul, Silas, and Timothy had personally instructed them while in Thessalonica. What Paul was now writing was nothing new.

Paul reminded the Thessalonian believers of their need to please God. He was complimenting them on their spiritual progress. Even so, they must not relax, and he urged them to do so **more and more**. The progress of these Thessalonians brought sincere joy and delight, but Paul always expected and urged people to do "more and more." Paul himself modeled that kind of living.

4:2. From the very beginning Paul and the others had given clear moral instruction on the life that was expected from those who chose to follow Christ. Living in a way that pleases God is not optional, but a moral necessity and obligation. The Thessalonians knew this from the start. No one could claim ignorance. Pleasing God is the point of life. As our Creator and Savior, he has the right to tell us how to live . . . and to expect us to obey.

The moral instructions which the missionaries gave the Thessalonians were not concocted by these men, but these teachings came by the **authority of the Lord Jesus.** Paul, Silas, and Timothy may have been the messengers, but the truth originated in God. It is an echo of what Paul wrote in 2 Corinthians 5:20: "We are therefore Christ's ambassadors, as though God were making his appeal through us." The words spoken and written were weighted with the authority of God himself. This places on believers the responsibility of obedience. It also brings sobriety to what follows as Paul wrote of purity, love, and Christ's return.

In a day when the authority of the Word of God is not taken seriously, this sober reminder is needed. Those who teach must make a clear distinction between what the Bible says and human opinions. The seasoned teacher of preachers, Dr. Haddon Robinson, always asked people who were speaking, "Where did you get that?" This is a good question, and it is one we should ask ourselves when teaching or giving advice.

4:3. Most people are eager to know God's will. They attend seminars and read books on how to find it. Behind the interest is a desire to have God make our choices for us. "I am praying for God to show me his will about whether or not to take this job," some say. Others ask, "Pray that my son will know God's will about which college to attend."

God's revealed will is very specific. There is no guess work, no need for searching or seminars. There is only the choice of whether we obey when we know what God desires.

One of the specifics of God's will is that his followers participate in the process of sanctification—being set apart and dedicated to God. Since God is holy, his followers must also be holy. This is reflected in a pure life . . . keeping oneself from **sexual immorality.**

4:4. First Paul stated the Christian moral standard positively: **control [your] own body in a way that is holy and honorable.**

Paul instructed us to **learn** self-control. Control does not come automatically but involves work and discipline as well as clear instruction in Christian ethics. Self-control is an evidence of God's Spirit at work within us, but it requires our vigorous cooperation.

In this context, **body** refers to one's own body, which is to be controlled and held in holiness as something set apart for God's use.

4:5. Paul then stated the ethical mandate negatively: **not . . . like the heathen, who do not know God.**

Either we take control of our bodies and their desires, or those desires will control us in unholy lusts. The world around us is a case study in this problem. We live in a culture in which sexual obsession and perversion are rampant. This is displayed graphically day after day through broken lives, the media, conversations, and social confusion. Christians are to stand apart from such a culture.

The manner of life for a Christian is self-control, not through rigorous rules and disciplines—though these can be helpful—but by turning our bodies over to the Lord. Listen to Romans 6:13: "Do not offer the parts of your body to sin, as instruments of wickedness, but rather offer yourselves to God . . . and offer the parts of your body to him as instruments of righteousness."

And again, in Romans 6:19, Paul writes: "You used to offer the parts of your body in slavery to impurity and to ever-increasing wickedness, so now offer them in slavery to righteousness leading to holiness."

True self-control, true distinction from the unbelieving world, means having the will to give ourselves to God, to the control of his truth and his Spirit. To be pure, as God demands, is not a whim of the moment, but a habit of holy obedience to God, perfected and strengthened over time.

4:6–8. Paul next supplied the motivation for sexual purity. Three strong reasons emerge: (1) God's punishment on the disobedient (v. 6b), (2) it is the life God has called us to live (v. 7), and (3) to reject it is to reject God and the Spirit he has given us (v. 8).

4:6. Paul declared, **The Lord will punish men for all such sins.** Paul was not talking about the physical or relational consequences which sexual sins create. He was looking ahead to the day of judgment when Christ, who judges the world, will punish all who commit sexual sin. It is an appeal to look down the road, to realize that the day of God's judgment is more certain than tomorrow morning. There is no escaping it, and we would do well to live with a greater realization of that great day's inevitability. Fear of consequences is good motivation.

God always desires to forgive. For those who have participated in sexual sin there is always hope. God's forgiveness is extended to those who confess, repent, and seek God. But this cannot be glib agreement. What is needed is the heart-penetrating cry for God's cleansing and forgiveness. God will not punish what he has forgiven, though consequences of our sin may follow.

There is no distinction between believers and unbelievers here. Sexual sins will be punished. God's will may be difficult, but it is not confusing.

4:7. God calls us to purity as a way of life: **to live a holy life.**

God himself calls the individual. He brings us into union with Christ; he has made every spiritual transformation possible. It is God who places us in his kingdom. Impurity is inconsistent with such a work and such a calling.

We have not simply been saved *from* something (God's wrath), but we have been bought *for* someone (God) in order to showcase God's glory and character.

It is hard for us to imagine being owned by someone else. The truth is that every "man is a slave to whatever has mastered him" (2 Pet. 2:19) and we are all mastered by something. As believers, our call from God is to be mastered by him.

4:8. Those who do not follow these instructions do **not reject man but God, who gives you his Holy Spirit.** The person who ignores the demand for sexual purity is not setting aside a law of man, but is disdaining God himself. The demand for purity springs from God's essence.

These demands of God are strengthened by the fact that his Spirit lives within each believer. The construction of the sentence emphasizes the Spirit's holiness, tying in with this whole section on pure living. It places an undeniable obligation upon the Christian to live in harmony with the *Holy* Spirit of God within. To live any other way is to repudiate the most precious gift given by God.

B Our Call to Love (4:9–10)

Supporting Idea: *Christlike love is not something we attain, a state of being or an emotion; it is an ongoing action that we constantly strive to improve.*

4:9. With the words **Now about brotherly love,** Paul moved on to something new, yet not so new. He was still describing "how to live in order to please God" (vv. 1–2).

Paul again commended the Thessalonians, remarking that when it comes to brotherly love, he did not need to say a thing. The church in Thessalonica was a caring community. It had that kind of reputation. Love was, and still is, the hallmark of the Christian community. In fact, it is the supreme call on the life of any believer.

The word used here for love is *philadelphia*—brotherly, family love. It is affection marked by strong action. This word describes people who meet the needs of others; it is not mere talk or superficial socializing.

Paul did not need to instruct the Thessalonians about love, not only because they were living it out so well, but also because they had **been taught by God.** This refers to the direct ministry of the Spirit of God upon the hearts of those who belong to him. God himself instructs, guides, urges. "God has poured out his love into our hearts by the Holy Spirit, whom he has given us" (Rom. 5:5). We then pour out this love to one another. It is a direct work of God.

4:10. Although love is a work of God, it takes willing and obedient hearts. So Paul turned to these people and said, "Great job!" These Thessalonians loved **all the brothers throughout Macedonia.** True to the Spirit of

God, the love of these Christians was generous and broad; it was not self-protective or clannish. They expressed their love widely and unsparingly.

There is not a point in this life when we decide we have arrived and everything is settled. There is no complete maturity level where we sit back and gaze at the past for the rest of life. There is always the challenge of moving forward and doing more of what Christ has commanded. All believers need to keep growing in love.

Ⓒ Our Call to a Christian Lifestyle (4:11–12)

SUPPORTING IDEA: *We should work hard at living wholesome, responsible lives, not only to please God, but to achieve a good reputation for Christ's church and his people.*

4:11. Paul's concerns for the church surfaced in three areas: restlessness, meddlesomeness, and idleness.

First, Paul told these believers to be ambitious toward a **quiet life**. He used an electric word *(ambition)* and coupled it with a low-energy word *(quiet)*. Paul wanted them to see that a tranquil, restful life does require effort. It is easy to get carried away in spiritual excitement and emotional issues, but we must purposefully aim toward balance and calm. This is what Christ calls us to practice.

Second, Paul turned to the problem of meddlesomeness. He admonished, **mind your own business**. Every person's first priority is to handle his own affairs and responsibilities.

Third, he instructed them to **work with your hands**. This was not a divine command for everyone to do manual labor, though it certainly blesses such work. Paul's intention was to keep these people responsible in their daily living. Work is a reflection of our Christian life and ethics; it must not be neglected. Christianity should never be separated from daily routine and obligations. It finds its most eloquent expression in the common traffic of commerce, farming, nursing, construction, and all other forms of work.

4:12. Why all this fuss? Why Paul's concern about whether they were working or idle? Two reasons.

First, because Paul wanted to **win the respect of outsiders**. He was not concerned about popularity. Nor did he need the unbelieving community to validate or approve the church. Instead, he wanted us to realize that how we live is noticed . . . and remembered. If we are habitually late for work, or gain a reputation as the office gossip, it hurts the name of Christ. Unbelievers do not separate our faith from our behavior—nor should we. If the church is to be slandered, let it be without grounds. Our desire as believers should be to live exemplary lives.

Second, Paul was concerned that these believers **not be dependent on anybody**. This was a call to financial independence. We are not to make ourselves a burden to anyone, although those who are truly in need may accept the generosity of others (2 Cor. 8–9). To presume upon brotherly love and generosity and so evade the responsibility of work and providing for oneself or family was not acceptable to Paul.

D The Future of All Believers (4:13–18)

SUPPORTING IDEA: *No matter how busy we are, how pressing our problems, how overwhelming our circumstances, a day is coming when Christ shall return. That certain future gives courage and strength for today.*

4:13. Paul was about to clear up some misunderstandings regarding death and the coming of Christ which were causing the Thessalonians a good deal of anxiety. Evidently these young Christians felt that those who died before the return of Christ would miss out. They must have thought there was a special advantage to being alive at Christ's return. This meant, in their minds, that there was a disadvantage for those who did not make it.

Paul was concerned that the Thessalonians quit sorrowing and grieving like everyone else around them. People outside of Christ have no basis for facing death with hope. In the pagan world death was grim and full of despair. In our own time it is a mystery many people ignore. Consequently, deep anguish and sorrow were often expressed for the dead person. It was this kind of sorrowing which Paul wanted the Thessalonians to stop.

The death of a Christian is something very different from the death of an unbeliever. The difference is the hope, the assurance, of resurrection.

To straighten out their thinking and calm their fears, Paul went on to describe the coming of Christ and the place of the living and the dead in that magnificent event.

4:14. First Paul made an assertion of faith: **We believe that Jesus died and rose again.** This is the bedrock of our faith. Paul then tied the truth of Christ to the unknown future. Whatever Christ *does,* his people follow. Wherever Christ *is,* his people are there. Christ died and rose again. Christians who die (fall asleep) will rise again. Christ will return again. Those who have died will return with him. All of this is carried out by God's power.

4:15. Paul next introduced something new, a special revelation **according to the Lord's own word.** He received direct word from Christ about what followed.

Paul's primary concern was not to teach an eschatological lesson but to assure and encourage the young church at Thessalonica. He did this by stating with the authority of Christ's words, that everyone who is alive on earth at the time of Christ's coming will *not* go before those who have died. Paul was pointing the believers away from grief toward hope regarding those who had died. The dead loved ones will not miss out or come in in second place.

4:16–17. Paul then handed the readers a program of sorts, an order of service. Christ is coming, and this is how it will occur.

- The Lord, Christ himself, will come down.
- There will be a lot of noise.
- The dead believers will rise first.
- Christians who are still alive on earth will rise next.
- Everyone meets together with Christ in the air.
- Eternity begins!

The Lord himself will come down. The rapture of believers is a very personal affair. Christ himself will be there in his great and shining glory.

With a loud command, with the voice of the archangel, and with the trumpet call of God. It is debated whether this describes one great sound, or whether two or three distinct sounds will occur. The "shout" or "loud command" could signify the shout of triumph expressed by Christ, the conqueror of death, as he descends from heaven. Whether it is one or more sounds, the coming of Christ will apparently be a noisy event.

It is also debated whether unbelievers will be aware of his coming. This is not clarified. It could be that, like those who accompanied Saul on the road to Damascus, something will be heard, but the source or significance will not be comprehended.

The dead in Christ will rise first. The dead believer is still **in Christ.** Nothing can separate us from Christ once we belong to him—not even death. Yet, though their souls are with Christ, they are to receive resurrected bodies. It is this rising that Paul spoke of. God will bring with Jesus those who have died (v. 14). The first order of business is their resurrection to glorified bodies.

After that, we who are still alive . . . will be caught up. There is probably no great time span implied here, for everything will happen in "the twinkling of an eye" (1 Cor. 15:52). There will be people from every nation on earth when Christ returns, and these will be "caught up." The word can be translated "snatched, swept up, carried away by force." The Lord literally "snatches" the bodies of the living, and they are transformed and their bodies glorified.

These two groups, the living and the dead, will join Christ in the clouds. This is a great company. All believers back through the centuries will join those who are living at that moment, forming the church united with its head, Christ. And then **we will be with the Lord forever.**

4:18. Paul's conclusion: **Therefore** (in view of this) **encourage each other with these words.**

MAIN IDEA REVIEW: *The point of life is to please God, to learn what brings him honor and delight. By living a worthy life today, we will then be prepared for that great day when Christ returns and ushers us into the eternal Now.*

III. CONCLUSION

Timely Advice

Time flies, we say;
Alas, but no—
Time stays,
We go.

—author unknown

Paul did not know this short poem, but he did have two eternal perspectives that motivated his short time on earth:

- He had seen the risen Christ. In a special revelation he was given a unique call to Christ. This was an event that showed him paradise (Acts 9:3–6; 22:6–10; 2 Cor. 12:1–6).

- He believed in the "soon-to-be" physical return of Christ to earth, with the accompanying resurrection and judgment (1 Cor. 3:10–15; 2 Cor. 5:10).

With those in mind, and with the compelling motivation of Christ's love (2 Cor. 5:14–15), Paul wanted to live for Christ without shame.

This chapter is a call for us to do the same—live holy lives, pleasing God, loving others.

It is apparent that we are not naturally inclined to live this way. Our sexual drive and the temptation to hate, hold grudges, snub or discard one another are powerful. Paul addressed this directly, describing the consequences of disobedience. He then explained details about Christ's return, answering the Thessalonians' questions about the sequence of that event which had bothered them.

His answer is good theology—information as well as great motivation for obedience and readiness. Of all people, Christians have hope and incentive if we will think in a wise and godly way. And then act that way as we go. Time stays, we go. That is, until that day described in this chapter.

PRINCIPLES

- We know most of what is God's will for our lives through the Bible, including sexual purity. We know enough to keep us busy being and doing what God desires.
- Knowing how to love one another is not the issue; it is *wanting* to do the unselfish actions of love.
- Faithful obedience to God is one way Christians gain the respect of unbelievers.
- God wants us to know that those who died as Christians will not miss the return of Christ. They will receive the same glorified bodies at his return as those who are still alive.

APPLICATIONS

- People who care about God's will must diligently guard their sexual purity.
- We would do well to worry less about where we live or work, and to worry more about what kind of people we are.
- Schedule times and ways to love others.
- We should encourage bereaved people with the facts of the future resurrection, not just sentiment.

IV. LIFE APPLICATION

Under Construction

In the 1960s, there was a song made popular not so much for its tune as for its message. It spoke of the sameness of everyone's life—same cars, same universities, same kinds of kids, same ambitions, same "little houses made of ticky-tacky . . . and they all look just the same." It was the refrain of an era—that conformity was to be avoided at all costs. Despite the frustration, even in the sixties there was nothing radically new. The American dream was examined by a younger generation and found wanting, but nothing satisfying or novel was offered in its place. It was simply mimicry of another sort, and it was found to be equally empty.

The problem is that we all conform to something. Conformity is a fact of life. It is the stuff on which societies and civilizations are built. It is our tendency to conform that makes it possible for us to live in relative peace with one another. But conformity can have its downside.

As Christians, we often take the same approach to our inner lives, our character. We become content to aspire to sameness. We are satisfied with small gains or no apparent losses.

I think that Paul might consider such lives "ticky-tacky." He was never satisfied, never at rest in his pursuit of becoming like Christ. He wrote it with energy in Philippians 3:12–4:1: "Forgetting what is behind and straining toward what is ahead, I press on toward the goal" (3:13–14). It was that same drive toward increasing maturity, the same yearning to become like Christ that found expression in his letter to the Thessalonians: "we instructed you how to live in order to please God, as in fact you are living. Now we ask you and urge you in the Lord Jesus to do this *more* and *more*" (1 Thess. 4:1, emphasis added).

Never content with being like everyone else, Paul aspired to more noble purposes—being like Christ. This ambition drove distractions away. It caused a holy restlessness that kept him working and loving, giving and trusting more and more. It was not that he was a non-conformist; he was a conformist of the highest order. He had simply left behind all smaller ambitions and aimed toward conformity to Christ.

We can choose to be easily satisfied like those around us, building "ticky-tacky" lives that look just the same. Or, as C. S. Lewis described it, you can

> "imagine yourself as a living house. God comes in to rebuild that house. At first, perhaps, you can understand what he is doing. He is getting the drains right and stopping the leaks in the roof and so on: you knew that those jobs needed doing and so you are not surprised. But presently he starts knocking the house about in a way that hurts abominably and does not seem to make sense. What on earth is he up to? The explanation is that he is building quite a different house from the one you thought of—throwing out a new wing here, putting on an extra floor there, running up towers, making courtyards. You thought you were going to be made a decent little cottage: but he is building a palace" (Lewis, *Mere Christianity*, 174).

V. PRAYER

God of all creation, by the power of the resurrected Christ create in me a holy desire. By your Spirit fire my will to follow after you in increasing devotion. I refuse apathy and forsake the ambitions of society that would swallow me in mediocrity and blind me to the nobler goal of being like Jesus. Amen.

VI. DEEPER DISCOVERIES

A. Purity (vv. 3–8)

When many young people seek the will of God, they are typically thinking about college, or work, or perhaps job location. Wanting to know God's will is a great desire for life, but it needs to be balanced with the fact that most of God's will is already known—in the Bible.

Paul introduced the subject of sexual purity by saying, "It is God's will that you should be sanctified" (v. 3). Then he proceeded to talk about controlling one's own body so as not to hurt others or take advantage of them sexually.

Sanctification means to be set apart for holy use. No person can be used by God if his or her life is not pure sexually. Throughout the Bible, sexuality has implications beyond any physical act. It is viewed as a likeness of spiritual union and fidelity. God has consistently presented himself as the bridegroom and his people as the bride. Turning away from obedience and love for God has been likened to adultery. More personally, God calls individuals to sexual purity since we are mysteriously joined with him through the Holy Spirit: "Do you not know that your bodies are members of Christ himself? . . . Do you not know that your body is a temple of the Holy Spirit, who is in you, whom you have received from God? You are not your own; you were bought at a price. Therefore honor God with your body" (1 Cor. 6:15,19–20). If you want to know the will of God, this is a good place to start.

B. Mind Your Own Business (v. 11)

Paul's statement that we should "mind our own business" is not a directive for personal isolation. He was speaking about being a "busybody," worrying too much about the behavior of others while neglecting personal responsibilities.

We are responsible for our own lives and are accountable before God for how we live them. In that sense, everybody is to pull his own weight, contributing to the work of ministry and developing Christlike character and habits. The one person you can exercise control over is yourself.

When you mind your own business, you believe that, in one sense, life is just between you and God. You are accountable to God alone. You care about others, but you carry your own load. In Galatians, Paul wrote, "Carry each other's burdens, and in this way you will fulfill the law of Christ" (Gal. 6:2). A little later he adds, "Each one should carry his own load" (Gal. 6:5).

These verses seem contradictory, except the word translated "burdens" and the one rendered as "load" have very different meanings. One concerns carrying the pain of others and the problems they face. We should pitch in and help them carry that load. The other word focuses on personal responsibility and the load of accountability that each person has before God. In this case, no one can help us. Here we stand alone.

It is this latter idea that Paul was concerned with in writing to the Thessalonians. We are to mind the business that is ours and get to work, no matter what anyone else does.

C. Return of Christ (vv. 14–18)

The return of Christ and the resurrection of believers are based on the first resurrection when Christ crashed through death and hell: "We believe that Jesus died and rose again and so we believe" (v. 14). A parallel passage in 1 Corinthians 15 adds logical argument when Paul writes, "For if the dead are not raised, then Christ has not been raised either. And if Christ has not been raised, your faith is futile; you are still in your sins. Then those also who have fallen asleep in Christ are lost. . . . But Christ has indeed been raised from the dead" (1 Cor. 15:16–18,20). Christ is the foundation and authority for our present purpose and future expectations.

And the return of Christ (the resurrection of the dead, the uniting with Christ of the living) is based on the authority of God himself: "According to the Lord's own word . . . The Lord himself will come down" (1 Thess. 4:15–16). God is the cause, the power, the initiator, and the focus of the snatching of all believers into eternity.

Life past, present, and future drives toward the final and everlasting glory of God. The first chapter of Ephesians repeats again and again that all of this is "for the praise of his glory."

The resurrection of Christ began the recovery process of all that rightfully belongs to God—which is everything. It happens in this way:

1. First, Christ will be resurrected, defeating the power of death and sin through the legitimate power of God.

2. When Christ returns, the dead in Christ will be resurrected and united with him as his rightful possession.

3. After that, those who are still living at the time of his appearance will be snatched from the earth to be joined with him in the air—again, as his rightful possession.

4. Christ then will proceed to defeat all powers, authorities, and dominions (1 Cor. 15), crushing his enemies, the last being death.

5. Everything—flowers, elephants, trees, rivers, rocks, all that exists—will be released to Christ's rightful rule, freed from the twisted domination of Satan (Rom. 8:21). Christ will reign, and everyone and everything will acknowledge and submit to his authority (Phil. 2:10).

6. Then Christ himself will submit to the Father so that God "may be all in all" (1 Cor. 15:28).

There may be debate among theologians about sequences and events, but Christ's return is as certain as God himself. He will come. He will rule. He will be glorified. Knowing this should produce two things in the believer: a life lived in obedience to God and courage.

VII. TEACHING OUTLINE

A. INTRODUCTION

1. Lead Story: Where Are We Headed?
2. Context: While sexual immorality seems rampant these days, it has always been an area of great temptation and failure on the part of both believers and unbelievers. It certainly was in New Testament times and at Thessolonica. Paul gave sensible warnings about this problem, explained what pure love for one another was like, and then detailed a great answer to questions about the return of Christ.

B. COMMENTARY

1. Our Call to Holiness (4:1–8)
   a. Paul's teachings about life (4:1–2)
   b. God's will about sexual purity (4:3–6a)
   c. God's judgment for offenders (4:6b–8)
2. Our Call to Love (4:9–10)
   a. The teaching by God (4:9)
   b. The obedience by Christians (4:10)
3. Our Call to a Christian Lifestyle (4:11–12)
   a. Proper care for one's self (4:11)
   b. Resulting respect from others (4:12)
4. The Future of All Believers (4:13–18)
   a. The basis for this teaching (4:13–14)
   b. The sequence of the events (4:15–17)
   c. The encouragement from this teaching (4:18)

C. CONCLUSION: UNDER CONSTRUCTION

VIII. ISSUES FOR DISCUSSION

1. What is God's will? Has it already been revealed or is it about what job to take or where to live or whether we should marry? What are the wishes of God for us in what he writes to us in the Bible?
2. Why is sexual morality so important?
3. What helps you stay clean sexually?
4. How does brotherly love show in daily life?
5. Can you rehearse the sequence of events about the return of Christ in your own words? What excites you most about it?
6. What is unique about the Christian resurrection theme when compared with other religions?

1 Thessalonians 5

Our Future Hope and Our Present Life

Quote

"*It* is since Christians have largely ceased to

think of the other world that they have

become so ineffective in this."

C . S . L e w i s

1 Thessalonians 5

IN A NUTSHELL

The Lord's return will be a big surprise to many people. But for Christians, the Lord's return and the work of Christ on the cross are great motivations for obedience. As Paul concluded his letter to the Thessalonians, he included specific commands for them to follow and then prayed for them to walk in God's grace.

Our Future Hope and Our Present Life

I. INTRODUCTION

Be Ready

I wonder how often people think about Christ's return. Not just with an intellectual head nodding, or a whimsical sigh punctuating life's pressures, but with serious expectation. I confess that I must work hard at confronting my day or peering into the week's possibilities through the lens of Christ's future triumph and inevitable return.

Yet Jesus thought that the promise and certainty of his return held tremendous implications for life now . . . and later. In his travels around the Palestinian countryside, he wove stories about wedding feasts, virgins and lamp oil, household servants, and fig trees—each with a pointed warning about the need for readiness when he returned. Just as his earthly life forced people to points of decision, so his return will reveal the course those decisions took. "When the Son of Man comes, will he find faith on the earth?" (Luke 18:8). Will we be ready?

In this final chapter of 1 Thessalonians, Paul revisited Christ's warnings by reminding his readers that we should not be slumbering. Sleep is not the position of readiness. It belongs to the night, that time of dimmed perceptions when we quit our work, take it easy, and resist everything but our own comfort. Snuggled down in the covers, wrapped in our own warmth, we do not want to be awakened.

Yet before spiritual sleep actually overtakes us, drowsiness tugs, warning of trouble and eventual danger. It is that twilight time in which we waver between two worlds. Without vigilance, the world of the spirit becomes more fuzzy and the world of sleep, the non-spiritual, grows more real. We yawn a lot. Eventually, we close our eyes.

To prevent spiritual snoozing, Paul gave warning of the eventual outcome of being unprepared, the promise of readiness, and practical instructions on living a life pleasing to God.

II. COMMENTARY

MAIN IDEA: *The church is living in a significant period, the last days, so we should stay awake to how we can live for Christ and walk in his light. This includes some specific ways to treat each other both inside and outside the church. By God's grace we can do it!*

A The Times (5:1–3)

SUPPORTING IDEA: *Nobody knows when Christ will come again. It is a secret kept with God. But he will come.*

5:1. Although Paul was still writing concerning the coming of Christ, he shifted his focus away from how the Lord will come to what that coming will mean for different people. Evidently the Thessalonians had been taught concerning the return of Christ, for Paul began by saying, **about times and dates we do not need to write to you.** He then went on to reinforce what he must have talked with them about.

The "dates" and "times" can be translated as *epochs* and *crises*. This phrase refers to a *time period* and to the *conditions* of a particular time. Both are secrets, hidden with God (Acts 1:7), not known by anyone else, even the angels or Jesus (Matt. 24:36).

5:2. Paul declared, **The Lord will come like a thief in the night.** This possibly refers to the "times" in verse 1. The imagery is taken from Jesus' teaching in Luke 12:39–40: "If the owner of the house had known at what hour the thief was coming, he would not have let his house be broken into. You also must be ready, because the Son of Man will come at an hour when you do not expect him." The suddenness and surprise of Christ's coming was well understood. A thief does not call up and ask if he can stop by at 2:30 in the morning. He just comes . . . when most people are sleeping.

5:3. Paul expanded on Christ's return by using the imagery of a pregnant woman's labor pains. Just when everyone is thinking things are fine, when no one seems worried or concerned, when life is going well, then Christ appears. But the contrast is even more dramatic. People are saying and thinking **peace and safety**, while **destruction** is actually what happens.

The people who will be caught by surprise are the unbelievers, the great masses of people throughout the world. It is not clear whether they are feeling secure and well economically and politically, or whether they feel "safe" spiritually, believing there is no God to worry about. Whatever the source of their security, it will be suddenly and irrevocably shattered: **they will not escape.**

The destruction is not physical death, but the spiritual separation and judgment which Christ brings. Christ the judge has come at last, and the verdict is hopeless ruin, the loss of all that gives purpose. Like a woman in labor, the judgment comes upon the unbelieving world suddenly, inevitably, with pain. There is no reversing the matter.

B Our General Lifestyle (5:4–11)

SUPPORTING IDEA: *Because of what Christ has done for us, our commitment to him is a commitment to his light, a lifestyle just the opposite of moral darkness and its consequential wrath.*

5:4. Paul then began to discuss the implications of Christ's return for the believer before his great coming. To the unbeliever, Jesus will come like a thief in the night, but for the believer his return will come as no surprise, nor will he come like a robber who destroys the owner's possessions. Those who believe **are not in darkness.**

In the Bible, *darkness* typically refers to moral or spiritual blindness, disobedience, or separation. This sphere of darkness is where the unbelieving world lives. Paul's contrast is sharp: you (the Thessalonians and all believers) are not living in unbelief, spiritual darkness, moral confusion: "For he has rescued us from the dominion of darkness and brought us into the kingdom of the Son he loves" (Col. 1:13). For believers, Christ's coming is nothing to fear.

5:5. Christians are **all sons of the light . . . sons of the day.** Having just said what Christians are *not,* Paul asserted what they *are.* The contrast is bold and unmistakable. Unlike an unbeliever, a Christian is in relationship with **the light,** with God and Christ. Not only that, but the Christian lives in moral and spiritual enlightenment. His life and understanding are affected by his faith in Christ.

To draw the contrast with bold strokes, Paul again stated, **we do not belong to the night or to the darkness.** There can be no confusion. The Christian is different in life and destiny from the unbeliever.

5:6. Now the reasonable conclusion: Being in the light, having been rescued from the darkness, looking to a future with God, not being subject to his wrath—these should make a difference in how we live.

Paul urged, **Let us not be like others, who are asleep.** The comparison is most likely to the unbeliever, though it may also target the Christian who is apathetic. Whoever these people were, they were "asleep."

Falling asleep is a picture of what can happen to us spiritually, ethically, or morally if we are not watchful. We simply drift off. Drowsiness begins, we become comfortable, our hearts become insensitive. Spiritual drowsiness slowly paralyzes the spirit. The person who was once vibrant and wide awake in following Christ can become lethargic and lazy about issues of the spirit.

As you drive down the road and your eyelids become heavy, it is best to open a window, turn up the radio, or pull over for a rest. Spiritually, at the first sign of sleepiness, when church becomes a bit boring, or prayer drops off a bit and you do not seem to care as much—make some corrections. At the very least, ask God to renew your heart, open your spirit to his renewing work, and find accountability with another believer. Falling asleep at the wheel can have disastrous results; so can falling asleep spiritually.

We are to be **alert and self-controlled**. To be alert is the opposite of being asleep. An alert person is aware, sensitive to life around him, and morally and spiritually awake.

5:7. Paul reflected back to his analogy of night and day. He had already defined those outside of Christ as being of the night, and those whose faith is in Christ as being of the day (v. 5). Remembering that Christians are of the day, he emphasized the need for readiness and alertness by reminding the readers that sleepiness and drunkenness belong to habits of the night. These behaviors should not characterize those of us who are of the day.

5:8. Paul then turned to one of his favorite metaphors—armor (Eph. 6:13–17)—to describe the readiness, seriousness, and combatant qualities of a Christian.

We are to have on the **breastplate** of **faith and love**. These two virtues, like the breastplate, protect the heart. Faith guards it within, keeping us in close relationship with Christ. Love guards our hearts in our outward behavior toward others, keeping us pure and expressive of the spiritual vitality within.

Along with this, we are to keep on the **helmet** of the **hope of salvation**. Our head is the control center of our life; it processes our thoughts and emotions; it analyzes life. The certainty of our salvation, when Christ comes for us (as described by Paul in 1 Thess. 4:14–17), protects our thinking from being overwhelmed by the evil around us. Hope is certainty, not wishful thinking. Christ will come and we shall live with him forever. This reality guards us in times of persecution, temptation, weariness, and all other dangers that come from living in a hostile environment.

5:9. God has appointed us to salvation, not wrath. This is a continuation in thought from verse 8. Our salvation is certain; there can be no wavering on the issue. God appointed, or destined, us to gain salvation. He has offered us the means to grace, and we must exercise determined and persevering faith to see salvation realized in fullness when Christ appears.

In the same way, God did not appoint, or destine, us to suffer his wrath. Wrath is the judgment of God upon unbelief. For the Christian, there is no fear of Christ's appearing: "Therefore, there is now no condemnation for those who are in Christ Jesus" (Rom. 8:1).

5:10. According to Paul, the life of the believer is secure, determined, safe in the hands of God. Christ died so that **whether awake or asleep, we may live together with Him.**

Paul's use of the "asleep" metaphor goes back to its usage in 1 Thessalonians 4:15, referring to death, not moral failure as in 5:6–7. Christians who die, "sleep" in the sense that it is not the end. One day the trumpet of God will arouse the dead to bodily transformation.

5:11. This assurance of salvation, of transformation into the image of Christ, should encourage us. As we are encouraged, we must continually talk about it and remind one another of our future so that we do not grow weary or lose heart in the spiritual battles which rage. Every Christian has a responsibility to encourage others in the faith. In an age which is prone to criticism and fault-finding, the same fault-finding attitude can creep into the church. It can become natural to talk about others or critique their performance instead of examining our own hearts or encouraging others toward godliness.

While encouragement inspires us to keep on track spiritually, **building each other up** deals with investing in others. We should add to other people in such a way that they will be spiritually stronger. In this way, we encourage maturity and fortification of character. We need to look upon all persons as those for whom Christ died. They are eternal soul-spirits just as valuable as we are. We have a responsibility to encourage them to remain faithful and growing until the end.

Strong, Specific Commands for Life (5:12–22)

> **SUPPORTING IDEA:** *There are some specific ways to display the changes Christ brings into our lives.*

1. Behavior toward church leaders (5:12–13)

5:12. Paul turned to some practical matters of church life. The first involves the relationship between the congregation or community and its church leaders. Paul first called the congregation to give respect to **those who work hard among you, who are over you in the Lord.** Honor is due to church leaders, whether they are paid staff or officers who give their time and energy (elders, deacons). Spiritual leadership is difficult and weighted with responsibility. These leaders are engaged in hard work. One of their "thankless" duties is to **admonish.** This deals with pointing out faults or mistakes, errors in individuals or the community. Those who perform this task take on a difficult responsibility, and they are to be respected and honored.

There are implications for the leaders as well. They are to **work hard.** It is good work, and they are to get their energy from God. Part of the job description of the church leader is to "stand before" or **be over** others **in the Lord**. This is not a dictatorship, but a way of lovingly and authoritatively teaching the Word of God to the people. Leaders are also to point out wrongs, sins, and failures in the lives of their people and congregation. This is not a favorite task, but it is essential to the health of believers and the church.

5:13. Not only are we to honor our leaders; we are to think of them in a special, affectionate way. We are to **love** them. The basis for this love is **their work**. Church leaders are performing a good work for Christ and his people. This deserves our highest respect and love.

Paul then turned our attention toward the person sitting next to us, or across the aisle, and commanded us **to live in peace with each other**. This is a maintenance program for a healthy church: keep the peace.

To live in peace means to go as far as possible to live in harmony with others, or "as far as it depends on you" (Rom. 12:18). Many people who would not rob a bank or tell a blatant lie will sin against this clear command. They speak or act in ways that are divisive. People who act this way hurt not only themselves and other persons, but they also hurt the church. People outside the church notice such things and stay away.

2. Instructions for all the church (5:14–15)

5:14. Paul next launched into some short, staccato instructions and commands for Christian living. He focused on three types of people in the Thessalonian church who presented different concerns for him. He spoke about the **idle**, the **timid**, and the **weak**.

The **idle** were to be **warned**. There were those in the Thessalonian church who were so certain of the imminent return of Christ that they became lazy in their daily living. If Christ is coming back soon, they may have reasoned, what is the point of the daily grind? In their neglect they became careless in their responsibilities, spent too much time chatting over the back fence, and contributed little to the general welfare of the church.

Today the attitude is opposite to that first-century expectation, but the result is the same. Christ seems so long in coming, and life keeps rolling along at a predictable clip. We become idle in our Christian responsibilities. Too absorbed in the daily routine, we fail to use our gifts, time, and lives for others and the church. Idleness springs from distorted thinking, and such thinking deserves a warning: it is wrong—stop it!

An Alaskan dog musher described to me the differences between the huskies in the straps of his sled. "Some of them are known as dishonest dogs," he said. "They learn how to fake it, to pretend they are working hard by leaning against the harness without really pulling." Maybe we should examine ourselves to see if we are "dishonest" by failing to do our share of Christ's work.

The **timid** were to be **encouraged**. These were people who had become discouraged, perhaps depressed. They may have felt this way because of difficult circumstances, or because they despaired of living up to the high standards of the Christian faith. These people needed to be helped, not warned. They needed to hear, "You can do it."

The **weak** were to be **helped**. These were the spiritually weak in Paul's time, and they are still found in every church. Perhaps they lack knowledge or experience; it could be that they struggle with certain sins which continually defeat them; they may lack courage or find it difficult to trust God. They are weak in the faith and need to be helped along the way. We all identify with this group of people at some time or other.

In our weakness and inability to conquer sin, we find that Christ helped us by the sacrifice of his life. Can we who have been so blessed do any less for others in their time of need?

Everyone should be dealt with in **patience**. "People work" can be frustrating at times. We are all so different. We mature at different rates, have different personalities and backgrounds, likes, dislikes, and habits. These factors can make it complex and difficult when we are called on to warn, help, instruct, or encourage others.

Love is what helps us **be patient with everyone**. Love is patient. It does not seek its own way. Because of our selfish tendencies, we need patience from others, even as we need to be patient. Perhaps that is why God can be so patient with us. He recognizes that our mistakes, our bungling efforts, our one step forward and three steps back are valuable learning exercises in growing in grace and character.

5:15. Paul was concerned not only with relationships within the church, but relationships outside the church. He gave commands for behavior **to each other and to everyone else.**

The payback rule is common: You get me—I will get you. You shove me—you had better be ready. Getting even, exacting our own sense of "justice," is a strong human tendency.

Jesus was different. He contradicted just about everything we naturally do. He often began his moral lessons with "you have heard" and then called for a change by following up with "but I tell you" (Matt. 5:21–30; 33–37; 38–42; 43–47). He brought a new way to live. He is the new way.

Only as we abide in Christ and entrust our grievances, hardships, and the wrongs we suffer to him can we live with this command. It is not natural, but it is possible. It marks a distinctly Christian approach to life. Paul detailed this approach by quoting Proverbs 25:21–22 in the Book of Romans when he called us to live in peace, to not take revenge. He told us, "If your enemy is hungry, feed him; if he is thirsty, give him something to drink" (Rom. 12:20), then added "Do not be overcome by evil, but overcome evil with good" (Rom. 12:21). And so Paul told the Thessalonians to be kind to each other and to everyone else. This means everyone both inside and outside the church.

3. Inner attitudes (5:16–18)

5:16. Paul admonished, **Be joyful always.** This is short and to the point. The key, however, is the word *always.* Paul meant this literally. Christian joy is not bound by circumstances or hindered by difficulties. In fact, joy in the New Testament is often coupled with sorrow or suffering.

The Thessalonian believers had already experienced this strange duet, like an inspiring song played in minor key (1 Thess. 1:6). When the sorrow or suffering results from being identified with Christ, the Holy Spirit creates a supernatural joy—a wellness of soul that cannot be dampened by adverse situations. The explanation may be found in 2 Corinthians 4:16–18: "For our light and momentary troubles are achieving for us an eternal glory that far outweighs them all."

But we should remember that we have a part in this joy. We are the ones commanded to be joyful. It is a choice, a deliberate response that focuses on the grace and goodness of God. As the writer to the Hebrews directed us, "Let us fix our eyes on Jesus, the author and perfecter of our faith, who for the joy set before him endured the cross, scorning its shame, and sat down at the right hand of the throne of God. Consider him who endured such opposition from sinful men, so that you will not grow weary and lose heart" (Heb. 12:2–3).

5:17. The next staccato note follows: **pray continually.** This means never stop praying. Paul was a busy missionary, and he wrote about the Christian's duty to fulfill daily responsibilities, so this is not a command about speaking non-stop prayers. It refers, however, to the attitude of prayer, or reverence before God. The Christian's life of righteousness and his approach to relationships and responsibilities should be such that he maintains a constant attitude of being in God's presence. Such a person will pray often and about many things, including requests, praise, and thanksgiving. This command also means that we should never quit praying.

5:18. The next command requires trust in the sovereignty of Christ: **give thanks in all circumstances.** It recognizes God's eminence in all events.

A thankful spirit does not come naturally to most of us. Certainly it pushes us beyond our natural capacities when difficult or painful situations invade our life. This command to be thankful, no matter what happens, is possible only by God's grace. When we can agree with God that he works all things out for good to those who love him and are committed to obedience (Rom. 8:28), then we can thank him.

For those who wonder about God's will, here it is emphatically stated: **this is God's will for you in Christ Jesus.** There is no need for searching, seminars, books, or "fleeces." God's will is that we are to be joyful, prayerful, and thankful because we are his children.

4. Personal responsibility and spiritual integrity (5:19–22)

5:19. This verse is a caution against dousing water on the fire of God's Spirit: **Do not put out the Spirit's fire.** This can happen in any heart when the Holy Spirit is stifled, allowing thoughts or actions which are contrary to the character or practices of God. The fire of the Spirit is suppressed when he is rejected, when his convicting power, righteousness, and judgment (John 16:8–11) are ignored. We douse the Spirit's influence in our life through doubt, we drench him with anger, we drown his power with immorality.

The Holy Spirit himself cannot be put out. He is God. We can, however, stifle his work in our life. We quench the Spirit, or grieve him, when we do not reach for those attitudes and graces which are peculiarly his— love, joy, and peace (Gal. 5:22–23). The Spirit's fire is quenched when his presence is ignored or his guidance and conviction in our hearts are suppressed and rejected.

5:20. Paul declared, **Do not treat prophecies with contempt.** Others have translated this verse, "Despise not prophecies." This is a present tense verb, addressed to "you" (plural), and therefore intended for the entire church.

Exoutheneo, the Greek word for "despise" or "contempt," is a very strong word. It means to act as if the thing in question means nothing.

Many interpreters understand this negative command from Paul to mean that in the church services at Thessalonica, some believers were so worried about the misuse of the charismatic gifts that they allowed none at all. Just the opposite problem occurred in Corinth, where Paul tried to temper and balance the uncontrolled use of such gifts.

Scholars are divided today on whether prophecies—direct revelation from God—are still God's gift to the church or whether these ceased with the completion of the New Testament. Certainly the revelation of God through the Bible is the standard against which all else must be measured.

Perhaps the main way we "despise" prophecies today is that we neglect or ignore the Bible's message by not doing what it says. Such behavior quenches the Spirit who guided the writing of the Bible and despises the prophecies themselves.

Another more indirect application of this verse would be when we belittle gifts or ministries of other Christians because we think ours is more important.

5:21–22. Paul advised the Thessalonians to **Test everything.** The word *everything* is universal; it leaves nothing free from examination by spiritual standards and understanding. Paul did not explain how to carry out this testing. But certainly the fire of the Spirit (his convicting, guidance, and illumination), the instructions from the apostles and missionaries, and the written revelation of God are the lenses through which we must scrutinize everything.

The clear purpose of this testing was to **hold on to the good**, and to **avoid every kind of evil**. The good has its origin in God; evil is a distortion of that good. Evil is twisting and destructive. We must not flirt with evil.

Benediction (5:23–28)

> **SUPPORTING IDEA:** *All these instructions about our lifestyle can be accomplished only by the help of the Lord. We should seriously pray for his assistance and presence.*

5:23. After all these commands and instructions, Paul offered the hope and possibility of living this extraordinary life: **May God himself, the God of peace, sanctify you through and through.** Christianity is not a teeth-gritting effort, an ascetic call. Though personal effort and responsibility are required, we are offered the very hand of God. He pulls us up to a higher and more glorious way of living.

We are not left on our own. The **God of peace** sets us apart for his use. Only those who live in peace with God—who have entered through the way of Christ's reconciliation—can be sanctified. To be sanctified is to be "set apart" or "consecrated" for holy use.

God works to make us sacred, or holy, **through and through**, in every part of our lives. Paul emphasized this as he prayed that their **whole spirit, soul, and body be kept blameless at the coming of our Lord Jesus Christ.** He prayed that our entire being—our personal, spiritual inner life, the true person; our body, the vehicle for our earthly journey—would be totally under the holy claims of Christ.

To be found **blameless** does not mean earthly perfection. Paul was expressing his desire that no one would be able to make an indictment against the Christian's life. It is the same idea as expressed in Philippians 2:14–15: "Do everything without complaining or arguing, so that you may become blameless and pure, children of God without fault in a crooked and depraved generation."

5:24. The follower of Christ is never left alone: **The one who calls you is faithful and he will do it.** Here is great comfort and assurance. We are never abandoned. God's faithfulness is the undergirding of our faith. Our hope and trust are placed in a trustworthy God. The call of God is not separated from his faithful enabling. In our struggles we can rest in him.

5:25–28. Paul closed his first letter to the Thessalonians with three personal requests to the church.

He asked them to **pray for us.** As the missionaries had remembered the Thessalonians, now these believers were to remember Paul, Silas, and Timothy before God. Prayer was not a ritual or an empty duty to Paul. He saw it as the power of God unleashed, the place where the Christian was transformed in the presence of God.

In asking for their prayers, Paul was also identifying with these Christians. He recognized that, although he was an apostle, he was still human. An adventurer in the Christian life, he was facing hardships, struggles, weariness, and temptations just as they did—in every way their brother.

5:26. Paul then told the Thessalonians to **greet all the brothers with a holy kiss.** A kiss upon the cheek was a warm greeting practiced widely in that culture, and still is today. The distinction was Paul's description of this greeting as a "holy" kiss. This was a pure, holy greeting that was never to degenerate into romantic or sexual feelings. Love and affection are marks of the church, but these distinctions must always be kept blameless and holy.

5:27. First Thessalonians was far more than just a friendly correspondence. This becomes clear in the next command: **I charge you before the Lord.** Paul put these believers under oath, and he did so before the Lord. He was binding them to **have this letter read to all the brothers.** Paul had written from his heart, and he had written on some important matters for everyone in the congregation. This letter was not simply to be circulated, but to be read aloud when the Thessalonians gathered for worship.

5:28. As he began, so Paul ended—with grace: **The grace of our Lord Jesus Christ be with you.** The grace of God is the well-spring of all God's goodness to us. Forgiveness, salvation, peace, the gift of his Holy Spirit, the maturing of our lives in holiness, the stirring of our hearts and will to follow him—all these are of grace.

MAIN IDEA REVIEW: *The church is living in a significant period, the last days, so we should stay awake to how we can live for Christ and walk in his light. This includes some specific ways to treat each other both inside and outside the church. By God's grace we can do it!*

III. CONCLUSION

"Have a Good Day"

Most of us say goodbye to someone by using whatever clichè is in vogue: "See you soon." "Take it easy." "So long." "Have a good day." There is nothing wrong with this.

Paul, on the other hand, wished people God's grace—the kind favor of God which we need no matter who we know or what our circumstances!

Along with wishes for God's grace, Paul also concluded his letter with a long list of specific responsibilities for every believer. Undergirding them all was Paul's main priority of living for Christ instead of self. The question behind all the decisions we face is always, "Who are we living for?"

I once spent a good part of a Saturday morning arguing in a very civil, kind exchange with a new acquaintance about a number of issues he could not resolve:

- We covered creation and what I thought were clear proofs of the design of the Creator.
- We weighed both sides of the question of God's sovereignty and our free will. I thought I handled the perplexities in a way that would have made my seminary profs proud.
- We spent a good forty-five minutes on why God "imposes" (my friend's word) his moral code on us.

Finally, at the end of those three questions and a little over two hours later, my friend said candidly, "I guess I just want to run my own life."

"Why didn't you say that earlier?" I asked. "We could have saved some time."

While I will never know if that was a good use of our time, I do know he finally got to a basic question: submission. Sometimes this is the real issue behind our hesitancy to obey.

Paul summed it up by writing: "We are convinced that one died for all . . . that those who live should no longer live for themselves but for him who died for them and was raised again" (2 Cor. 5:14–15).

That is the issue, whether it is a long list of commands as in this chapter or any other act of obedience our Lord requires. Our response to this issue will determine whether we have a good day, in the best sense.

PRINCIPLES

- Only God the Father knows the time of our Lord's return to earth.
- Self-controlled, disciplined living is a mark of the Holy Spirit in our lives.
- People who care about the Lord's return to earth will be conscientious to live life for his pleasure today.
- There is a Christian way to act toward all people who come into our lives—and it is known as love and grace.

APPLICATIONS

- Studying prophecy is good, but it is better to live in obedience to the prophetic Word of God.

- We are to live with habits, character, and purposes that can withstand the glare of daylight exposure—the scrutiny of God. We are not to live a dark life, hidden in its intentions or practices.
- Show respect for your Christian leaders and parents.
- Trust God to do his part in our sanctification and growth as we do our part.

IV. LIFE APPLICATION

Creating Conflict

"So next time you come you have only to find the lamppost and look for those two hills and walk through the wood til you reach my house. . . . But remember—you must bring the others with you. I might have to be very angry with you if you came alone."

"I'll do my best," said Edmund.

"And, by the way," said the Queen, "you needn't tell them about me."

With these simple words, C. S. Lewis, in his book *The Lion, the Witch and the Wardrobe,* hands his character, Edmund, the script which will set his course. His mission is to bring his brother and sisters back, not only to Narnia, but to the White Witch's house. And, to conduct his plans deceitfully. His goals and motives will determine his conduct.

On the opposite side of the page, the other children (Lucy, Susan, and Peter) have decided that the White Witch is an evil which must be stopped, or at least fought. With everlasting winter ruling Narnia and the witch turning all good creatures to stone, Lucy expresses what the others believe: "I mean we must do something." And so, the author has scripted their course as well, but it is contrary to Edmund's.

Lewis has written into his tale what all good storytellers include—conflict. With differing scripts, his characters will come into opposition with each other . . . and this keeps the reader reading.

Conflict, tension, the unsettled nature of the story and its characters—these keep us in a darkened theater or bind us to the pages of a book. The key to such conflict is that the characters, inescapably linked together, live by a different script. They are set at odds. But while conflict is marvelous in movies and literature, it is quite another thing in real life. Most of us invest a great deal of energy trying to create a conflict-free environment for ourselves.

But we live in a universe engaged in cosmic hostility. The earth is, quite literally, the setting for an epic story created by the clash of life and death, holiness and depravity, wisdom and foolishness, order and chaos. There is no avoiding it. The struggle between Satan and God, darkness and light, hell and heaven, is more pervasive in life than in the best of apocalyptic fables.

Just as fictional tension is created through characters with differing texts to follow, real-life conflicts occur by the same means. As Christians, we have been given a script which determines our goals and conduct—to live lives worthy of God's calling—so that our "whole spirit, soul and body [will] be kept blameless at the coming of our Lord Jesus Christ" (5:23). To assure this, we are to "test everything. Hold on to the good. Avoid every kind of evil" (5:21–22). All of this is at odds with a society which does not embrace faith in Jesus Christ or even an admission of the divine.

We should not go searching for conflict. Nor does conflict have to be mean-spirited. But there should be little surprise at the obvious reality that we exist in conflict with the thinking, goals, and values that litter the landscape of our world. When we try to minimize the differences, we wander from the script and improvise our way to bland compromise and mediocre living. We become "like others, who are asleep" (5:6).

When Paul wrote about the coming of Christ, his purpose was to inspire us to a higher purpose and more holy lifestyle. When he wrote about our existence as sons of light, his purpose was not to create an us-vs.-them mentality, but to transform our outlook on daily living.

Christ has promised that we shall see him face to face, live forever with him, share in his kingdom and glory. These truths should determine what occupies our thinking, our time, our investments, our lives. It will set us in conflict with all other claims. But in the midst of hostility we are called to be alert and "self-controlled, putting on faith and love as a breastplate, and the hope of salvation as a helmet" (5:8).

V. PRAYER

Jesus, triumphant and eternal, we honor and delight in you. With bold and relentless desire, you have rescued us from the terrors of an eternity without you. It is hard to imagine or comprehend the fate from which you have saved us. Even so, stir in us the flames of your purpose that we may boldly live before others your mercy and hope. Amen.

VI. DEEPER DISCOVERIES

A. Darkness and Light (vv. 4–5)

"God is light, in him there is no darkness at all" (1 John 1:5). There is nothing confusing in this statement. Everything God does is good and righteous. All his thoughts, plans, motives, and acts are perfect. He operates in the bright sunlight, not under cover of night. He has no need to hide his activities.

People, on the other hand, often seek the cover of darkness. We operate at times behind people's backs, or in the shadows where no one can see us clearly, where our thoughts or motives cannot be detected.

When our Lord calls us to be people of the daylight, he is using the term metaphorically. Because the moral light of Christ is in our lives, we are to live out in the open, unashamed, guiltless. We can speak about each other openly because we speak in love. We can open our business books to scrutiny because we deal honestly. We can invite people into our homes because we have relationships built on love and mutual respect. We belong to the day.

When Paul wrote of our belonging to "the day," he discussed our need for self-control. Christ is our example as he grew in "grace and truth." He did not sneak around while on earth, hiding his intentions or beliefs, operating in a covert manner. He proclaimed his love and mission openly.

It is intriguing that when Christ was crucified, darkness was imposed upon the earth in the middle of the day. "It was now about the sixth hour, and darkness came over the whole land until the ninth hour, for the sun stopped shining" (Luke 23:44–45). This darkness was a symbol of the judgment he was taking in our place as all our acts of the night were placed upon him.

When we understand this great grace of our Lord, we will want all the more to "walk in the light, as he is in the light" (1 John 1:7). We will do so with gratitude for his holiness and what he did when he forgave us and helped us to follow him . . . in the daylight.

B. Respect for Leaders (vv. 12–13)

Paul's words about respect for those who work hard as spiritual leaders are very clear: "Hold them in the highest regard" because of their work.

This does not mean that pastors are responsible for enforcing this rule. You cannot demand respect; you earn it over time through love and by living and teaching the Word of God.

Parents can teach their children proper respect for their spiritual leaders—starting with the Sunday school teacher of the little children. Respect does not mean idolizing such leaders. There should be no hero worship. It is Christ whom we honor as Lord. He is complete, perfect. Everybody else needs his grace day by day.

VII. TEACHING OUTLINE

A. INTRODUCTION
1. Lead Story: Be Ready
2. Context: As Paul concluded his letter of love and concern, he reminded us about the return of Christ, using the analogy of that

great day to remind us to walk in the light. He then listed some commands that should characterize every believer.

B. COMMENTARY

1. The Times (5:1–3)
   a. The common knowledge of Jesus' return (5:1–2)
   b. The characteristics of the time (5:3)
2. Our General Lifestyle (5:4–11)
   a. Life in the light (5:4–8)
   b. Salvation for those who follow this lifestyle (5:9–11)
3. Strong, Specific Commands for Life (5:12–22)
   a. Behavior toward church leaders (5:12–13)
   b. Instructions for all the church (5:14–15)
   c. Inner attitudes (5:16–18)
   d. Personal Responsibility and Spiritual Integrity (5:19–22)
4. Benediction (5:23–28)
   a. Paul's prayer for purity (5:23–24)
   b. Final instructions and blessing (5:25–28)

C. CONCLUSION: CREATING CONFLICT

VIII. ISSUES FOR DISCUSSION

1. What is "the day of the Lord"? When will it begin? In what specific ways can you be ready?
2. Give some examples of ways that light should characterize our lives. Can you name some ways in which the thinking or actions of Christians can become darkened?
3. When it comes to daily righteousness or personal obedience, what is our responsibility and what is God's?
4. Why do you suppose God cares so much about how we treat other Christians as well as those outside the church? How do our dealings with others reflect our belief system?
5. When reading the instructions about how to treat each other (5:12–15), what part is personal and what belongs to the church?
6. How can you be "joyful always" when life brings so much pain?
7. Why are God's commands so uncompromising: "always," "continually," "all," "everything," "every kind"? (5:16–22). Why cannot he be more lenient? What differences would it make?

Introduction to

2 Thessalonians

LETTER PROFILE: SECOND THESSALONIANS

- Letter written by Paul, somewhere between A.D. 51 and 52.
- Sent to a young, inexperienced assembly of believers in the city of Thessalonica, many of whom were Gentiles.
- Letter written by Paul, but with the greeting and support of Timothy and Silas who had been with Paul when he first traveled to Thessalonica.
- Paul praised the Thessalonians for their faith and love; assured them that their suffering was not in vain; and encouraged them by pointing to the future destruction of the wicked and the certain glory for those who belong to Christ. Paul concluded by offering solidarity with these suffering Christians, standing with them in prayer.

AUTHOR PROFILE: PAUL

- Jewish-born in Tarsus, near the Lebanese border in modern Turkey.
- Roman citizen.
- Prominent, Jewish religious leader, highly educated as a Pharisee.
- Persecuted Christians before his own dramatic conversion in A.D. 35.
- Visited Thessalonica on his second missionary journey about A.D. 51 (see Acts 17). There he witnessed instant conversions followed by strong persecution.
- Known for his tireless pioneer work to Gentiles.
- Imprisoned by Nero's regime in A.D. 67 in Rome (see 2 Tim. 4), where he was executed the next year.

CITY PROFILE: THESSALONICA

- An urban center of the Roman Empire, the city of Thessalonica had a strong Greek culture; it was built in 315 B.C. by Cassander, a general under Alexander the Great.

- Located in European Macedonia, present-day Balkans; the city's population in the first century was about two hundred thousand.
- Thessalonica, the capital of Macedonia, was a booming commercial center located at the crossroads of the great road from the north and the main east-west trade route.
- Many foreign merchants lived in the city, making Thessalonica an ethnically and culturally diverse city.

2 Thessalonians 1

God's Justice

I. **INTRODUCTION**
When Is Enough, Enough?

II. **COMMENTARY**
A verse-by-verse explanation of the chapter.

III. **CONCLUSION**
"And the Winner Is . . ."
An overview of the principles and applications from the chapter.

IV. **LIFE APPLICATION**
Woe Is Me
Melding the chapter to life.

V. **PRAYER**
Tying the chapter to life with God.

VI. **DEEPER DISCOVERIES**
Historical, geographical, and grammatical enrichment of the commentary.

VII. **TEACHING OUTLINE**
Suggested step-by-step group study of the chapter.

VIII. **ISSUES FOR DISCUSSION**
Zeroing the chapter in on daily life.

"*O*ut of our beliefs are born deeds; out of our deeds we form habits; out of our habits grows our character; and on our character we build our destiny."

Henry Hancock

2 Thessalonians 1

I N   A   N U T S H E L L

*P*aul began with a greeting to the Thessalonian church. He complimented them for their growing faith and love and their perseverance in difficulties. He assured them that the hardships they endured strengthened their lives and created a worthiness in them as they suffered for Christ's kingdom. Paul wrote of God's coming judgment on those who reject Christ and promote evil. At the same time, he encouraged the believers that Christ's coming would usher in their awaited glory.

God's Justice

I. INTRODUCTION

When Is Enough, Enough?

*S*uppose someone tried to convince you that the goal of life was to have all the fun you wanted—for ten minutes. Indulge yourself, place no limits, disregard all the rules and laws, ignore the feelings of others. You would find personal fulfillment if, for ten uninterrupted minutes, you lived without restraint.

I presume you would consider such an offer foolish. After all, there is more to life than just ten minutes.

Then, assume the offer was extended to one hour: "Do whatever you feel like doing, whatever passions or desires compel you. Take what you want, use whatever you see, cater to your every whim."

Foolish, even for an hour.

Then, another proposition. What about a day? Certainly you deserve one day to give in to your cravings. One day to release your desires without the constraint of conscience, the weight of other opinions, the burden of standards. "Wouldn't it be fun? Wouldn't it be a relief?"

Still not worth it, you decide. The consequences are too great.

He keeps at you. A month? A year?

"No," you argue. "Life is more than a day or a month, or even a year."

"What about twenty years?"

At what point does self-indulgence become worth it?

If it is wrong to give into passions, selfishness, inconsiderate behaviors, and sin for ten minutes, do we ever reach a place where such conduct becomes reasonable? If it is foolish to throw off restraint for a short time, how much more foolish to indulge ourselves for longer periods . . . for a lifetime.

In light of eternity, sin is never worth any of our time.

Paul wrote to the Thessalonians commending their endurance in suffering and persecution. Rather than crumbling under the pressures of a godless society or giving in to their culture's standards, they chose to say "No" to the world and "Yes" to righteousness. They understood that life consisted of more than this hour, this day, or this week. Life extended through the years and beyond, into eternity where Christ would pronounce judgment on every life and deed. For those who indulged their passions and lived a self-consumed life, refusing his mercy and righteousness, there would be punishment. For those who responded in faith to God's grace, committing themselves to Christ's commands and holiness, there would be glory and reward.

For the next ten minutes, dedicate yourself to self-discipline and right living. Then add ten minutes more, then an hour. As we keep our eyes on life's true goal—the pleasure of God in eternity—we can live life faithfully, ready for Christ's return.

II. COMMENTARY

MAIN IDEA: *Unlike other letters, Paul made no assertions of his apostleship or authority in 2 Thessalonians. Instead, he wrote a very personal, gentle letter to the believers in Thessalonica who were suffering for their faith. He urged their continued perseverance, good behavior, love, and faith. He reminded them of Christ's coming, at which time the unbeliever would receive punishment, while the Christian would obtain honor, glory, and the eternal presence of Christ Jesus.*

Greeting (1:1–2)

SUPPORTING IDEA: *The church exists only in God the Father and his Son Jesus, in whom reside grace and peace.*

1:1–2. Within a short time of Paul's first letter, the Thessalonian Christians received yet another letter, co-authored by Paul, Silas, and Timothy. Since the three missionaries were still together, most likely only a few months separated the two writings.

They wrote **to the church of the Thessalonians in God our Father and the Lord Jesus Christ.** This is a good description for any local church—grounded in a particular city or town, belonging to the community, but connected to our Lord. The church is an assembly of people, called out from the city's throng to worship Christ, then sent back into the city to proclaim and live his goodness. We are citizens of two worlds.

It is tempting, when reading Paul's letters, to skip over the first verse or two and "get on to what the letter is about." The words *grace* and *peace* so often salute the reader that they seem as significant and meaningful as our greeting, "Hi, how are ya?" Just standard form.

But this is bedrock theology at the start. These two words address significant dilemmas which all people face: the struggle for personal significance and the assault of personal guilt and failure. Paul directed us to the answer: **God our Father and the Lord Jesus Christ.**

God is the wellspring of grace. He has a passion to give, and this extravagance issues from his love. Grace is any action or gift freely given; it cannot be earned or retained by personal effort. And when we are speaking of God's grace, it covers everything: "For who makes you different from anyone else? What do you have that you did not receive? And if you did receive it, why do you boast as though you did not?" (1 Cor. 4:7). But even though God's grace does not depend upon us, it can be hindered by us through sin, ingratitude, and refusal.

Peace can be achieved only through Jesus Christ. Peace deals with our legal standing in the court of God's justice. No person could ever survive the divine judgment without divine intervention. The cross and resurrection give us access to God through faith in Christ; we are admitted into his presence. Peace from God also brings wholeness, restoring the fragmented condition of humankind. Through Christ, we are able to grow and develop into a complete self and personality as God designed. We also join other redeemed persons to form a unified community as he purposed.

𝔹 Thanksgiving (1:3–4)

SUPPORTING IDEA: *After praying that the Thessalonians would experience God's grace and tranquility of soul, Paul offered thanksgiving for these believers because they continued to develop in faith and love. This church, although experiencing hardship, was an example to other churches because of their community life and brotherly kindness.*

1:3. Paul's opening statement, **We ought always to thank God for you,** sounds a bit like grinding duty. While obligation is felt in these words, it is not guilt-induced. Paul did, in fact, feel a duty to give thanks, but the duty was not to the Thessalonians, but to God. Paul literally had an outstanding debt before God, and it was a debt of thanks. Hearing of the spiritual life and development in the Thessalonians, he knew that God's faithfulness undergirded their progress. Consequently, an ongoing offering of thanks was due God.

The Thessalonians were the occasion of Paul's thanksgiving, but God was the source, for it was God working in partnership with them "to will and to act according to his good purpose" (Phil. 2:13), which had caused their faith and love to increase. **Faith** refers to the outworkings of Christian belief. It is not just doctrinal dogma, but coherence of belief and action.

Love, action to meet the needs of others, was continually increasing like a river overflowing its banks. This overflowing was demonstrated by all the Thessalonian believers. We often find it easy to select certain people whom we will love or befriend, maybe those close to our own age who share similar interests. But Paul praised these Thessalonians because they expressed love indiscriminately toward all the brethren.

1:4. This is a transition verse, combining delight with a hint of what will follow, as Paul turned his attention to the hardships these believers confronted each day.

Despite some of the internal problems of the church, such as laziness and misconceptions about Christ's return, Paul recognized some sterling qualities in these believers. He encouraged them by pointing these qualities out: **we boast about your perseverance and faith in all the persecutions and trials you are enduring.** Love (v. 3), faith, and perseverance (made possible through hope), form the eternal triad. Paul not only commended them for these qualities, he also spread the news to other churches. He was thrilled at the genuine nature of their faith.

The persecutions and trials they encountered were varied, yet unspecified. These could have been anything which resulted from faith in Christ and from seeking to live righteously in a hostile culture. Their perseverance was not a meek "I can take it" but a steadfast, heroic strength from God. Such continuance under difficulties results from an abiding trust in God's goodness and sovereignty.

Ⓒ Encouragement—Christ Is Coming (1:5–10)

SUPPORTING IDEA: *The Thessalonians' ability to endure hardship showed the power of God in their lives. This evidence should assure them of a glorious future when Christ returns, for he would find them worthy of the grace he had bestowed on them. Those who were tormenting them in this life would face judgment in the future, when true justice would fall upon all creation.*

1:5. Paul declared, **All this is evidence that God's judgment is right.** All what? It hardly seems likely that the persecutions were evidence of God's righteous judgment. Most likely it was the Thessalonian believers' ability and power to persevere and stand in the midst of unjust hardship that was the evidence pointing to God's judgment. The truth of the gospel, the transformation of their lives, and the certainty of the future justice of God were proved by their ability to withstand the various trials. In addition, their lives proved God's indwelling power. The Thessalonians' endurance came from something besides human capacity. By their lives they validated God's work and strength and the transforming energy of his Spirit.

Suffering with strength not only proves the power of God; it also proves the saving faith held by these Christians: **as a result you will be counted worthy of the kingdom of God.** They did not *attain* their salvation through suffering; they demonstrated it, thus establishing their worthiness to inherit the joys and benefits of God's favor when Christ establishes his kingdom.

1:6–7. Paul wanted to encourage these believers further by directing their attention to the future. **God is just,** he declared, and then he pointed to the evidence for this truth.

That God is just can be consolation, encouragement, or warning. Unlike human judges and justice systems that are flawed, infected by personal bias and limited understanding, God is the measure of his justice. God is unchanging, uncompromising, impartial, and righteous. We can be certain that God's judgments are fair, above appeal, without dispute.

One demonstration of God's fairness is that **he will pay back trouble to those who trouble you.** Every act takes place before his God's holy gaze. He deals out justice, matching punishment with sin.

Conversely, those who are now being troubled will, at that time, receive **relief,** or rest. This is not a rest from work, but an easing of stress and trouble. It seems likely that Christians will in some way "work" forever, but the future envisions a "work" unhindered by external sniping and quarreling. This relief will come when Christ returns to earth.

In modern times, people are fascinated with space. This curiosity fluctuates, depending on social and political conditions on earth. When life seems relatively settled, we gaze toward the stars. When life seems to unravel, we become a bit more myopic. Even so, from simple mythologies to scientific theorizing, life beyond earth is a constant curiosity to earthlings. Unlike the alien invasions depicted in sci-fi literature, the actual assault upon earth will come when Jesus Christ is revealed from heaven **in blazing fire with his powerful angels.**

Christ will be revealed **from heaven.** The second appearing of Christ has been termed the *parousia* (his "coming presence"), and the *epiphany* (the "shining forth"). Here it is called the *apocalypse* or "unveiling." The word indicates a type of revelation, a disclosure of what already exists (Rom. 16:25). Just as the servant of Elisha had his eyes opened so he could see heaven's horses and chariots of fire upon the hills (2 Kgs. 6), so will the eyes of all people see the reality of what already exists—Christ the judge.

The power belongs to Christ, and this power is given him by the Father. He will be joined by angels, messengers of his will, "mighty ones who do his bidding, who obey his word" (Ps. 103:20). Jesus will be revealed in the blaze of his glory and the consuming fire of his justice. It is a future of judicial power and rightness, and it establishes moral direction and certainty for us today. Our moral and ethical center is found in the holiness of God and the inevitability of his judgment.

1:8. Paul then explained who would receive Christ's judgment. It is reserved for **those who do not know God and do not obey the gospel of our Lord Jesus.** Various opinions exist as to whether one or two groups are in mind here, or if Paul is giving a different description of a certain type of people.

The phrase "those who do not know God" possibly refers to people who, not having heard the gospel, nevertheless stand guilty because they refuse to acknowledge the general revelation of God. "The wrath of God is being revealed from heaven . . . since what may be known about God is plain to them, because God has made it plain to them. For since the creation of the world God's invisible qualities—his eternal power and divine nature—have been clearly seen, being understood from what has been made, so that men are without excuse" (Rom. 1:18a,19–20).

The phrase "those who do not obey the gospel" may refer to people who have been exposed to the truth of Jesus Christ, yet have refused it. Having turned their backs, they have not obeyed. They have denied his sovereign right as Lord.

1:9. Having described those who would be judged by Jesus, Paul stated the nature of Christ's judgment. There will be no deliberations, no appeals, no lessening of the sentence, no possibilities for parole. Judgment will be final and irrevocable. The punishment will be **everlasting destruction.**

We do not know exactly what Paul meant by this "destruction." What is certain, however, is that those who have rejected Christ—and so become enemies of God—will receive a punishment commensurate with such a high crime. As the author of Hebrews wrote, "It is a dreadful thing to fall into the hands of the living God" (Heb. 10:31). This is not annihilation or extinction. These people are sentenced to eternal punishment and separation from God, the source of life.

These people who have rejected God while in this life on earth will be shut out **from the presence of the Lord and from the majesty of his power.** This, then, is hell. As physical beings, we tend to think of the punishment of hell as excruciating pain, the damned dancing and writhing in flames. But the greatest pain is spiritual, as evidenced by Christ's own cry of agony from the cross, not at the nails or spear, but at his being forsaken by God the Father. Paul's description of eternal punishment is in keeping with Jesus' experience. Paul sketches the punishment of hell in terms of separation from God.

In contrast, heaven holds delight and wholeness for body and soul. Here the complete person will find fulfillment of desire by being joined in unhindered fellowship with the God for whom he was created. Hell, its opposite, is the banishment from this completeness—the futility and agony of incompleteness—as people are severed from the purpose for which they were given life.

1:10. But for the believer, Christ's coming will begin the eternal magnificence of his presence, the ceaseless experience of our desire—God himself.

When Jesus comes he will be **glorified in his holy people.** Christ will not only display *his* glory, but in some way this glory will be shown in those who belong to him. This is the day Paul had in mind when he wrote, "Our light and momentary troubles are achieving for us an eternal glory that far out-weighs them all" (2 Cor. 4:17). The future kept him pressing on in the present. That is why he could say, "We do not lose heart" (2 Cor. 4:16).

This future includes all who believe the testimony of Christ and the Scriptures. Indeed, the redemption from the kingdom of darkness which Christ accomplished, and the transformation which awaits his people at the completion of salvation, belong to the work of Christ, the keeping grace of the Spirit, and the power of God: "Worthy is the Lamb, who was slain, to receive power and wealth and wisdom and strength and honor and glory and praise! . . . To him who sits on the throne and to the Lamb be praise and honor and glory and power, for ever and ever" (Rev. 5:12–13).

SUPPORTING IDEA: *Paul's relationship with the people in the various churches went beyond teacher, to friend and spiritual father. He labored for them and constantly prayed for them. He concluded this section of his letter by offering a prayer for God's power in their lives, so that Christ might be glorified.*

D Prayer for Believers in Hardships (1:11–12)

1:11. Paul then gave an outline of the prayers he offered on behalf of the Thessalonians. This prayer was based, in part, on the preceding description of their present suffering, endurance, and faith, and their future justice, rest, and glory. This was no out-of-sight, out-of-mind relationship. Paul not only felt the weight of responsibility to teach, preach, and correct, but to pray day after day in their behalf.

Paul's prayer was that **God may count you worthy of his calling.** No one deserves to be called by God (referring to his call to salvation); no one merits such grace. Yet, God extended his love and call to the Thessalonians to enter into the kingdom of his Son through faith. After accepting this call, the believers are compelled to live in a way that is fitting, or worthy, of such an honor (Eph. 4:1–3). We are to demonstrate God's transforming grace through our behavior.

We can be counted worthy if God's power is working within us. The good purposes and acts prompted by faith come from the regenerated believer. These are consistent desires and actions that issue from faith—wholeness of mind, spirit, and body—founded in harmonious belief and life. But even these will be ineffectual if we attempt them on our own. Effectiveness is totally dependent upon the power of God. It is an affirmation of Jesus' words in John 15:5, "I am the vine; you are the branches. If a man remains in me and I in him, he will bear much fruit; *apart from me you can do nothing*" (emphasis added).

1:12. The point of this prayer is **that the name of our Lord Jesus may be glorified in you, and you in him.** The purpose and driving energy in history is the glory of God in Christ Jesus: "To bring all things in heaven and on earth together under one head, even Christ" (Eph. 1:10). Our lives in the present prepare us for the future. In the future, the glory of God will be proclaimed through the redemption and worthiness of his people. We will be his glory. Because we are coheirs with him, we will also receive glory, sharing in the honor of our Lord.

How do we explain the glorification of the believer? How is it that enemies of God are made children of God, that people of disobedience become the servants of Christ, that those dead in sin are made alive in Jesus, that suffering turns to joy, that poverty inherits God's riches? Only by the grace of God. There is no other explanation. Both mystery and glory, it is beyond understanding. We can only receive it with awe and thanksgiving. "To him who is able to keep you from falling and to present you before his glorious presence without fault and with great joy—to the only God our Saviour be glory, majesty, power and authority, through Jesus Christ our Lord, before all ages, now and forevermore!" (Jude 24–25).

> **MAIN IDEA REVIEW:** *Unlike other letters, Paul made no assertions of his apostleship or authority in 2 Thessalonians. Instead, he wrote a very personal, gentle letter to the believers in Thessalonica who were suffering for their faith. He urged their continued perseverance, good behavior, love, and faith. He reminded them of Christ's coming, at which time the unbeliever would receive punishment, while the Christian would obtain honor, glory, and the eternal presence of Christ Jesus.*

III. CONCLUSION

"And the Winner Is . . ."

Suppose you were playing halfback in the Super Bowl. Someone approaches you before kickoff and tells you that he already knows the outcome of the game. Absolutely, positively, your team will win. This guy is trustworthy and reliable; you have no doubt he is right. But here is the rub—only those who play their hardest will receive a Super Bowl ring.

So what will you do? Run hard, go all out, take risks? Or be content to run a few patterns, catch a couple of passes, and sit on the bench for a while? After all, your team will win. This is the dilemma Christians face every day. Our team is guaranteed the victory "when the Lord Jesus is revealed from heaven in blazing fire with his powerful angels" (2 Thess. 1:7).

But what will we do in the meantime?

Many Christians, confident that they will go to heaven, spend their time on earth sitting on the bench. They attend church, pass up opportunities to help in ministry, are preoccupied with the playbook, and like to watch missionaries out on the front lines of faith. But they rarely stretch beyond their own comfort zone.

Paul encouraged the Thessalonians, and us, to devote ourselves to godly living. This is not an option for Christians, but it should be our consuming passion so that "God may count [us] worthy of his calling, and that by his power he may fulfill . . . every act prompted by [our] faith" (2 Thess. 1:11). God is guaranteed the ultimate victory, but we are not guaranteed the reward unless we do our part, persevering in faith, holiness, and love.

PRINCIPLES

- The church exists solely because of Christ and exclusively for his glory.
- Faith and love must continually increase in a believer's life.
- Persevering through life's difficulties and hardships validates our faith and trust in Christ.
- God will act as impartial judge over all creation some day.
- Though life in this present time may be full of injustice, a day will come when the ungodly will suffer punishment and those obedient to the gospel will experience God's eternal peace.
- Christians are to live worthy of God's saving grace.
- Hell and heaven are real places of eternal existence.
- Christians should pray for one another.

APPLICATIONS

- We should never consider the church "ours" in a possessive, controlling sense. The church belongs to Christ. The decisions we make in regard to our local congregation should be driven by our desire to glorify the Lord through our gatherings.
- True spirituality is never static, we either progress or lose ground. Our goal should include continual development of the graces of faith and love.
- We should not be surprised by difficulties. Faith, honestly pursued, will make us stronger in times of hardship.
- Our life on earth proceeds for a short time . . . then eternity. We should order our lives with the understanding that God will judge all people some day.
- The realities of hell and heaven should motivate us to tell the gospel to others, praying for their salvation.

IV. LIFE APPLICATION

Woe Is Me

In the modern world, hardship is horrifying. We admire those who exhibit an inner spirit of triumph in the midst of suffering or poverty. But we would rather have our character refined by other means. Give us a book or a seminar, but do not give us trouble.

Oddly enough, the Bible portrays the life of faith as one bombarded by difficulties. You do not have to read far in the Old Testament to discover that righteous people suffered because of their friendship with God and their dedication to righteousness. Those who chose to align themselves with holiness convicted the ungodly, causing hostile reactions or disbelief. Abel was murdered, Noah was mocked and ridiculed, and the prophets were abused because they challenged the status quo and spoke for God.

In the New Testament, we find the same thing. Jesus prepared his disciples for the inevitable difficulties in the life of faith when he stated, "In this world you will have trouble" (John 16:33). James, his half brother, added, "Consider it pure joy, my brothers, whenever you face trials of many kinds, because you know that the testing of your faith develops perseverance. Perseverance must finish its work so that you may be mature and complete, not lacking anything" (Jas. 1:2–4). Peter joined the dialogue on suffering by writing, "Since Christ suffered in his body, arm yourselves also with the same attitude, because he who has suffered in his body is done with sin" (1 Pet. 4:1). Here in 2 Thessalonians, Paul commended the believers because they continued in faith, enduring trials and persecutions (2 Thess. 1:4).

Many of us live in a nation driven by the myth of unending success and material well-being. This fantasy cannot tolerate failure, poverty, and rejection. Some Christians have unwittingly cast their responses on the side of society. They consider difficulties unfair or think they come about because of some personal deficiency.

The Thessalonians, however, did not appear stunned by their ill treatment. We do not find them depressed, whining, or reeling under the scorn of their neighbors. Nowhere do we discover reports of anti-government hostilities because their rights were not upheld. They assumed that their cultural environment would treat them with antagonism. In short, they were not shocked by the behavior of the wicked.

They not only survived the fires of persecution; they bore these difficulties with noble grace and bold trust. They grew in their faith and love as the winds of hatred swirled around them. They focused beyond the moment to the great purposes of God.

Perhaps we feel uneasy and defeated by injustice and hardship because we correlate goodness with personal happiness, comfort, social acceptance or the absence of problems. But if these are our expectations, we will inevitably become disillusioned. While we acknowledge that God does not promise an easy life, we keep hoping that we might be the exception.

We must come to understand that the "good" which God is determined to accomplish in our lives is to make us like Christ. We can live above our circumstances. Every wonderful or crummy thing that happens to us is not excluded from the creative finger of God. Nothing in our experience is wasted. He is committed to our transformation and will use everything at his disposal to shape our character, faith, obedience, and love.

When we embrace this kind of good, we are released from the small ambitions of this life. The worthiness of our life does not depend on the success of our efforts but on becoming more and more like Jesus Christ. God is in charge of the creative process by which we are being changed into the likeness of his Son. Our part is to surrender in faith, believing the declarations of God to be true and the character of God to be indisputably good.

V. PRAYER

Sovereign Father, help me loosen my grip on the enticements of this world. Take away my longing for ease. Each day as I read your Word, remind me that you are the purpose of life. Amen.

VI. DEEPER DISCOVERIES

A. Grace (v. 2)

People spend a great deal of energy and mental anguish striving to gain acceptance and legitimacy. Can God accept us? Can we perform enough kindnesses, give enough money, recite enough prayers, join enough boards or ministries?

Can we prove by our industry that we are worthy of respect? If we work hard enough, can we justify our position? Can we demonstrate to others that we are special in some way, and thus not get lost in the crowd? If we achieve more, if we know the right people, can we find assurance that our life means something to somebody?

But God's values are different than the fear-induced human system. Grace cannot be achieved; it rejects all sweat and labor. Grace cannot be won; it opposes all competition and comparisons. Grace gives wing to the actions of a generous heart, for it exists totally by the will of the giver. Whether we are talking about the rescue of souls or the sending of rain, these are bestowed by God.

When we presume that we can gain God's favor through our good behavior, we trample on grace. With this attitude, we consider his gifts our payment, our just due. The only proper response to God's grace is enduring trust and abiding thankfulness.

B. God Is Just (v. 10)

When Paul wrote, "God is just" (2 Thess. 1:6), he penned a statement similar to John's declaration, "God is love" (1 John. 4:16). Love, life, and justice are defined by God. These values contain meaning only because of who God is.

In fact, we cannot define God; we can only declare who he is, and from that, we can then define qualities and characteristics which we see reflected in the created order. Justice, love, and life are inseparable from his essence. We cannot comprehend or conceive of justice without God. These values and core ethics would cease to be without him.

For example, someone might say, "Knute is kind." By that, he would mean that I possess certain characteristics and actions with which we associate goodness. But no one would be foolish enough to think that I am the quintessence of kindness. Webster did not consult me or my character when defining the word.

Justice, on the other hand, cannot be known without the nature of God. His essence determines the term itself and our understanding of it. True justice requires impartiality and rightness. These simply do not exist, except imperfectly, in our world. If these qualities are absent in their pure form, then they do not originate in human logic or because of cultural expediency. These virtues exist because they reside perfectly in God. They reside perfectly in God because he determines the standard.

This is why, as we look forward to the future when God judges the earth and all people, we can be confident of justice being meted out properly. We do not have to fear that anyone will escape the retribution which evil deserves or fail to receive the reward which God's grace has determined. God cannot act contrary to himself; he cannot act unjustly.

VII. TEACHING OUTLINE

A. INTRODUCTION

1. Lead Story: When Is Enough, Enough?
2. Context: Paul wrote a second letter to the Thessalonian church, probably because he heard reports of certain recurrent problems within the congregation. But he wrote with kindness. These friends had exhibited great strides in their love and faith and in their endurance of persecutions. He reminded the believers of Christ's coming

judgment upon the world and his return, in which all Christians would participate and share in his glory.

3. Transition: Paul provided a good example for all of us. In our zeal to correct problems or cure wrongs, we sometimes ignore the good qualities and progress of those who desire to follow Christ. We need to encourage one another, not with flattery, but with honest appreciation for the positive steps of faith we see. We should find courage in God's promise to establish justice throughout the world. Nothing escapes the eye of God, so we need not shrink back from hardship or suffering. We must wait patiently, confident in God's ability as judge.

B. COMMENTARY

1. Greeting (1:1–2)
2. Thanksgiving (1:3–4)
3. Encouragement—Christ Is Coming (1:5–10)
4. Prayer for Believers in Hardships (1:11–12)

C. CONCLUSION: WOE IS ME

VIII. ISSUES FOR DISCUSSION

1. Discuss the qualities you appreciate in a Christian you know personally.
2. For what qualities are you best known? Do they elicit thanks from others?
3. Talk about some of the hardships you are experiencing and how God is using them to strengthen your faith.
4. What are you doing to prepare for Christ's return?

2 Thessalonians 2

The Day of the Lord

I. **INTRODUCTION**
21 Questions

II. **COMMENTARY**
A verse-by-verse explanation of the chapter.

III. **CONCLUSION**
To Be Like God
An overview of the principles and applications from the chapter.

IV. **LIFE APPLICATION**
Beginnings and Endings
Melding the chapter to life.

V. **PRAYER**
Tying the chapter to life with God.

VI. **DEEPER DISCOVERIES**
Historical, geographical, and grammatical enrichment of the commentary.

VII. **TEACHING OUTLINE**
Suggested step-by-step group study of the chapter.

VIII. **ISSUES FOR DISCUSSION**
Zeroing the chapter in on daily life.

Quote

"*The* great value of the doctrine of the Second Coming is that it guarantees that history is going somewhere."

William   Barclay

2 Thessalonians 2

IN A NUTSHELL

This chapter describes, in part, the culmination of history—the coming of Christ to destroy the works of Satan. Paul outlined the revelation of the man of lawlessness, his activities in the world, the power of lawlessness which works within the world's people and systems, Christ's destruction of the Antichrist's works, and the great delusion of unbelievers.

The Day of the Lord

I. INTRODUCTION

21 Questions

*W*hen playing the game "21 Questions," one individual (let us call him Bob) tries to figure out what another person (Betty) is thinking by asking specific questions. Betty tries to keep Bob from uncovering her idea by providing only vague and evasive answers.

When it comes to biblical prophecy, sometimes it seems as though we are engaged in a game of "21 Questions" with God. We turn to Old Testament prophetic books, or read Revelation in the New Testament, and often feel more confused than enlightened.

We cannot presume to know the mind of God or his reasoning behind his actions. But I suspect part of his purpose in keeping prophetic information metaphorical and non-specific is to increase our faith. He gives just enough information to reveal the basic outline of the future. This means we can find assurance in God's ultimate triumph without charting our lives independently. God envelopes human existence in mystery, keeping us slightly off balance, so we will depend upon him.

Nonetheless, people continue to predict specific times, dates, and places when Christ will return or when the Antichrist will appear. They try to identify the leading characters of earth's final days, naming individuals and speculating on how the nations will be aligned. Books on the subject abound.

Then, after all the rhetoric, the supposed Antichrist fades from public life, or dies, and the anticipated day of Christ's appearance comes and goes. People are left disappointed, disillusioned, or cynical.

God never gives us specific dates or times for Jesus' return, but he does allow us to look into the future and gain a panoramic view of what lies ahead. We know society will continue to degenerate, and the earth itself will convulse as the end approaches. We also know that a person, chosen by Satan, will rise as a world leader, promising to usher the nations into peace. He will exact an enormous toll as he unites the world behind him. His purposes are diabolical, anti-God, and utterly repressive. Even so, a great apostasy will occur as millions betray their faith and follow him.

Paul wrote of this Antichrist and the ultimate fate which awaits those who refuse to believe in Jesus Christ. His purpose was to encourage us. By catching a glimpse of Christ's victory and evil's doom, the apostle hoped to inspire courage, perseverance, and hope in the present. By refusing to chart the specifics, he prevented us from becoming obsessed with the end times to the exclusion of the present moment. At the same time, he told us enough so that we can prepare for that ultimate day. God does not leave us in the dark, unsuspecting of his plans.

Paul's outline of the last days instills comfort. God does not abandon his people; he warns them of difficulty so they can prepare themselves. Best of all, we know with certainty that he will triumph.

So we study 2 Thessalonians, investigating the plan of God as he reveals it. Then we live one day at a time, devoting ourselves to righteousness as we anticipate that day when we will share in his glory.

II. COMMENTARY

> **MAIN IDEA:** Misinformation had circulated throughout the Thessalonian church regarding Christ's coming. Paul set the record straight by explaining the events which must occur before the Lord's return. He wrote of the Antichrist's power and works within the world, the delusion he will create among those who refuse God, and the future coming of Jesus Christ to destroy Satan and all that belongs to him. Paul assured the Thessalonians that they had not been excluded from this great event. It was yet to occur.

The End of the World (2:1–12)

> **SUPPORTING IDEA:** Paul attempted to put the Thessalonians' minds at rest regarding the great day of the Lord. Some false notions had gained acceptance within the church. Paul refuted these by clarifying the events which will lead up to Christ's return.

1. Rumors (2:1–2)

2:1–2. Paul immediately plunged into the main topic of concern: **the coming of our Lord Jesus Christ and our being gathered to him.** These are not two topics, but two parts of the same event, just as he had described them in 1 Thessalonians 4:13–18.

This anticipated event still caused problems and misunderstanding among the Thessalonian believers. In his first letter to the Thessalonians, Paul had tried to calm their concern regarding those Christians who died before Christ's return. They had adopted the idea that only those believers living when Christ came back would be united with him for his triumphant conquering of earth.

Now, new rumors were afoot. People were teaching that the day of the Lord had come and gone. Now even greater questions troubled them. Could they have missed the trumpet call? Had they been excluded from this great event? Consequently, Paul launched into a narrative of "that day," the main theme for this portion of his letter. The point of the writing, however, was not to sketch eschatological curiosities, but to encourage these Christians so they would **not easily become unsettled or alarmed.**

Paul was applying curative counsel. Whispers, rumors, and claims, most probably by false teachers, were raising questions, causing concern, and unsettling the Thessalonian believers. The word translated "unsettled" is used in the passive tense, meaning the object is being acted upon by something outside itself (the Thessalonians' agitation coming from outside reports or people). These reports and claims that the day of the Lord had already occurred were shaking previous beliefs. New and inexperienced in this life of faith, the Thessalonians were allowing every new claim to grab their attention and imagination. Rather than thinking clearly, they became emotional and irrational in their responses.

These false reports were also causing **alarm.** This is an even stronger word conveying fright, perhaps even shock and panic. Whether these reports were from false teachers or those with overactive imaginations, Paul mentioned three sources of disturbance: prophecy, report, and letter.

It may be that the word of **prophecy** was linked to Paul (a misunderstanding of his teachings), or that someone else claimed prophetic inspiration from God. Whomever the source, it was hard for the Thessalonians to ignore what was represented as direct revelation from the Lord. After all, who wants to be the first doubter?

There were also **reports**—a whisper here, a rumor there, a "someone told me." Again, these may have been linked to Paul's oral teachings but, like the childhood game of "telephone," the message had become garbled. In addition, it was always tempting to give credence to claims of direct knowledge or messages credited to someone influential, such as an apostle.

The **letter** was *supposed* to have come from Paul or the three missionaries. The church may even have had a letter in hand. If so, it was bogus. But the point Paul made was that whatever the source, none were to be believed because the truth existed apart from the messenger. The day of the Lord had not yet come.

2. The man of lawlessness (2:3–4)

2:3. Since Paul did not want these believers to be led into falsehood, deceived by spinners of tales, he unfolded for them what the day of the Lord would be like, the events leading to it, and its culmination in judgment.

Before that great day comes, Paul declared, the **rebellion** must occur. The word used here is *apostasia,* or apostasy. Before the day of the Lord, there will be a great denial, a deliberate turning away by those who profess to belong to Christ. It will be a rebellion. Having once allied themselves with Christ, they will abandon him. Within the recognized church there will come a time when people will forsake their faith. Throughout history there have been defections from the faith. But the apostasy about which he wrote to the Thessalonians would be of greater magnitude and would signal the coming of the end.

The other precursor to the day of the Lord will be the revealing of the **man of lawlessness . . . the man doomed to destruction.** That he will be "revealed" indicates that he will be a real man, living on earth, whose identity is not known, or at least not understood, until a particular time. Then the mask will be taken off and his true identity will be revealed.

The **man of lawlessness** will be a person so given to sin that he will become the embodiment of it. Here is a man so overcome with evil that no flicker of light can be detected. It is hard to imagine how horrible that will be, especially in light of some of the diabolical figures throughout history which this man will overshadow.

This man of lawlessness is **doomed to destruction.** He will not be annihilated, but he will suffer the eternal torment and agony which such an assault upon God will bring. This man is doomed, utterly lost, irrevocably sentenced in judgment to everlasting agony apart from God.

2:4. The reason for such catastrophic and unpardonable judgment was explained by Paul: **he will oppose and will exalt himself over everything that is called God or is worshiped.**

This man will oppose everything connected with the divine—not only Christianity but anything that has to do with theism. This man will wage war against everything that hints at religion, faith, or spirituality. He will try to eradicate worship of any kind: prayers, songs, gatherings, and shrines.

The man of sin will set himself up **in God's temple,** or more literally, put himself into God's seat in the inner sanctuary of the temple, **proclaiming himself to be God.** This will be more than a taking over of some building. The man of sin will understand the implications and claims that attend taking his seat in the sanctuary of God. He will anoint himself as divine. He will usurp the rightful place of God and declare himself as the one to be worshiped.

3. Waiting the proper time (2:5–7)

2:5. Paul interrupted his teaching with an exclamatory aside: **Don't you remember . . . I used to tell you these things?** It was a rhetorical question intended to jog the Thessalonians' minds. This was nothing new; this was a reinforcement of what they had heard. Why had they gotten off course and become excited by other teachings? Having already received the truth of what will come, why were they being deceived and sidetracked?

No teaching should ever replace the Word of God. No interpretation should undercut what is clearly taught in Scripture. Stick to the apostles' teaching; stay with the Word of God. There will always be new twists and theories, new claims to entice, but the Word of God remains steady and dependable. It is absolute and trustworthy.

2:6. Paul picked up his description of the end times, particularly as it regarded the Antichrist. This man who embodies sin was being restrained; something was **holding him back.** There is a controlling purpose in the affairs of men and of Satan as well. Although he is ruler of this present system and world, Satan and his activities are still restrained by the sovereignty of God.

Even when events seem out of control, still there is the restraining hand of God. In the last days, God will act with deliberate purpose in holding back Satan's workman: **so that [the man of sin] may be revealed at the proper time.** Just as Christ had an advent, entering history at the proper time ("when the time had fully come," Gal. 4:4), so the Antichrist will have a proper time for his revealing. This will be a strategic time in history, not only for this man to be known, but a time perfectly suited for this man in the moral evolution of the world.

2:7. Though the coming of the "lawless one" is on the horizon, **the power of lawlessness is already at work.** This work is supernatural. It is designed and empowered by Satan, his minions, and all who do his bidding. Just as all good things come from God, so all evil is empowered by the energy of Satan. However, we are not talking equals. This is not a dynamic struggle against forces of equal power or ability. Satan has great power and we should not ignore it. But God reigns over all—even Satan. That is why God restrains Satan's activities. That is why the culmination of history and time is settled. That is why there is no nail-biting anxiety as to whether Christ will triumph.

Even so, until that time, Satan is allowed enormous influence and power, capturing the souls of billions. Though held back from the full vent of his evil, the power and energy of wickedness continues to work and build toward the day of the Antichrist's revealing. The evil we experience and see around us today, and which has been generated throughout the last two thousand years, is not so chaotic as it may appear. It has a purpose, driving toward the day of the Antichrist. Satan is busy exercising lawlessness in view of the day of his overthrow of God's rule.

Though there is a containment of evil now, there will come a day when the present restraint will be removed: **but the one who now holds it back . . . is taken out of the way.**

There are many candidates set forth by scholars as to who this "one" is who restrains Satan and his forces. The most logical course would be to determine who could possibly hold such power as to restrain the powers of Satan. No mere man could. His limits of time and power would make that impossible. So the "one" must also be superhuman. This places God at the forefront of possibilities. Yet, God does not abandon the world when the Antichrist is revealed. So the most reasonable explanation as to who holds back the boiling powers of evil is the Holy Spirit.

The Holy Spirit is now in the world in special ministry: to "convict the world of guilt in regard to sin and righteousness and judgment" (John 16:8). This is a work which he does on his own. In addition, the Spirit dwells in the spirit of every believer. As such, the church and those individuals in it are also a restraining force of God in the world. The Holy Spirit works on his own, but he also works through the believer and the church to hold back Satan until his proper time.

When the time for the Antichrist comes, however, the Holy Spirit will depart; he will be **taken out of the way**. This must refer to the rapture of the church when Christ comes to gather us, to snatch us up to be with him. Though still omnipresent as a member of the Godhead, the Spirit's unique working relationship within people will end. It is at that moment in history that the Holy Spirit will depart from his involvement in the affairs of mankind.

4. Christ's coming (2:8)

2:8. With the believers and Holy Spirit gone, the restraint will be removed **and then the lawless one will be revealed**, allowing Satan and his Antichrist to unleash their fury and abominations.

Paul did not finish his sentence before he added, **whom the Lord Jesus will overthrow with the breath of his mouth and destroy by the splendor of his coming**. Paul did not give the Antichrist much time, and it is conceivable that God will not either. The duration of his rule and power is unknown, but most agree that it will not be an extensive time.

Satan has been building toward this time of rebellion when he can hurl his evil in the face of God and his creation. But this will be over simply by the breath of Christ's mouth. This will not be a long, bloody battle. This will not be a back-and-forth contest. Satan's chosen man will be destroyed by Jesus with one blow of his breath. The Antichrist will be overthrown and destroyed.

The residual effect of the Antichrist's reign will be destroyed by the glory of Christ's presence. The systems, the power structures, the religious perversions he created will crumble with Christ's second advent.

5. The work of Antichrist (2:9–12)

2:9. The portrayal of the man of sin (Antichrist) has parallels to the Son of Man (Christ). Both have a coming and a revealing—when people become aware of what is already in their midst. One proclaims the truth and the other proclaims a lie. Both demonstrate power through signs, miracles, and wonders—one from the truth and the other a counterfeit. Each will claim exclusive worship. Both are empowered—Christ by God and the Antichrist by Satan.

The lawless one lives **in accordance with the work of Satan**. The word translated "work" is *energeo,* from which the word *energy* is derived. This word is not limited to outworking actions, but deals more directly with inward power. It is used of God's power working in the believer: "for it is God who works in you to will and to act according to his good purpose" (Phil. 2:13). This word is also used of Satan's empowering his chosen man (2 Thess. 2:9). The "work" is an energy which comes from beyond the individual, and it is supernatural in origin.

Miracles, signs, and wonders were testimonies of Jesus' claim as Messiah. They also validated the authority of the apostles and the apostolic church. Since Satan deals in mimicry and deception, he will also use miracles, signs, and wonders to affirm the Antichrist's demands for worship and power.

Miracles, translated from the Greek *dunamis,* is yet another word for power. This describes inherent, supernatural ability. Here in 2 Thessalonians 2:9 it is singular in form and so points more directly to the *power* causing the act rather than the act itself.

Signs (*semeia*) are tokens, deeds done in order to confirm authority or power. In the case of the Antichrist, he will perform supernatural feats, energized by Satan, for the purpose of authenticating his claims for worship and obedience.

The **wonders** (*teras*) include anything strange or spectacular which cause people to be amazed. The word is always used in combination with the word *signs*. Signs deal with the purpose—to validate authority—while wonders deal with the effect—to cause a sensation. The people will be awestruck, and the performer of the signs and wonders will be admired and treated with reverence and honor.

Christ performed miracles, signs, and wonders, and the lawless one will also. The difference is that the Antichrist's miracles and signs are designated *pseudous,* or false. The Antichrist's miracles originate from the realm of falsehood and lies because they are empowered by the father of lies, Satan. Antichrist and Satan have no legitimate claim to authority or worship, so their supernatural works are designed to entrap people and steal what rightfully belongs to God. In this way, everything they do is "pseudo" or false.

2:10. Not only would the lawless one traffic in miracles, signs, and wonders, but **in every sort of evil that deceives**. Paul employed words that have no limits. What Satan can devise, and what Antichrist will enact, are beyond the imaginations of mere mortals.

It should be remembered that evil is being used to ensnare people, to lure them away from what is true. Most likely this is not the evil of terror, but evil which attracts the base and natural inclinations of fallen humanity—power, narcissism, sexual degradation, and moral blindness that elevates selfishness, just to name a few. But these ancient sins will be loosed with a fury unseen or experienced before.

Satan will use **every sort of evil that deceives those who are perishing.** His purpose is to secure people for himself, thereby stealing from God what rightfully belongs to him—the crown of his creation, mankind.

Paul's use of the present tense, **who are perishing,** indicates that these people are in process. Though blinded and deceived, they have chosen the path toward destruction on which they are traveling. These are not innocents whom Satan snatches, but people who continually and persistently choose unrighteousness, sin, and falsehood. They **refused to love the truth and so be saved.**

These are people who willfully spurn the saving grace of God. That is why they are in a state of perishing, a process which results in eternal destruction rather than salvation. God has held out the truth and opportunity of rescue, but they have refused. God's intention has always been deliverance. Even so, there are many who persist in their course away from God. These people follow the way of death; they willfully choose it and thus bear the responsibility for their own judgment.

2:11. Paul declared, **For this reason God sends them a powerful delusion.** After humankind continually refused God and embraced wickedness and self-exaltation, "God gave them over" (Rom. 1:24). Likewise, in these last days, men and women refuse the truth, running after evil and conceit, and so "God sends them a powerful delusion." In each case the judgment is just, resulting from their own choices. Since they prefer lies, God obliges them with delusions. The ultimate delusion is their acceptance of the Antichrist and his claims for worship. It is *the* Lie, because it is in opposition to *the* Truth, that God has given Christ all authority.

We must remember that God does not cause these people to believe the lie, or to follow delusions. They have already proved themselves contrary to righteousness and open to evil. These people have repeatedly embraced wickedness so that their character is formed by evil.

2:12. The consequences of such sin are always judgment and death (Rom. 6:23). In this day when Satan rules through the man of lawlessness, **all will be condemned who have not believed the truth but have delighted in wickedness.** By willfully rejecting the truth, these people reap for themselves the natural consequence of such rebellion. Those who reject truth inevitably follow after unrighteousness.

Truth and wickedness are mutually exclusive. You follow either one or the other. There is no neutrality in issues of life and morality, righteousness and wickedness. Rejecting truth will always pull a person to evil. The further a person allows himself to continue in sin, the more deeply entrenched he becomes, and the more hardened his heart and conscience. But at each point, every person chooses, making God's judgment fair and just.

B Paul's Personal Remarks (2:13–15)

> **SUPPORTING IDEA:** *Having described the utter ruin of the disobedient through willfulness and deception, Paul encouraged the Thessalonians by placing them in an entirely different category. They had believed the truth, were loved by God, and were called to share in his glory. Paul wanted them to stand firm in the truth of what he taught them, not shaken by false rumors.*

2:13. Paul repeated his opening comment of 2 Thessalonians 1:3, **we ought always to thank God for you.** Paul wanted the Thessalonians to take courage, especially in contrast to those facing certain doom. Paul, Silas, and Timothy felt an obligation to pray continually for these believers. From observing their love and life, it was obvious that God had saved them. The missionaries understood the necessity of giving God thanks because these were **brothers loved by the Lord.**

Paul wrote in affectionate terms in order to encourage the Thessalonians. Despite their persecutions and difficulties, they were loved by God and continually prayed for by the missionaries.

Those who persecute Christians and cause violence to the gospel may seem to have the upper hand. But as Paul explained, their judgment and destruction are certain. These Thessalonian believers could also rest assured that they were chosen for salvation in eternity past by God's good pleasure and his personal care (Eph. 1:4). This salvation was initiated **through the sanctifying work of the Spirit and through belief in the truth.** This set them apart for future reward when their salvation would be completed.

Sanctification is a process by which the believer becomes increasingly holy. The Holy Spirit affects this process in conjunction with the individual, who must choose continually to believe the truth. The Holy Spirit works through the word of truth, and the truth becomes energized by our faith— our willful decision to believe and obey. When faith and the Spirit work in harmony, the believer develops more like Christ, becoming increasingly useful in the work of God and his kingdom.

2:14. God chose the Thessalonians before "the creation of the world" (Eph. 1:4), but the actual call came to them at a specific time **through our gospel** which the missionaries preached to them in their city.

Redeeming his creation not only brings glory to God; it also brings glory to those who believe, for they will **share in the glory of our Lord Jesus Christ.** In contrast to those who await judgment because they do not believe the truth of God, the Thessalonians could be confident that salvation and glory await those who believe and live in obedience. "For our light and momentary troubles are achieving for us an eternal glory that far outweighs them all. So we fix our eyes not on what is seen, but on what is unseen" (2 Cor. 4:17–18a).

2:15. The consequence of knowing our future should bring endurance, faith, determination, and confidence for today. The Thessalonians were told to **stand firm and hold to the teachings** [Paul, Silas, and Timothy] **passed on to you.**

The appeal to stand firm addressed the Thessalonians' current situation and distress. Rather than becoming **easily unsettled or alarmed** (2 Thess. 2:2), Paul advocated strength and firmness by abiding in the teachings which he gave them verbally and by letter. These teachings included everything from salvation to daily conduct to the coming glory. Some teachers had tried to introduce new ideas and practices into the apostolic traditions and beliefs. Others would likely follow because false teachings were a constant problem in the early church. Paul wanted the believers to hold on to the instructions and teachings he had given them so they would not be persuaded and led astray by some other "gospel."

C Prayer (2:16–17)

> **SUPPORTING IDEA:** *Paul offered a prayer on behalf of these precious believers.*

2:16. After instructing the Thessalonians, Paul offered a prayer of blessing, calling for divine help so his instruction would be received with the power to perform what was required. He called on **our Lord Jesus Christ himself and God our Father.**

Jesus Christ our Lord intercedes for the believer, yet he is called upon equally with God the Father **who loved us and by his grace gave us eternal encouragement and good hope.**

Encouragement and hope are present realities for the believer. The comfort and courage that God gives the Christian are in stark contrast to what the world gives. God's comfort and courage reach to the depths of the soul and spirit. They are not fleeting or contrived; neither are they attained through self-effort. These are graces, gifts from God to his children. In the face of difficulty, discouragement, persecution, and shattered dreams, God brings encouragement. He also gives **good hope**—the certainty of a good future.

2:17. Both eternal encouragement and good hope should shore up and **encourage** [our] **hearts and strengthen** [us] **in every good deed and word.** This covers the totality of our experience, from our inner state to our outer life. Paul had in mind the progressive maturing of the Christian. He prayed for a harmonious life, for our words and actions to exist in consistency with our beliefs.

> **MAIN IDEA REVIEW:** *Misinformation had circulated throughout the Thessalonian church regarding Christ's coming. Paul set the record straight by explaining the events which must occur before the Lord's return. He wrote of the Antichrist's power and works within the world, the delusion he will create among those who refuse God, and the future coming of Jesus Christ to destroy Satan and all that belongs to him. Paul assured the Thessalonians that they had not been excluded from this great event. It was yet to occur.*

III. CONCLUSION

To Be Like God

In the beginning, Satan tempted Eve with a lie, appealing to one of the strongest desires in the human heart—the longing to be god-like (Gen. 3:5–6). Since that moment when Eve succumbed and Adam joined her, the human race has tried to usurp God's rightful place of authority and dominion.

But the will to overthrow God's supremacy extends beyond the earth's sphere into the far reaches of the cosmos. Satan's own fall resulted from his determination to gain the throne of God: "I will ascend to heaven; I will raise my throne above the stars of God; I will sit enthroned on the mount of assembly, on the utmost heights of the sacred mountain. I will ascend above the tops of the clouds; I will make myself like the Most High" (Isa. 14:13–14). In his lust for independence, Satan led a revolt of angels against God. Since then, Satan has dedicated himself to continual battle with God, extending his attack into creation.

Paul stated in this chapter of 2 Thessalonians that a spirit of lawlessness which repudiates God's laws is at work in all people and all human institutions. Behind this disregard for order and submission, Satan's shadow lurks. The moral disintegration all around us, the rebellion toward authority, and the attitude of self-determination will some day find their consummate expression in the Antichrist, the man of lawlessness.

Recently, at the funeral of a well-known person in our area, a pastor eulogized, "She was the master of her fate, the captain of her soul, and everyone knew that." Was that a compliment? Most likely he meant it as such. She ran her own life. She did what she thought best. She was nobody's fool. She said what she wanted. She was a self-determined woman.

But by insisting on making our own choices and doing things our own way, we may exclude ourselves from the grace of God and set ourselves in opposition to him. God's grace welcomes us to submit to him in love, enjoying the goodness of his blessings and the promise of his presence. Even as Christians, we must make the daily decision to submit to his power and authority.

At the end of time, when Christ finally triumphs "with the breath of his mouth and . . . the splendor of his coming" (2 Thess. 2:8), everyone will stare at Satan and his Antichrist and wonder, "Is this the man who shook the earth and made kingdoms tremble, the man who made the world a desert, who overthrew its cities and would not let his captives go home?" (Isa. 14:16–17). Though Satan seems formidable now, his doom is certain. At the time of Christ's conquest, Satan's terror will be nullified so that "at the name of Jesus every knee should bow, in heaven and on earth and under the earth, and every tongue confess that Jesus Christ is Lord, to the glory of God the Father" (Phil. 2:10–11).

PRINCIPLES

- God's revealed truth is complete.
- The future looms inevitably before all people, resulting in promise for believers and judgment for those who refuse God's Son.
- The man of lawlessness will appear in time, marking the end of history. He will oppose God and all God represents.
- The Antichrist will perform false miracles, signs, and wonders in order to lure non-Christians into adoring and worshiping him.
- A great apostasy will occur within the organized church as those who claimed belief in God will abandon the faith.
- Christ will come and destroy Satan's representative by his breath and the splendor of his appearance.
- People perish and receive God's judgment because they willfully refuse his truth and grace.
- By his goodness, God has called people to receive his salvation.
- Christians will share in Christ's glory.

APPLICATIONS

- We should never allow new ideas or theological interpretations to disrupt or shake our trust in God's revealed Word. Handed down through the centuries, his Word is protected by his Spirit and preserved by traditional orthodoxy.
- The certainty of God's judgment on unbelievers should awaken our compassion to proclaim the gospel and live its truths.
- Knowing that deception remains a lethal tool of Satan, we should pursue intimacy with God and holiness in our lives. We should

not succumb to laziness or apathy regarding sin, prayer, self-discipline, and love.

- We should pray for the unsaved and for one another.

IV. LIFE APPLICATION

Beginnings and Endings

It does not take long to begin something. Then, we become engaged in whatever we chose to start—a journey, a book, some process, a game, our dinner. But beginnings are no small matter. They determine a whole chain of events, as well as perhaps the eventual outcome.

"In the beginning God created . . ." (Gen. 1:1). So begins the Bible, and life—the singular expression of God. If we ignore, discount, or minimize that commencement, we do so at our peril. Acknowledging God as Creator proclaims him as ultimate authority. It is this claim to power which sets him at odds with the world.

The theories to explain the origins of man are not so much a scientific debate of evidence and reason as they are a time-worn rebuttal to God's authority. Created beings are always under the sovereignty of God. If we acknowledge this simple truth, man is cast off his soapbox of self-proclaimed importance. Even though we have shown ourselves incompetent to handle the little power we possess, we are committed to holding on to it and grabbing for more—to the very end.

Those who refuse God are like the child who proclaims to his family that he is an orphan. His mother and father are there, along with his brother and sister. Yet, he insists he does not belong to them, has never seen them before, and does not know why they all ended up in the same house. Since he is an orphan, his parents have no claim upon him. So he announces that from now on he will set his own rules. Never mind that he enjoys the warmth of the home, the food in the cupboards, and the soft quilt upon his bed (none of which he labored for).

This child has struck off on his own, torn up his birth certificate, become independent. He has thrown off the restraints of parental authority and is free to stay up as late as he wishes, eat only the food he likes, come home when he decides, and indulge in every pleasure. But his decision has not changed the facts of the matter, the truth of his origins. His self-styled freedom has, however, changed his outcome. He is now "free" to get sick on junk food, become overwhelmed by fatigue, miss family outings, sit alone in his room, skip the hugs and kisses his siblings enjoy, and exclude himself from any inheritance.

When we agree that "in the beginning God created," we admit that there is transcendent authority. Without God there can be no justice, only the ignorance of the crowd or the whims of the powerful. Without justice there can be no mercy, only bribery or retribution. Without God there can be no holiness; without holiness, no morality. Without morality there can be no order or safety, only acts of convenience and personal preference. Without God there can be no goodness. With no consistent standard, we are abandoned to shifting opinions. Without goodness there can be no punishment for evil, only violence and chaos.

For centuries, man has rejected God as the first cause of this world. His rejection has determined his ultimate end, for the degenerative process will culminate when mankind utterly casts off God, accepting in his place the man of Satan's own choosing—the Antichrist. Paul, in describing the final days of humanity, characterized Satan's emissary as lawless and the power he wields as lawlessness—the total repudiation of authority.

But God initiated another beginning, a new creation. Paul wrote, "From the beginning God chose you to be saved through the sanctifying work of the Spirit and through belief in the truth" (2 Thess. 2:13). Those who trust God as truth agree with the first beginning which established God as sovereign through creative authority. They also submit to the truth of the second beginning which established God as Sovereign through redemptive authority.

The first creation suffered the trauma of sin's judgment. The second creation, while enduring the effects of sin, will be saved from God's wrath. Those who refuse to believe these creative acts of God's authority refuse the goodness and salvation which he extends to all people. Those who confess him as sovereign, Creator of heaven and earth, and Creator of a purified people through the death and resurrection of Jesus will participate in a new order—now and into eternity.

Until we reach the time of our full salvation, we must order our lives under the truth of God, the law of his love and righteousness. We must determine to live out the power of his goodness, rejecting the temptations and distractions of a world allied against the God of all grace.

V. PRAYER

Author of life, judge and sovereign, I know that the punishment of the wicked, the irrevocable destruction of those who refuse you, is more certain than tomorrow's sunrise. Yet, I give more thought to the morning's tasks than I do to the duties of faith and love by which eternity is judged. May I number my days properly, dedicated to goodness and truth. Amen.

VI. DEEPER DISCOVERIES

The Trinity (vv. 1, 13–14)

The word *Trinity* does not appear in the Bible. It is a word devised as shorthand for a complex and mysterious theological belief. But while we cannot find the word within the Scriptures, in this second chapter of Thessalonians, we see the persons of the Godhead acting distinctly and harmoniously.

God the Father. Paul wrote that the Antichrist would set himself up in "God's temple" (2 Thess. 2:4). "God's temple" describes not only a setting but also God's ultimate authority. God alone deserves worship; he alone commands the respect and worship of all the created order.

Later in the chapter, Paul wrote that "God chose you to be saved" (v. 13). Here again, God acts as potentate, exercising his will unhindered. He performs what the human mind cannot conceive. He selects according to his purpose, yet he does not violate our will by his choice.

Paul also declared that "God our Father . . . loved us and by his grace gave us eternal encouragement and good hope" (2:16). The Father works on our behalf, loving us regardless of our achievements and in spite of our sin. For those who trust in his Son, his love breaks like a flood, sweeping us into the glory of his grace—eternal life and blessing.

God the Son. The Son has always existed, thoroughly God and eternal. Incarnated as Jesus the Christ, the crucified one, and resurrected by the power of God's might, he brings salvation to all people. Paul stated that those who confess their faith in him and commit to obedience will "share in the glory of our Lord Jesus Christ" (2:14). Jesus, completely God and completely human, reaches across the estrangement which sin creates, and lifts us into God's family. At his return, "we shall be gathered to him" (2:1). Our future rests in his claiming us, and in the wonder of his presence which we shall enjoy forever. In love he makes us heirs together with him, bestowing on us the endowment which God shall bestow upon him on that future day of glory.

Paul prayed that "our Lord Jesus Christ himself . . . [will] encourage your hearts and strengthen you" (2:16). Christ continues to work for us and in us, penetrating the heart with courage and strength so we can obey him. On our own, we remain powerless.

God the Holy Spirit. From other Scriptures we know that the Holy Spirit indwells the believer because of Jesus Christ (Acts 2:38–39; Rom. 8:9; 1 Cor. 6:19). We also learn here in 2 Thessalonians that the Spirit carries out a "sanctifying work" (2:13) in believers. Through enlightening the Scriptures, awakening our consciences, convicting us of sin, and enabling us to act righteously, he makes us holy and useful for sacred work.

For the world in general, the Spirit's work is to "convict the world of guilt in regard to sin and righteousness and judgment" (John 16:8). In addition, the Holy Spirit restrains evil, keeping it within the sovereign parameters which the Father has established (2 Thess. 2:6–7).

These distinct three—Father, Son, and Spirit—are somehow one, a unity. We simply cannot comprehend it. Our only response is trust and worship. We praise God, "from Whom all blessings flow." We praise, "Father, Son, and Holy Ghost." In awe we whisper, "Holy, Holy, Holy."

VII. TEACHING OUTLINE

A. INTRODUCTION

1. Lead Story: 21 Questions

2. Context: The Thessalonian Christians were agitated because false teachers claimed the second coming of Christ had already occurred. Paul wrote to put their minds at rest, describing the events which must precede Christ's coming. He also encouraged the believers by assuring them of their future—the eternal presence of Christ and a share in his glory. He confirmed their need to remain secure in the truth of the gospel as he taught it to them.

3. Transition: Few people today believe Christ has already come. We tend to live as though he may never arrive. But Paul's sketches of earth's final days should assure us that, whatever the time frame, we are inevitably speeding toward that great and conclusive time of history. Such knowledge should determine our priorities, aligning them with God's mission of redemption, love, and goodness. We should also take courage to proclaim and live God's righteousness. Truth and goodness will find their reward, and disobedience will determine its punishment.

B. COMMENTARY

1. The End of the World (2:1–12)

   a. Rumors (2:1–2)

   b. The man of lawlessness (2:3–4)

   c. Waiting the proper time (2:5–7)

   d. Christ's coming (2:8)

   e. The work of Antichrist (2:9–12)

2. Paul's Personal Remarks (2:13–15)

3. Prayer (2:16–17)

C. CONCLUSION: BEGINNINGS AND ENDINGS

VIII. ISSUES FOR DISCUSSION

1. Paul warned Christians not to believe lies and rumors about the last days. How can we recognize these rumors and yet still prepare for the last days?
2. Can you identify different ways in which the spirit of lawlessness is evidenced today?
3. How does Paul's description of the end times give you courage for living today?

2 Thessalonians 3

Instructions on
Daily Living

> **Quote**
>
> "If we refuse to practice, it is not God's grace that fails when a crisis comes, but our own nature . . . God regenerates us and puts us in contact with all His divine resources, but He cannot make us walk according to His will."
>
> Oswald Chambers

2 Thessalonians 3

 IN A NUTSHELL

Godly and useful living requires self-discipline and purposeful choices. We do not advance in our Christian faith automatically; it takes determination and right choices. Paul commanded the Thessalonians to focus on respectable and responsible living and to hold tightly to orthodox belief. In these ways they would be useful in God's kingdom.

Instructions on Daily Living

I. INTRODUCTION

Do Not Wish for Sausages

A man and his wife were walking along a city street one day, enjoying the sunshine and looking in shop windows. Their feet hurt after a while, so they sat on a bench to rest a bit before moving on. A stranger sat beside them and said, "You have been randomly selected to receive three wishes. You may wish for whatever you like and it will be granted. Remember, however, you have only three wishes." He smiled, then left.

The man and his wife puzzled over this odd occurrence. "Well, I can tell you this," said the man. "This has made me very hungry. I wish I could think this over while eating a plate of sausages."

Immediately, a plate of sausages appeared.

"What a stupid wish!" his wife shouted. "What a waste! Look at you, nothing but a plate of sausages for all this. I wish those confounded sausages were hanging on your nose!"

And it was so.

This was quite a predicament. The man was uncomfortable and humiliated sitting there with sausages hanging from his nose. His wife was embarrassed as well. They did some loud whispering between them, along with some wild gesturing, and eventually the man persuaded his wife to use their last wish to remove the sausages from his nose.

And so she did.

It is easy to waste life on small purposes—to blunder through our days without direction, busy yet getting nowhere. A man or woman without purpose makes no progress in life, even if circumstances seem favorable. They simply put in time. Then, when pain, adversity, disappointment, or hardship comes along, they are ill-prepared to face it. But a person with determination, especially one who aims at pleasing God, understands the goal toward which his life moves. He makes his choices wisely. He perseveres though difficulty because he focuses on his final destination, his objective.

This last chapter of 2 Thessalonians is a call to noble living, to adopting the high standard of godliness in order to glorify Christ. God becomes our purpose, our reason for living.

We may not have wishes to squander, but each person has a life that can either be wasted or made useful. It all depends on whether we seek to live out the high purposes of serving our Lord.

II. COMMENTARY

> **MAIN IDEA:** *Paul requested prayer for the missionaries, that the gospel might spread effectively through their ministry. He told the Thessalonians of his confidence that they would follow through on all his instructions. He then warned them again, as he had in his first letter, to engage in daily life with integrity and purpose. Laziness was shameful and disobedience was intolerable.*

A Prayer Requests (3:1–2)

> **SUPPORTING IDEA:** *Paul shared a prayer request. He wanted the Thessalonian believers to participate in his ministry by praying that the gospel would move forward and that people would respond in faith. He wanted them to pray for the missionaries' deliverance from evil people.*

3:1. Paul left the eschatological teachings of chapter 2 and moved on to instructions for daily living. He began by asking the Thessalonians to **pray for us.** This request for himself, Timothy, and Silas shows the human side of these three great men. Like everyone else, they depended on the prayers of others to carry on their work and remain steadfast in their lives.

Paul's request reminds us that we never reach a place in our Christian maturity or service where we progress beyond the need of prayer. Prayer remains essential to the life and work of all believers, not as a ritual, but as an honest interaction of longing and trust with our Lord. Prayer that agrees with Christ's will always result in divine empowerment. We are foolish if we assume that the work of God can be carried forward without prayer.

First, Paul requested prayer that the gospel **may spread rapidly and be honored.** The verb translated "spread" actually means "run," carrying the idea of continual movement forward. While the word *spread* sounds a bit aimless, even impersonal, "run" conveys an animated energy exercised with direction and purpose. Such was Paul's desire for the gospel message.

He also desired that the gospel be honored, seen as valuable and admired for its inherent transforming power. Paul mentioned the Thessalonians as proof of the realism of his prayer request. He also complimented them for the manner in which they received the gospel.

3:2. Second, Paul asked the Thessalonian believers to pray that he, Silas, and Timothy would be delivered **from wicked and evil men.** The three missionaries continually suffered for the gospel, just as the Thessalonians did. Paul's request for personal safety and rescue issued not from the desire for personal ease, but from his longing for the gospel to move ahead unhindered.

Paul's description of the opposition as wicked and evil portrays those who were blatantly unrighteous and sinful. The word *evil* describes active hatred. Evidently, these people purposefully and maliciously confronted Paul, Silas, and Timothy. The Thessalonians had experienced similar opposition, so they understood the serious nature of Paul's request (Acts 17:5–9). Paul then added the statement, **for not everyone has faith.** The gospel produces either faith and joyful obedience or a contentious refusal of God's truth. The gospel does not always find receptive hearts.

B Encouragement to Continue in Faith (3:3–4)

SUPPORTING IDEA: *While people may disappoint and fail us, God remains faithful to those who belong to him. He protects us from the attacks of Satan and evil men. Paul expressed his confidence that the Thessalonians would continue to obey the true teachings of the gospel.*

3:3. People may prove fickle, even deceitful, but **the Lord is faithful.** Paul often used contrasts to make his point and drive home the truth more forcefully. Just as he contrasted Jesus and the Antichrist, here he contrasted faithless men with a faithful Lord. Whatever humans can hurl against the Christian, God always triumphs, because he is faithful and unrelenting in his purposes. He has made a covenant between himself and humankind and sealed it with the blood of Jesus Christ. God remains trustworthy and dependable in his covenant relationships.

Knowing this truth instills confidence that God **will strengthen and protect you from the evil one.** Paul gave strong affirmation that God would accomplish inner stability and outer protection for the Christian. Despite the persecutions, despite evil men, despite Satan himself, God's commitment to his children assures us that no one shall prevail against us. This does not mean we will not suffer difficulties, hardships, or even martyrdom (as was obvious from their own experiences). But it does mean that nothing can overcome those who belong to Christ. God is in control, and he keeps a protective guard around the believer. When Christians experience harm or even death because of righteousness, it is not evil which triumphs, but the plan of God which succeeds.

3:4. After declaring that the Lord works faithfully on behalf of believers, Paul commended the Thessalonians for their devotion as they continued **to do the things we command.** The Christian life always has these two forces at work: the power of God and the willful obedience of the believer. Christianity is an engaged faith with an interacting Lord.

Paul's confidence rested in the Lord. He was certain that God would produce in these Christians a willingness to obey (Phil. 2:13) and that they would continue to respond in faith, just as they had in the past.

3:5. Paul recognized that the Thessalonians continued to encounter persecution and that false teachers infiltrated the best of churches, so he offered a prayer: **May the Lord direct your hearts into God's love and Christ's perseverance.**

Paul understood that Christ's involvement with the human spirit created the proper conditions for believers to respond in faith. He prayed for Christ's intervention so the inner spirit of the Thessalonians could fully experience the love of God. He desired for them a deep, experiential comprehension of God's love, an understanding of which would produce in them steadfast obedience and love (Phil. 1:9–10).

Paul's prayer that their hearts be directed into Christ's perseverance contains a twofold meaning. First, misunderstandings about Christ's second coming had disrupted the Thessalonian church, producing anxiety and impatience concerning his return. Through his prayer, Paul wanted to produce patience in these people. Second, their own hardships required a steady faith. Christ was their example, as he "learned obedience from what he suffered" (Heb. 5:8). Paul's prayer also contained the same theme he so eloquently wrote of when he described the sufferings and humility of Christ, which he urged believers to imitate (Phil. 2).

C A Matter of Discipline (3:6–13)

SUPPORTING IDEA: *Some believers in Thessalonica were so preoccupied with the return of Christ that they neglected the daily necessities of living, sponging off others and creating disruptions. Paul commanded everyone to work, providing for their own needs. Those who refused this command were to be disciplined.*

3:6. In this verse Paul comes to a serious disciplinary matter in the church. He approached the issue with a mixture of command and plea: **In the name of the Lord Jesus Christ, we command you, brothers.**

At the outset he made it clear that the authority and undergirding of this command were given in the character of Christ Jesus and, as such, carried extreme seriousness. But his use of the word *brothers* kept the command from harshness, conveying concern and affection. Nevertheless, this was a command. Paul expected the instructions to be carried out thoroughly and without compromise.

The command was **to keep away from every brother who is idle and does not live according to the teaching you received from us.** In matters of discipline Paul sometimes commended ostracizing the offending person in order to produce a shame leading to repentance (1 Cor. 5:5,11). The members of the assembly were to withdraw fellowship so the person would feel the consequences of his action. These consequences would prove the individual's heart. He would either repent or display prideful indifference.

The command was also to be carried out for "every brother," removing the possibility of favoritism or misuse. Paul also recognized that this offending person would remain a brother, a member of the community of believers. He did not call for excommunication. Paul initiated a disciplinary measure in order to keep the church orderly and to maintain its good reputation. His purpose was to restore the offending person.

The offense was idleness and the intentional rejection of teachings which Paul had given the church. Paul had touched on this problem in his first letter (1 Thess. 5:14), but evidently the problem persisted. He now addressed the issue more thoroughly.

These people were not only lazy; they were expecting others to support them financially by giving them food and other supplies. They were capable of supporting themselves, but they were looking to others for support, deliberately neglecting their own responsibilities.

3:7–8. Having described the offense, Paul then gave examples and reasons to show why this kind of behavior should not be tolerated. He uses two arguments for discipline: apostolic example and apostolic teaching. First, he appealed to his own lifestyle when the missionaries were in Thessalonica: **We were not idle when we were with you, nor did we eat anyone's food without paying for it . . . we worked night and day.**

The missionaries' hard work was a well-known fact among the Thessalonian believers. Paul appealed to this common knowledge. Everyone, including those now behaving in disobedience, knew that Paul, Silas, and Timothy modeled hard work, earning their way while at the same time establishing the church, instructing the believers, and sharing their lives (1 Thess. 2:8). Following the lifestyle of the missionaries was recognized as a worthy goal (1:6), and the Thessalonians had complied in many respects.

Now Paul appealed to that same commendable desire to imitate the apostolic example. The missionaries had not exploited anyone; neither should they. Paul asked no more from the Thessalonians than he demanded of himself.

His statement that they did not eat anyone's food without paying for it was not a recommendation to refuse a meal given out of generosity. Paul wanted to establish the principle of responsible independence; he did not want capable Christians to become dependent on the generosity of others.

Christians, especially those "in the Lord's work," should develop a reputation for industry, not indolence. Those causing the problems in Thessalonica probably presumed upon the goodness of others for their daily living.

They may have claimed this as a right, either through poverty or because they were "busy with God's work." Paul did not see working for the Lord as an excuse for a parasitic lifestyle which took advantage of the kindness of fellow believers. Unrelenting in their work, the missionaries had pushed themselves **so that we would not be a burden to any of you.**

3:9. Examples are given with a purpose, and the missionaries' pattern of life was no exception. Paul stated emphatically that the reason they worked so hard and long among the Thessalonians, the reason they refused to be supported by them, was to leave **a model for you to follow.**

Paul always had a great concern that the church should be upright and blameless in the larger community. He instructed the churches to conduct themselves honorably so the church of Jesus Christ would embody good behavior and love. Lazy and meddlesome people do not contribute to the sterling reputation Paul sought for the church.

Working diligently also insulated the missionaries against any accusations of greed, personal gain, and comfort. Outsiders were constantly throwing charges at them. Paul wanted such allegations proved false and unfounded because of their good conduct.

Even so, Paul acknowledged that, as ministers, they did have the right to be provided for: **not because we do not have the right to such help.** While Paul was eager that everyone should work, he did not want them to go to extremes by denying pay or support to legitimate ministers of the gospel. This was their right and due. However, the idle believers of Thessalonica had no rightful claim to such support.

Paul also contrasted the motives of the missionaries and the idle. The loafers in Thessalonica reaped personal benefit. But the missionaries, who deserved support, refused it for the benefit of others.

3:10. While Paul, Silas, and Timothy were in Thessalonica, they must have seen indications that this lazy attitude and lifestyle posed a problem. Even then they had instructed them, **If a man will not work, he shall not eat.** The apostle had given them this rule face-to-face. Now, because they had neglected following it, he repeated the command.

The command did not apply to those who could not work for some debilitating reason, but to those who "will not work." Paul directed his disdain toward those who sponge off others, whatever their stated reasons—misguided asceticism, work beneath their ability or desire, or too busy. Paul's point was that no one within the Christian community should presume upon the charity of others, nor should they shrink from work. Every person was responsible to provide for himself and his family. For those capable of work, any other course was wrong.

3:11. Paul moved from the general to the specific. Having stated and explained the Christian view on work and laziness, he now focused on the

Thessalonians by stating, **We hear that some among you are idle.** This report of indolence was the occasion for the foregoing instruction.

Paul's reference to "some" suggests this was not a widespread problem involving a large number of people. Even so, Paul wanted to deal with the problem before it got out of hand. Sin in any form can spread and infect others.

Paul described the offenders: **They are not busy; they are busybodies.** Paul used word play to give his portrayal a sharp edge. These people did not work in a beneficial or useful way; they worked in a useless manner. Busy with everybody else's problems, they failed to tend to their own affairs.

3:12. To these individuals Paul appealed on behalf of **the Lord Jesus Christ.** Christ is the authority and standard for behavior.

Paul told these people **to settle down and earn the bread they eat.** They needed to show an outward calm which reflected an inner peace—quite the opposite of what they demonstrated in their busy, fussy, agitated actions. They needed to change! As an apostle, Paul commanded it. These people must have a settled nature which was reflected in their work. Rather than living off the goodness of others, they needed to find jobs and provide their own keep. They must *earn* their *own* bread.

3:13. Paul then turned his attention to encouraging everyone else—those who followed his teachings and instructions. He hoped to motivate this larger group of people, the **brothers,** to continue in faithful and proper living: **never tire of doing what is right.** Though general in its appeal, this exhortation may have had specific application to the parasitic disruption that the slothful had caused. Perhaps some believers wondered what benefit came from working hard, providing for oneself, and being kind, when others were living well without any labor. Paul wanted no such discouragement to seep into the attitude of these believers, causing them to lose heart or slacken in their devotion.

A Warning (3:14–15)

> **SUPPORTING IDEA:** *The disobedient must receive discipline.*

3:14. Paul then outlined steps for church discipline if these individuals should continue rejecting the command to earn their own living. Paul wanted the hard-working core of the church to understand their responsibility in discharging discipline.

Church discipline must be exercised without prejudice: **If anyone does not obey our instruction . . . take special note of him.** Do not associate with him. The obedient must set the disobedient apart for discipline. Since the letter was read to the entire congregation in a public meeting, no one could claim ignorance of Paul's command. In the same way, no one could claim immunity from carrying out the demands of participating in the discipline. Rather than shunning or ostracizing the offenders, Paul wanted the church to take official action.

Paul's direction to **not associate with** the offending persons is peer pressure at its best. He counseled the church to exercise firmness in order to bring the brother back to repentance and right living. The purpose of this discipline was to make the offending persons **feel ashamed.** The result of such shame would be restoration and healthy participation in the church. It would benefit the believer by bringing him out of sinful living and setting him in the right direction. Shame can cause a person to reconsider his behavior, to look inward and think about his life.

3:15. Paul also understood the dangers of discipline. The act of disassociation tempts one to look upon the offending person with disdain and contempt. So Paul issued this warning to the faithful: **do not regard him as an enemy, but warn him as a brother.**

In cases of discipline, restoration must stay at the forefront of our thinking—not punishment. We must retain the binding relationship within God's family; the discipline is exercised against a "brother."

In addition, the Thessalonians must warn the disobedient person as well. Action most often necessitates explanation. The disobedient brother should imagine no hidden agendas or misunderstandings. Required discipline seeks correction out of compassion; this must be plain to all. A disobedient Christian must know what wrong he commits and why close fellowship is being withheld. The warning comes to him as a brother, in gentleness and love.

E Conclusion (3:16–18)

> **SUPPORTING IDEA:** *Paul signed his name, extending blessing to the Thessalonians in the hope that they might experience God's grace and peace.*

3:16. Paul offered a prayer on behalf of these beloved believers, asking that **the Lord of peace himself give you peace.** Paul drew attention to the Lord as the giver. Peace is the desire, but it is the Lord Jesus Christ himself who arrests our attention and captivates our thoughts. Paul directed our gaze toward the Lord, who intervenes on behalf of his children. From him comes the gift of peace. We cannot attain it on our own, but we wait for it in trusting anticipation—a peace born of God. The peace Paul prayed for exists apart from circumstance.

His brief prayer concluded with **the Lord be with all of you.** Paul desired that all the believers in the church, even those currently living in disobedience, experience the reality of God's presence. The spiritual truth of God's continual presence keeps a person growing and following in obedience.

3:17. At the end of the letter, Paul authenticated it by writing: **I, Paul, write this greeting in my own hand, which is the distinguishing mark in all my letters. This is how I write.** Later Paul generally dictated his letters to a scribe or assistant. Many scholars believe these to the Thessalonians were Paul's first correspondence. So he described from the start what would authenticate the letters as his—his signature, his penmanship.

Other letters were rumored to have come from Paul when, in truth, they had not. In order for churches to distinguish the genuine from the false, Paul adopted the practice of penning a greeting or some portion of the letter in his own handwriting as proof of his authorship and authority. His comment, "This is how I write," seems to direct their attention to the style of his hand-writing so everyone would recognize it.

This was important because his letters carried such crucial doctrinal information, revelation, instruction on church life, personal holiness, and, in this case, matters of church discipline. Since these established foundational Christian thinking and practice, the stamp of apostleship was critical.

3:18. Paul ended his letter with a blessing: **The grace of our Lord Jesus Christ be with you all.** He covered a great deal of ground in this short let-ter—encouragements, prayers, the coming of Christ, the revealing of the Antichrist, our future hope, and discipline for unruly believers. In the end, Paul blessed them, calling forth the undeserving gifts of God, his grace.

At the beginning of 2 Thessalonians Paul desired the grace of God for the Thessalonians, and in the end he desired nothing less. At all points in life we cling to the benevolence and generosity of God.

MAIN IDEA REVIEW: *Paul requested prayer for the missionar-ies, that the gospel might spread effectively through their ministry. He told the Thessalonians of his confidence that they would follow through on all his instructions. He then warned them again, as he had in his first letter, to engage in daily life with integrity and pur-pose. Laziness was shameful and disobedience was intolerable.*

III. CONCLUSION

The Size of Your "Wanna"

At a recent Olympics, one coach commented on the marvelous athletes com-peting there. "The difference between those who take home the gold and all the others," he declared, "is the size of their 'wanna.'" Their want to. Their willpower.

Paul talked a great deal about perseverance and endurance, particularly as they relate to gaining strength from God to successfully live the life of faith.

I was reminded of this every time I watched the beginning of *Wide World of Sports* Saturday afternoons on television. It always started with fast-action scenes from sporting competition, with announcer Jim McKay's voice in the background—"The thrill of victory and the agony of defeat."

As he spoke of defeat, a ski jumper was shown losing control at the bottom of the ski jump, falling in a discombobulated heap. And the poor guy did it every Saturday afternoon!

But there is also agony in victory. There are grueling hours of training and, quite often, your body works through pain as you approach the finish line or the end of the game.

I run because it is good for me, although it is agony most of the time. I think I was built for basketball, though there is nothing outstanding about my height. Or, maybe I was built for baseball—centerfield (where I played in my Little League days and later in college). Then again, perhaps checkers is what I was built for.

But, I run—in spite of my build. Whether ease or pain. The alarm goes off and my feet hit the floor (most days).

Overall, life is not fair. Solomon moaned, "The race is not to the swift" (Eccl. 9:11). But those who train well, run well. Spiritual justice awaits its day. So, as Paul said, we "beat" our bodies (1 Cor. 9:27). That means we "black-and-blue" our spirits to get them to listen to higher orders and do what is best in the long run. And the long run is what life is about.

It is not whether my testimony sparkled when I first gave it after receiving Christ as Savior, but what kind of shine has been in my life during the pressure times of the last few months. The great human race is a marathon.

Paul wrote to the Thessalonians about the future, that great day we all anticipate when Christ returns. But we should not neglect today. Paul wanted these believers to commit themselves to living worthy lives, running with endurance toward the goal to which Christ had called them.

PRINCIPLES

- The spread of the gospel to other people depends upon the prayers and faithful work of Christians.
- The gospel does not always find receptive hearts.
- God is faithful in every respect.
- All Christians who can work should do so with integrity and industry.
- Christians should model responsible behavior before their families and others.
- Believers should help people but not presume to run their lives.

- Disobedience among believers should not be ignored. Church discipline should be imposed, especially in cases of willful waywardness.
- Churches must enact discipline unapologetically, yet with gentle care and concern.
- The goal of church discipline is restoration.

APPLICATIONS

- Prayer is not only a gift but a hard work in which the believer must engage for the welfare of others and the continued progress of the gospel. We need to develop greater compassion and self-discipline in this area.
- Rather than become discouraged when people reject the gospel, we must pray more fervently that God will open the minds of unbelievers.
- Christians should build a reputation for hard work, personal integrity, and a willingness to go beyond the minimum requirements of a job.
- We should also develop a reputation for kindness, helpfulness, and tact. We should refuse to gossip, use our time wisely, and not succumb to laziness.
- Everyone in the church has a responsibility to keep other Christians accountable in their personal lives through meaningful friendships and encouragement.
- Churches should develop a standard, unbiased process of disciplinary action for those who sin and require intervention.

IV. LIFE APPLICATION

Heavy Industry

Work was originally an expression of God's image, a reflection of the creative impulse. But the entrance of sin into the world rocked the established order with confusion and imbalance. From that moment, nothing remained safe from the possibility of perversion and corruption.

In the Genesis account of human history, God spoke to Adam saying, "Cursed is the ground because of you; through painful toil you will eat of it all the days of your life. It will produce thorns and thistles for you, and you will eat the plants of the field. By the sweat of your brow you will eat your food until you return to the ground, since from it you were taken" (Gen. 3:17b–19). Since that time, tension has existed between people and their work.

As a consequence, people approach work in one of four basic ways—through neglect, hatred, idolatry, or balanced esteem. In each case, a person's assessment of work reflects his idea of God as well as his view of himself.

In Thessalonica, labor problems divided the church. A few believers refused to work, presuming upon the kindness and charity of other Christians. These idle people claimed exemption from daily work because they busied themselves in ministry, helping other people. But their economy operated contrary to God's values. They viewed people occupied in "the Lord's work" as holding greater importance, and so deserving greater privilege. To them, work operated on a hierarchical system, with daily labor and secular jobs at the bottom. In reality, their neglect of work stemmed from arrogance. These people enjoyed a self-imposed unemployment designed for their own benefit.

People today fall into the same delusion when they refuse to work because certain jobs are beneath their dignity or training. God views all legitimate work as useful and sacred, as long as it is carried out to his glory.

Perhaps a more prevalent problem today is that of hating work. This attitude has existed since sin tainted work. Indeed, many people refer to work as a "necessary evil."

In our own day, the machine, the clock, and the development of transportation have conspired to alienate people from the thing that should bring them a measure of satisfaction—their work. The machine has dehumanized the work environment, speeding production while insulating workers from meaningful interaction with others. The clock has mechanized man, training him to respond to whistles and bells. Modern people have become so time-conscious that they can hear within their brains the constant ticking of the clock partitioning their hours into isolated categories of duty and leisure. Transportation has torn man's work from a meaningful context, making his labor a small piece of a greater whole that he rarely sees.

As a result, many people despise their jobs. In the process they belittle God's directives and gifts.

Conversely, other people elevate their jobs, idolizing labor and personal accomplishments. Unlike those in earlier times who viewed work as a response to God's goodness, man has now eliminated God from the equation, making work a means to his personal identity. Productivity has become equated with worth. Those who aspire to a meaningful and purpose-filled life cannot conceive of it outside the arena of paid labor.

Such an approach, however, leads either to recurring frustration or denial of work's inability to bring true meaning to life. Once work or work's rewards (such as money, vacations, benefits) become the central purpose in life, we supplant God in our search for identity, security, and meaning.

The biblical approach to work values diligence without enslavement to the job, offers personal satisfaction without regard to occupation, and esteems labor without glorifying it.

The Christian recognizes that personal worth comes only through a relationship with Jesus Christ. People cannot merit or work themselves into a position of importance. At the same time, our security rests in the sovereign will and goodness of God. Life's meaning resides in our devotion to God and his glory, not in what we produce. Any legitimate work can bring meaning to life and honor to Christ.

The Christian needs to approach work not as a means to personal ends, but as an expression of God's blessing. Our work can provide ways for us to express God's original intent—that selfhood, safety, and significance issue from God's grace.

V. PRAYER

Lord, it is easy to get caught up in the frantic search for meaning, presuming I can become significant and important through what I do. Help me to relax. Then, as I work, help me to do so with energy out of response to your goodness and love. Amen.

VI. DEEPER DISCOVERIES

Self-Discipline (vv. 4–5,13)

Paul did not tell the Thessalonians to exercise self-discipline, but he intimated this as he wrote, "We have confidence in the Lord that you are doing and will continue to do the things we command." Following Christ in continuing spiritual progress and development takes self-discipline. Godliness runs contrary to our natural inclinations.

The term for self-discipline means to take possession or custody of something. No one will be able to take possession of the self without self-will and effort. Our wills must yield to the higher purpose of godliness. Then, in partnership with God's Spirit, this trait will grow stronger. But we must take a part in this effort. Peter tells us to "add to your faith goodness; and to goodness, knowledge; and to knowledge, self-control" (2 Pet. 1:5–6), noting that if we increase in these qualities we will be effective and productive in our Christian life (1:8).

But self-mastery cannot succeed without the Holy Spirit. People are limited in their ability to conquer themselves. Even at our most noble moments, we cannot achieve on our own what is possible only through the enabling power of God's Spirit. In Galatians 5:22, self-control is listed as one of the Spirit's fruits, clustered with love, joy, peace, patience, kindness, goodness, faithfulness, and gentleness. All these qualities hang together as evidence of God's Spirit working and developing a Christian's life. The lack of self-control causes spiritual degeneration. Paul listed this along with other sinful behaviors which mark the chaotic final days of earth (2 Tim. 3:3).

If we cannot conquer ourselves, we cannot advance in our spiritual growth. And without self-control we fail at every other Christian endeavor. That is why Paul listed self-control as a requirement for church leadership (1 Tim. 3:3; Titus 1:8; 2:2). Actually, self-control means leaving the control to God. It means removing ourselves from the chair of authority and allowing God to replace our desires, motives, purposes, and character with his own.

If we commit ourselves to this from the start, we will face temptations and times of crisis with the strength of God's Spirit. We will not stumble as often, confused and confounded about what to do. Our inner self will know beforehand whose voice to follow.

VII. TEACHING OUTLINE

A. INTRODUCTION

1. Lead Story: Do Not Wish for Sausages
2. Context: Paul wanted the Thessalonians to continue maturing in faith and godliness. He asked for prayer and then offered his own prayer for the Thessalonians. Paul then turned his attention to a matter he had addressed in his first letter—idleness among believers. Evidently this problem had not been resolved, so he dealt more thoroughly with the issue in this chapter. All Christians who are able to do so must work, providing for their own daily needs and not depending on others for their personal support. As in so many cases, Paul's major concern was for the church and the gospel to maintain a good reputation within the community and so enhance the views of the gospel by non-believers. He closed with a blessing of grace and peace.
3. Transition: Christians need strong prayer support from one another. The battles against evil and personal weaknesses are just as prevalent as they were in Paul's day. Yet we often rely on personal determination rather than depend on Christian community and prayer for added strength.
4. In addition, believers today must create a balanced view of work. Work comes from God, and we should exhibit diligence and integrity in our jobs. But we must also rest, finding refreshment in God, others, and his creation. For the Christian, work should be evaluated by the gospel and our mission to the world. We should responsibly

provide for ourselves and our family, but we need to engage also in charity among those less fortunate than we are.

B. COMMENTARY
1. Prayer Requests (3:1–2)
2. Encouragement to Continue in Faith (3:3–4)
3. A Matter of Discipline (3:6–13)
4. A Warning (3:14–15)
5. Conclusion (3:16–18)

C. CONCLUSION: HEAVY INDUSTRY

VIII. ISSUES FOR DISCUSSION

1. What do you consider your job, and how do you see it in relation to God's kingdom?
2. What is your attitude toward work?
3. Do you know someone who models a balanced view of work? Discuss how that person's actions show his or her heart attitude.
4. Discuss society's responses toward the unemployed, those on welfare, or in low-status jobs. Has studying this chapter challenged or changed your position? In what way?

Introduction to

1 Timothy

LETTER PROFILE: FIRST TIMOTHY

- This letter was probably the first of the three letters which came to be known as the Pastoral Epistles (1 and 2 Timothy and Titus). They have guided pastors and churches for centuries.
- Paul sent the letter to Timothy, his protégé and spiritual son.
- The letter was delivered to Timothy in the city of Ephesus, where he had remained in order to deal with certain problems in the church.
- Paul gave instructions on preserving truth in the church and outlined standards for worship; he also emphasized personal integrity and Christian character for church government and leadership.
- Paul closed the letter with strong teaching about finances, especially as they relate to contentment and personal goals for a godly life. Detailed instructions were also given on the church's role in caring for widows.

AUTHOR PROFILE: PAUL

- Paul, a Jew, was born in Tarsus, a city near the Lebanese border in modern Turkey. The citizens of the city zealously studied culture and academic disciplines.
- Paul was a Roman citizen. Whether his citizenship came by birth or payment is uncertain, but clearly he enjoyed the full range of privileges accorded a citizen of Rome.
- He was a prominent Jewish leader, highly educated as a Pharisee and, before his conversion to Christianity, a leading persecutor of the church.
- Paul visited Ephesus on his second and third missionary journeys (Acts 16–20).
- He was known for his tireless pioneer work among the Gentiles.
- Imprisoned by Nero's regime in Rome, Paul was beheaded around A.D. 68.

CITY PROFILE: EPHESUS

- Ephesus was a major trading center and seaport on the Aegean Sea during Paul's time. Today the city lies seven miles inland due to the accumulation of silt from the Cayster River.
- Ephesus was home to one of the seven wonders of the ancient world—the temple of the goddess Artemis. For the Ephesians, the temple and worship of Artemis represented economic opportunity as well as civic pride.
- The city had a reputation as a center for the learning and practice of magical arts.
- Like other major cities in the Roman Empire, Ephesus enjoyed a measure of civic self-rule.

1 Timothy 1

False Teachings Versus Truth

"*For* religion is not a matter of arrangements or places

or words, but of life and love, of mercy and obedience, of

persons in a passion of faith."

E u g e n e   H .   P e t e r s o n

1 Timothy 1

I N   A   N U T S H E L L

*P*aul greeted his good friend and spiritual son, Timothy, then got right into warnings about false teaching and legalism—opposites of true faith and grace. Paul then explained how God's truth worked in his own life and urged Timothy to embrace faithfulness.

False Teachings
Versus Truth

I. INTRODUCTION

Lifeguards and Road Maps

I once met a young man who had spent the summer as a lifeguard at a lake. During those months he had pulled five people to shore, saving their lives. But the interesting thing to me was his comment about something all five had in common. "Not one of them," he said, "asked me for help or yelled for me to come."

Caught in a struggle between life and death, these people refused to admit their dilemma.

On the lighter side, most women recognize men's denial of need when it comes to asking directions while driving. They will hear confident assertions like, "I am not lost," or "I will find my way," as they speed toward the wrong destination.

There are probably a number of explanations for such responses—an independent nature, self-protection, selfishness, pride. Most of them are rooted in our sinfulness. They keep us from seeking direction or rescue, from finding mercy or grace.

In this first chapter of 1 Timothy, Paul spoke to the fundamentals of the faith—who Christ is, what he has done, how we can know God. He also taught the need to guard our hearts and faith carefully, to seek help and understanding through God's revelatory Word—our source of authoritative truth. As Paul instructed and gave his personal witness, it became clear that God desires to save everyone, that his grace is abundant toward all people, that his love has broken through the barrier of sin. He wants to rescue us, to give us direction, to show us truth.

But we must first admit we are drowning. We must acknowledge we are lost.

II. COMMENTARY

> **MAIN IDEA:** *Adhering to true faith and doctrine results in changed lives, which becomes evident in our behavior and church unity. When we become involved in what is false or wander from the goals of the faith, this also becomes apparent in our behavior and in our hearts.*

A Greeting (1:1–2)

> **SUPPORTING IDEA:** *Hope and salvation are the themes of this letter, especially as experienced within the church. Paul encouraged Timothy in a difficult task and then approved him before the congregation.*

1:1–2. These verses refer to the Father, who gave the Son to be our salvation. Therefore, God, three in one, is our Savior as much as the sacrificed Son. Paul's introductory greeting to Timothy and the church at Ephesus comes loaded with authority. In his opening sentence, he drew attention to his apostleship, stating that it came **by the command of God our Savior and of Christ Jesus our hope.** Right at the start he gave clues about the themes of the letter: salvation and hope.

As we believe in the Son and rest in his finished work of paying for our sins on the cross, he takes away our fears of punishment. He removes our guilt. He assures us of heaven. In short, he is **our hope.** There is none without him.

The letter was addressed to Timothy (v. 2), but it was intended to be read before the entire assembly at Ephesus. By addressing Timothy as **my true son in the faith,** Paul accomplished two intentions—to encourage Timothy, who was faced with a difficult task of untangling problems within the church, and to let the church know that Timothy came with the authority and approval of Paul. Paul "fathered" Timothy by helping him grow in the faith and ministry (2 Tim. 1:5).

Paul concluded his greeting with a blessing: **grace, mercy and peace.** All three are unmerited good will from God toward those who believe. *Grace* covers everything that God gives to those who are his; it is his generosity provoked only by his love. *Mercy* includes that special attention and care which God extends to the person in need. *Peace* describes the heart at rest and in harmony with God; it includes a tranquillity of the soul independent of circumstances. All of these come only from God the Father and Christ Jesus our Lord.

Ⓑ Understanding the Law (1:3–5)

SUPPORTING IDEA: *Some people add to the gospel as given through the accepted canon of Scripture. Others create controversy through strange ideas or legalistic requirements. Then there are those who claim to have special knowledge regarding God or faith. All these people should be kept from leadership in the church and urged to return to true faith. The true goal of our faith and life should be to glorify God through love, faith, and purity.*

1. Description of false teachings (1:3–4)

1:3. From the church's beginning there have been heresies, rumors, and defections. In the first century, new churches were being formed and established churches were learning to create community and order. During these beginning years, false doctrine attacked the foundations of the faith. Some of the attacks came from without, but others that sprang from within. Timothy, therefore, had been told to stay in Ephesus instead of continuing into Macedonia with Paul. He was to **command certain men not to teach false doctrines any longer.**

The false doctrines under question did not concern areas of conscience—those things which each believer is free to decide based on personal conviction. They undermined basics of faith and belief. Once truth is asserted, Satan quickly introduces what is false in order to bring confusion, distortion, and misbelief. Pluralism has its attraction, voicing tolerance and respect for opposing viewpoints, but it is dangerous when adopted in matters of faith. Not all proposed "truths" can be true.

Paul called these false doctrines *hetero* teaching, meaning teaching "of another kind." These teachings were simply untrue. The standard for truth was the Old Testament, the words of Christ, and the teaching of the apostles. All else was wrong, false, untrue.

If Christians become grounded in the truth of their faith, false teaching can be stopped before it spreads. If we can learn what the Bible says and then learn to obey it, we are less prone to deception. Otherwise, we fit Paul's description of the immature believer who is "tossed back and forth by the waves, and blown here and there by every wind of teaching and by the cunning and craftiness of men in their deceitful scheming" (Eph. 4:14).

1:4. Paul condemned the false teachings which were being propagated in Ephesus, calling them **myths and endless genealogies.**

The **myths** of the first century were more than fairy tales; they were legends used primarily to promote immorality. These were stories taken from the past and used to justify behavior which was contrary to God's call to righteousness. There were teachers who used the Old Testament as a "happy hunting ground"—to use John R. W. Stott's description—for invented allegories and frivolous spiritualizing. Every truth was turned to symbol, every event became a metaphor so that soon they had "proof texts" for their own ideas, biases, and desires.

Rip a verse out of context, read between the lines and, presto, you have whatever you like.

The phrase **endless genealogies** refers to histories and prophetic speculations rising out of guesswork and the desire to be different. Such people became the special interpreters of Scripture; they claimed special knowledge.

Paul recognized that these teachings resulted in division. The strange doctrines, the myths, the genealogies—**these promote controversies rather than God's work.**

Rather than equipping the church, these false teachers were creating factions, confusions, and disrepute for the church of Christ. To put it bluntly, these people trafficked in disruption rather than **God's work—which is by faith.**

God reveals the content; we believe it in faith. "Faith comes from hearing the message, and the message is heard through the word of Christ" (Rom. 10:17). We are all called to build our lives on the foundation of our Lord's words (Matt. 7:24–27).

2. The true goal (1:5)

1:5. Paul came right to the point. The reason he wanted Timothy to stop these people from continuing in their false beliefs and to prevent them from spreading destructive ideas was **love.** The issue of false teachings is not purely doctrinal. It concerns conduct as well.

Instead of controversy, our lives should be marked by love—first for God, then for others.

Many people in the world think of God only in negative terms. They blame him for everything from hurricanes to famine, from economic collapse to car wrecks. This verse jumps out as a correction to such people. God wants the world to operate in a different way. His goal for us is love.

God's definition of love is not sentimental. It is a love that is trustworthy and active. It springs **from a pure heart and a good conscience and a sincere faith.**

A **pure heart** refers to wholeness within the inner, spiritual dimension of a person. The heart is considered the control center of thoughts, motives, and spiritual life. The pure heart is cleansed from sin in these areas. Therefore, love which springs from a pure heart is sacrificial (1 Cor. 13), free of selfish motives, godly, honorable.

A **good conscience** had a slightly different meaning for the Ephesians than it does today in Western societies. For first-century people, conscience dealt with a person's conduct within the chosen group. A good conscience meant living according to the standards and practices which the group (in this case the church) deemed proper and acceptable. It meant living without shame among one's peers or companions. We view the conscience as if it is concerned with right and wrong on an individual basis. We would do well to recapture the ancient meaning and sense of accountability.

Sincere faith assures correct behavior because it comes from the revelation of God. The Word of God provides the directives for Christian conduct and belief.

Paul's desire for the church was to produce people who embraced correct doctrine as formed through the Old Testament, the prophets, Christ and the apostles; people whom Christ had cleansed from sin and who were living in that forgiveness through the continual purifying of their heart. Paul's vision was that followers of Christ would form a community of sound conduct that kept its members accountable in their behavior and life. He hoped the end result would be a distinctive people known for their love.

The False Teachers (1:6–7)

SUPPORTING IDEA: *The church should hold its leaders accountable, requiring orthodoxy in doctrine and purity in faith, so the church may be preserved in unity and love.*

1:6. According to Paul, some of the believers had **wandered away from these and turned to meaningless talk.** The false teachers had turned a different way, their inner spirits becoming muddied by sin and wrong thinking, their behavior ineffective and at odds within the church, their reputations built on controversy rather than love. Because of this, what they taught was meaningless. It was fruitless, or empty, and wrong.

Paul gave some descriptions of false teachers throughout 1 Timothy:

- They emphasized fables and genealogies (1:4–7; 4:7).
- They emphasized rigid asceticism, renouncing marriage and certain foods (4:3,8).
- They professed a special knowledge of God (6:20).

1:7. Paul asserted that these people **want to be teachers of the law.** It seems that the driving force of these teachers was to attract admiration and respect, to gain the title "teacher of the law." They wanted others to regard them as authoritative interpreters of Scripture. They wanted a following. But no matter their desire, **they do not know what they are talking about.** Their ideas and intricate systems of thinking were groundless. There was no truth in them, despite their confidence. They could assert a position, even when the structure of thought and belief was wrong. But sincerity does not automatically translate into truth.

ⅅ Understanding the True Purpose of the Law (1:8–10)

SUPPORTING IDEA: *The purpose of the law is to draw clear parameters for godly living, to show us what God is like, and to point us to our need for salvation.*

1:8. Paul declared, **We know that the law is good if one uses it properly.** Of course the law is good, but like many good things it can be misused. The good of the law is clear:

- It shows us what God is like and what he wants us to be and do.
- The Ten Commandments are a guide for right and wrong in our daily choices.
- The law stands as an indictment for all those who do not receive Christ and his righteousness. By the law comes the knowledge of sin (Rom. 3:19). Psalm 19:7 says, "The law of the LORD is perfect."
- The law reveals sin.

1:9–10. Paul went on to elaborate on the "proper use" of the law as he put forth three pairs or groups of sinners: **lawbreakers and rebels; the ungodly and sinful; the unholy and irreligious.**

This catalog of sins covers everything and everyone—those who by outward acts disobey the standard of God; those who defile themselves inwardly as in coveting, hatred, disrespect; and those who are defiantly opposed to God's authority. No one escapes the judgment of the law.

From these broad categories Paul selected perhaps the most abhorrent sins, each with a deliberate tie to "the law"—the Ten Commandments. He listed **those who kill their fathers or mothers,** as opposed to the command to honor your father and mother (Exod. 20:12); murderers, in contrast to the command not to kill (Exod. 20:13); adulterers and perverts are set against the command not to commit adultery (Exod. 20:14); slave traders are contrasted with the law not to steal (Exod. 20:15), and liars and perjurers contradict the command not to give false testimony against your neighbor (Exod. 20:16).

The purpose of the law is to point out how good and holy the Lord is and how righteous his doctrines are. It points out our inability to live righteously as God demands. The law points out our guilt and sentences us to condemnation (Rom. 3:19–20). But the law also guides us to the gospel as given in the apostolic writings. It shows us our need for the Savior (Gal. 3:24).

The law does not save us; it points us to the one who can. How amazing then that so many people say they live their lives by following rules or doing the best they can. The words of the hymn, "Rock of Ages," expresses our total dependence on God alone: "Not the labor of my hands / Can fulfill the law's demands / All for sin could not atone / Thou must save, and Thou alone."

To conclude his list, Paul included **whatever else is contrary to the sound doctrine.** Sound doctrine produces mature, healthy Christians. Sound doctrine will result in transformed individuals who are morally fit and who love "from a pure heart and a good conscience and a sincere faith" (1 Tim. 1:5). True doctrine is not theoretical. It changes lives and produces a new kind of person.

The Glorious Gospel (1:11)

SUPPORTING IDEA: *The good news of God's saving mercy and gracious forgiveness through Jesus Christ is, indeed, glorious. It is a treasure from God.*

1:11. Paul's message was built upon the law, the prophets, and special revelation from Christ himself. Paul was entrusted with God's message of grace to all people—including the Gentiles. He was the great proclaimer of God's sacrifice and generous forgiveness to everyone who believes. Paul understood the privilege and high call that God had given him: **the glorious gospel of the blessed God.**

The gospel or "good news" is that Jesus suffered in our place. He died a death reserved for lawbreakers, experiencing the condemnation of the law on our behalf: "Christ redeemed us from the curse of the law by becoming a curse for us, for it is written: 'Cursed is everyone who is hung on a tree'" (Gal. 3:13). Because of this, Christ offers forgiveness if we admit our inadequacy to live by God's righteous standards (law), acknowledge that we are lawbreakers, and trust in Christ alone for our forgiveness and acceptance before God, who is holy.

But the gospel also includes the fruitfulness of a life given to God. Within the glorious gospel of forgiveness, godly conduct and character are also assumed. The true gospel reveals a God who is powerful and willing to forgive and who is able to keep those who live by faith, bringing about "a new creation" (2 Cor. 5:17).

Understanding the Work of Grace (1:12–17)

SUPPORTING IDEA: *No one is beyond the scope or power of God to save and recreate into his likeness. God is extravagant in his love and mercy. He has shown mercy to all of us, because all are sinners. We become the exhibit piece of God's mercy, love, and faithfulness to those we live with and meet along life's way.*

1. The example of Paul's conversion (1:12–14)

1:12. Paul offered his personal testimony as a contrast to the false teachers and leaders in the Ephesian church. Paul's words (doctrine) matched his life; his manner corresponded with the truth. When our character and lifestyle harmonize with our beliefs, we become a powerful example of God's truth and reality. Paul was an example to all believers, and specifically to Timothy and church leaders, of how life and doctrine must complement each other.

Paul began his personal testimony by directing attention to Christ: **I thank Christ Jesus our Lord, who has given me strength**. Whatever Paul was able to point to in his life as exemplary was because of Christ Jesus. Paul had an amazing life of powerful ministry for God. His life and work brought about tremendous results for God's kingdom. Even so, Paul knew it was because of God from start to finish. He was the giver of power and strength.

Paul's thankfulness continued: **God considered me faithful, appointing me to his service**. Paul had demonstrated faithfulness throughout his ministry, and in God's economy this resulted in greater ministry and responsibility. God knew Paul would be faithful and so put upon him the great responsibility of taking the gospel throughout the known world. Even so, "it is God who works in [us]" (Phil. 2:13). So Paul gave thanks, because he knew that who and what he was came from God: "Not that we are competent in ourselves to claim anything for ourselves, but our competence comes from God" (2 Cor. 3:5).

Paul did not select his role in life. God clearly and specifically called him: "This man [Paul] is my chosen instrument to carry my name before the Gentiles and their kings and before the people of Israel" (Acts 9:15). He was appointed by God.

1:13. Paul had not always been a missionary in Christ's service. Looking back at his life, he described himself prior to his conversion as a **blasphemer and a persecutor and a violent man**.

We first met Paul (then called Saul) at the stoning of Stephen (Acts 7:57–58; 8:1). While an angry mob surrounded Stephen, throwing rocks at him until he was battered to death, Saul witnessed the execution with approval. A few verses later we gain a clearer portrait of this zealot: "Saul began to destroy the church. Going from house to house, he dragged off men and women and put them in prison" (Acts 8:3).

Here is blasphemy, persecution, and violence from the hands of Saul. He opposed the work of God; he was contemptuous of Christ. He harassed the people of God. He was brutal, having people imprisoned and perhaps killed for their faith in Christ the Lord.

Even so, he was **shown mercy**. In a dramatic encounter with the living Christ, Paul was rescued from his unbelief. He was saved from his rebellion (Acts 9).

1:14. There is no doubt in Paul's mind that his salvation was due to **the grace of our Lord . . . poured out on me abundantly.** Having just recounted how he lived before his encounter with the risen Christ on the road to Damascus, his rescue from sin can only be attributed to the overflowing grace of God. It was poured out. The Greek verb actually has the prefix *huper,* or "hyper" we would say. It means over, above, beyond, in excess. Paul struggled for words to express the greatness of God's grace.

Not only was he saved; he was changed, receiving the abundance of **faith and love that are in Christ Jesus.** The flood from which grace springs also brings forth faith and love. All are gifts of God; all are evidences of those who are captured by the gracious salvation of God in Christ. Perhaps Paul was drawing a contrast between himself and the false teachers with whom Timothy had to deal. People may claim to know God, but the truth of this love will be revealed by their faith and love.

2. The explanation of the gospel (1:15–17)

1:15. Paul declared, **Here is a trustworthy saying.** "Pay attention!" he told them, because what he would now write was true, beyond debate. It carried the same force as Jesus' declaration, "I tell you."

And what was this undeniable truth? **Christ Jesus came into the world to save sinners.** That was the point of his incarnation. Before Jesus was born, his mission was announced: You are to give him the name Jesus, because he will save his people from their sins" (Matt. 1:21). He proclaimed his own intentions, stating, "It is not the healthy who need a doctor, but the sick. I have not come to call the righteous, but sinners" (Mark 2:17). And that truth had been sounded by the apostolic witness: "But God demonstrates his own love for us in this: While we were still sinners, Christ died for us" (Rom. 5:8).

Many people refuse to believe the truth that they are sinners. It is too hard to admit. They cannot admit that "all have sinned and fall short of the glory of God" (Rom. 3:23)—including them.

Paul pointed to his own experience as he spoke of sinners, claiming **of whom I am the worst.**

Paul could go back in his mind and point to his religiosity: "a Hebrew of Hebrews; in regard to the law, a Pharisee . . . as for legalistic righteousness, faultless" (Phil. 3:5–6). Even so, despite admirable efforts, Paul knew his own heart and mind, his selfishness, his motives, and recognized that nothing he could do would satisfy the holiness of God. He was a sinner in need of grace.

It is the place each person must come to, an admission that *Christ Jesus came into the world to save sinners—of whom I am the worst.*

1:16. Paul offered himself as a case study of God's goodness, mercy, and patience. Although he was the worst of sinners, God saved him. He was forgiven, transformed. His persecution of the church made Paul the perfect example of God's mercy: **I was shown mercy so that in me, the worst of sinners, Christ Jesus might display his unlimited patience.**

Paul believed that God had selected him, the worst, so that no one then or today could say, "I am too bad, too sinful. God could never forgive me." But no matter how deep the sin, our Lord is able to penetrate deeper with his love and forgiveness. God's patience is unlimited. Literally, it has no limit. It never runs out, never becomes exhausted. It is as eternal as he is.

Paul was an **example for those who would believe on Him and receive eternal life.** The false teachers, in their self-indulgent pursuit of glory, were examples of God's righteous and holy intolerance of sin. God's patience brings hope to those who struggle and search in life, for those whose past or present is littered with sin. But God will not be mocked; those who refuse his grace will suffer his wrath.

Belief on Christ is necessary to salvation. This is not adherence to dogma, but a personal trust in the sacrificial death of Christ upon the cross and in his victorious resurrection. The demons acknowledge the existence of Jesus Christ and they tremble (Jas. 2:19), but they do not rest in Christ's work on the cross. Belief encompasses trust, dependence, and obedience. It is a belief that changes our lives now and for eternity.

1:17. Having recounted God's grace, mercy, love, and faithfulness toward himself and all who believe, Paul then burst into praise, offering a personal doxology.

To the **King eternal**—the God of power and sovereignty over all the affairs of men and angels; **immortal**—eternal, beyond the reaches of death or decay, above all the created order; **invisible**—beyond the constraints of the physical, beyond the approach of humankind; **the only God**—not only his supremacy, but his exclusive claim as authority, the foundation of Christian belief that God is—to this trustworthy, incomparable, self-existent God who is rich in mercy and love be **honor and glory for ever and ever.**

Remaining Faithful to the Call (1:18–20)

> **SUPPORTING IDEA:** God's truth obligates the believer to live responsibly and faithfully; there are grave consequences for those who turn aside from God's truth and calling.

1:18. This same God whom Paul praised has called Timothy into his service: **in keeping with the prophecies once made about you.** Such a call, while placing obligations upon Timothy, was meant also to reassure the young man of God's greatness and grace. These prophecies, given in the past, were words given from God defining what kind of person Timothy was and would become. The calling affirmed his gifts and God's investment in him for spreading the gospel and bringing him glory.

For those called to ministry today, it is equally good to remember that entry into God's service is just that—service to God. The church and its people are to be served with love, faithfulness, sound teaching, and discipline. Still, it is to God that final responsibility and devotion belong. God himself enlists and equips his servants.

Paul called Timothy to remain obedient and true to God's selection of him as his minister/worker so that he **may fight the good fight.**

The good fight is the struggle which all Christians engage in when their efforts are focused toward honoring Christ and accepting responsibility for personal holiness. It is about keeping the faith individually as well as in the church. Paul used this phrase again at the close of his letter when he reminded Timothy to "fight *the good fight* of the faith. Take hold of the eternal life to which you were called when you made your good confession" (1 Tim. 6:12, emphasis added). Toward the end of his own life, Paul offered himself as an example for Timothy to follow, stating, "I have fought *the good fight,* I have finished the race, I have kept the faith" (2 Tim. 4:7, emphasis added). This is a militaristic term that admits to a hostile environment: "our struggle is not against flesh and blood, but against the rulers, against the authorities, against the powers of this dark world and against the spiritual forces of evil in the heavenly realms" (Eph. 6:12).

1:19. Paul continued by describing what was personally involved in "fighting the good fight," instructing Timothy to **[hold] on to faith and a good conscience.** Faith is the complete gospel, the pure doctrine and knowledge of Jesus Christ and God. In dealing with false teachers, Timothy must be certain of truth and hold on to it and not be pulled into error. Satan deals in deception, and truth is the response which defeats such arrogance. A good conscience is a life lived blameless before God and others. It is not perfection. But it is a life against which no one can bring a legitimate charge. Such a person is free of guilt before God and before the community of believers. Paul wanted Timothy to maintain what he believed and to act on it.

Timothy had huge responsibilities ahead of him. Paul was handing the torch of ministry to this young son of the faith. But in many ways our responsibilities are exactly the same. We also have the faith delivered to us through the Scriptures. We also carry a conscience that scolds us when we sin and affirms us when we believe and live the faith. The command to fight the good fight, to hold on to faith and a good conscience is continuous, stretching down through the centuries to all believers.

With the challenge came a warning for those who reject divine instruction: **some . . . have shipwrecked their faith.** Strange doctrine, wrong motives, sinful habits—and a life can be lost through the abandonment of faith.

1:20. Paul put forth two examples of men who had shipwrecked their faith: **Hymenaeus and Alexander.** These leaders within the Ephesian church were spreading false ideas about God and Christ.

Paul stated that **he handed [them] over to Satan to be taught not to blaspheme.** The discipline that Paul imposed is also described in 1 Corinthians 5. In that case it involved a man involved in immoral behavior. In both instances, the sinning person was dismissed from the church. He was taken out of the protective community of the church and Christ's kingdom and handed over to the kingdom of this world, ruled by Satan. Alone in Satan's domain, the disciplined person would realize his errors, recognize the truth and goodness of God's kingdom, and choose to repent and return to God and the church in faith.

Obviously not everyone will repent, but the church is called to practice this loving discipline so people will awaken to their sin and turn back to their Lord.

MAIN IDEA REVIEW: *Adhering to true faith and doctrine results in changed lives, which becomes evident in our behavior and church unity. When we become involved in what is false or wander from the goals of the faith, this also becomes apparent in our behavior and in our hearts.*

III. CONCLUSION

"At Least I Am Better than Charlie Sedgewick"

People have said it for years—"Well, I am not as bad as So-and-so." (I have always used the pretend name of Charlie Sedgewick.) They may be talking about a bad temper, time with family, giving money, or even some athletic ability. We can always find someone who is worse at something than we are.

One time I was shooting a one-minute spot for television, talking about the Christian life, and using basketball as an analogy. Holding the basketball and standing on the court, I bragged, "I can beat Charlie Sedgewick one-on-one." I could imagine the viewers' looks of bewilderment as they asked, "Who?" But then I countered, "But why not talk about beating Mark Price?" (an NBA star playing with the Cleveland Cavaliers at the time).

I got a note from a viewer whose name was Charlie S. (close to Sedgewick) who said he was not so sure I *could* beat him! Touché! I also played Mark Price once in a pickup game and got killed!

We can always play a comparison game with other people and find someone who, by contrast, is a little worse than we are. But our standard for life is not someone in the crowd. It is Christ himself. God tells us to be perfect, to be like Christ, to look to him as our standard of righteousness.

Paul had some accomplishments he could brag about and some things that brought him shame, but he refused to compare himself to others. In fact, in the light of God's character, Paul called himself "the worst of sinners." He recognized the gap which existed between his sinful heart and the holy God.

When we see ourselves as weak and frail, in need of Christ, then we will want to stay close to the Lord and his teachings as this first chapter of 1 Timothy challenges us to do. Otherwise we play the comparison game, and this leads to pride. Then someone like Charlie Sedgewick will look your way and say, "Well, at least I am not as bad as . . ."

PRINCIPLES

- Spiritual truth comes from God. People devise myths and deviations from that truth.
- The law is perfect and good, but we are not able to keep it.
- The more we understand grace and God's goodness, the more we are aware of our own sinfulness.
- Shipwreck comes to people who throw away their moral and spiritual compass—the prophecies and truth given by God for our fight of faith.

APPLICATIONS

- We need to study the Scriptures and continually learn the contents of the faith. We lose a "good conscience" when we allow our own "myths" or interpretations to supplant true faith.
- We do best when we are honest about our sinfulness, as Paul was. We respond best to this truth by abiding in Christ.
- We are called to faithfulness in the fight of the faith. Thus, it is healthy to make ourselves accountable to one or two other believers and to have a strategy for study, ministry to others, and church involvement.

IV. LIFE APPLICATION

What the World Needs Now

Love. We all long to possess it, but I wonder how many of us aspire to give it away. We want to be love's recipient, but do we desire to be the instrument of its power?

As Christians we are told to love our enemies (Matt. 5:44), to love God (Matt. 22:37), to love one another (1 Pet. 1:22; John 13:34), to love our neighbors (Matt. 19:19; Rom. 13:10), to love our spouses (Eph. 5:25). In fact, we are to do everything in love (1 Cor. 16:14), for "the only thing that counts is faith expressing itself through love" (Gal. 5:6). There are no exclusion clauses. We are to express sincere love in every relationship we can imagine, from God to home, from the community of believers to those outside the faith; we are to include even those who mistreat us and position themselves as our enemies. Love is required, encouraged, described (1 Cor. 13). It is the jewel in the eternal triad, outshining faith and hope.

But while love is the great obsession, it is also the great disappointment. People go through life desperate for love but poverty-stricken in their hearts. In a society built on fear, love has become one more item of suspicion. So we escape into self-love, media fantasy, cynicism, or bland compromise, doubting that our heart's desire will ever intersect with the ideal.

I suspect we find that our own efforts to live in love are often tainted, weak, or conditional. How often do we extend love to those who are difficult to love?

In the opening chapter of 1 Timothy, Paul tells us how true love is formed. It comes from **a pure heart and a good conscience and a sincere faith.**

A pure heart is unmixed. Like gold, it does not contain trace elements like sin or selfishness. True biblical love exists within the inner spirit of a person who is blameless before God. This cannot be created out of the normal struggles of the human heart. A pure heart is possible only through the cleansing of God's Spirit as we open our souls to his guidance.

Genuine love is possible only when our consciences are untainted. This self-awareness is sensitive to right and wrong as God prescribes it. Such a person comprehends what is proper behavior for those who claim Christ as Lord and then determines to live in conformity to God's commands and in harmony with other believers. We cannot have disputes with other Christians or live in a way that is contrary to the church and expect to have the resources to love fully.

But the foundational element of love is a sincere faith. It must center in God, who is Love. Faith involves correct belief about God and his personhood. It also encompasses the fruits of such conviction and relationship. Genuine faith cannot be contained; it expresses itself in day-by-day living. Love that is Godlike comes only from those people who are cleansed by God, obedient to his righteousness, and authentic in the profession and the living of their faith.

V. PRAYER

Father of all that is good and true, teach us to love as you do, with sincerity and a pure heart, that we may draw from the wellspring of your generosity and kindness. Keep us from error as we go about our days, so that our thoughts of you may be true, our actions right, our motives blameless. Amen.

VI. DEEPER DISCOVERIES

A. Ephesus (v. 3)

Paul often centered his evangelistic activities in major metropolitan centers from which the gospel could spread. Perhaps he chose Ephesus for this reason. One of the greatest cities of the Roman Empire, Ephesus was known for its spectacular temple to the goddess Artemis (the Roman Diana). This temple at the time of its splendor was considered one of the seven wonders of the ancient world.

Located on the coast of the Aegean Sea, the ancient city was a busy port town and trade center. As with all commercial centers, Ephesus provided a cosmopolitan atmosphere, combining Greek and Roman cultures. The city was also a worship center, and it attracted large numbers of pilgrims and religious seekers.

Artemis was an ancient goddess of mixed associations. She was identified with fertility and childbirth. Though worshiped long before Greek or Roman dominance, she eventually merged with her Roman counterpart Diana, becoming known as goddess of the hunt and goddess of the moon.

Ephesus was also a center for the practice of the magical arts. The people believed strongly in amulets, potions, magical words, and spells. During Paul's three-year stay in Ephesus, it is possible that he was regarded as a powerful magician. Acts 19:11–12 states that in Ephesus "God did extraordinary miracles through Paul, so that even handkerchiefs and aprons that had touched him were taken to the sick, and their illnesses were cured and the evil spirits left them." In spite of Paul's miracles in Ephesus, the people were not always receptive to the gospel (see Acts 19:8–9,13–16,23–41).

B. The Law (vv. 8–11)

A Presbyterian church in Florida made famous the question, "If you died and went to heaven and God said to you, 'Why should I let you into heaven,' what would you say?" Hypothetical as it is, the question puts everything on the table and reveals the object of our trust.

Often people will answer, "I keep the Ten Commandments." One man told me this, but he could not name even three of them.

But such an answer is inadequate, especially when we see the law illuminated by Jesus in the Sermon on the Mount. Jesus went to the heart of the law, past actions to thoughts and motivation, revealing the true desire of God that people live in holiness. It is not a matter of rules, but of spirit.

But the law cannot justify or save or forgive anyone. The law points out our sin. It confronts us with a standard too high to attain. It mirrors a God beyond us, whom we cannot know or please without his help. The law is meant to drive us to Christ.

One of the clearest statements in the Bible regarding this truth is Romans 3:20: "Therefore no one will be declared righteous in his sight by observing the law." This does not need any explanation. And yet people continue to rely on effort, good deeds, or keeping of the law (God's or their own) to attain heaven.

Laws are judgments. Even civil laws are established as judgments against certain behaviors. As Paul wrote to Timothy, the law is meant for "lawbreakers and rebels, the ungodly and sinful, the unholy and irreligious" (1 Tim. 1:9). The law condemns us all.

But God is rich in mercy and does not give us the law in order to leave us in a state of despair. He reveals the standard of his character so we may understand our tremendous need. He then offers a way out of the dilemma. It is Christ. Through Christ's death on the cross, he satisfies the demands of the law and the curse of its judgment. His resurrection proved him victorious.

So the law drives us to Christ, and then Christ drives us back to the law. Now we can plunge to the depths of its intent, not by chaining ourselves to legalisms, but by loving obedience issuing from a changed heart. We are no longer left in despair, but we are given hope.

VII. TEACHING OUTLINE

A. INTRODUCTION

1. Lead Story: Lifeguards and Road Maps
2. Context: In the first chapter of 1 Timothy, Paul warned about false doctrine and teachers, urging Timothy to hold on to the true faith. Paul also gave personal testimony to the mercy of God in saving him.
3. Transition: Today we are assaulted on every side by cults, false teachings, and the pull of society for our allegiance. It is easy to believe that following certain patterns of behavior secures us in our faith, much like the Jews of the New Testament relied on the law. But true Christian faith is relational and full-orbed, demanding a coherence between thought and actions. From out of this relationship with Christ comes sincere praise and adoration. When we realize the

greatness of our salvation, perseverance in the face of difficulties then becomes possible.

B. COMMENTARY

1. Greeting (1:1–2)
2. Understanding the Law (1:3–5)
   a. Description of false teachings (1:3–4)
   b. The true goal (1:5)
3. The false teachers (1:6–7)
4. Understanding the True Purpose of the Law (1:8–10)
5. The Glorious Gospel (1:11)
6. Understanding the Work of Grace (1:12–17)
   a. The example of Paul's conversion (1:12–14)
   b. The explanation of the gospel (1:15–17)
7. Remaining Faithful to the Call (1:18–20)

C. CONCLUSION: WHAT THE WORLD NEEDS NOW

VIII. ISSUES FOR DISCUSSION

1. Do you recognize the false teachings of today? Discuss some of them. How can we defend ourselves against them?
2. Since the law is "made not for the righteous," does it serve any purpose in a Christian's daily life? Do we still need to teach the law at church? Why?
3. In what sense does the law point to grace? Do people with "greater sins" need more grace than others do to be forgiven?
4. What lessons in gratitude can we learn from Paul's statements about personal grace and salvation? How will true gratitude influence us when we are tempted by habitual sins?
5. Write a one-sentence doxology of thanks to God for your salvation.
6. Discuss ways people shipwreck their faith. How can we stay the course ourselves?

1 Timothy 2

Orderly Worship

I. INTRODUCTION
Feuding in the Ballpark

II. COMMENTARY
A verse-by-verse explanation of the chapter.

III. CONCLUSION
God's Design for the Future

An overview of the principles and applications from the chapter.

IV. LIFE APPLICATION
Weaver Birds: Order and Complexity

Melding the chapter to life.

V. PRAYER
Tying the chapter to life with God.

VI. DEEPER DISCOVERIES
Historical, geographical, and grammatical enrichment of the commentary.

VII. TEACHING OUTLINE
Suggested step-by-step group study of the chapter.

VIII. ISSUES FOR DISCUSSION
Zeroing the chapter in on daily life.

"That which is not in the interests of the hive cannot be in the interests of the bee."

Marcus Aurelius

1 Timothy 2

IN A NUTSHELL

Paul's rules for public worship services emphasized the need to pray for everyone, especially leaders. The goal was to focus on God and to have an environment in which people could come to know Christ the Savior. Paul instructed believers about spiritual leadership and women about quiet submission.

Orderly Worship

I. INTRODUCTION

Feuding in the Ballpark

*I*t was sandlot baseball at its best, there at the corner of Rudy and Edgewood Roads in Harrisburg, Pennsylvania. It was not unlike the pickup games that take place on streets and small lots all over the country every evening in the summer. But this time we were arguing about a call at home plate.

No one hires umpires for these games; the judgments are made by personal honesty or committee. Jack Angelo said he was safe. Eddie Cramer and I both knew he was out by a country mile.

"Safe!"

"Out!"

Back and forth we went.

It seemed everybody on Eddie Cramer's team agreed with us. Jack's teammates backed him up. We finally settled it with a flip of a coin, but to no one's satisfaction.

Baseball needs umpires—to hold us to the proper standard.

The church, too, needs guidelines to hold us to God's standards. This chapter includes some of these rules, particularly on public worship.

In studying these verses we must remember that God is *totally other*. His ways are not our ways. Even so, he wants our ways to become his ways, because he knows what is best. He is truth.

This short chapter of 1 Timothy gives the best ways for the people of God to worship. These rules may seem specifically first century, but they hold principles for people of all times.

This chapter also contains one of the most controversial verses in the Bible, about the place of women in the church. There are many ways to understand this. Ask for wisdom as you study the chapter and for grace toward others who may disagree with the conclusion that becomes your conviction!

Remember as you study these hard sayings that God is the only one who is truly wise. Our limited knowledge should keep us humble and searching.

II. COMMENTARY

MAIN IDEA: *God desires order, peace, and holiness in our lives, in our worship, and in our relationships within the church and our communities. This reflects the order, constancy, and righteous character of God. When we live this way, God is revealed, and people will embrace him as Savior.*

A Call to Depend upon God (2:1–7)

SUPPORTING IDEA: *The desire of God is that all people will be saved and come to a knowledge of the truth. The starting point for us is not in strategies, but in prayer and full dependence upon God as we labor with him in this great privilege.*

1. By praying for others (2:1–4)

2:1–2. Paul had just written of the wonderful grace of God exhibited in Christ who "came into the world to save sinners" (1:15), followed by remembrance of two men who had professed Christ (1:20), and yet whose faith became "shipwrecked." It must have reminded him of the many people who still had not heard of Christ, and also of the dangers inherent in the life of faith. He told Timothy that the first order of the church is to pray for all people: **that requests, prayers, intercession and thanksgiving be made for everyone—for kings and all those in authority.**

We need not make too much of the various words which Paul used: requests (entreaties), prayers (reverent, worshipful conversation), intercession (confident, familiar talk rather than the popular notion of speaking on behalf of another), and thanksgiving (often linked with holiness and therefore proper every time we bow before God). Paul labored the point in order to spread before us the comprehensive nature of prayer and also to underscore this serious command.

In our public worship, prayer should be our first order of concern and participation. Prayer is not to be a filler between hymns or a routine before the sermon. Paul wrote to the Philippians, "In everything, by prayer and petition, with thanksgiving, present your requests to God" (Phil. 4:6). He urged the Colossians and us, "Devote yourselves to prayer" (Col. 4:2). Prayer is a uniting with God. It is to be entered into with awe and joy, with respect and a sense of responsibility. We are engaged in the worldwide mission of glorifying God, especially as demonstrated through the spread of the gospel as people come to salvation through Jesus Christ.

It should be remembered that God has instituted government for our benefit. When government operates well, it is a significant ally to the gospel.

Knowing that the mission of the church is to reveal and disperse the truth of Jesus Christ, Paul emphasized the need to pray for those in authority. This was written during the reign of Nero as emperor of Rome. Even under his degenerate and harsh rule, the Roman Empire provided a useful structure for extending the reach of God's truth.

In our own time, we must also recognize that corporate prayer is not only a central expression of worship, but a requirement. Regardless of political loyalties or persuasions, churches should pray for national and local governmental leaders, uniting the hearts of many for these influential people.

Governmental leaders and bureaucratic policies have a direct bearing on our freedom to **live peaceful and quiet lives in all godliness and holiness.**

Peaceful literally means "tranquil." This word refers to the absence of outside disturbances. **Quiet** refers to a composed, discreet order. Certainly we desire our nation to be peaceful and quiet. Paul implied that God is willing to help us achieve this. "The king's heart is in the hand of the LORD; he directs it like a watercourse wherever he pleases" (Prov. 21:1).

The point of desiring a benign environment, however, is not for our own comfort. It is for the expression of **godliness and holiness**; it is for Christian witness. Paul still had in view the observing community and world, the spread of the gospel, the salvation of the lost. This became apparent as he continued.

2:3–4. The full expression of our transformed lives and faith in God **is good, and pleases God our Savior.** God is not silent about what pleases him and glorifies his name. Such lives are used by God **who wants all men to be saved and to come to a knowledge of the truth.**

God's desire is for everyone to be saved. But this is not an issue of sovereign will. It is not an edict handed down regardless of what people think, believe, or do. God's desire may be one thing, but he has subjected it to our willful responses. The second half of God's desire for all people is the universal availability of the truth. This shows the expansive nature of the church's mission. God's plan is for the evangelization of all nations and peoples.

2. By confessing who Christ is (2:5–6)

2:5. Paul then pointed to the critical claims of the gospel: **there is one God and one mediator between God and men, the man Christ Jesus.**

The great football coach Vince Lombardi stood in front of his team, the Green Bay Packers, after a horrendous loss. The players expected a strong diatribe. Instead, Lombardi went to the center of the classroom and picked up a football. He held it up and said, "Gentlemen, this is a football." The coach took the players back to the basics.

Paul did the same for the Ephesians and us. The declaration of the exclusivity of God and Christ is basic to the Christian message. Yet it is a point on which many people stumble. Even those who agree that there is one God often refuse the claim of Jesus as the only way to knowing God.

For some people the chief virtue of the day is tolerance, and the great hope is pluralism. They discard truth for sincerity. Certainly we honor the freedom to believe whatever one wishes, as long as it does not hurt another person. That is fundamental to democratic self-rule and civility. But it is quite another matter to say that everyone is right simply because they "believe" something. That makes faith instead of objective truth the test for validity. We must go back to the basics.

The revealed, divine word through Paul is that there is only one way to forming a relationship with God, and this is through the man Christ Jesus. This underscores the universality of the gospel—all people come the same way to God. Not only must they come the same way, through Jesus, but salvation is available to all, Jew and Gentile alike.

Salvation comes through the **man Christ Jesus**. He is fully God and fully man. "The Word was God. . . . The Word became flesh and made his dwelling among us. We have seen his glory, the glory of the One and Only, who came from the Father, full of grace and truth" (John 1:1,14).

Jesus is not one among many. He is the *One* and *only*.

He is the answer to Job's ancient cry about God: "He is not a man like me that I might answer him, / that we might confront each other in court. / If only there were someone to arbitrate between us, / to lay his hand upon us both" (Job 9:32–33).

Jesus bridges the gap between sinful humanity and the righteous God. He settles the legal demand for justice.

2:6. In Job's lament, he longed for "someone to remove God's rod from me. . . . Then I would speak up without fear of him" (Job 9:34–35). Again, Jesus is the answer to Job's cry.

Paul, having announced Christ as the mediator/arbitrator, then told how this Anointed One (the Christ) removed the rod, allowing those who trust in him to approach God in confidence: He **gave himself as a ransom for all men**.

Christ's gift to the world was a self-giving sacrifice. He explained to his disciples, "No one takes [my life] from me, but I lay it down of my own accord. I have authority to lay it down and authority to take it up again" (John 10:18).

The word for ransom is *antilutron*. The root word signifies a loosing or freeing. It was often used in reference to buying a slave's freedom. Paul's attachment of a prefix to this word added to it the significance of the vicarious nature of Christ's payment. He is the substitute, the "instead of" payment for sin.

In his perfection and sacrificial death Jesus satisfied the holy laws of God which stated, "without the shedding of blood there is no forgiveness" (Heb. 9:22). Over and over the scene is replayed through the histories of the Old

Testament and throughout the life of Christ—people choosing a spotless lamb to be sacrificed on the altar of the temple in order that their sins might be forgiven. But then Jesus became that substitute sacrifice for all. We can hear John the Baptist shout with joy as he saw Jesus walking along the banks of the Jordan River: "Look, the Lamb of God, who takes away the sin of the world!" (John 1:29).

This coming of Christ and his death for all humanity, according to Paul, is **the testimony given in its proper time.** Christ is the witness of the Father's love, the pursuing desire of God to bring his creation back to himself. Christ came "when the time had fully come" (Gal. 4:4)—when the timing was perfect for his revealing and the salvation of all people.

3. By remembering who we are (2:7)

2:7. Paul knew who he was; he knew his calling. Such understanding is a great dynamic for a good life. He was **a herald and an apostle . . . a teacher of the true faith to the Gentiles.**

God had spoken to Paul: "I will rescue you from your own people and from the Gentiles. I am sending you to them to open their eyes and turn them from darkness to light, and from the power of Satan to God, so that they may receive forgiveness of sins and a place among those who are sanctified by faith in me" (Acts 26:17–18).

Paul had been put into service by God himself. He understood that he was the herald, not the creative writer; the ambassador, not the king. So he told others the revelation of God. He depended upon God and viewed himself as his slave, a representative on earth of the God of heaven and earth. It is a wonderful paragraph that shows Paul's dependence upon God, calling us to the same understanding and commitment. This King of kings still seeks human representatives, people who will glorify him by the way they live.

Paul knew his message of the universality of God's salvation would be challenged, as would the claim that Jesus is the sole means to that salvation. So he backed his message with his own integrity: **I am telling the truth, I am not lying.** He wanted three things to be very clear: (1) all truth comes from God, (2) salvation is available to all, and (3) the church and its people are God's means of spreading the truth of salvation to all people.

B A Call to Order (2:8–15)

SUPPORTING IDEA: *Personal integrity and the way we conduct ourselves in corporate worship affect our spiritual capabilities, church unity, and the perception of Christ by those outside the church. God has prescribed leadership in harmony with the way he created us. Leadership is not based upon worth or importance, but upon the need for order and clarity, recognizing the inherent strengths of men and women.*

1. Instructions for men (2:8)

Paul next turned his concern to orderly, proper worship. Though his comments were directed to particular disturbances and troubles within the Ephesian church, we can extract principles that are applicable to all times and cultures.

2:8. Paul wrote, **I want men everywhere to lift up holy hands in prayer.** His first directive for worship was given to men. He did not use the generic word signifying mankind, but a word specifically targeting males.

In the original Greek text the sentence begins, "*Therefore,* I want men." This connective word takes us back to the beginning of the preceding paragraph where Paul urged the congregation to pray especially for those in authority. He reasoned that if Christians could live in peace and harmony, this would create an environment for the spread of the gospel. With the salvation of the lost in mind, Paul looked at the men of the church and instructed them in effective prayer.

As followers of Jesus Christ, we are encouraged to "approach the throne of grace with confidence" (Heb. 4:16) and to come with the affection and security of a child, by the Spirit crying, "*Abba,* Father" (Rom. 8:15). Even so, we must remember that in prayer we are approaching God himself. Along with reassurance comes warning: we must be in proper relationship with our holy God.

Paul's emphasis was on holiness, not physical posturing. The most general demeanor for prayer in the ancient world, for pagans, Jews, and Christians alike, was to stand with hands outstretched and uplifted, palms turned upwards. The frescoes in the Roman catacombs provide vivid illustrations from the life of the early church. The Jews ceremonially washed their hands before prayer as a symbol of spiritual cleanness because the hands represented the condition of a person's soul and heart. "Who may ascend the hill of the Lord? Who may stand in his holy place? He who has clean hands and a pure heart" (Ps. 24:3–4). It was in the spirit of such understanding and practice that Paul instructed men to pray with holy hands—to pray out of a character of righteousness, of complete devotion to God, unpolluted with sin. The implication is that our standing before God must be right.

In addition, Paul called for proper relationship among believers: Prayers must issue forth to God **without anger or disputing.**

The Spirit of God promotes unity, harmony, and order; these are divine qualities. Any time we pervert our identity in Christ and become entangled in divisions, factions, and chaos, the church's mission is compromised, and our prayers are hindered. Our standing with others must be right.

2. Instructions for women (2:9–10)

2:9–10. Next Paul directed his attention to the women. He wanted them to **dress modestly, with decency and propriety.** He then went on to list some things which he deemed inappropriate for women to wear in public worship services: **braided hair or gold or pearls or expensive clothes.**

Paul never intended his letter to be a fashion guide. We must define modesty and decency in the context of our own culture. His targeting of specific practices of dress was aimed at the women in Ephesus where these particular styles were disrupting and interfering with worship. Perhaps some insensitive women were flaunting their dress and jewelry before the poor in a way that caused a disturbance in the church. These adornments were common among wealthy women of that time. The church is to be a place of equality before God, where distinctions in wealth, occupation, gender, or race do not exist.

Paul's call to modesty could also have sexual overtones, recognizing that men easily get distracted and tempted by visual stimuli. A woman of good works calls attention to God and promotes worship. A preoccupation with glamour can cause a mind to wander and possibly awaken lust.

The section is almost identical to 1 Peter 3:3–4 with its call to inner beauty and a quiet and gentle spirit. Our **good deeds** as Christian women (and men) are to call attention to God, not ourselves. Character, not clothing should identify us and promote proper corporate worship.

3. Spiritual leadership (2:11–15)

The following verses are difficult for most people, especially considering our culture's changing attitudes about men and women. Many Christians differ about the application of this passage today. Some believe the instructions remain frozen in the first century, applicable and intended for that time only. Others sense a more universal theme. In attempting to draw meaning from these verses, it is wise to proceed with care. We need to balance Paul's instructions here with other passages of Scripture where Paul and others esteemed the value of women in ministry, regarding them as equal partakers in the grace of God (Gal. 3:26–29).

2:11–12. To learn **in quietness and full submission** does not mean women should never talk. Quietness here means peaceableness. It could be that as women experienced new freedoms within the Christian community, they began to throw off restraint. Their disagreements, questions, and assertions then became not a learning experience but a disruption that worked against true worship. Paul did not want the women to be contentious. His main concern was the establishment of orderly worship.

Full submission has to do with the overall decorum of women. It has nothing to do with their ability to think or the importance of one person over another. Rather, God has an order for leadership and a preference for character which, in the case of women, includes the qualities of peacefulness, gentleness, and the willingness to surrender questions of spiritual authority to the male. Women were free to question, contemplate, and formulate ideas, but the characteristics of peace and submission were to prevail.

Many Christians take exception with Paul's next assertion: **I do not permit a woman to teach or to have authority over a man.** They believe these instructions are purely cultural and that there is no application for today. There is continued debate regarding its implications.

Clearly Paul did not teach that women are inferior to men. But this text does support the idea that men and women are different (some would disagree with this). These teachings about authority have nothing to do with a woman being president of the United States or a corporation. It is specifically about spiritual leadership in the church. (The same hierarchy of authority is extended to the home in Eph. 5:22–33; Col. 3:18–19; and 1 Pet. 3:1–7, with clear commands and responsibilities extended to the husband.)

Paul concluded this sentence with the startling statement: **she [women] must be silent.** Again, this is not a gag order on women. It means that they are not to writhe under the spiritual authority of the church leaders. Paul's continued concern is for order, for respect, for a good reputation within the community.

The word for "silent" is used as a noun in 2 Thessalonians 3:12 where people are urged to "settle down." In Acts 11:18 it is used in reference to people who had no further objections; literally they "held their peace." And Paul instructed everyone in 1 Thessalonians 4:11: "Make it your ambition to lead a quiet life." This does not mean we are never to mumble a word. Rather, we are to rest in the sovereign teaching and will of God. It is this kind of silence which Paul required of women in worship.

2:13–14. Paul supportd his instructions for men and women upon a theological structure which reaches back to the order of creation and sin's entrance into human affairs. It is a section which is hard to understand in its implications. Probably no teacher is totally convinced of his or her interpretation, and we should not hesitate to admit the difficulty of this section. But it is inspired of God, and so we must attempt to understand what Paul was saying.

He declared, **For Adam was formed first, then Eve.** It appears that Paul was implying a hierarchy from the very start, even before sin. The order of creation evidenced a role structure which placed man in leadership and woman in a supportive position. Perhaps the difference between life before and after the fall is that these structures and positions of authority changed from joyful harmony to festering conflict, from loving leadership to insensitive authoritarianism, from willing submission to agitated compliance. However, by returning to the Genesis account, Paul affirmed that these structures existed from the start and were still valid and operative.

Many Christians understand this section as a cultural issue which had application in first-century society but which does not apply to today. They see it in much the same way as 1 Corinthians 11 which also uses the Genesis account as a basis for women covering their heads in public worship. It is a good reminder that each section of the Bible must be dealt with on its own claim and in concert with other passages of Scripture.

2:14. Paul continued to draw on the Genesis record as he wrote, **Adam was not the one deceived; it was the woman who was deceived and became a sinner.** Paul was not trying to cast all blame for humanity's mess upon Eve or women in general. Nor was he portraying Adam as better or more spiritual. On the contrary, Adam's sin was more blatant, more intentional.

It is good to remember that Paul was writing a personal letter to a fellow minister and a specific group of believers. Timothy's mission was made clear from the start (1 Tim. 1:3); he was sorting out truth and deception, order and chaos, propriety and license. It is highly possible that this reference to Eve's deception is a link in understanding Paul's concerns—women in the Ephesian church were usurping the authority of the church leaders. Perhaps they were also being carried along by the deceptions of the false teachers.

Male leadership is called for in the church (and other biblical texts call for it in the home). God has designed it this way. Women are to accept this in quietness, to be at peace and harmony with this truth. It produces order, harmony, and structure, and is meant to reduce disruptions, divisions, and uncertainties.

What God says is often contrary to our natural inclinations. But we must remember that we see through the skewed lens of fallen humanity. Even the whole issue of forgiveness grates against our desire for revenge. So we need not always understand the logic of God's instructions, but we do need to think carefully and then obey.

If you think verses 13 and 14 are difficult to interpret, read verse 15!

2:15. Paul declared, **Women will be saved through childbearing.** Which women? What kind of "saved"—eternal salvation? Whose childbearing? Here are two possibilities:

Believing women will be physically protected during childbearing. This has not always been the case, nor does it seem to have much to do with the context in 1 Timothy.

Godly women will find fulfillment and safe passage in life by bearing children. This would imply God has a definitive plan for the roles of men and women.

Though universal in scope, the promise of salvation has conditions. It is extended to those who **continue in faith, love and holiness with propriety.** Though addressed specifically to women since they were the cause of concern at the moment, it is a universal principle—salvation rests with those who bear the marks of genuine Christianity.

> **MAIN IDEA REVIEW:** *God desires order, peace, and holiness in our lives, in our worship, and in our relationships within the church and our communities. This reflects the order, constancy, and righteous character of God. When we live this way, God is revealed and people will embrace him as Savior.*

III. CONCLUSION

God's Design for the Future

She was just eighteen months old and had just had lunch. She knew what was ahead—lunch was always followed by a bath and then a nap. Her joys were simple—time spent with her mother and father, playing, reading, and bonding.

Fortunately, her parents taught her love and gave her time and affection. So this is the life she knew, and it would become a part of her, something she would pass on someday. God has designed the family, as well as the church, as communities which pass on his grace and love.

Many children live in the midst of turmoil, divorce, family strife, or neglect. They never know the goodness of loving relationships. Many more children grow up with no church experience. Their understanding is very spotty when it comes to God, grace, and truth.

Certainly God can call children directly, and others can introduce them to the goodness of God in Christ, but habits are formed early. The great majority of people who put their faith in Christ do it before their teenage years.

The model of church that we present is so important—for our children and for unbelievers in our communities who hear about or visit the church.

This chapter has some hard rules for public worship. But all that God expects of his church is important to the legacy of the church and also for the context in which love is taught. We must not fail him or our children.

PRINCIPLES

- God gives definite instructions about worship, although they do not always meet with approval by many Christians. He gives us a lot of flexibility in our worship styles, music, order of service, and programming. But in areas where he has spoken, we should obey.
- God wants everyone to be saved, but he does not force them. Free will is a generous gift.

- The closer our relationship with God, the more we will have his concern for everyone to be saved.
- Modesty is for all time.
- God makes a distinction between men and women. We should, too.

APPLICATIONS

- Church services should include prayers for government leaders.
- The only salvation for mankind is Christ. This must determine our goals for life and love for others.
- Church leaders must adopt—before questions arise—specific policies about male and female leadership and teaching responsibilities.

IV. LIFE APPLICATION

Weaver Birds: Order and Complexity

God has shown himself as a God of order from the very beginning. Taking a shapeless and empty planet, he made earth into an intricate and highly complex arrangement of life.

From our very youngest years onward, we try to make order of our world. But in this struggle to create order, we sometimes try to erase all distinctions between people, or we isolate ourselves from those different from us. We struggle in and out of belonging; we waver between doubt and faith; we fly between connection and detachment.

Asia and Africa are home to weaver birds, an amazing species. These birds construct nests by weaving. Taking strips of broad leaves, palm fronds, grasses, or reeds, the male birds select a suitable branch in a tree out of harm's way and begin attaching these ribbons. They tie them to the branches by using their beaks to make knots while their feet hold everything in place. Back and forth they weave and knot their strips, like a weaver at a loom.

Within this species are masked weavers, baya, grosbeak, grey-headed sociable, and Cassin weavers. Each bird weaves its own style of nest. Some have an entry tube; others have chambers and antechambers; some hang like a droplet from a branch; others are built in clusters like small city-fortresses.

Why? Why not a single kind of bird with one particular type of home? Why all these assortments and variations?

Environmental differences are one key, but this is only a partial explanation. Beneath all the variety there is form and purpose. Within the structure of order is God's exuberance and delight in variety and creativity.

Life is crowded with details. Life is crowded with purpose. In the order and complexity that God has designed, everything is in place to bring beauty and function, to trail its way back to God who is beyond definition.

Order should not be equated with monotony or convention. That God desires order is evidence of divine direction, purpose, and harmony; it is confirmation that he engineers every minute detail of life with interconnected meaning.

Why then do we Christians think we are the exception to this design, this structure? God calls his people to an orderly existence. The church showcases this by the way its leadership functions, by the assignment of roles and duties, by the way it conducts itself in worship, and by how it handles disagreements and conflict.

For both men and women in the church, leadership roles have been designed to create a well-functioning whole. There is plenty of space within the organism to express talents and gifts, to reach deeply into creativity and individual distinctives, to display God's harmonious design.

V. PRAYER

Holy Trinity, three yet one, teach us, your church, to worship you in unity. Give us the wisdom to use our differences for good, weaving them into a harmonious community of your love. Keep us from petty divisions, selfish disputes, and minds that wander to our own concerns. When we come together as your people, move in our hearts so that we may bring our spirits, our praise, our wills undivided and unhindered into your presence. Amen.

VI. DEEPER DISCOVERIES

A. Requests, Prayers, Intercession (v. 1)

For many Christians, prayer is an enigma. But it is one of the clearest indicators of the depth and extent of our trust in God.

Often prayer is a ritual—a routine before meals or bedtime. It is invoked as a safeguard for travel. It is sighed in desperation when there is nothing left to do. We mouth words that sound "right"; we create prayer lists or schedules to keep us on track. Occasionally a prayer seems answered, and we may wonder how that happened. Other times our words seem to float heavenward, dissipating in the clouds. We become used to our one-sided conversations and expect little else.

But God never calls us to empty habits. He never instructs us to pursue form without content, action without purpose or result. So when we are told to pray continually, to enter prayer with boldness, to pray for rulers, society, and neighbors. He is not giving us something with which to fill our empty moments, some pious act to make us feel good.

Prayer does make a difference, in ourselves, in our world. To picture this imagine two overlapping circles. Circle #1 represents our prayers. We ask for a lot of things, often very personal things. We may ask for healing, a job, the restoration of our marriage, a new home. Our requests cover a wide variety of concerns. That is what God wants us to do. He desires that our hearts be open and our trust childlike. Circle #2 represents God's will. These are things he wants to accomplish.

The intersection of these two circles signifies answered prayer. Where our desires overlap God's intentions, we can be assured our prayers will be answered. Sometimes it is a matter of being able to participate and enjoy working alongside God in the purposes and events he has already determined. At other times his actions and our involvement depend on our asking. At times he tethers his will to our willingness.

Much of what passes for unanswered prayer is simply an exposure of the selfishness of our hearts. This does not mean we hide these from God. He knows our condition better than we do. But we can learn to recognize our selfish tendencies and have these cleansed by God. This will result in more powerful prayer as our narrow desires expand into God's desires.

There are times when we ask for things from God which may not be for our best or the best of others. We must learn to release to God his rightful sovereignty and wisdom.

Perhaps most intriguing are those things in circle #2 which would occur if we would only pray for them. These "unclaimed blessings" seem an oxymoron, yet they are those things which we "do not have, because [we] do not ask" (Jas. 4:2).

So what are we to do? Spray our prayers heavenward like buckshot, hoping we will hit God's will once in a while? This is not the right approach. Here are some conclusions we can reach about prayer.

- We should keep praying. Whether God responds with "Yes," "No," or "Wait," our part is to expose our hearts and wills to the Father and to participate continually in his work in our lives through prayer.
- We should not become discouraged if we do not get what we ask for. God is infinitely wise, while our understanding is limited. Often we think there is only one possible course of action. Only later may we recognize that God knew the situation better than we did. Prayer can be a submission to the magnificence of God's wisdom and power.
- That God listens to us and answers prayers at all is a wonderful gift of his grace. He welcomes us into his presence. He allows us

to join with him to work in our world. For that we can be humbly thankful.

- God's will is centered on creating godly character in us and in extending his active reign throughout creation. We ought to focus on that kind of praying. This does not mean the humdrum of daily life is unimportant to us or to him, but that it all fits within the greater purposes of his kingdom.

- We should oppose those teachings that claim we can demand from God, as though he is under obligation to our whims and desires. That is simply not the case. It may work for vending machines where we put our coins in and claim a prize, but God is not in the heavens to cater to us. We are here for him.

- Our prayers will intersect with his will as our spirits grow and develop in step with his Spirit. As we come to value Christ above all else, we will find our prayers following after the glory and purposes of God. We will understand God's love for the world, and our requests will reflect this. His answers will be welcomed with joy.

B. Women as Leaders (vv. 11–12)

When interpreting a verse or paragraph in the Bible, there are three contexts that must be remembered to arrive at the intended truth:

- the immediate context of the paragraph or verse,
- the surrounding context of the book or letter, and
- the encompassing context of the entire Bible.

No teaching will contradict any other part of the Bible, because it contains the harmonious counsel of God. Certain verses or passages may amplify or extend the range of understanding of particular themes or ideas, but they will never contradict the foundations of Scripture.

For instance, James wrote in uncompromising terms about the necessity of works for faith. When compared with Paul's statements in Romans that justification is by faith alone, these teachings may appear contradictory. But they are consistent.

The two writers were emphasizing particular perspectives, different angles on the same issue. Paul was anxious that his readers understand that a relationship with God cannot be earned. James, in total agreement, emphasized the quality of such faith. He wanted his readers to understand that faith is no tipping of the hat toward God, no creedal statement, but a life-encompassing involvement with God. Such trust cannot be restrained. Works will be present as evidence of a person's genuine faith.

An understanding of the place of women in the local church must be approached with the same cautions. We must take into account the immediate context (as in 1 Timothy), but we must also consider other Scriptures that speak of women and their relationship to God, the church, and each member to the other.

On its own, this verse sounds as if women are never to utter a sound at church: "let the women keep silent." But we must consider the difficulties and situations which Timothy was facing (see Commentary on 1 Tim. 2:11–12), be aware of the cultural context in which he was living, and remember how God views women.

In Galatians 3:28, Paul wrote that in Christ there is neither male nor female. Throughout Acts it is apparent that women were vital workers in the ministry. In fact, women were among the most responsive to Paul's message as he traveled from city to city. Jesus also enjoined women to follow him. Even his speaking to the Samaritan woman was considered scandalous.

God has always placed value on all people—of all social, economic, and racial categories. Even so, he does establish an order to his creation. It is based on duties and responsibilities, not personal worth. Scripture teaches that men are to be the spiritual leaders and guardians in the church and home. The qualifications for elders and husbands requires a selfless love, with a clear understanding that they are responsible to God himself. The man is responsible for spiritual guidance, leadership, and vision in the home and church.

VII. TEACHING OUTLINE

A. INTRODUCTION

1. Lead Story: Feuding in the Ballpark

2. Context: Paul gave principles for prayer (especially for government leaders) and for public worship (for men and women).

3. Transition: One of the great privileges of the church and its people is prayer. Throughout history, the church has been exemplary in praying for people in power. We should be no different. As individuals we often feel powerless against the machinery of institutions and government. But when we grasp the compassion and the power of the sovereign God, it should compel us to pray more. As citizens of our society, we must also be sensitive to its traditions and forms. The church should always work hard to maintain a good reputation among unbelievers. One of the best ways we do this is by conducting ourselves with dignity and honor when we come together to worship.

B. COMMENTARY

1. A Call to Depend upon God (2:1–7)
   a. By praying for others (2:1–4)
   b. By confessing who Christ is (2:5–6)
   c. By remembering who we are (2:7)
2. A Call to Order (2:8–15)
   a. Instructions for men (2:8)
   b. Instructions for women (2:9–10)
   c. Spiritual leadership (2:11–15)

C. CONCLUSION: WEAVER BIRDS: ORDER AND COMPLEXITY

VIII. ISSUES FOR DISCUSSION

1. Do you tend to pray more for health and physical issues than for leaders and character issues? If so, why?
2. Why do you pray at all?
3. Discuss what our attitude in prayer should be.
4. Are Paul's instructions on modesty and lifestyle for women applicable today? Why or why not? Give examples.
5. What is your church's position on the role of women in church leadership, ordination, and teaching? Why are there so many different opinions among Christians on this subject?

1 Timothy 3

Church Leadership and Government

"*U*nholiness in a preacher's life will either stop his mouth from reproving, or the people's ears from receiving."

William Gurnell

1 Timothy 3

IN A NUTSHELL

*P*aul explained the leadership and character qualities which church elders, deacons, and their wives must have, with special emphasis on character, family, and faithfulness. He concluded the chapter with a hymn of confession summarizing our beliefs about Jesus the Christ.

Church Leadership
and Government

I. INTRODUCTION

Rewriting the Six O'Clock News

I wonder what it would be like to enter the season of political campaigning and have no one speak about the legislation a candidate passed or opposed, bills on which he voted yes or no, proposals he made for laws or budgets, or his ideas on programs and institutions.

What would it be like if all we were told was how the candidate treated his family? What if the campaign ads flashed images of ordinary life—picnics with neighbors, dinners around the kitchen table, talking with friends, helping someone in trouble, resolving a conflict, or getting angry in a traffic jam? What if we saw charts not on how much money they had raised but how much money they had given away to others and the amount of their family budget?

What if we heard about the little points of life that reveal character. Would it make a difference? It should.

Our inner spirit is unmasked in the way we live, the life decisions we make. That is why Paul saw personal character as the major qualification for church leadership. How a person conducts himself indicates how he manages life and areas of responsibility. For the church, there can be no compromise in the area of personal integrity.

In talking to the Pharisees, Jesus said, "You clean the outside of the cup and dish, but inside they are full of greed and self-indulgence . . . First clean the inside of the cup and dish, and then the outside also will be clean" (Matt. 23:25–26). Our inner lives determine our outward behavior.

II. COMMENTARY

> **MAIN IDEA:** *Church leadership is a noble and respectable position that requires nobility of character. Paul called everyone to live exemplary lives as he wrote of the high value God places on the church and the close relationship it has with Christ.*

A What a Pastor Should Be (3:1–7)

> **SUPPORTING IDEA:** *Leaders in the church have many duties that can change with time and culture. The qualities that are timeless and the main standard for pastors and other leaders require a blameless character. Paul described the outward evidences of such character.*

1. The pastor's desire (3:1)

3:1. According to Paul, **any person who aspires to the office of pastor, who sets his heart** on it, **desires a noble task.**

The office which involves guiding, leading, and serving the church has honor and goodness in itself. It is a position which God desires for the local church and which he finds honorable because the pastor guides in matters of the spirit. Because the office has honor, the person who desires to do the job, who literally "reaches out" after it, must be honorable.

In the days of the early church, a couple of things may have made the office of pastor seem less than desirable. First, the persecution of the church may have made being a pastor appear less than appealing. Also, the position may have fallen into disrepute due to false teachers and those who used the office for personal or financial advancement. Even so, Paul wanted to be clear that the position and function of pastoring was good and needful. It was not to be looked down upon, nor was it to be shunned.

The position described here, *episkopos*, is variously translated as "overseer" or "bishop." Over time, these terms, particularly *bishop*, have come to be associated with ecclesiastical denominations. In Acts and other places this leadership position is called *presbuteros*, or "elder." Today the term *pastor* is widely used, based on the model of shepherding and guiding given to us by the Great Shepherd, Jesus Christ. All these terms have come to represent those who are charged with overseeing the spiritual affairs of the church.

Scripture has listed the duties for this position in a number of places: to lead (Acts 20:28); equip (Eph. 4:12); rule (1 Tim. 3:4–5); teach (1 Tim. 3:2; 2 Tim. 2:15); shepherd (1 Pet. 5:1–4); and to set an example for others (1 Pet. 5:3). With these serious responsibilities, it is no wonder the qualifications were high.

2. The pastor's goals (3:2–7)

3:2. For the person desiring or under consideration for the position of pastoral leadership, Paul listed character qualities which were evidenced by certain observable behaviors. These were manners which should characterize the pastor's life.

First, he must be **above reproach**—blameless. Paul was not suggesting perfection, for no one could reach that. He did mean that this person should have no legitimate charge brought against him, either in a legal court or by other people. There should be no grounds for true accusation because this person deals with sin between himself and God and others.

The pastor must also be **the husband of but one wife**. Literally, he must be a "one-woman man." This means that the pastor must be committed to the covenant of marriage; he must be faithful to his wife. This is loyal oneness.

Some interpreters believe this qualification means that the overseer could not be in a second marriage, whether by death of a spouse or after divorce. Churches have various policies related to the interpretation of this phrase as they systematize qualifications for ordination or the pastorate. Of this we can be sure—the pastorate requires a strong modeling of marriage and loyalty.

He must also be **temperate**, or balanced, not given to extremes. *Temperate* comes from a word meaning "sober," or "calm in judgment." It carries the idea of objective thinking and clear perspective. A temperate person is free from the influences of passion, lust, emotion, or personal gain.

All Christians are called to be **self-controlled**; this is an evidence of the Spirit's life within. Here Paul required that leaders model this quality. A pastor is to be in control of himself, not given to anger, personal ambition, or passions. He is to be sensible and in charge of his life.

Peter told all Christians to be "self-controlled and alert. Your enemy the devil prowls around like a roaring lion looking for someone to devour" (1 Pet. 5:8). Without the power of God's Spirit, the human spirit is left alone to navigate the forces of evil and personal weaknesses. By the Spirit whom God has placed in all believers, we are given the ability to live beyond these evil influences; we are enabled to have a self that is controlled not by fallen nature but by God's kingdom goodness.

A pastor should also be **respectable**, his life well-ordered. He is to be harmonious within and without. His behavior should not be at odds with his inner spirit and soul.

The word **hospitable** means "open to strangers." It reflects a vulnerability to others, a desire to care for guests and those in need. Hospitality was highly valued by the Mediterranean cultures where there were few inns and those which existed were often disreputable. But having fancy hotels and fast-food restaurants does not relieve any of us from this call to hospitality. All believers are instructed to practice hospitality (Rom. 12:13). Even if our guests do not require a bed or a meal, we should provide them with a warm and accepting atmosphere—a place of refuge. The pastor is no exception. He must lead in this area as an example to others.

The pastor must be **able to teach.** The functions of the pastor are often described as "pastor-teacher" because teaching has become such a central duty of the job. The pastor must be able to communicate God's Word in a clear way. He must understand Christian doctrine and live it, guiding others in their pursuit of God and godliness.

3:3. This verse is about controls. There are four "nots" given in a row: **not given to drunkenness, not violent . . . not quarrelsome, not a lover of money.**

The prohibition against **drunkenness** is a call for pastors not to "sit beside wine." Drunkenness nullifies self-control, which all believers are expected to exhibit. The pastor is called to self-control in a special way. Leaders controlled by chemical substances of any sort cannot think clearly or lead with integrity.

Likewise, a **violent** person lacks self-control. Such a person is controlled by emotions that are rooted in selfishness and an attitude of judgment. Obviously, people with such a turbulent inner spirit would be unqualified to lead anywhere, but particularly in God's church.

In contrast, the pastor is to be **gentle** in his dealings with people. The English word carries the idea of softness, even tenderness. But the Greek word portrays fairness, equity, and moderation. The pastor is not to be swayed by people of position; he is not to deal in favoritism. Instead, he must be just.

It follows that a pastor would not be **quarrelsome.** This instruction from Paul was not simply to squelch fights and arguments; it was intended to promote an inner spirit that would not even allow contentious behavior. A quarrelsome person is, like an angry individual, self-seeking and disrespectful of others. Such a person considers only himself, never the opinions of others.

The pastor, according to Paul, is also not to be **a lover of money.** Such a person will have a detachment from wealth and its distractions. He will be an example of generosity and faithful dependence on God. His goals and decisions will not be influenced by paychecks and benefits. Instead, a pastor has only one devotion, one treasure—God himself: "No one can serve two masters. Either he will hate the one and love the other, or he will be devoted to the one and despise the other. You cannot serve both God and Money" (Matt. 6:24).

3:4–5. Since the pastor deals with people, the test of his leadership and management capabilities is noted by observing his home: **He must manage his own family well and see that his children obey him with proper**

respect. If you cannot exercise leadership at home, you should not attempt to lead the family of God. If the husband does not lead spiritually and with vision in the close relationships of family, it is doubtful that he can lead the church in those same areas.

In John Bunyan's *Pilgrim's Progress,* Talkative is described as "a saint abroad, and a devil at home." This can happen. Outside we play the part of church leader, but at home where we are most real, most vulnerable and unmasked, our true nature is exposed. Failure in the home indicates some serious troubles. These must be attended to before a person attempts to lead others.

Every home experiences tension from time to time, but the mood of the family should be obedience, love, honor, and respect. Titus 1:6 adds that the children must "believe and [not be] open to the charge of being wild or disobedient." Eli, high priest in Israel when Samuel was in training, was judged with death because he "failed to restrain" his sons when he knew they were living a life of sin (1 Sam. 3:13). The pastor must be an example of management in this first priority—his own family.

Equally, the church must honor privacy in the personal life of its pastor and his family. No wife or children of a pastor should be placed in positions of undue pressure or tension just because they are the pastor's family. This places unnecessary burdens upon the household.

3:6. Paul also taught that the pastor **must not be a recent convert, or he may become conceited.** The word translated "recent convert" is *neophuton,* meaning "newly planted." It is the word from which we derive neophyte, one who is just beginning a new kind of life: a novice. This is not to suggest that time necessarily guarantees maturity. Many people who claim the name of Christ remain at the initial stages of faith for a lifetime. The writer to the Hebrews reprimanded his readers for their continuing immaturity (Heb. 5:11–14).

But those new to the faith cannot have the necessary spiritual maturity which church leadership requires. Though a recent convert may be adept in finances or business management, for church leadership there is a more fundamental requirement—the spiritual depth of the individual that can only develop persistently and faithfully over time.

Paul recognized that the new believer who had an undeveloped faith could easily become proud if thrust too quickly into church leadership. Such pride would cause him to **fall under the same judgment as the devil.**

There are a couple of ways to interpret Paul's warning of judgment. It could refer to the conceit Satan exhibited when he tried to usurp God's authority and power. He was judged by being banished from heaven and condemned for eternity. If the "I will" statements of Isaiah 14 do point to Satan, it is a striking example of the arrogance and dangers of pride as well as the judgment of God. Or Paul's statement may point to pride as a means by which the devil gains leverage over the believer. It may be that pride, like anger, offers Satan a foothold in the life of a Christian, affording Satan the means to exploit the believer as well as damage the church. Pride is always competitive, uncooperative. For leaders in the church, this is contrary to unity, the harmony that should characterize the community of faith.

Pride and self-will are inherent in our fallen nature. They pose a constant danger. It takes spiritual development and grace to overcome these tendencies and temptations. Only the spiritually mature, seasoned by time and God's grace, are equipped to face the challenges of spiritual leadership.

3:7. The pastor or church leader is an ambassador for the church and for Christ, so he is to have **a good reputation with outsiders.** Like Jesus, he is to increase in wisdom and "in favor with God and men" (Luke 2:52).

Sometimes the pastor or church leader becomes so involved in work and ministry within the walls of the church that "outsiders" do not even know him. This can create a reputation of sorts, one that can be interpreted as elitist or unconcerned. The point is that we always create a reputation for ourselves. Paul was concerned, as we should be, that our reputation is good. We should live so that our "daily life may win the respect of outsiders" (1 Thess. 4:12).

Paul's concern with the opinions of unbelievers was not for the sake of popularity. His overriding passion was the evangelistic mandate to tell others of the saving grace of God. We damage this message when our lives do not exhibit the qualities of godliness. Paul did not want unnecessary hindrances and distractions placed in the way of others coming to Christ. A suspect reputation among church leaders gives the gospel message a bad reputation among unbelievers.

If the church is to be offensive to society, then it must be for the sake of the cross—not our hypocrisy, misuse of liberty, or bad behavior. Paul's emphasis was not on trying to meld with society but on living pure, good lives against which no one can find fault (1 Pet. 3:13–17).

These seven verses describe the challenges for a person who wants to pastor a church. These are also the criteria for the church searching for a pastor. It is not enough to be a good speaker, an efficient manager, a charismatic personality. The pastor must demonstrate an ongoing spiritual development and a character of the highest quality.

B What a Deacon Should Be (3:8–13)

SUPPORTING IDEA: *Paul described the qualities of a deacon, those who serve people in the name of Christ and the church. He did this so the church would know how to select for this office men and women who serve well and please God.*

1. Qualifications for men (3:8–10,12–13)

3:8. The word **deacon** means "servant." Paul discussed what sort of character and lifestyle deacons were to maintain; he did not precisely define what deacons did, their particular tasks or duties. This leaves a lot of room for flexibility in this office.

The men chosen in Acts 6 to "wait on tables" and see that the "widows" were not "being overlooked" are often considered the first deacons. Some churches apply the title of *deacon* to any person who holds an office or has a job responsibility in the church. Others believe deacons are responsible for managing church property and supervising the pastoral care of the congregation. In some churches the deacons function as the governing board.

The main issue here, however, is that God has strong views about what kind of people he wants to represent and lead the church. Those who desire to lead in the church and those responsible for enlisting leaders should follow these qualifications.

Paul indicated the deacon is to be **worthy of respect.** He must be of a serious mind about spiritual and leadership issues. He is to have an inner character which calls forth respect from the people with whom he serves. It does not mean he should be stern or unbending, but that his life should evoke admiration.

The deacon is also to be **sincere,** literally "not double tongued." He must be known for truthfulness. His word must be reliable. His "yes" must be yes, and his "no," no (Jas. 5:12).

The qualification that the deacon should not be **indulging in much wine** is the same admonition as that for the pastor (see 1 Tim. 3:3).

Paul always distanced himself from those who taught or preached for the sake of money. It is not surprising that he warned against deacons **pursuing dishonest gain.** Perhaps stories were still circulating about Judas pocketing the disciples' money for himself while presenting himself as a true follower of Jesus. Paul understood the lure of money, so he was careful in the area of finances, making certain that neither he nor the churches could be accused of greed or money-making schemes (1 Thess. 2:5; 2 Cor. 8:20–21).

3:9. The deacon must also **keep hold of the deep truths of the faith.** This is a warning against allowing into leadership people who are ungrounded in the Christian faith or who adhere to strange or unfounded doctrines. This practice had created deep problems in the Ephesian church as false teachers assumed leadership positions.

The **deep truths** of the faith most likely deal with the whole body of revelation from God to mankind. But there are cardinal truths such as the incarnation of Christ (1 Tim. 3:16), the indwelling of the Spirit in our lives (Eph. 1:13–14), the unity of Jesus as God and man (Phil. 2:6–8), the gospel of Christ and the good news of salvation (1 Cor. 15:2–5; Acts 4:10–12), the mystery of lawlessness (2 Thess. 2:7), and the return of Jesus Christ (Acts 1:9–11). There is a body of truth to be believed.

These truths must be held with conviction and become a part of the church leader's life and heart. But not only must God's revelation be believed; it must be held **with a clear conscience.** In the first century, the conscience was seen as the seat of the will. To hold truth with a clear conscience was not only to agree intellectually but volitionally as well. Intellect and mind must agree with life and purpose. Doctrine must penetrate to the person's will so that his conscience before God and others is blameless as he lives biblical truth in his daily life.

3:10. Paul underscored the importance of a leader being blameless, stating that deacons **must first be tested.** This is not a formal, written exam but the test of public scrutiny. A life which withstands observation is the best credential for a ministry of service. If no charge can stand, then the person is free to serve.

3:12. The deacon is held to the same standard as the overseer. He **must be the husband of but one wife** (see 1 Tim. 3:2 for the explanation as it applies to elders). In the same way, the deacon must also **manage his children and his household well** (the same as elders, 1 Tim. 3:5).

3:13. As he concluded the qualifications for pastor and deacons within the church, Paul ended as he began—by elevating the positions of leadership and those who serve.

Paul was writing to a church suffering from a crisis in leadership. False teachers had brought division to the church and led some people away from true faith. In this atmosphere, Paul wanted to restore leadership to its rightful place and restore the people's respect for the office. He told the Ephesians that leadership within the church is a noble task and that it has its rewards—before people and before God.

Those who have served well gain an excellent standing before Christ and the church. They achieve a good reputation with all people and are favored by God.

They also gain **great assurance in their faith in Christ Jesus.** This may relate to a boldness that develops as a person faithfully follows Christ. It may also mean that people of such character and obedient leadership attain a confidence in their prayers and service as they keep expanding their ministries—they grow closer to Christ. This is a worthwhile reward indeed!

2. Qualifications for women (3:11)

Godly character is valued by God in all his followers. The qualifications for women require the same depth of character, even though their leadership or service may not be as public as men's.

3:11. The big debate swirling around this verse is whether these qualifications were intended for the wives of deacons or for women who served in the church in some official capacity. We cannot argue too conclusively for either position.

Either way, these women were to be **worthy of respect.** Paul was always concerned that followers of Christ, particularly those associated with church leadership, demonstrate a life in which the Spirit was working. These women were to live in such a way that they earned the respect of all people.

Paul then gave a couple of markers to guide our understanding of what a respectable life is. First, such women should **not [be] malicious talkers.** Women do not have a corner on gossip; men also have trouble taming the tongue. But it may be that women, since they are naturally more communicative, are more susceptible to this problem. No matter who is tempted to hurt others through words, the faithful Christian should have no part in it.

Instead, these women were to be **temperate and trustworthy in everything.** These qualifications parallel the pastor and deacon's call to self-control and sincerity.

3. The servant's heart (3:12–13)

Chapter 9 of Mark contains the account of the disciples arguing about which of them would be greatest in the kingdom of God. We can imagine Peter's claim for boldness, faith, and leadership. John may have staked his claim on his kindness or special friendship with Jesus. James may have pointed to his acts of service, his practical work. Whatever their assertions, they must have recognized the arrogance of their discussion. When Jesus asked them what they were arguing about, they "kept quiet" (Mark 9:34).

Of course Jesus knew the nature of the discussion, and so he sat down with the Twelve and taught: "If anyone wants to be first, he must be the very last, and the servant *(deacon)* of all" (Mark 9:35).

That is how the Creator of the universe and Lord of this life defines greatness—to be a deacon (or deaconess). Those who hold the title of deacon certainly should model this attitude and lifestyle.

What the Church Is (3:14–16)

SUPPORTING IDEA: *Without Christ, the church would not exist. We must know who we belong to and what he expects of us and then align ourselves accordingly.*

1. How God sees the church (3:14–15)

God has established only three institutions—government, marriage and family, and the church. In post-Christian America all three of these are being either discarded or treated with suspicion. In modern America, church has become peripheral.

Yet God firmly established the church, bestowing it with honor and declaring that even hell itself could not overwhelm it. Despite society's no-confidence vote, it is paramount that we learn how God views the church and what he expects from it.

3:14–15. Paul first described the church as **God's household.** The household of the first century was a bit different from what we have in modern times. Not only did the ancient home consist of parents and children; it also encompassed extended family, workers, and stewards. It was the framework and microcosm of society at large. Within the household were various age groups, genders, duties, responsibilities. Over this diversity was the master, who kept the house in order, and stewards, who bore responsibility to the master for those in his charge. The household is a picture of the church in variety and structure, bringing together a mix of talents and gifts, men and women, adults and children, professionals and laborers. all of them are cared for and guided by stewards—pastors and deacons responsible to the Master.

The household is also a picture of the warmth and refuge which family provides. We are to treat one another with the love and respect of brothers and sisters, mothers and fathers. The church is to exemplify to the world a place of acceptance, love, and protection as offered by the other members and by God himself. We are members of God's household (Eph. 2:19).

As Christians we are also members of **the church of the living God.** We are his assembly, his gathering. The emphasis is on God, who is alive. This group, known as the church, is distinctive from all other groups, because the one who has called us is an ever-living, ever-present God. This is no club meeting based on ideology, the religion of ritual, or idols. The church meets to worship the living God, even as its members have the Spirit of God within them.

The church is a gathering of new relationships, a place of protection and refuge. Paul characterized the church as **the pillar and foundation of the truth.**

All that is true comes from God, and he has designated the church as guardian and proclaimer of the truth. The church provides the framework for safeguarding orthodoxy and living its claims. The church is "built on the foundation of the apostles and prophets, with Christ Jesus himself as the chief cornerstone" (Eph. 2:20).

The Word of God must be taught in all churches. This imagery of the church as the supporting structure of essential truth is a reminder that we must base the central issues of belief and practice upon the authoritative Word of God.

The church protects the truth from the attacks of falsehood. Paul's call for pure doctrine is also a call for pure people. Central to the truth of the gospel is the transformed life of the Christian.

2. How we live as the church (3:14–15)

3:14–15. After describing how we are part of God's household, Paul interwove through these verses guidelines for **how people ought to conduct themselves** as God's people and gathered assembly. The purpose of Paul's instructions on order, worship, and leadership was to make vivid the high calling of the Christian and the church—their remarkable way of living as individuals and as a group—to the glory of God.

Leaders of some nations have on staff a person known as the chief of protocol. His or her job is to tell people how to act when dignitaries arrive—when to stand, manners of greeting, and other etiquette.

The Bible is the protocol book for life—for all we do. As followers of Christ we are responsible to live lives that are deserving of his gift of grace. We are to be holy as God is holy (1 Pet. 1:15); we are to conduct ourselves "in a manner worthy of the gospel of Christ" (Phil. 1:27).

3. How Christ relates to the church (3:16)

3:16. Paul concluded this section with a confession on the **mystery of godliness**. This was probably a hymn well-known in first-century Christendom and often used in public worship services. Paul may have included these familiar words to provoke the listeners to evaluate their conduct and life in view of this confession.

Paul declared, **He appeared in a body.** This refers to the incarnation of Christ, the coming of God into the world. God and godliness were revealed to humanity as God became flesh. The Word of all time, the truth of all eternity, the wisdom of God, the very Son became like us, living in our midst.

Christ was also **vindicated by the Spirit.** He was declared acceptable to God in his sacrificial death for the sins of all people. He was proclaimed the Son of God through his resurrection and ascension into heaven. This was done by the Holy Spirit, who "raised Jesus from the dead" (Rom. 8:11, see also Rom. 1:4).

The next line of the hymn states that Jesus **was seen by angels.** In keeping with the victorious tone of the previous line, this statement is a shout of triumph. The vindicated Christ, the resurrected Lord, was shown to the angels, his ministering spirits.

Jesus was also **preached among the nations.** Again, the glory of the risen Christ continued as his salvation and life were communicated throughout the world. This proclamation is now the duty of the church.

The result of this preaching is that Jesus is **believed on in the world.** This is the continuing legacy of godliness. Salvation is perpetual in power as the living Christ is believed on by individuals of every nation, tribe, and people group. The richness of our salvation must be treasured if we are to share it with others.

Paul ended his hymn excerpt with the declaration that Christ was **taken up in glory**. The Son was raised in power, and he ascended to his place at the right hand of the Father. He is Lord, reigning at the top of all the created order. He rules with majesty and power. Christ's ascension is assurance of his return. It is the proof of his ever-present reality and power and his claims on our lives.

In this confession of the mystery of godliness, Paul called us to pay attention to the importance and calling of the church. Founded by Christ, built on him and by him, the church is called to be a preview of his kingdom. This occurs as his people serve and love in obedience to their living Lord. Let us live worthy of the call of God, serving his church.

MAIN IDEA REVIEW: *Church leadership is a noble and respectable position that requires nobility of character. Paul called everyone to live exemplary lives as he wrote of the high value God places on the church and the close relationship it has with Christ.*

III. CONCLUSION

A Curriculum for Life

In his book, *Teaching as a Conserving Activity,* Neil Postman wrote, "A curriculum is a specially constructed information system whose purpose, in its totality, is to influence, teach, train, or cultivate the mind and character." As such, curriculums are not simply yearly plans used by schoolteachers. In fact, curriculums are not limited to schools at all. Systems of influence and training are used by business and the media as well as the church.

Knowing this, it is important to do more than analyze the content of the curriculum, to see what is being taught. We must look behind the words and assumptions, taking into account those people who create the systems.

Balance is necessary because no teacher or purveyor of ideas is perfect. Ideas and beliefs spring from the inner regions of our character; they do not exist separate from us.

When you take your child to church and leave him or her with someone for an hour, you expect that person to convey biblical truths. But intellectual stimulation is only a part of the curriculum for Christian living. You want that teacher to *live* that biblical truth as well. That teacher should be consistent in belief *and* practice. The same thing is true of pastors and other church leaders.

God has strong qualifications for those who direct and guide, who represent him and enact his curriculum for living. It is important for the church to adhere to these biblical criteria for all church leaders.

PRINCIPLES

- Church leaders are meant to be models in character, family life, and relationships.
- There are clear guidelines about how church people should live and behave. Church leaders have a greater weight of responsibility because of their influence on others.
- Our Christian commitment is based upon the life of Christ—his incarnation, ascension, and redemptive achievements.
- We are God's people on earth, his representatives. We must live in close relationship with him. Our lives should model the intimacy and power we receive from him.

APPLICATIONS

- Young people who want to serve as pastors in the church should be guided on their mission by the church and by strong leaders who have matured in spirit and grace.
- All churches should adopt the standards for pastors, deacons, and deaconesses listed in this chapter; these qualifications are not optional.
- Married people who serve in official positions in the church should have sound, growing marriages.
- While there is a lot of room for differences on minor points of the faith, there is a particular way to conduct ourselves in the family of God; it requires depth of character and godliness.
- Tributes to Christ for all he is and all he has accomplished can never be overdone. He is the foundation of our faith and practice.

IV. LIFE APPLICATION

Gardening Hints

Jesus used a lot of agricultural images for his spiritual lessons. He spoke about vineyards and wheat fields, planting and harvesting, soil analysis, controlling pests and weeds, and grafting.

I have a friend who enjoys plants. Raised in the city, his encounters with agriculture have been limited to potted plants and seed packets. Plants with him have a slim chance. Begonias, ferns, spider plants, English ivy—it does not matter. They begin healthy but then droop and die. He's been known to kill even a philodendron (oft considered the herbaceous Energizer bunny of the plant world).

Though he is constantly sweeping petals and leaves off the floor, it does not keep him from trying. He will bring home a new plant. The old plant is dislodged from its pot. Then, in a puff of dust, the spent plant is tossed into the garbage. The new plant assumes its place.

The problem is, he always forgets to water. What you tend grows. What you do not, will not—it is as simple as that.

What is true for plants also applies to the spirit. It takes a commitment to feed the areas of our spirit that will respond to the will of God. And it takes equal determination to starve the influences that deter us from living godly lives.

Our lives develop in an environment, but we are the ones who decide what we feed within that environmental mix of personal choices, friends, family, desires and ambitions, media, time investments, and values.

Whenever I open my mouth, think a thought, watch TV, read a book or magazine, or make a decision, I feed something. It is a principle that works both ways, for good or ill. Starve a bad habit, like sarcasm, and my spirit and character grow. Dehydrate a loving attitude, and I shrivel within.

That is why Paul was so explicit about church conduct and personal character for Christians. We represent the living God. Our lives are not a performance but a revelation of our inner spirit which is united with Christ. If our relationship to God is developing in dependence and intimacy or if it is drifting and estranged, the truth of our relationship to God and his Spirit will be demonstrated through the way we live and the choices we make.

Remember, what you feed, grows. What you do not, will not.

V. PRAYER

God of all truth, keep me receptive to your Spirit's guidance so I will live honestly, acknowledging my sins and errors, choosing your goodness and righteousness. Protect me from pretending, rationalizing, becoming lazy in my daily life. Give me an alertness so that I will perceive the true issues and implications of my decisions. Give me boldness to follow in your way. Amen.

VI. DEEPER DISCOVERIES

Church Government (vv. 2,8,11)

Paul referred to overseers, deacons, and possibly deaconesses. The terms are not as critical as the function and responsibilities each provided within the local church. The crucial point is that God established particular roles so the church would operate smoothly and orderly.

Three main systems of church government have developed over the years: episcopal, presbyterian, congregational.

1. The word *episcopal* is taken from the Greek word *episkopos,* found in 1 Timothy 3:2 and translated in the NIV as "overseer." In current church structures, the episcopal form is organized by a hierarchy of leadership. Dioceses are territories which are administered by the church and governed by a bishop. Bishops are elected by the clerics and lay leaders at diocesan conventions, and they serve in administrative functions. Beyond this there is a supreme court of the church. In the Episcopal church the general convention meets every three years to discuss church policy, administration, and theological issues. There is also an executive council which exercises executive functions in the intervening years. There is also a senior leader. In the Roman Church it is the pope; in the Episcopal church it is the presiding bishop who is elected by the general convention.

   This basic organizational approach is used by the Methodists, Episcopalians, Roman Catholics, and others.

2. The word *presbyterian* comes from the Greek word *presbuteros,* used in 1 Timothy 5:17, and translated as "elder." Both *presbuteros* and *episkopos* are used interchangeably throughout Scripture. The Presbyterian form of church government consists of a hierarchy of courts. First, the kirk session, which is the local church with its minister and elders; then the presbytery, which is composed of ministers and representative elders from a geographic area; next are the synods, which are made up of members of several presbyteries covering a larger territory. Finally, there is the supreme legislative and administrative court, the general assembly, composed of equal numbers of ministers and elders.

   Ministers in the Presbyterian system are elected by the local church, but ordination comes as an act of the presbytery after completion of strict educational requirements. Ministers typically preach and teach. Elders are ordained for particular offices in the church.

   This particular system of government is used by the Presbyterian church and some Reformed churches. Selected aspects of this governmental structure are used by independent and Congregational churches as well.

3. The Congregational form of government derives its name because of its emphasis on local congregations. These churches function independently and autonomously, using a democratic approach to church government with Christ as the sole head of the church. All members are considered "priests unto God" with responsibility to serve in the administration and decisions of the church. Sometimes these churches form associations based on doctrinal agreements, but there

are no authoritative or legislative bodies to which the local church is subject.

This form of government is used by many independent churches which exist outside specific denominational adherences. This type of government is also used by certain Congregational and Baptist churches.

In any church government on the local level, no one person should have sole responsibility for the decisions of the church. If there is only one official pastor or minister, then that person gathers around him a board or session of elders or mature Christians. Together they pray and study the Scriptures to determine the application of principles for specific situations within the church. This sharing of responsibility is designed by God to protect the solitary pastor from being overburdened, the church from apathy, the individual pastor from the temptations of power, and the local church from mindless compliance.

Deacons and/or deaconesses seem to refer to any other job in the local church that is officially recognized as a serving position. If Acts 6 indeed describes the first deacons, as many believe, then their first job was to ensure a just distribution of food to both Hebrew and Greek widows in Jerusalem. Today deacons care for homebound persons, teach Sunday school, decide financial matters, visit in the hospitals, serve ordinances, or, as in many Baptist churches, serve as the official leadership board of the church.

The church is to be organized with many people contributing to its work and sharing in its responsibilities. The church has a role to play in the life of believers and in the community. Its government and organization assure that no essential matter is forgotten, that it functions with integrity and purpose. However we organize the church, Christ is always the head.

VII. TEACHING OUTLINE

A. INTRODUCTION

1. Lead Story: Rewriting the Six O'Clock News
2. Context: Every organization needs structure. In chapter 3, Paul laid the foundation for church government and order, emphasizing the importance of personal character and conduct in its leaders.
3. Transition: We have become a niche society in the West. We think that people with expertise are fit for leadership, based on their expertise alone. Even in the church we are tempted to do this, selecting bankers and accountants as trustees and professionals such as doctors and lawyers for leadership positions. Though each of these might be fit for the job, their vocation alone does not qualify them for

church leadership. Godly character, as demonstrated within the community of believers and within the community at large, is the fundamental qualification for church leaders.

B. COMMENTARY
1. What a Pastor Should Be (3:1–7)
   a. The pastor's desire (3:1)
   b. The pastor's goals (3:2–7)
2. What a Deacon Should Be (3:8–13)
   a. Qualifications for men (3:8–10,12–13)
   b. Qualifications for women (3:11)
   c. The servant's heart (3:12–13)
3. What the Church Is (3:14–16)
   a. How God sees the church (3:14–15)
   b. How we live as the church (3:14–15)
   c. How Christ relates to the church (3:16)

C. CONCLUSION: GARDENING HINTS

VIII. ISSUES FOR DISCUSSION

1. Why are the standards so strong for an elder or pastor in the church? Could anyone be perfect in all these areas? What do these qualifications say about God's concern for his church?
2. Discuss the differences between the standards for elders/pastors and the deacons. What are the common characteristics for both?
3. Discuss the implications of applying the standards of 1 Timothy 3:4–5 personally and practically. What if a pastor has ongoing problems in his family, with a child, or his marriage? How should the church respond? What is the pastor's responsibility?
4. How are we to live in the church today? If you truly believe the confession of faith at the conclusion of 1 Timothy 3, what difference does that make in your life?

1 Timothy 4

Christian Godliness
and Discipline

I. INTRODUCTION
Hoopster Par Excellence

II. COMMENTARY
A verse-by-verse explanation of the chapter.

III. CONCLUSION
Snub Clubs

An overview of the principles and applications from the chapter.

IV. LIFE APPLICATION
Swimming with the Orcas

Melding the chapter to life.

V. PRAYER
Tying the chapter to life with God.

VI. DEEPER DISCOVERIES
Historical, geographical, and grammatical enrichment of the commentary.

VII. TEACHING OUTLINE
Suggested step-by-step group study of the chapter.

VIII. ISSUES FOR DISCUSSION
Zeroing the chapter in on daily life.

"*And if you will here stop and ask yourself why you are not as pious as the primitive Christians were, your own heart will tell you that it is neither through ignorance nor inability, but purely because you never thoroughly intended it.*"

William Law

1 Timothy 4

IN A NUTSHELL

Paul got very specific as he discussed false teachings which were rooted in legalism. He also gave personal commands for Timothy to stay faithful in leading God's people and diligent in personal godliness.

Christian Godliness and Discipline

I. INTRODUCTION

Hoopster Par Excellence

*M*ark Price was an all-star guard for many years with Cleveland's pro-basketball team, the Cavaliers. His basketball skills were supreme, but he stood a little under six feet and had an average frame. Yet he played well among giants.

Once, in front of a group of men and boys at church, he was asked how someone his size had become so exceptional in basketball.

Mark reflected on the many Friday nights he was alone in the gym shooting foul shots and long-range shots while everyone else was out on a date or hanging out with friends.

He remembered the hard work with his father, shooting and correcting, shooting and correcting, dribbling and passing—then doing it all over again. In high school he was all-state; at Georgia Tech he was all-conference. Then he was signed by the pros.

Physical strength and excellence require conditioning and training, dedication and hard work. Spiritual strength and maturity require the same. But not many people will discipline their spirits. Too often we become satisfied with mediocrity or with watching *others* live for Christ.

Physical training has some limited value, but development and exercise of the spirit benefit our lives now and for eternity. This chapter of 1 Timothy is about the value of disciplining ourselves for life.

II. COMMENTARY

> **MAIN IDEA:** *The outward life of a person flows from his or her inner spirit. Those who discipline themselves to follow after Jesus Christ, who are focused on living out the truth of God's revelation, will develop a life of growing intimacy with Christ. They will delight God, producing goodness and godliness in what they do.*

Days of Trouble (4:1–5)

> **SUPPORTING IDEA:** *Paul described deviant doctrines, bad teaching, and useless practices that pull us away from God's grace and truth. He focused on how to respond to falsehood and how to live righteously.*

1. Timing (4:1)

4:1. Paul turned from his triumphant hymn of Christ to a stark warning: **the Spirit clearly says that in later times** troublesome things will happen within the church.

The phrase **later times** refers not to some coming event but to the sweep of time from Christ's ascension to his future return. It covers everything in between, from Paul and the early church, to Luther and the Reformation, to Wesley and the Great Awakening, to us. These are the "later times," the last days. This great epoch of the church is the final stage of human history before the triumphal return of Jesus Christ.

These words from Paul are just as relevant to our churches as they were for those in the first century. They will continue to be valid for believers in the future last days. The troubles which Paul describes have been happening throughout history to the present time, at other times with guerrilla tactics and scattered damage, often with frontal assaults and great devastation to the church.

Paul predicted that **some will abandon the faith.** Apostasy has been around as long as human history. Paul dealt with it in his own day (1 Tim. 1:19; 2 Tim. 2:17–18), and the casualty list is high in our time. Even so, the church will triumph.

2. The teachers (4:1–2)

To deny the truth and abandon the faith, people would follow **deceiving spirits and things taught by demons.** Despite the assault of the physical world upon our senses, we live in a spirit-saturated environment. There is not a moment when we are outside the interplay of spirituality, for we are spirit beings. The very faculty of the human will is spiritual. Whatever we choose to believe or do is founded in our spiritual nature.

When Paul wrote about following deceiving spirits and things taught by demons, he was not necessarily envisioning Satan worship or drug-led transcendentalist theology. There is a wide variety of ways in which Satan peddles his twisted inventions. All deceptions come from Satan's realm, but he uses many genteel ways to fashion these lies, spreading ideas which are anti-God.

The apostle John wrote, "Every spirit that acknowledges that Jesus Christ has come in the flesh is from God, but every spirit that does not acknowledge Jesus is not from God. This is the spirit of the Antichrist, which you have heard is coming and even now is already in the world" (1 John 4:2–3).

John's words cover a whole range of teachings, some religious in nature such as cults and various world religions and others antireligious as in popular philosophies. All find their source in demons. The false teachings find receptivity in those who are **hypocritical liars, whose consciences have been seared as with a hot iron.** Such people perpetuate the lies of Satan and his hosts.

Not only were these false teachers peddling in lies; they were doing so under the guise of spirituality, under the pretense of being godly. Hypocrisy was anathema to Jesus; it received particular condemnation from him. Such a posture misrepresents God to others; it has a potent capacity for leading others away from the loving Father. Paul warned the Ephesian believers, "Even from your own number men will arise and distort the truth in order to draw away disciples after them" (Acts 20:30).

Paul described the psychological workings of false teachers: their **consciences have been seared.** "Such people are not serving our Lord Christ, but their own appetites. By smooth talk and flattery they deceive the minds of naive people" (Rom. 16:18). The conscience is the human capability to discern right and wrong, and it is connected to the will. A good conscience, one guided by faith, enables a person to navigate life's moral issues. But a seared conscience is left scarred, unable to assess truth and error, incapable of producing godly behavior.

Sometimes we think in apocalyptic terms relative to the dangers and evil of the "last days." Certainly as time draws to a close, evil increases. But evil does not always present itself as crime, drugs, and brutality. Such manifestations issue from a degeneration of beliefs, values, ideas, and conscience that have filtered through society for a long time. Evil frequently begins in decent places—in philosophical discussions at the university, in debates at seminary, in sermons at church. Falsehood often comes dressed up and attractive.

God's simple call to faith in his Son is often abused either through legalism or libertarianism. In Paul's day, the tendency in the church was toward legalism, which he proceeded to describe.

3. False teaching (4:3)

Rules are good when used to maintain proper boundaries in life and to create a harmonious and orderly existence. But when adherence to rules becomes an attempt to placate God or to earn righteousness or salvation, they become deadly. Rules elevate human achievement and devalue the goodness of God. There is only one way to restore and maintain relationship with the holy God—trust in his Son, Jesus Christ.

4:3. Paul wrote of the legalists as those who **forbid people to marry and order them to abstain from certain foods.**

Legalism enslaves people to joyless toil. Such systems misrepresent the God of grace and belittle the work of Christ on the cross. They lead people down a path of grinding effort, at the end of which there is no God—only insecurities, mental anguish, and more labor.

The particulars of a legalistic system are not as important as its assumptions. In fact, the legalist often uses convincing arguments that have the ring of truth. Forbidding people to marry, for instance, may have come from Jesus' own teaching about Paradise-to-come in which there would be no marriage. Abstaining from certain foods may have been rooted in the Genesis account of paradise-past when vegetarianism seems to have been the rule.

There is nothing wrong with singleness, nor is there anything wrong with maintaining a strict diet. But the Word of God is twisted when these particulars are put forth as demands, as absolutes in gaining God's approval. Nowhere in Scripture is marriage forbidden. In fact, it is honored and instituted by God from Creation. Paul described the advantages of single life as allowing extra time for serving God, but he did not make singleness a rule.

Dietary restrictions were a Jewish concern dating back to the giving of the Law, but in Acts 10 God opened up the storehouses of creation. Nothing which comes from God is forbidden as long as it is **received with thanksgiving by those who believe and who know the truth.**

Disciplines are good in controlling our spirit and guiding us, but they must never become law. The law of God for righteousness has been fulfilled by Christ; our task is to abide in him.

4. Correct teaching (4:4–5)

4:4–5. Paul did not refute the antimarriage argument because he had implied his endorsement earlier in 1 Timothy (3:2,12). But he did face the food issue by asserting that **everything God created is good.** He told the Corinthians, "Food does not bring us near to God; we are no worse if we do not eat, and no better if we do" (1 Cor. 8:8).

Paul also declared: **Nothing is to be rejected if it is received with thanksgiving, because it is consecrated by the word of God and prayer.** This statement extends beyond diet, creating a context for understanding life and godliness. The touch of God purifies. In him there is no darkness at all.

Everything that comes from God is good. In addition, prayer and Scripture go along with thanksgiving. By these a transformation takes place as a believer acknowledges God as the source of all that is good.

Ⓑ The Good Minister of Christ Jesus (4:6–16)

SUPPORTING IDEA: *In contrast to the false teachers, the good follower of Christ is one who adheres to correct doctrine, teaches it to others, exalts Christ as Lord, and disciplines himself to be a model for godly living.*

1. The good minister (4:6)

4:6. The following instructions were directed to Timothy, a minister of the gospel, and to all Christian leaders. But Paul's words were not for the select few. They apply to all believers in Christ.

Paul referred back to the warnings he has just given about false teachings. He told Timothy, **If you point these things out to the brothers, you will be a good minister of Christ Jesus.** Leaders cannot afford to let doctrinal compromise or wrong ideas creep into their congregations. These fundamental issues of faith and right action must be guarded.

Further, Paul reminded all Christians that a good minister is one who continues in **the truths of the faith and the good teaching.** Constant spiritual nourishment is essential. Out of it our lives and teaching flow. Ministry work must never become so demanding that the first priority of spending time in personal spiritual renewal and growth is ignored. Ministry will lose its power and effectiveness when leaders neglect their spiritual development.

2. Warnings and directions (4:7–11)

4:7. Not everything promoted as spiritual is good for our development. Some things fall under the category of **godless myths and old wives' tales.** These are to be strictly avoided, Paul declared. In our own time these may come in the guise of new theologies, popular spiritual movements, curiosities about numbers, pyramids, and dates. We must be aware of all the false and distracting "knowledge" that presents itself as spiritual and then stay far from it and warn others of its ungodly results. To be able to discern the false from the true, a believer must be solidly grounded in the truth of God.

We can safeguard ourselves and those we lead or influence by training ourselves **to be godly.** In contrast to the legalism of the false teachers, who supposed that godliness had to do with laws of self-denial, true godliness centers on a life lived in the truth of God's revealed Word.

The Greek word *gymnazo* is translated "train." It means to exercise ourselves. Doing this takes discipline and purposeful decision. Nobody ever wakes up "trained" or stumbles into exercise. The person who benefits most from exercise does it routinely and with determination. The athlete stretches and runs because these exercises lead him toward the greater goal of fitness. In the same way, prayer, fasting, Bible study, and other disciplines are not ends in themselves but means to a fuller relationship with God. We pursue righteousness, peace, and love because we pursue God.

4:8. Paul declared, **Physical training is of some value, but godliness has value for all things**. Physical training is limited to just that—the physical dimensions of life. Godliness, on the other hand, penetrates every aspect of life. Godliness affects everything: our view of self, marriage, parenting, business, civic responsibilities, environmental outlook, relationship with our next-door neighbors. Nothing escapes godliness; it covers everything.

Godliness is not limited only to the present; it also extends to our life to come: **Godliness [holds] promise for both the present life and the life to come**. It does not matter if a person invests in physical exercise or careful dietary plans. Inevitably, death confronts us. Jesus addressed this truth when he said, "What good is it for a man to gain the whole world, yet forfeit his soul?" (Mark 8:36). What we become in this life we carry into eternity.

4:9–10. Spiritual growth and nourishment and disciplines for godliness do not exist in a vacuum. They must be grounded in the living Christ. Paul underscored this idea by stating, **This is a trustworthy saying that deserves full acceptance**. This is the thing for which the apostles and followers of Christ **labor and strive**. They had one purpose in their work. They committed themselves to one urgent and pressing goal—the spread of the gospel.

Their hope was not in performance, legalisms, or mere talk. The touchstone of faith for all who believe is that **hope** is placed **in the living God, who is the Savior of all men**. The God we follow is living, interactive, and present in our lives. Our confidence rests in a God who is ever-living.

Since only God is the Savior of all people, only one message brings hope to the human condition. If there is only one way by which people can be saved into a new realm of God's rule and righteousness, then it is imperative that we tell others about this way.

Although God is the Savior of all, not everyone will be saved. Abiding trust is the requisite for such salvation. He is the Savior **especially of those who believe**. There will be those who refuse, some who cling to idols. They will fulfill Jonah's ancient and prophetic voice, "Those who cling to worthless idols forfeit the grace that could be theirs" (Jon. 2:8).

Those who put their hope in the living God acknowledge the truth and embrace the truth. They believe that "Jesus is the Christ, the Son of God" and know that "by believing [they] have life in his name" (John 20:31). We do not believe and then add works to our faith, just to make sure. We do not believe and then make up additional rules for righteousness. We put full trust in Christ, resting in his righteousness.

Our spiritual discipline and godly training are designed not to gain favor with God but to reinforce our trust in him.

4:11. Paul's instruction was for Timothy and all church leaders to **command and teach** others about the Savior. Grace is no side issue. Legalism is no weak enemy. Rules are great for discipline but not for righteousness.

3. Conduct (4:12)

4:12. Chronological age does not necessarily bring spiritual maturity (Heb. 5:11–14). Deep devotion and spiritual strength as well as apathy and weakness can be found among young and old alike. Paul's encouragement to Timothy, **Don't let anyone look down on you because you are young,** should remind us that the issue for leadership is never age but spiritual development. True spiritual progress is more than exegetical expertise; it is marked by exemplary conduct and love.

But whatever the response of those around us, age is never an excuse for speaking or leading. As Christians we are to **set an example in speech, in life, in love, in faith and in purity.**

Speech and **life** encompass the observable aspects of life. It is how we conduct ourselves. Speech is a valid indicator of a person's character, "for out of the overflow of the heart the mouth speaks" (Matt. 12:34). Of course, the point is not to muzzle our mouths, for we can be silent and very wicked. The principle is to pursue Christ so diligently that the inner spirit is purified, producing only good and appropriate things to say. The same is true of our outward acts, our lifestyle.

Faith and **love** are the essence of the Christian life. Faith is our knowledge and confidence in Christ, our deep reliance on what he has done and what he declares as truth. Love is the Holy Spirit's action in our life, the evidence of our relationship with the God who rules.

Purity refers to sexual conduct and integrity of heart. Sexuality seems to be a mysterious picture of our relationship to God. God is very particular about how we treat our bodies and honor others. Sexual purity is a symbol of spiritual consecration. Misconduct in this area of life ruins fellowship with Christ and destroys a person's influence and reputation with others.

Authentic spirituality cannot be separated from inner righteousness. Christianity which is honest and genuine envelopes the entire person, from inner heart and spirit to outward behavior.

4. Worship (4:13)

4:13. Paul told Timothy to give his energies to the **public reading of Scripture, to preaching and to teaching** when the church came together.

The **public reading of Scripture**, along with **teaching**, was an accepted custom of the Jews in the synagogues (Acts 13:15). This practice is carried over to Christian worship. Reading God's Word is a command for church life, but God does allow flexibility in how services are conducted. There are many variations and styles of worship which may be used, as long as they point to Christ and his grace. But within stylistic and cultural preferences, there are certain essentials that must undergird worship. One of these essentials is the public reading of Scripture.

The Word of God is powerful (Heb. 4:12); creates change (Isa. 55:11); is essential for life (Deut. 8:3). Too often our familiarity with the Bible causes us to forget that these written words contain the very breath of God—his wisdom and intelligence, yearnings, energy, strategies, and humor. The Bible is a bit of the mind and personality of God laid open for us.

The public reading of God's Word prepares our minds and hearts for the preaching or teaching which follows. The Holy Spirit acts through the revealed truth which God has given. As the church reads and affirms what God has declared, the Spirit is freed to instruct, convict, and guide.

The public reading of Scripture also hedges the church against error. The problems facing Timothy and the Ephesians centered on false teaching. The corporate reading of truth is a defense against falsehood.

Preaching (exhorting) and **teaching** (explaining) are also essentials of public worship. **Preaching** deals with encouragement, exhortation, and warnings from which the preacher intends to elicit a response from the hearers. **Teaching** is regarded as instructional. A teacher explains the principles of Scripture in more intellectual terms.

The point is not to create some rigid rules, but to understand that both teaching and preaching are Spirit-given gifts which must be exercised for the good of the fellowship of believers.

5. Spiritual gifts and God's call (4:14)

4:14. Although this verse is an intensely personal message to Timothy regarding his spiritual gift, the same directive can be leveled to all Christians, especially those who lead: **Do not neglect your gift.**

Each Christian leader has been specifically gifted in some way by God for ministry. The peculiar ability is given for the benefit of the church. With the gift comes a God-exacted responsibility which cannot be shunned.

The gift Paul referred to here was some capability which Timothy was given. This was not some inherent ability. It came **through a prophetic message when the body of elders laid their hands on you.** It seems likely that this was Timothy's ordination into ministry, a ceremony of approval by mature Christian leaders signified by the laying on of hands. This was an affirmation of God's call upon Timothy's life for special ministry to God and his church. It made him responsible to both—the God who called him and the people whom he served.

6. Endurance (4:15)

4:15. Having outlined what is required for being a good minister before God and his people—what, in fact, is involved in true Christian living—Paul told Timothy to **be diligent** in all these things. The word **diligence** means "to keep at it," "to practice with serious intent." This is not a once-in-a-while proposition. This is day-to-day dedication.

Paul reinforced this appeal: **give yourself wholly to [these matters]**. Literally this means, "be in these." Live them, breathe them, immerse yourself in them. This is your *life*, not a job. As Thomas Carlyle said, "No man ever became a saint in his sleep." This admonition was directed toward all who claim to be followers of Christ. Such a life does not happen automatically without concerted effort and desire. As Jesus said, "If you hold to my teaching, you are really my disciples" (John 8:31). A true follower or disciple of Christ abides, or lives, in what Jesus taught.

If we live in God's teaching, pursuing him every waking moment, **everyone [will] see your progress**. A life growing progressively close to God, dynamically changing, cannot be hidden. Christianity is not a matter of creed but of life.

Timothy was to lead the way by pouring himself into Christian life and ministry. The church would respond because it would see **progress**, the authentic presence of Christ in his people.

4:16. Paul recapped what he has just written in detail: **watch your life and doctrine closely**. Ultimately, Timothy could effectively control only himself. We are the only person over whom we have immediate authority. My ability to lead and influence others is connected to my ability to manage and live my own life well. The Christian life hinges on conduct (life) as empowered by God's Spirit and correct faith (doctrine).

Paul could not emphasize it enough: **persevere in [Christian life and doctrine]**. Perseverance is evidence of salvation; a disciplined person is willing to continue in God's way. Such commitment will be tried again and again.

The result of such continuance and devotion is that it would **save both yourself and your hearers**. Salvation is a process. It has a beginning point at conversion and its full realization when we are united with Christ. In between is the process of becoming more Christlike in our person and behavior. Exemplary living and God's truth will safeguard the leader and those whom he leads. A leader's perseverance in godliness will save his congregation from the dangers of false teachings which can shipwreck faith and cause ruin to the soul.

MAIN IDEA REVIEW: *The outward life of a person flows from his or her inner spirit. Those who discipline themselves to follow after Jesus Christ, who are focused on living out the truth of God's revelation, will develop a life of growing intimacy with Christ. They will delight God, producing goodness and godliness in what they do.*

III. CONCLUSION

Snub Clubs

People sometimes form little clubs to exclude people who do not share the same secrets or have the same knowledge as the club founders. It can become a matter of pride that they know a little more than others do, and they do not hesitate to flaunt their superiority.

Some "clubs," founded on personal interpretations of Scripture, criticize those who do not use the same terminology or quote the same experts as the club members.

In this chapter Paul warned Timothy to beware of those who do not stick with the mission of the church. The church's task is to build maturity into believers so they can live worthy of the God who has called them and extend the gospel to those who have not heard. This alone builds unity in Christ's church.

Church unity is important in God's eyes. He desires that believers unite within his Spirit:

- No clubs,
- One church,
- One family,
- One Spirit.

PRINCIPLES

- Legalisms and rules are always an easy way to distort grace and give ourselves some credit.
- Believers are called to have a training strategy for developing godliness in their lives.
- Man-made opinions and "godless myths and old wives' tales" can distract us from the truths of the faith if we are not well-rooted in Scripture.
- The young can have positive influence and leadership positions in the church as long as they live exemplary Christian lives.
- All followers should nurture and use the gifts given to them by the Holy Spirit in order to serve others.

APPLICATIONS

- Through God's Spirit we should find the liberty that sets us free from all the roles that we think earn us a righteous standing before God.
- It is good for every Christian to stay in shape physically, but it is far more important to exercise ourselves toward spiritual maturity.
- Church leaders should shepherd toward vocational ministry all those in the church who have an interest in studying and teaching the Scriptures.
- Perseverance and faithfulness are characteristic of those who are determined to follow Christ—practicing candor, accountability, prayer, and spiritual disciplines.

IV. LIFE APPLICATION

Swimming with the Orcas

Summer was officially underway. Memorial Day had been blistering hot, so Bryan rented a kayak, then hopped a ferry to San Juan Island, one of the larger spots within Washington State's San Juan archipelago. After pitching his tent, he launched his kayak into the soft ripples of Haro Strait. It was a warm evening, and the mild breezes off the water felt good after the day's heat.

Though not an expert kayaker, Bryan was in good health and fit. He stowed his life jacket under the shock cords in front of him and headed toward Limekiln Park, a favorite place for viewing orcas.

When he arrived, a pod of seven whales surfaced, including a young calf. People on shore watched as Bryan maneuvered in among them. One of the whales breached very close to the solitary kayaker several times. The orcas rolled, shot their heads above the water, and leaped into the air.

The sun began to set, but enough daylight lingered in the sky so that the crowd on the beach could see Bryan paddle toward open water along with the whales. Eventually the evening gave way to the blackness of a moonless night.

Early the following morning, Bryan's empty kayak was recovered six and a half miles south of Limekiln Point, his life jacket still secured to the kayak. A search and rescue effort was mounted, but Bryan's body was never found. (Matt Broze and George Gronseth, *Sea Kayaker, Deep Trouble*, [Camden, Maine: Ragged Mountain Press, 1997]).

It is easy to be deceived. Most likely Bryan anticipated a summer evening of easy paddling upon the inland waters between San Juan and Vancouver

Islands. The tides were not tricky; the breezes remained mild; the sun was shining; the orcas were playing—nothing appeared alarming. Yet Bryan ventured into waters he was ill-equipped to handle. Worse, he paddled in among untamed animals whose instincts for self-protection and survival outweighed Bryan's apparent innocence. The thrill of being among these beautiful, leaping giants dulled Bryan's alertness to the danger around him.

In this chapter, Paul repeatedly warns Timothy about the dangers of veering off course, the hazards of wandering into intriguing but pointless arguments and theological conjectures. New ideas may seem harmless, confined to philosophical jousting and talk, but deviations from orthodoxy prove not only powerful (**some will abandon the faith**, 4:1) but diabolical (**coming from deceiving spirits and things taught by demons**, 4:1).

Like the calm, inviting waters of Haro Strait, deception presents itself in appealing ways. Often, false ideas seem reasonable, charming us through a universal desire to earn approval through personal effort. Paul points out that those who **forbid people to marry and order them to abstain from certain foods** are actually promoting false ideas, beckoning others to follow. Such restrictions, if followed, don't seem that harmful. Certainly they don't smack of heresy or the terrors of divine disapproval; yet Paul forcefully and repeatedly issues warnings against paddling in among these "wild" ideas. Allowing ourselves to toy with, or practice, a few of these deviations, sets us on a dangerous course toward the open waters of spiritual ruin.

Paul remains adamant—**set an example . . . in speech, in life, in love, in faith and in purity . . . devote yourself to the public reading of Scripture, to preaching and to teaching**(4:12,13). And, at the conclusion of this chapter, he stresses to Timothy: **Watch your life and doctrine closely. Persevere in them, because if you do, you will save both yourself and your hearers** (4:16).

However fascinating a new fad may be, however benign a practice may appear, Christians who venture into uncharted ideas risk their spiritual lives upon the hidden shoals of false doctrine and among the predators who promise new experiences. Christians must devote themselves to the orthodox beliefs and observances which the Scriptures promote and the Holy Spirit empowers.

V. PRAYER

Giver of good gifts, by your Spirit open my eyes to the bountiful goodness which surrounds me—simple things which you provide, such as sleep, food, a soul at peace. Protect me from the arrogance which assumes I have gained my possessions, my friends, my family, my job. Then from my heart I will give genuine thanks for your mercy and kindness. Amen.

VI. DEEPER DISCOVERIES

A. Last Days (v. 1)

Eschatology is the study of "the last days," or end times. Many books on the subject are sold, and alarmist theories are invented regularly. Each crisis in the Middle East produces another batch of books that quickly become outdated because the author's predictions failed. Even the movie industry borrows names associated with the final days of earth, such as apocalypse or Armageddon. There is a fascination with things considered mysterious or cataclysmic.

But all the attention, and especially the misunderstandings associated with the last days, makes many people cynical. The truth of Scripture is thrown in with all the false prophecies and imagery and is equally discounted. We need to hear God on the matter. We can be sure of at least these truths about the end times:

- The "last days" began when Christ left earth after his resurrection.
- Nobody knows when Christ is coming back. No group or individual has an inside path on when the end will come. Even Jesus said that he did not know the day or the hour of his return. Only the Father knows.
- God always calls us to righteousness and light in the midst of darkness, to holiness in a world that turns away from him. We are to remain faithful until Christ returns.
- We are to live as if every day could be our last, honoring Christ as Lord and fully expecting his return at any moment.
- We are to live fully engaged in the world. We are not to hibernate or separate ourselves from the normal interactions of life. God desires that Christians influence the world for him, even as the world becomes more sinful and opposed to the truth. People are his first love. They are the objects of his salvation. God delays his return in Christ because he loves his creation, the people he made. He calls us to share that love until he comes.

B. Asceticism (vv. 1–3)

Paul began chapter 4 of 1 Timothy with a scathing description of people who teach false ideas in the guise of truth. He called them hypocritical liars, people without conscience, followers of demonic speculations. Yet when Paul described their teachings, he pointed to two practices which seem rather unexceptional: forbidding people to marry and abstaining from certain foods.

What Paul detected in these teachings, however, was an attack upon the person of God and his grace toward mankind. In his own time, it was the possible infiltration of an early expression of gnosticism which posed a threat.

Christianity and gnosticism use some of the same imagery. Both speak of the tension between light and darkness, good and evil, life and death, spirit and flesh, God and the world. These similarities of language and outlook made gnosticism a dangerous opponent of Christianity.

Both Christianity and gnosticism believed in the battle against good and evil and the necessity of the spirit overcoming the passions of the flesh. Some of the Ten Commandments relate to subduing the physical aspects of life. Jesus also called believers to deny self. Paul's letters are filled with instructions to put off the desires of the flesh, to focus on the spirit, to exercise self-discipline. Even so, there were crucial differences between Christianity and gnosticism.

Classic dualism views good and evil as essentially equal in power; the Christian truth acknowledges God as sovereign, even over the powers of darkness. Gnosticism also held all matter to be evil. This notion lay behind the false teachers forbidding marriage and the eating of particular foods. Paul refuted the idea in 1 Timothy 4:3–4, citing God as Creator of all matter.

Another critical difference between Christianity and gnosticism was the nature of man's redemption. The gnostic believed that man's true self, his soul, held a portion of divinity. They believed each person was essentially connected with primal man, or first man. Primal man's fallenness was inherited, but so was the spark of divinity which he had before his fall into darkness. This, too, has Christian overtones. However, for the gnostic, redemption came through man's refusal of all things associated with evil—namely, physical existence and matter. It was also achieved through man's personal efforts at maximizing his inherent spirituality.

In contrast, the Christian acknowledges that he cannot achieve spiritual life or maturity without the intervention of a personal God. Once God has renewed his spirit, the goal of the Christian is to extend this redemption to all the created order. The physical world is not to be shunned but rescued until that day when Christ himself will redeem his world.

Paul kept current with the philosophies and religious thinking of his time. Those philosophical systems which contained resemblances of Jewish or Christian faith posed the greatest threat because they easily infiltrated and polluted the singular Christian outlook. By knowing the popular theories of life, origins, and ultimate purpose, he was able to detect deviations from truth and protect the purity of the gospel. We must also proclaim and live the righteousness of Christ.

VII. TEACHING OUTLINE

A. INTRODUCTION

1. Lead story: Hoopster Par Excellence
2. Context: In this chapter, Paul assured Timothy that the opposition and difficulties he was facing in Ephesus were to be expected, since these were the end times. The false teachers were to be resisted and exposed for the heresy they peddled. To stand firm in such an environment, Timothy must pursue Christ diligently, keeping his gospel pure.
3. Transition: People are always attracted to rules and human effort to achieve, often carrying this over into their practice of religion. It is easier to follow strict rules and feel we have contributed to our own salvation than it is to admit our helplessness and inability to gain God's approval. This is both the attraction and danger of legalism. But the life of faith cannot be condensed into lists and rules. It demands a personal relationship with God first. Out of this relationship will come the desire and the discipline to follow his will.

B. COMMENTARY

1. Days of Trouble (4:1–5)
   a. Timing (4:1)
   b. The teachers (4:1–2)
   c. False teaching (4:3)
   d. Correct teaching (4:4–5)
2. The Good Minister of Christ Jesus (4:6–16)
   a. The good minister (4:6)
   b. Warnings and directions (4:7–11)
   c. Conduct (4:12)
   d. Worship (4:13)
   e. Spiritual gifts and God's call (4:14)
   f. Endurance (4:15)

C. CONCLUSION: SWIMMING WITH THE ORCAS

VIII. ISSUES FOR DISCUSSION

1. Do you see any connection between Paul's warnings about the last days and what is happening around us today? Give some examples.

2. Are there rules in your life which God did not make? Do you think you need to reevaluate these rules in light of this chapter?
3. In what ways will good spiritual training help you avoid deviant doctrines? Which is harder for you to maintain—spiritual or physical training? Why?
4. Identify and discuss your spiritual gifts and how you can use them for the good of others and the church.

1 Timothy 5

Relationships and Responsibilities Within the Church

"*I*f we love, we can never observe the other person with detachment, for he is always and at every moment a living claim to our love and service."

Dietrich Bonhoeffer

1 Timothy 5

IN A NUTSHELL

*C*hapter 5 has specific instructions about how the pastor should relate to the various people within the church. Paul described worthy and unworthy widows and the church's responsibility for them. Then he called the church to honor its pastors, gave Timothy some medical advice, and concluded with another comment about people's character.

Relationships and Responsibilities Within the Church

I. INTRODUCTION

Just the Facts, Ma'am

*J*ournalism has always claimed unbiased reporting. Though in recent years the media's image has suffered, the common perception of its objectivity continues to preserve its force in public life as the guardian of truth and distributor of information.

But the nagging question persists about whether a journalist can be impartial. Behind every report, from the simplest to the most complex, is a grid of values, intentions, and assumptions held by the reporter. It is this matrix which determines the tone as well as the inclusion or exclusion of events, interviews, and background information. Add to this mix the drive to track down something the reporter suspects is true, and objectivity all but disappears.

But the journalist is not alone in this tangle of fact, opinion, and desire. We all filter our choices through an intricate system of preferences, values, emotions, and experiences.

How, then, are we to understand Paul's insistence on objectivity—his command to avoid all favoritism?

As imitators of a God who acts consistently with his nature, we are under obligation to live from the power of his indwelling character in us (Eph. 6:9; Col. 3:25). Expediency, personality, position, or public pressure should never sway a Christian's decision or weaken his resolve to do what is right (Jas. 2:1,9).

In writing to Timothy, Paul gave parameters for enacting justice within the church, providing safeguards against personal opinion and politics. Whether it is interpersonal relationships, extending financial aid to the needy, investigating accusations against a leader, or disciplining someone who has sinned, impartial judgment is required because we act on behalf of God.

Anticipating the temptation to compromise, Paul demanded a detachment from the opinions of others and even from ourselves. He emphasized personal responsibility and godliness as the foundations for distributing Christian compassion and mercy without prejudice.

II. COMMENTARY

MAIN IDEA: *The leader must be exemplary in his interpersonal behavior, associating with all age groups and economic classes, modeling truth and godliness with dignity and grace. The church also has responsibilities toward its members, particularly in providing for widows and leaders. Church benevolence and support must adhere to strict guidelines.*

A The Church Leader's Relationships (5:1–2)

SUPPORTING IDEA: *Throughout the Bible various metaphors are applied to the church to emphasize particular qualities. In these verses Paul described the relationship between the pastor and the members of his congregation in terms of a family. As a family unit, believers are to interact with love and honor.*

5:1. People are sensitive to their own weaknesses. Drawing attention to their failings is often painful. Even so, a pastor must not shrink from the obligation to exhort and correct. The heart of the pastor and the manner in which he approaches others is crucial determining whether the rebuke and guidance will be positive or counterproductive. When done in a judgmental or heartless way, rebuke can cause more harm than good. This is why Paul gave careful instruction on how a leader should approach the people under his care.

He told Timothy and all pastors to teach or correct **an older man . . . as if he were your father.** In the West we have tried to obliterate generational differences through a familiarity which borders on presumption. But Paul wisely counseled a respect for age. Honoring a person because of age does not mean the pastor holds back correction when needed. But he should exercise correction in a gentle and respectful manner and not with authoritarian coldness. The same holds true in dealing with **older women** who are to be treated **as mothers.**

The pastor will also have to interact with peers or those younger than himself. In those situations he should **treat younger men as brothers.** The pastor should not be condescending. Rather, this is a call to mutual respect and equality. The same applies in dealing with **younger women** whom the pastor is to treat **as sisters, with absolute purity.**

The additional clause is a reminder that the pastor must be above all suspicion sexually and relationally with those under his care. In his letters, Paul recognized women friends, but as always their friendship was centered in ministry. Lydia was a great help to the church and to Paul personally (Acts 16:14–15), and several women in the closing chapter of Romans were thanked for their hard work (Rom. 16:3–15). Paul's warning to Timothy was that the pastor must not take advantage of his position and compromise the name of Christ.

B Specific Care for Widows (5:3–16)

SUPPORTING IDEA: *God always cares for those who exist on the margins of society. He has established certain structures, the church and family, to provide help and compassion for those who are left alone. But each party has specific responsibilities in receiving and enacting God's provision.*

1. Defining widows (5:3–4)

5:3. Paul launched into a detailed explanation about the care of widows. Why were widows such a major concern? There were some abuses occurring within the church which needed correction. Paul was simply exposing the nature of God, whom the church is to model—a nature which has always demonstrated compassion for the powerless.

Paul began his discussion by urging the church to **give proper recognition** (honor) **to . . . widows.** This refers to financial or material support and care. The same word is used later in 1 Timothy 5:17 in reference to paying pastors. But being a widow was not the only criterion that qualified a person for financial support by the church. They must be **widows who are really in need,** widows in the full sense of the word. These must be women who were totally alone in the world, who were without resources.

5:4. True need is the starting point for any church considering the support of a widow. The church is under no obligation to care for widows who have family members still living: **if a widow has children or grandchildren, these should learn first of all to put their religion into practice by caring for their own family.**

Asian and African cultures, with their inclusion of extended family and cross-generational relationships, have a much better understanding of family cohesion and care than do Western societies. Our idolizing of independence often severs us from the sense of gratitude and long-term reciprocity which God intends for a family.

While no parent invests time and energy into raising children simply to be repaid for it, the ties and obligations of family relationships do not rest entirely upon parents. Children and grandchildren have the opportunity to give back time, love, and material support. They should also grow up with the expectation that this is their privilege and duty, especially to those widowed within their family. The church should be vocal and supportive in instilling these values in children and grandchildren.

It is to our shame that in Western nations the children often leave parents to their own devices or to social welfare programs. It certainly should not be so among God's people.

Paul understood that those who gave proper care to their family had **put their religion into practice,** and **this is pleasing to God.** This is the practicality of faith, the essence of belief, for God tells us to honor our parents (Deut. 5:16; Eph. 6:1–2). This is one way in which we carry out our trust in God's values.

2. Worthy and unworthy widows (5:5–6)

5:5. Having distinguished between widows according to need, Paul focused on a widow's spiritual state. In this way he further limited the conditions under which the church could use its financial resources.

Paul began with what might be termed "the worthy widow." This was a woman destitute, **who is really in need and left all alone.** Once again he called attention to her circumstances, her lack of resources both financial (v. 3) and familial (v. 4). But even these were not enough to commend her for church support. The worthy widow was also a woman **who puts her hope in God.** This was evidenced as she **continues night and day to pray and to ask God for help.**

The limited resources of the church must be extended only to those who reflect the church's mission and spiritual communion with God. The worthy widow relied upon the grace of God, and in this hope she was confident of his provision. Day by day she waited persistently and expectantly for God's care.

5:6. In stark contrast, the unworthy widow was one **who lives for pleasure.** The church should not support such a widow, for she had invested her hope in this world. God stands aside and allows her desire; he expects the church to do the same. She will be granted her pleasure, however long it may last and whatever results it may reap. We can be certain, however, that it will not last long enough or bring fulfilling life, for she is pronounced **dead even while she lives.**

A widow like this becomes proof that the one who tries to "save his life will lose it, but whoever loses his life for me [Christ] will find it" (Matt. 16:25). The widow who lived selfishly, for her own pleasure, was not due the support of family or church. Helping her financially implied agreement and supported her in her waywardness.

3. Christian obligation (5:7–8)

5:7. Paul wanted Timothy to **give the people these instructions**; the entire congregation was in mind as he wrote. They were to understand thoroughly all his instructions **so that no one may be open to blame.**

5:8. One of the ways Paul wanted believers to be blameless, even to those outside the faith, was in family care. He returned again to the theme of verse 4, emphasizing that someone who **does not provide for his relatives**, particularly immediate family, **has denied the faith.** He may have had in mind the false teachers who were disparaging marriage (1 Tim. 4:3) and, by implication, the entire family structure with its duties and responsibilities.

There are different ways to disown the faith. A person can repudiate it outright or deny it by lifestyle. Titus 1:16 describes people who "claim to know God, but by their actions they deny him."

We must remember that these instructions were given to believers, followers of Jesus Christ. So if a widow had living relatives who were believers and they neglected to care for her, the church was not simply to pick up the slack and assume the family's responsibility. The first thing the church should do was to correct the family and hold it accountable for its lack of love, its irresponsibility, and the damage it incurred against the reputation of the church. Any family member who neglected his first obligation to family **has denied the faith and is worse than an unbeliever.**

4. Qualifications for church-supported ministry (5:9–10)

5:9–10. Apparently there was a **list of widows** in the early church. This list registered widows who had dedicated themselves to ministry in such a way that they qualified for financial support by the church. As with any person dedicated to service (like pastors and deacons), certain characteristics must be evident in the candidate.

In regard to widows dedicated to service, she was to be **over sixty.** This was considered the age of retirement in the first century. Also, in contrast to the younger women addressed in verse 11 and following, being over sixty would typically have placed these women past the "marriageable" age. This would have safeguarded them from abandoning their commitment to ministry.

A widow was also to have **been faithful to her husband** when he was alive. Literally, she was to be known as a "one-man woman." Does this mean that a woman was unqualified for church-supported ministry if she had been married twice? This seems unlikely or Paul's encouragement to younger widows to remarry would have disqualified them for this special service in their older years. Instead, being a "one-man woman" speaks of faithfulness and loyalty. This is reminiscent of the qualifications for elders and deacons in 1 Timothy 3:2,12.

In addition, the widow was to be **well known for her good deeds**. Paul then provided a partial list of these deeds, none of which required exceptional Christian faith and courage. But this is the glory of the gospel and of Christ among us. He honors even the common activities of daily life.

The widow's good deeds included **bringing up children**, caring for their physical and spiritual welfare and development. Her life must be characterized by **hospitality**, the opening of her home to strangers and to those in need. Paul also included in his list **washing the feet of the saints**. Foot washing was a job usually reserved for slaves, but these women followed in the way of Christ, who exalted this dirty and lowly task, sanctifying it as an expression of love (John 13:4–15).

The widow was also to have a reputation for helping people in distress. Paul concluded with a catchall phrase that covered anything deemed good: she was to be known for **helping those in trouble and . . . all kinds of good deeds**.

These are not the traits recommended for women within the pages of popular women's magazines. But God's ways are not our ways. They often run counter to our natural inclinations. All these qualities portray a woman with an open heart and home, given to the care of others in the name of Christ. They are the qualities which bring joy and purpose to life.

These descriptions were meant as a guideline for churches helping widows. They are also a reminder of what God sees as virtues in any woman, indeed, in any follower. True faith shows in loyalty and love—especially at home but also in service to others.

Paul's statements also make a strong argument against applying a retirement mentality to Christian living. Service to Christ and others is not reserved for the young. In fact, physically and mentally capable people entering retirement often have more discretionary time to devote to church ministry, teaching, discipling, and missions.

5. Younger widows (5:11–15)

5:11–12. In case the church was tempted to overlook the first qualification for the registry of widows, Paul emphasized the age factor by stating, **do not put [younger widows] on such a list**. Paul's overriding concern was for the reputation and welfare of the believing community, the church. It was this passion which drove his instructions about younger widows.

Paul recognized that people go through different stages of life. Desires and ambitions have a tendency to change as we grow older. His first observation was that **when their sensual desires overcome their dedication to Christ, [young widows] want to marry**.

This may be the simple recognition that sexual desires are more active in younger women. Paul gave similar advice in 1 Corinthians 7:8–9. It is possible that after dedicating themselves to service in the church they become restless in their singleness. Passions and personal desire grow strong. They turn away from their commitment to Christ and his church to get married. By rejecting this first pledge (either of ministry or faith) **they bring judgment on themselves.** First Corinthians 7:32–35 is a good companion text for understanding Paul's view of marriage and its obligations.

5:13. Another reason Paul wanted younger widows excluded from the list of widows was because they **get into the habit of being idle.** They become **gossips and busybodies, saying things they ought not to.**

These women appeared to have no strong purpose in life. In vivid contrast to the widow given to prayer and good deeds (vv. 5,10), these women tended to waste their time. Rather than busy themselves in works of service, speaking encouragement and directing others to Christ, they were busy in everyone's affairs, running here and there, exchanging stories. They spread not love and faith but selfishness and distrust.

5:14. In order to protect younger women from falling in with the general Ephesian population of gadabouts, Paul advised **younger widows to marry, to have children, to manage their homes.**

This is not settling for second best, for Paul had already commended the faith of others as exhibited in these same engagements of life—a good home, well-trained children. It is in these areas that God's kingdom can take hold and spread and so allow **the enemy no opportunity for slander.** Channeling the energies of the individual believer to good works robbed Satan of the chance to infiltrate the heart and thinking of these young women; the church was then free from disgrace before the unbelieving community.

5:15. Sadly, casualties of the faith always exist. Though true doctrine is guarded, correction is given, and love is extended, still there will be those who **turn away to follow Satan.**

Following Satan can take many forms. It could be that these women were the same as those in 2 Timothy 3:6 who were "weak-willed" and "loaded down with sins" and so became swayed by the false teachers. Paul labeled these false doctrines as demonic (1 Tim. 4:1). It may also be that the women became enamored with society's values and its pleasures. But there is no middle ground in life: "friendship with the world is hatred toward God" (Jas. 4:4); "If anyone loves the world, the love of the Father is not in him" (1 John 2:15); Paul delivers the unfaithful over to Satan, the world system (1 Tim. 1:19–20).

5:16. Paul concluded the section on widows by drawing a line back to the family. Women are not just recipients of welfare; they may also be the deliverers of compassion. If a believing woman has widows in her family, **she should help them and not let the church be burdened.**

The church, then, is not to give indiscriminate handouts. Each family bears the primary responsibility for providing for its own "needy." The church should not weaken this God-given duty by assuming the care of everyone.

Nor is need alone sufficient reason for financial support. For the sake of the church's reputation, the church should give financial backing only to those who exhibit true need along with spiritual maturity and service. By implication, since the church is obligated to care for these people, the name of Christ is dishonored if this duty is neglected.

Paul gave directives for a purposeful life: an older widow's good deeds, a younger woman's godly home. God and his church confirm the significance of every person, regardless of age, sex, or marital status.

God has set forth a welfare structure of compassion which guards against abuse, recognizes true need, and affirms the dignity and value of each individual.

Special Counsel About Pastors (5:17–25)

> **SUPPORTING IDEA:** *Managing church leadership requires a balance of respect, impartiality, and appropriate discipline. It requires a recognition and appreciation for hard work and caution in appointing people to such a vital task.*

1. Recognition of church leaders (5:17–18)

5:17. Some people read this verse and think it refers to two groups of elders: the administrators **who direct the affairs of the church well,** and **those whose work is preaching and teaching.** Most likely, however, Paul was speaking of pastors in general. Teaching was a task for all pastors (1 Tim. 3:2).

The more important point, however, was that those pastors who apply themselves to their job should do it well. Those who serve faithfully before God are deserving of **double honor.**

"Double honor" could mean they deserved twice as much pay, but this poses some difficulties: double what he got last year? double someone else who did not do as well? double from the church down the road? double what he expected? Paul probably intended that the pastor receive honor in double form: through fair pay and the respect and obedience of the congregation.

Certainly he was eager that the church recognize the dignity and value of the pastor who did his job conscientiously (1 Tim. 3:1). The word **work,** used in conjunction with preaching and teaching, emphasizes energy, labor, working to the point of weariness. At the same time, the church must respect the life of their pastor by protecting him from overwork and low pay.

5:18. To give biblical credence to Paul's claim that a pastor should be given an honorable wage, he cited two scriptural precedents representative of all the created order. The first comes from the law: **do not muzzle an ox**

(Deut. 25:4); the second points to Jesus' teaching: **the worker deserves his wages** (Luke 10:7).

2. Protection and correction of leaders (5:19–20)

5:19. Because leaders are always more open to unfair criticisms, gossip, and allegations, **no accusation** against a pastor or elder should be considered **unless it is brought by two or three witnesses.** The roots of this counsel are founded in the timeless wisdom of God as given to ancient Israel (Deut. 19:15). It was confirmed by Jesus (Matt. 18:15–17) and Paul (see also 2 Cor. 13:1).

Stories abound about churches where one person made an accusation against a pastor or leader. The word spread and, like "feathers thrown to the wind," could never be recaptured even though the claim was untrue. Paul's instruction here is a wise way to approach any damaging claims against another person.

5:20. But there may be occasions when a church leader is found guilty of sin. If so, that leader is **to be rebuked publicly, so that the others may take warning.** The rebuke is intended to produce repentance in the sinner and to emphasize to the congregation the seriousness of sin. It is also a statement regarding the influence of a leader and how his actions affect those under his care. With the hope that restoration will occur, those who have broken congregational trust must appear before those whom they have violated.

This is another clear biblical directive that is often ignored today in deference to saving the offending person from embarrassment. It should not be so.

3. How to lead leaders (5:21–22)

5:21. The temptation for many people, even those in leadership, is to avoid the uncomfortable, especially when it involves disciplinary actions against a colleague. But Paul was unequivocal when he told Timothy to **keep these instructions without partiality, and to do nothing out of favoritism.** Objectivity and impartiality are important for a pastor if he is to lead well. The leader must exercise judgment in the same way that God discharges it— without favoritism.

Paul added special import to this instruction by giving his charge **in the sight of God and Christ Jesus and the elect angels.** Paul called as his witnesses God, the judge over all; Jesus Christ, the coming judge of the earth; and the elect angels, those who carry out the righteous judgments of God. Since the pastor and the church embody Christ in this present world, they must act in ways that do not compromise the nature of their Lord.

5:22. The undercurrent throughout this letter is unblemished Christian witness. This maintains its strength through pure doctrine and pure living. It almost seems unnecessary in view of all Paul has written that he should have to warn Timothy to **not be hasty in the laying on of hands.** The descriptions of false teachers and the list of qualifications for elders and deacons would seem to preclude hasty recruitment to the office of church leadership. But pressed by the necessity to fill jobs, or attracted by the personality of a candidate, churches sometimes minimize certain qualifications, gloss over "minor" problems, and become blind to potential difficulties. This is why Paul demanded impartiality when exercising leadership decisions. He also emphasized patient, careful selection of church leaders.

Paul ended this thought with a sober warning: **and do not share in the sins of others.** Careless selection of those called to represent God and his church can involve the appointing pastor in the sins of those selected. Through the laying on of hands, a leader identifies with the ordained person, touching him with blessing as well as approval. Haste or sloppiness in appointing people to ministry can also lead to personal compromise. What is overlooked in a fellow leader may be more easily excused in one's own life.

The conclusion of the matter? **Keep yourself pure.** This responsibility can never be delegated. Paul had already encouraged Timothy to "train [himself] to be godly" (1 Tim. 4:7). Each pastor, each professed believer, is responsible for his or her own soul in this area. The church and other Christians must help us in our spiritual journey, but we decide what disciplines will become part of our lives.

For example, there may be a wonderful health club just down the street from your house. It may offer the latest in diet plans, exercise equipment, and personal training. But if you do not take the time to eat the right foods, visit the club, or use the equipment, it will not make any difference in your life.

The same is true spiritually. A church can offer wonderful worship services, appropriate Bible classes, and spiritual mentoring, but we must take the personal steps toward growth. Attendance alone will never generate spiritual maturity.

4. Christian liberty (5:23)

5:23. After warning Timothy not to be dragged into the sins of others, Paul gave this young pastor a health tip: **stop drinking only water, and use a little wine because of your stomach and your frequent illnesses.** This sentence seems out of place, sandwiched between verses about sinfulness.

This verse should not be used as license to encourage the drinking of alcohol. It is more likely that, in order to clarify his directive for Timothy to keep himself pure, Paul put in this exception clause. He wanted to keep Timothy from being drawn into the same wrong thinking and practices as the false teachers who promoted a brand of asceticism (1 Tim. 4:2–3). Denial may have its place at times, but it is not law. Those who insist on particular codes of behavior without flexibility wander dangerously close to the legalism Jesus so vehemently opposed. Perhaps Timothy needed to be reminded of grace.

5. Reaping what we sow (5:24–25)

5:24–25. Everyone will realize the fruit of their life's efforts, whether good or ill, whether now or later.

Paul stated that **the sins of some men are obvious.** Some people are so given to sinful behavior that their sins precede them, **reaching the place of judgment ahead of them.** This phrase probably refers to the selection of church leaders. Some people are obviously unfit for the ministry.

Paul understood the human heart, so he warned Timothy that **the sins of others trail behind them.** These were people practiced in duplicitous living, who faked spirituality on the outside while a life of sin persisted within. That is why caution and patience is needed in appointing people to ministry. Time and observation will eventually reveal the inner spirit.

Whether sins are obvious or unseen, they do bear fruit. Our inner life cannot be totally hidden. Sin has a way of seeping out through attitude, careless speech, and unloving actions.

The flip side of this is that **in the same way good deeds are obvious.** Some people have a reputation for good deeds and service to others. Such individuals have passed some of the basic qualifications for church leadership. Even so, as Paul warned, caution is always in order and the candidate must meet all qualifications.

Other people are good in a quiet way, working behind the scenes. These good deeds, though unknown to others, **cannot be hidden.** Again, time will reveal them. Some people who seek church leadership may appear to fail the basic requirement of good deeds. Through patience their inner Christian character will be brought to light. True godliness cannot be kept secret.

Once again Paul restated a timeless principle: We reap what we sow. This is most often true in this life; it is unquestionably so in the life to come. God will reveal all that has been hidden, some for judgment, others for reward.

MAIN IDEA REVIEW: *The leader must be exemplary in his interpersonal behavior, associating with all age groups and economic classes, modeling truth and godliness with dignity and grace. The church also has responsibilities toward its members, particularly in providing for widows and leaders. Church benevolence and support must adhere to strict guidelines.*

III. CONCLUSION

Branches of a Family Tree

Most people do not know their great-grandfather's name. Few know what he looked like or how he made a living. Unless someone in the family is diligent in searching out relatives and creating a family tree, many of our relations are "lost," unknown to those born after them.

Fast-paced and frenetic, we disconnect from family, eager to branch out on our own. As the speed of change increases, so does fragmentation. Even if we remember family names, we have lost the cohesiveness which shared experiences and values bring. Each new generation has less understanding of those who preceded them.

Yet everyone is affected by the legacy of a family that stretches backward in time. Whether through genetic inheritance, habits, or collective experience, we are the combined result of many people through the years.

This can be for either good or ill. In this fifth chapter of 1 Timothy, Paul addressed many situations in terms of family—relationships within the church, the care of widows, the treatment of leaders by their congregation, or the reputation of the church. But for family to function at its best and provide a positive influence for the future, it must exhibit certain qualities:

- a deliberate respect and love for family members (5:1–2);
- a response of giving, compassion, and sacrifice (5:3–5);
- godly parameters for behavior (5:6,9–10,22);
- clear expectations, guidelines, and instructions (5:7,9–16,21);
- delineation of responsibilities for the common welfare (5:8);
- acknowledged methods and unbiased procedures of discipline (5:19–20); and
- celebration and reward for what is good (5:17–18,25).
- All these qualities contribute to the healthy functioning of the family. They also secure the future through a heritage of godliness.

How we live as individuals will affect those who come after us—our children, their children, and the spreading branches of our family tree. But we also influence those around us, either through works of goodness or selfishness, grafting new members into God's family or, through neglect, leaving them to wither and die. The church should model what a family ought to be, maintaining a rich heritage with secure roots that send out new branches to bud and grow into maturity.

PRINCIPLES

- Age deserves honor.
- Churches should teach the responsibility of the family to care for its own.
- The church should help take care of those believers in need who have no family to take care of them.
- Widows should aspire to godly living and service to others.

- Churches should pay their pastors fairly and give special honor to those who serve well.
- Pastors are accountable to the church.
- We will reap what we sow, sooner or later.

APPLICATIONS

- Church leaders should follow careful policies that guide their relationships with the opposite sex.
- Churches need a good system for caring for their elderly, widows, and other needy persons.
- It would be good for churches to have bylaws or policies for dealing with criticisms or charges made against their leaders.

IV. LIFE APPLICATION

Biology 101: Order and Disorder in the Body

In the dark inner world of our bodies there are billions of small, translucent globules crowded together, quivering like jellyfish. Each is a cell, capable of getting by on its own within the limits of its environment. These cells pulse and throb, push and bump, carrying out their jobs with common purpose—the health of the body.

There are times, however, when cells become renegades. Somewhere, quietly, a breakdown occurs. A cell reproduces beyond its borders and assumes control of an area for which it was not designed. It exceeds its function and purpose. Then, instead of contributing to our well-being, it becomes our enemy. Such cancers compress, push, shove, and displace good cells. If left unchecked, these ambitious cells can bring death, destroying the parent organism (us), and committing biologic suicide.

These same tendencies can extend to institutions. When Paul wrote to Timothy and the Ephesian church, he was careful to distinguish between the responsibilities and resources of the church and those of the family.

Both the church and the family have specific functions and limited resources. When one intrudes upon the other, a breakdown occurs. Neither the church nor the family functions in the way God intended. It brings weakness to both.

The church exists as God's holy community, his gathered witness to the world. Its primary function is to bring believers together for worship in order to honor Jesus Christ as Lord. The church is to teach biblical truth and hold believers accountable for their conduct and spiritual development. It is to function as a community of care for those who follow Christ. It is a gathering of diverse people drawn together and unified by their love and obedience to

Christ. Though the church is open to all people, its first obligation is to those who are followers of Christ.

God does not expect the church to meet every need in the world. When the church assumes responsibilities for which it was not designed, it is crippled. So is the institution whose duty it assumes.

Paul emphasized the need for the family to care for its own members, particularly widows. In our own day we might extend this family responsibility to providing spiritual training, education, and social activities.

None of these activities are wrong for the church. But a danger occurs when the church assumes the business for which the family was created. By releasing the family from more and more responsibilities, the very thing we wish to preserve and strengthen (the family) is weakened.

Perhaps the church should be putting back upon parents and families the obligations that God gave them. We should hold them accountable for the spiritual welfare and development of their children, the care and support of aging parents, and provision for family members without a job. When the church takes on these family responsibilities, the church is, in Paul's words, "burdened." In addition, the family becomes incompetent. The church and family might do better if the church would educate its members, provide ministry opportunities in which the entire family could participate, and then release them—to spend time together.

V. PRAYER

God of order and design, it is so easy to let others do for me what I should do for myself—to let the expert, the scholar, the organization shoulder my responsibilities; to quiver in the face of duty and feel inadequate. But you give ability and strength to meet the tasks you assign. Strengthen the church and the family to do their work well, supporting and strengthening each other. Amen.

VI. DEEPER DISCOVERIES

A. The Family (vv. 1–2)

The Scriptures often present the family as a model for community interaction and care. The Bible is filled with kinship terms that describe our relationship to God. We are to address him as "Our Father in heaven" (Matt. 6:9); he comforts "as a mother comforts her child" (Isa. 66:13); Jesus calls those who do his will his "brother and sister and mother" (Mark 3:35).

The Jews developed a family structure quite distinctive from some of the pagan cultures that surrounded them. From this Hebraic tradition the New Testament emerged, advancing upon the ancient understanding of family and elevating it to greater beauty and dignity. The character of God is delivered to us through the tribe, the clan, the family. He is revealed in the folkish mingling of love, nurture, discipline, and provision; the blending of sacrifice, heartache, tenderness, companionship, and inheritance.

Jesus brings to completeness what had been shadowed in God's interactions with Israel. He gives to those who believe in him the fullness of family, of community. As his sons and daughters, Christians participate in the love, sacrifice, companionship, and inheritance of God. As his children, we receive his discipline, tenderness, nurture, and provision. This same relational interplay is handed on to the church—as the family of God.

With these Jewish sensitivities and understandings about family, Paul wrote to Timothy about relationships within the church. That is why leaders are to treat older men with dignity and honor, to respect older women for their experience, age, and service. Relationships within the home are to teach leaders how to treat younger men as peers and younger women as sisters. We are family.

If we could grasp the implications of this, it would make a big difference in the witness of the church in society. If we would take it to heart and act on the full range of what a family is to be, the church and its people would be strengthened, and the power of God's love would be unleashed in the world.

B. Widows (vv. 3–16)

We gain our sense of place and our ability to function in the world primarily through our associations. The most powerful of these are family and culture. Without some connection to a group or community, our sense of our own humanity fails; we feel ill defined. Yet in all societies there are people who live on its margins. These people are defined not by their attachments but by their lack of attachment. In the Bible, these include the widow, the orphan, and the alien.

These people are utterly alone, isolated from cultural care, protection, and meaning. They are cut off from their past, essentially homeless, and disconnected from the future. Society rarely knows what to do with them.

God describes himself as defending "the cause of the fatherless and the widow, and [loving] the alien, giving him food and clothing" (Deut. 10:18). The psalmist sang that God is "a father to the fatherless, a defender of widows," and that he "sets the lonely in families" (Ps. 68:5–6).

God instructed Israel to "not deprive the alien or the fatherless of justice, or take the cloak of the widow as a pledge. Remember that you were slaves in Egypt and the LORD your God redeemed you from there" (Deut. 24:17). He told his people to leave wheat in the fields, olives on the branches, grapes on the vines "for the alien, the fatherless and the widow" (Deut. 24:19–22).

Israel also had laws for the protection of the widow and her material support. Her care was primarily carried out through the family. Father, sons, and brothers were legally bound to provide for their widows. When these resources were unavailable or inadequate, the Jewish community was to come to her aid.

This same concept is carried into the new covenant. One of the first issues of concern for the early church was the care of widows (Acts 6:1–4). Out of a crisis came the appointment of godly men for the purpose of food distribution to widows. James wrote, "Religion that God our Father accepts as pure and faultless is this: to look after orphans and widows in their distress" (Jas. 1:27). Paul's instructions regarding the care of widows was a more extensive treatment for the church of what God had always purposed. In responding to a specific need, Paul reinforced God's timeless principles.

As a God of compassion, he provides for and protects those who are shunned or mistreated by society. He identifies with the poor, the widow, the orphan, the foreigner. He calls his people to do the same. In our own society these marginalized people may include the abused, the addict, the homeless, the divorced. Christians and the church are to go to these people in compassion, identifying with their poverty and homelessness. Remembering the depth of our own need, we go as ministers of a loving and generous Lord who redeemed us.

VII. TEACHING OUTLINE

A. INTRODUCTION
1. Lead Story: Just the Facts, Ma'am
2. Context: Paul wrote about relationships within the church, especially how a pastor relates to his congregation. Widows were given particular attention, with specific instructions for church care and support. The financial support of pastors was discussed as well.
3. Transition: Paul's instructions are valid for the modern church also. They remind the church of its responsibilities to its pastors and members. Godliness and service to others are the criteria for receiving church support and care.

B. COMMENTARY
1. The Church Leader's Relationships (5:1–2)
2. Specific Care for Widows (5:3–16)
   a. Defining widows (5:3–4)
   b. Worthy and unworthy widows (5:5–6)
   c. Christian obligation (5:7–8)

d. Qualifications for church supported ministry (5:9–10)

e. Younger widows (5:11–15)

3. Special Counsel About Pastors (5:17–25)

a. Recognition of church leaders (5:17–18)

b. Protection and correction of leaders (5:19–20)

c. How to lead leaders (5:21–22)

d. Christian liberty (5:23)

e. Reaping what we sow (5:24–25)

C. CONCLUSION: BIOLOGY 101: ORDER AND DISORDER IN THE BODY

VIII. ISSUES FOR DISCUSSION

1. In our society, what precautions must church leaders take in relating to the opposite sex?

2. What are some specific practices by which a pastor can show respect for older men and women in the church?

3. In what ways does your church help widows? Are there qualifications for receiving this help? How do you see the church fitting in with government assistance programs?

4. Are there widows in your own family who need help? What can you do for them?

5. What criteria should be used to determine if a pastor is doing his work well? What does God say about rewarding those who do? How does your church apply this principle? Do you regularly show your appreciation to those in leadership?

6. What kind of reputation do you think you have in your church? Is it different from your reputation in the community? at work?

1 Timothy 6

Finding Contentment in God

Quote

"*We* are to work, knowing that nothing of ultimate value can be gained because everything of real value has already been given."

J . A . Walter

1 Timothy 6

I N A N U T S H E L L

Many new believers in the first century were slaves. Paul, in an unexpected reversal, gave them strong words on how to treat their masters. He discussed again the important issues of false teachers and people who love controversies and endless arguments. Much of the rest of this practical chapter is about money—how to be content, to avoid the love-of-money trap, and what to pursue instead. Paul's closing challenges about faithfulness (vv. 13–16) and keeping the truth (vv. 20–21) should be posted in our homes and hearts.

Finding Contentment in God

I. INTRODUCTION

Cadillac Coffins

*T*he comedian Bill Cosby tells the story of a wealthy man's funeral arrangements. Upon the man's death his family bustled about to fulfill the man's requests, ordering the right flowers, pressing into service the right minister, selecting the proper hymns.

The day of his burial arrived. His prepared body was eased into a casket, then placed in a shiny, chrome-trimmed automobile—he was to be buried in his prized Cadillac.

As the funeral cortege slowly moved down the street, some children watching from the curb saw the Cadillac bearing the dead man. They gazed in admiration as one little boy remarked, "Man, that is livin'."

Escalating incomes, the rise of personal debt, and rampant consumerism seem to support the notion that life consists of stuff. It is summed up in the slogan, "He who dies with the most toys wins." Others smile and quip, "Money is not the most important thing, but it is way ahead of whatever is in second place."

Most people live by such a philosophy. If we examine our priorities and habits, we might be surprised at how this view of life has crept into our own thinking. You do not have to be rich to make riches a priority or to be captivated by wealth.

"I know," we sigh on our way to the store, "money does not buy happiness." But what, exactly, does it buy? What does a preoccupation with material goodies get us? Admittedly, a little more comfort. Most certainly, a lot more headaches. Without a doubt, loss in the life to come.

Paul was open and candid in this closing chapter of 1 Timothy. He addressed two groups of people who seemed to have nothing in common— the slave and the rich. Both ends of the social spectrum, and all those in between, need to understand that contentment is not found in circumstances or stuff. Peace of soul is found in pursuing godliness, in chasing after God.

II. COMMENTARY

MAIN IDEA: *For most people, becoming a Christian does not entail a dramatic change in occupation, living conditions, salary, or neighborhood. Christ calls us to extend his kingdom from the place we now occupy, whether as CEO, student, mother, clerk, or migrant farmer. Contentment, the pursuit of godliness, and bold identification with Christ are foundational to effective Christian living.*

Ⓐ Slaves and Masters (6:1–2)

SUPPORTING IDEA: *Becoming a follower of Christ does not release a person from obligations or unpleasant conditions. Instead, being a Christian presents us with a higher standard in all circumstances and relationships.*

6:1. Though Paul did not condone slavery (he condemned the slave trader along with murderers in 1 Tim. 1:9–10), it is clear that for Christians, social redemption is secondary to personal redemption. Cultural changes occur out of the transformation of individual lives and the witness of the church. This is why Paul could write that **all who are under the yoke of slavery should consider their masters worthy of full respect.**

Paul understood that if the gospel became identified with social upheaval, as in the freeing of slaves or even the emancipation of women, the Christian faith would be seen as a threat to the existing order and peace. This was, in fact, a common accusation leveled at Christians. Paul wanted to guard the reputation of the gospel as much as possible so the kingdom of God did not become entangled with the kingdoms of earth, thereby hindering the true message of Christ. Consequently, Paul told slaves to give respect to their masters, **so that God's name and our teaching may not be slandered.**

Paul knew that salvation is not wrapped up in the alteration of society. No lasting change is brought about by political agitation or revolution. Such approaches do not solve the dilemma of man's relationship to God or the eternal destiny of the soul. Cultural liberation can occur and stabilize only when the people within the culture have been deeply changed. Only spiritual revolution can secure this.

It is also a fundamental doctrine of the Christian faith that all people are equal before God. The cross of Christ is the great leveler, with the powerful and the powerless coming to salvation the same, simple way. And so, though it may seem scandalous to us, God longs for the salvation of the oppressor as much as the oppressed.

When a hierarchy of authority exists, whether in government, social relationships, jobs, or within the church, God always requires the giving of honor and respect to those in power. In our own time and culture, this could certainly be applied to employee and employer relations. It reflects the divine order of God as our head.

6:2. A new dimension is introduced when slave and slave owner are both Christians. Though Christian faith makes many proclamations about freedom (Luke 4:18–19; John 8:32; 2 Cor. 3:17; Gal. 3:28), it does so in recognition of a spiritual reality that is not yet realized in the social context.

Christianity brings us into new relationships with one another, but the fullness of these relationships is not always achieved immediately or even in this life. That is why slaves **who have believing masters are not to show less respect for them because they are brothers.**

Some of the wealthy Christians of New Testament times had slaves and stewards in their households. Embracing Christianity did not free the slave from his situation, nor did it lessen his obligations of service to his master. Quite the opposite. Coming to Christ creates a new relationship not only between the individual and God but also between the individual and other people. Slave and master were now brothers, bonded together in God's family. This increased the obligation of service to one another.

In fact, entry into God's family holds the believer to a higher standard. The slave is to **serve them even better.** Why? **Because those who benefit from their service are believers, and dear to them.** Here is that exceptional love for which Christians and the church should be known—love that overrides roles, titles, jobs, and economic status and works for the benefit of others.

Of course Paul's instructions were based on mutual respect and submission to one another. The balancing instructions to masters are found in his letter to Philemon and also in Ephesian 6:9.

B Understanding Contentment (6:3–10)

SUPPORTING IDEA: *Paul profiled the twisted and unhealthy thinking which results in false teachings. Often it leads people to approach religion as a mercenary would—for profit and personal gain. But those distracted by the pursuit of money will open themselves up to harm. True purpose and peace are found in godliness.*

6:3. Paul had just told Timothy to teach the principles of honor, submission, obedience, and love as found in the slave-master relationship. Paul knew that Timothy would be challenged in this area, most likely by the false teachers. So the apostle set the standard by which true and false teachers and their doctrines were to be measured. It is simple on the face of it. False teaching is anything that **does not agree to the sound instruction of our Lord Jesus Christ and to godly teaching** (or teaching on godliness).

The **sound instruction** to which Paul referred is the same "glorious gospel" he spoke of in 1 Timothy 1:11. It encompasses the prophets, the words of Christ, and the teachings of the apostles, especially that which Paul himself received from Christ. It is sound, trustworthy, and true because of its source in God and its effective work in bringing about progressive godliness in the believer.

False teachers deviate from the revelation of God and their lives do not adhere to true godliness.

6:4–5. Paul began a scathing list profiling the heart of the false teacher; he then described the consequences of their teachings.

First to the source—the false teacher. **He is conceited and understands nothing.** Paul minced no words.

These false teachers thought they had special knowledge. Whether they claimed this came from revelation, intense study, or just being "blessed," these teachers thought they understood faith and God more deeply and more thoroughly than anyone else. They were elitist, setting themselves above others. But, despite their high opinion of themselves and their knowledge, Paul's conclusion was that such a teacher **understands nothing,** deluding himself as to real spirituality and true knowledge. It is reminiscent of Paul's remarks earlier in the letter when he declared the false teachers "do not know what they are talking about or what they so confidently affirm" (1 Tim. 1:7).

The false teacher also **has an unhealthy interest in controversies and quarrels about words.** These teachers actually enjoyed disputes. It was a competitiveness designed to place them in the winner's circle as they dissected words, arguing over nuances and shades of meaning, debating issues that could never be solved in this life.

The results were clear: **envy, strife, malicious talk, evil suspicions and constant friction between men of corrupt mind.**

Sin is always a tangle of evil. One sin breeds another, which spawns another, plunging the individual deeper and deeper into its snare. **Envy** is a dissatisfaction which pushes an individual to desire what another person has. This leads to **strife** (selfish competition) and **malicious talk** (the need to exalt oneself at the expense of others). Within such an atmosphere, **evil suspicions** are bound to develop as people whisper and distrust thrives. The end result is **constant friction**—tension and irritation.

The mind is the control center of our lives; from our thoughts come our actions. This is why we are told that our lives will be transformed through correct thinking (Rom. 12:2). The opposite is also true; wrong thinking produces a degenerate and wasted life. **Men of corrupt mind . . . have been robbed of the truth.** Once again Paul used contrasts. In 1 Timothy 6:3 he wrote that sound teaching produces godly behavior since it comes from

Christ, the source of truth. Here he connected corrupt thinking with the absence of truth, which produces false godliness.

True Christian faith produces humility, gentleness, unity, and giving. It is based in servanthood. But the false teachers, divorcing themselves from the truth, had unhealthy reasoning. False doctrines produce pride, contention, disharmony, and selfishness, which in turn produces greed. Such men **think that godliness is a means to financial gain.**

You do not have to watch religious television too long to begin thinking that much of it is simply big business—trinkets and financial deals for blessings, money that buys prayers. It can leave a person wondering if any unbelievers who watch such dealings would ever give true Christianity a try.

But using Christian faith for personal gain can also be more insidious. We can use Christian ministry for personal advancement and higher salaries. This is why it is crucial to examine our hearts and our thinking against the revelation of sound teaching.

Before we leave the topic of false teachings, here are some questions to ask about any teaching we encounter:

- Is it consistent with Scripture, true to the faith?
- Does it unite the church? Does it encourage unity and love?
- Does it promote godliness, strengthening the inner person above the outer person?

6:6. Paul had just shown how the false teachers equated gain, success, and personal well-being with money. They promoted a form of outer godliness and intricate academic systems in order to draw people into their influence and so secure their financial support. Religion brought them prestige and profits.

But . . . This little qualifier is an important word. Paul negated the premise and goal of the false teachers. Success and personal well-being have nothing to do with rules, crowd adoration, or material prosperity: it is **godliness with contentment [that] is great gain.**

For Paul, godliness was the entire scope of the faith—correct doctrine combined with new life, truth measured by right living. The spiritual goals and disciplines necessary to progress in Christlikeness are to be the consuming passion of all his followers. This has nothing to do with material wealth or poverty. Material possessions are irrelevant. The human soul was not created to find contentment in the accumulation of stuff. This is a phantom that too many people chase. Personal peace is found in intimate relationship with God—this is great gain.

6:7–8. Paul next provided some logic and reasonableness to his assertion that money and material wealth are unworthy goals: **we brought nothing into the world, and we can take nothing out of it.** No one comes into the world all dressed up clutching a shopping catalog. Nothing we own will follow us into the next world. We end life as we started it—empty-handed.

So in the interim, **if we have food and clothing, we will be content with that.** For Christians, God's "divine power has given us everything we need for life and godliness through our knowledge of him who called us by his own glory and goodness" (2 Pet. 1:3). Add clothing, given man's need for covering and protection; then add food, given the human need for physical development and health. Now we are set.

Paul was not developing a philosophy that equates the material world with evil. He was not advocating a Christian culture that requires poverty. He was drawing a definite line between possessions and true contentment. The former has no bearing on the latter.

6:9. Paul continued to add evidence supporting his statement that money and possessions do not add up to personal satisfaction. He described for his readers the downward spiral into which money and materialism pull an individual. It begins because **those who want to get rich fall into temptation and a trap.**

Money opens a whole new world of possibilities. I spoke once with a friend who remarked that when he and his wife were first married and had little money, they never went to the malls, never flipped through catalogs. They spent their time on walks, playing softball, sitting together reading. Later, as their income level rose, they began buying a few luxuries, acquired a mortgage, had to add to their insurance payments. They suddenly saw a lot more things they could buy, a lot more objects that drew their attention, time, and resources.

These "things" can be kept in balance, but it requires a constant critique of our daily living and choices. Balance demands an objective understanding of our culture's values and the ways money can entice us. If extreme care is not taken, the temptations that money can buy can entrap us into the values and pleasures which Satan peddles.

Once we become vulnerable to temptation, it is easier to fall into **many foolish and harmful desires.** Compromise leads to participation. James outlined this same process: "Each one is tempted when, by his own evil desire, he is dragged away and enticed. Then, after desire has conceived, it gives birth to sin" (Jas. 1:14–15). Many people have lost their integrity or abandoned their faith for fifteen minutes in the spotlight or for a little sensual pleasure.

Such things **plunge men into ruin and destruction.** Just as true gain is spiritual in nature, true ruin and destruction are spiritual as well.

Our deepest joys and well-being are to be found in God's kingdom. We are to be content with God—period. In the Old Testament, the Levitical priesthood received no portion in the division of the land; their portion was

God himself as they served before him day after day (Num. 18:20). Under the new covenant, Christians are priests unto God (1 Pet. 2:5). He alone is our inheritance. The question comes back to us, "Will we be content with him?"

Jesus said he came that we might have life and have it abundantly (John 10:10). He was not talking about houses and lands, bank accounts or cars. Though he is the giver of all good gifts (Jas. 1:17), his dearest gifts are of the soul.

6:10. This verse begins with some first-century folk wisdom, a saying common in Paul's day: **the love of money is a root of all kinds of evil.**

Money is not the only cause of misfortune and evil, but it is a powerful one. Love of money is the root, the life support for a variety of wrongs and destructive behaviors.

Look candidly at life. From a love of money grow thistles which choke out abundant living:

- The businessman determines to secure advancements and higher salaries, neglects his family, and loses their love and affection.
- The dreamer thinks he can gamble and make a fortune, hoping never to work again. He keeps trying, wasting his resources in hopes of a big win, losing friends and dignity instead.
- The housewife habitually buys new furniture and redecorates her home, neglecting to tithe or give to others because her comforts have made her insensitive to those in need.
- The pimp sells drugs or sex for the sake of money, fancy cars, expensive clothes.
- The guy down the street steals from others, his desire for things ruining his sense of personal worth.
- The mercenary kills for the sake of cash.
- A woman complains, gossips about a neighbor, snaps at her children and husband, making herself and those around her miserable because she is envious, bitter over what she does not have, always wanting more.

In order to end the evil behavior, each person must dig out its root—the love of money.

The drive for money can destroy relationships, resulting in immoral decisions and compromise. It can also bring spiritual ruin. Paul noted that **some people, eager for money, have wandered from the faith.**

Today our entire culture is built upon the accumulation of wealth and material possessions. It determines the success or failure of presidents. It is the foundation of free enterprise, the principle behind our system of credit cards and debt, banking, and loans. It is what drives the advertising, music, entertainment, and sports industries. Materialism and personal wealth are hammered into our thinking every day all day long.

It is easy to put Christian ministry, personal godliness, acts of justice and charity, and sacrificial giving on the peripheries of life—to see no connection between these Christian "ideals" and life as we experience it. The truth is that there is no compatibility.

Even so, we are forced to decide which offers truth and which offers illusions, which brings contentment and peace, and which leads to frustration and emptiness. It seems simple on the surface, but in our daily decisions the choices become hard; it is far easier to compromise then rationalize. Resistance to wealth's temptations becomes difficult. Though we would never deny the faith, it is easier (though just as deadly) to wander from it.

Paul's warning should not be minimized. Those who love money and wander from the faith have **pierced themselves with many griefs.**

Just as the rich young ruler who questioned Jesus was brought to a point of decision, so are we. It becomes a choice as to whether we will trust in God or the stuff around us. God allows us to make the choice. The young ruler decided to keep his riches. He walked away a wealthy man . . . but sad (Mark 10:17–24). There is always a price to be paid.

Paul was not against the drive to accomplish or the ambition to make a difference in the world or on the job. The Bible states clearly that we are to work hard, to be model employees or employers. But money should not be the driving force. It should be God's glory that pushes us—love of people, the mission of the church, our devotion to Christ.

C Christian Character and Life (6:11–16)

> **SUPPORTING IDEA:** *Those who have chosen to identify with and follow after Christ, those who dare call themselves Christians, are to exhibit God in this world. We do this through our words and lives—our public witness and private disciplines.*

6:11. Paul made an impassioned plea to Timothy—**you, man of God, flee from all this** (ungodliness). He was to live differently. So are all Christian believers.

Those who have chosen to follow Christ have an obligation to him. They are to run away from all the false teacher represents, the pride, the misguided thinking, the greed. But God never calls us to give up something without instructing us to embrace its alternative. We are told to put off the old nature and put on the new (Eph. 4:22–24); we are to stop lying and speak honestly, to put away crude speech and say only beneficial things (Eph. 4:25–29). The Christian is to escape from the traps and temptations of money, selfish ambition, and intellectual sophistry. We are to **pursue righteousness, godliness, faith, love, endurance and gentleness.**

These six qualities mark the life of a Christian. But they must be pursued with purpose. We are to "run with perseverance . . . [fixing] our eyes on

Jesus" (Heb. 12:1–2). Paul's list of characteristics closely matches the fruit of the Spirit described in Galatians 5:22.

6:12. Timothy was to chase after personal behaviors, attitudes, and habits which would reflect his companionship with Christ. He was also to **fight the good fight of the faith.** As a leader he was to defend truth.

There will always be attacks upon God's truth: professing Christians who propagate false teachings and those who encourage compromise. But the inspired beliefs must be fought for and upheld. This is not a skirmish but a sustained contest which the believer must see through to the end. This requires endurance and patience.

Paul told Timothy to **take hold of the eternal life to which you were called when you made your good confession in the presence of many witnesses.**

The eternal life which believers enter is not simply a future hope; it is also a present reality. We take hold of this eternal life when we live in the power and values of God's eternal kingdom. We will not experience the fullness of Christ's dominion until the future when he reigns over all the earth. But the eternal kind of life is still accessible at the present time. We touch upon it when we order our daily lives in harmony with God and his Spirit.

This new kind of life is what every believer is called to. It is not reserved for the elite. It is available to all who make the good confession—that Jesus Christ is God's Son, delivered to death for our sins and raised from the dead to secure eternal life for all who trust him.

True faith cannot be hidden. Timothy gave public witness that he believed and trusted in Jesus Christ. He had followed in the right way. Now Paul encouraged him to continue on with strength and clarity of purpose.

6:13. If all this were not enough, Paul wrote a serious mandate to Timothy. His prelude was filled with dignity, love, and a sobering reality. He gave his exhortation **in the sight of God, who gives life to everything.** This is not simply a nice-sounding phrase; it is a critical truth. God is sovereign over all life—everyone, the false teacher and the true, the powerful and the slave. All these exist by God's mercy and life-giving power. We are cared for by his strength and goodness. This should bring comfort as well as gratitude. This is the God whom Paul called as witness to the charge he gave Timothy.

All of us have a calling—it is to eternal life (1 Tim. 6:12). This life begins with faith and confession, and it grows in intimate fellowship with Christ, fulfilling his life through us in the world. Christ also had a calling—to reveal God in this world and to provide a way by which people could know God. This came through holy living, death for mankind's sins, and resurrection.

Paul delivered his command in the sight of **Christ Jesus, who while testifying before Pontius Pilate made the good confession.** In the course of Pilate's questioning, Jesus stated: "You are right in saying I am a king. In fact, for this reason I was born, and for this I came into the world, to testify to the truth. Everyone on the side of truth listens to me" (John 18:37). Jesus never wavered from the call of the Father upon his life. He persevered unto death.

6:14. Having called his witnesses, Paul then extended the charge to Timothy: **keep this command without spot or blame until the appearing of our Lord Jesus Christ.**

Timothy was to flee from unrighteousness and pursue the fullness of the Christian life. He was to devote himself to growing intimacy with Christ, to compassionate relationships with others, and unwavering guardianship of truth as found in Scripture. The full spectrum of life is to be lived under the reign of Christ, and it is to be done with consistency so that no sin interferes with such a life.

This is not a Sunday event but a lifelong pursuit and commitment **until the appearing of our Lord Jesus Christ.** The coming of Christ has sustained the church for centuries. It is to our shame that we do not have the same anticipation, the same high expectancy of the Lord's return. Such a glorious prospect keeps the difficulties as well as the temptations of this life in proper perspective.

6:15–16. This coming of Christ **God will bring about in his own time.** Even Jesus said, "It is not for you to know the times or dates the Father has set by his own authority" (Acts 1:7).

Paul again broke into adoration of the God whom he loved and served. It was meant to remind Timothy of the greatness of the one who had called him and to whom he ministered. Realizing the eminence of our God can diminish the opposing forces with which we must deal.

God, the blessed and only Ruler, the King of kings and Lord of lords— all these descriptions speak of his sovereignty, the vastness of his dominion.

This greatness was not evident at his first appearing, however. He came as a baby, naked and vulnerable. He served God and man, learning obedience through suffering (Heb. 5:7–8).

But at his second appearance he will come with might, with the word of his strength, invincible, clothed with majesty and glory. No king or president has any power except as given by God. Even this delegated authority is weak in comparison to the commanding strength of God.

The purpose of Jesus' first coming was to rescue sinners; the purpose of his Second Coming will be to save believers.

Paul stretched to describe this God who is beyond the created order. He began with God's transcendence: he **alone is immortal.** No one else and no other thing can claim this eternal existence. God has no beginning, no ending, no progression of growth or decline. Out of his life comes all other life. Out of his immortality he grants eternal life to others.

He **lives in unapproachable light, whom no one has seen or can see.** Light signifies purity, penetrating and blazing holiness. God is beyond the comprehension of humankind. He is also beyond our full knowing. He is so "other" than we are that no one can experience or approach the purity of his being. And it is to this God that **honor and might forever** are due.

Instructions for the Rich (6:17–19)

SUPPORTING IDEA: *Money is one of Paul's major concerns in this chapter—its temptations, disappointments, and destructiveness. Within every command and instruction, he directs us to recognize God's generosity and the fleeting nature of this world. Paul has talked to the poor, the charlatan, the Christian leader; now he addresses the rich.*

6:17. Christianity does not require a vow of poverty or the forsaking of wealth, for Paul wrote, **command those who are rich in this present world not to be arrogant.** Some followers of Christ will be wealthy by society's standards. Just as Paul told slaves to stay and serve their masters (1 Tim. 6:1–2), so also he left the rich person in his surroundings. Circumstance makes little difference in the value system of God. It is how a person behaves in their circumstances that makes the difference—either glorifying or discrediting the name of Christ. However, there are inherent dangers in having wealth.

Those who are rich can easily fall into arrogance. This is an ancient problem, and Israel provides a classic example. They possessed and settled the Promised Land after years of wanderings. God, foreseeing what would ultimately occur, warned the people that wealth could be their undoing. "When you eat and are satisfied, when you build fine houses and settle down, and when your herds and flocks grow large and your silver and gold increase and all you have is multiplied, then your heart will become proud and you will forget the LORD your God, who brought you out of Egypt, out of the land of slavery" (Deut. 8:12–14).

Abundance breeds pride—toward God and others. The person who has much begins to credit himself with his wealth. Creeping into his heart is the notion that he has done well on his own, that he can get by without God. Wealth also creates an economy of false values. Beneath the class wars and the tensions between rich and poor simmers the deception that worth is determined by possessions.

Another danger which confronts the wealthy is that they easily place confidence in what they see—their stuff. Paul told them not to **put their hope in wealth, which is so uncertain.** Jesus cautioned us about the uncertainty of money (Matt. 6:19). Each day we see the evidences of his warning—bankruptcy cases increase, the stock market fluctuates, governments fall and their monetary systems fail, prices escalate, and money drains away. There is no predictability when it comes to money; trusting it is risky.

Instead, wealthy believers are to hold their money with an open hand; they are to **put their hope in God, who richly provides us with everything for our enjoyment.** Putting hope in money is no different from the primitive man or woman who bows to an idol of wood or stone, expecting it to protect or provide. This is worshiping the creation instead of the Creator (Rom. 1:25). The Christian must never invest trust in things but in relationships—particularly with God, maker of all that exists (John 1:3).

A stronger, clearer statement about worthy trust could not be made than that given by Jeremiah: "Let not the wise man boast of his wisdom or the strong man boast of his strength or the rich man boast of his riches, but let him who boasts boast about this: 'that he understands and knows me, that I am the LORD, who exercises kindness, justice and righteousness on earth, for in these I delight,' declares the LORD" (Jer. 9:23–24). Riches are unworthy to be the center of our hearts.

6:18. Paul almost always countered the negative with the positive. If we are to refrain from something, then he tells us to engage in something else. If the rich are not to devote themselves to things, then they are to invest themselves in doing **good, to be rich in good deeds, and to be generous and willing to share.**

How we invest ourselves and our time is more valuable than money. God desires that we spend ourselves in doing good, helping others, benefiting those around us. It is a tendency of the wealthy to think that others exist for their benefit, to do their bidding. In God's eyes it is just the opposite. Those who have been richly blessed must give abundantly. Once again, God desires that we imitate him. Just as he richly provides us everything for our enjoyment, just as his mercy and love are without limit, so his people are to live with the same extravagance.

6:19. By imitating the generous nature of our Lord, **they will lay up treasure for themselves as a firm foundation for the coming age.** The treasure which accumulates in the life to come is not money, stock portfolios, or real estate. The treasure of which Paul spoke is spiritual, and it lasts for eternity.

This eternal wealth—the generous and giving life expressed in the world—is evidence of true faith in God. In this way it is a firm foundation for entry into eternity. How we use our time and our resources indicates where our heart truly belongs. If it is directed by the values and compassion of God, we **take hold of the life that is truly life.**

When compared to the rest of the world's peoples, most Americans would be placed in the "wealthy" category. This should lead each of us to examine our values:

- Which concerns me more: how much *money* I have or how much of me *God* has?

- Do I pray more about God supplying material items than I do about developing my character?

- Do I spend more time and money caring for my house and lawn than I do helping others?

- Am I confident about the future because my bank account is healthy or because my spirit is secure in Christ?

⒠ The Conclusion and Final Charge (6:20–21)

SUPPORTING IDEA: *Paul returned full circle, emphasizing the same concerns with which he began 1 Timothy: the purity of the gospel and the need to stay clear of false teachers.*

6:20–21. Paul issued a personal plea to Timothy: **guard what has been entrusted to your care.** This is no light matter. The gospel and doctrine, as given by the apostles, must be defended and preserved. Timothy had been equipped by God to do this; now he must set his heart and mind to the task. The work was entrusted to him, just as valuables are deposited in a bank for safety. Timothy was handed the responsibility of guarding the riches of the gospel against false teachers and keeping the church unified in the face of divisive teachings.

In order to carry out this work, Timothy must **turn away from godless chatter and the opposing ideas of what is falsely called knowledge.** These are the arrogant views of the false teachers, those who think academic pursuits and tangling with words are, in themselves, pathways to spirituality. They do not recognize the need for a comprehensive belief that changes the inner person and his behavior. Such people and their teachings appear wise, but they are actually empty.

These false teachers were not just little irritants which disrupted the church; they were dangerous. The spurious doctrines **which some have professed** have caused people to wander **from the faith.** This was soul-damaging. Such people appeared as religious teachers, but they were traitorous to the God who created them.

Paul ended as he began: **Grace be with you.** This was extended not only to Timothy, but to the congregation who listened to this letter and heard all of Paul's instructions. For the believers gathered in Ephesus, Paul desired God's grace, his abundant goodness and spiritual fullness.

We continue as we started in the Christian faith—by grace through faith (Eph. 2:8–10).

MAIN IDEA REVIEW: *For most people, becoming a Christian does not entail a dramatic change in occupation, living conditions, salary, or neighborhood. Christ calls us to extend his kingdom from the place we now occupy, whether as CEO, student, mother, clerk, or migrant farmer. Contentment, the pursuit of godliness, and bold identification with Christ are foundational to effective Christian living.*

III. CONCLUSION

"Man the Lifeboats"

The sinking of the Titanic on April 15, 1912, cost over fifteen hundred people their lives. Yet the whole disaster was avoidable. The day before, the giant ship had received six warnings about dangerous ice ahead. The last radio signal sent to the Titanic was answered curtly, "Shut up! Shut up! You're jamming my signal."

The radio room was busy with far more pressing concerns, sending messages ahead to Cape Race to arrange chauffeurs and baggage pickup for wealthy passengers. If only someone had heeded the warnings.

But nobody suspected that the mighty ocean liner with its enormous engines and polished decks, its glistening chandeliers and exquisite foods, was heading toward calamity. Nobody considered that the well-crafted ship and the well-appointed passengers were vulnerable to circumstances they could not foresee.

Money blinds us to the truth of life's insecurities. We cling tenaciously to its promises of happiness; we depend on it for our sense of well-being, our place in the social order. That dark night when the Titanic took on water, some people rushed about its decks seeking a way to escape. Others sold their seats in a lifeboat for cash.

Many people also flounder and drown spiritually. In spite of Scripture's warnings, they plow ahead as though they were exceptions to God's rule that focusing on money leads a person into temptation and ruin.

The best conclusion we can make about money is that we must keep it in its place. It can be used for Christ's glory, but it cannot bring true meaning. Money is to be held loosely; our reputation is to be made on goodness to God and others, not on the accumulation of goods.

On April 15, 1912, those who sold their place on a lifeboat for a bit of cash took it with them to a watery grave. Money can buy many things, but it cannot save a life or a soul (Matt. 16:26).

PRINCIPLES

- People who work for others should serve them respectfully.
- Proud, selfish people love to argue about words and to start quarrels. Christians are to avoid such conduct.
- Every good thing comes from God, who is generous to all. We must learn personal contentment in all circumstances.
- The love of money and the things it will buy are among the main competitors for our hearts.
- When we disobey the commands of our Lord, we are going up against the king of the universe.
- Rich people can do a great deal of good with their resources— good that lasts forever.
- Eternal life is a trust from God to us; he has secured the future of believers.

APPLICATIONS

- A "Christian day's work" may be even more than an "honest day's work." Christians might do well to ask their superiors what they think of their work.
- Churches must have clear strategies for helping people who are always causing controversies.
- Checkbook records tell a great deal about our hearts and where our treasures are. It might be good to look back over a few months of your checkbook and see what you love.
- All believers should make "the good confession" before their church, publicly acknowledging Christ as Lord and Savior.
- Believers who make good incomes should plan a systematic way to share regularly with people in need and to be "rich in good deeds."

IV. LIFE APPLICATION

The World Turned Upside Down

In the first century, those who decided to follow Jesus—whether slave or master, rich or poor, laborer or ruler—had to navigate the difficulties of living their faith in a hostile society. They had to come to terms with how they were going to carry out everyday living under an old social system, while they had entered a new spiritual order which claimed to transform all relationships.

Thousands of years later we are faced with the same challenge. One of the Christian's most difficult tasks is to learn how to live in this world without becoming a part of it—to live as a citizen of society without adopting its values.

Throughout the centuries, Christianity has witnessed men and women who found it impossible to reconcile life in this world with devotion to God. In seeking spiritual attainment, these people often treated the created world with contempt. Spiritual purification and advancement so consumed them that they pushed themselves deeper into introspection and further into absurdities. Struggling to obtain divine merit, they found no effort equal to the task.

This drive to achieve led to extremes as each devotee tried to outdo others in claiming God's favor through self-mortification. Many became hermits, living out solitary confinement in the desert. Simeon Stylites built a sixty-foot-high column in the Syrian wilderness and lived upon its top for thirty years without descending. St. Ciaran ate his bread with sand; others allowed their bodies to be eaten by flies or beetles.

Such efforts seem fantastic, even ludicrous. Not all ascetics went to such excesses, however. Many were able to balance a cloistered existence with positive interaction in society. But eccentricities always flow from efforts to merit what cannot be earned, and they certainly reveal a misunderstanding of faith and of God.

Within the church a running tension has continued between social encounter and withdrawal. Today, many Christians build strong ties between faith and Western values of success. Having lived with the benefits of national prosperity for so long, it is often difficult to understand the church in terms other than statistical growth, bureaucratic specialization, economic advancement, managerial efficiency, and personal actualization.

Then there are those who treat faith as a commodity, "evangelizing" through imprinted slogans on bumper stickers, T-shirts, and coffee mugs, melding faith with fad and fashion. Christianity is distinguished only by the lyrics. Either way, the church risks impotence, contributing to society and our neighbors little more than a religious rendition of pop culture.

By focusing on withdrawal or engagement, we make methods and rules the standard for spirituality. Separatists and conformists alike believe that God is best served by adopting or refraining from particular practices within the social order, elements which are neither sinful nor sacred.

God does work through the social context in which we live. He also works through the separated (sanctified) community of believers—the church. Just as yeast permeates dough, so the Spirit of God permeates a person and community, changing and altering character. The individual, united with other believers, moves through the social order, bringing Christ's goodness and redemption to all relationships. In this way, society grows toward goodness and a greater realization of Christian principles.

This final chapter of 1 Timothy argues well for engagement and detachment. Paul told Christians at both ends of the social scale to remain in their current situation, yet to live differently—apart from natural inclinations or social conditioning.

The Christian faith has fluidity and freedom. It does not insist on particular forms of dress, does not restrict diet, does not prescribe only one posture acceptable for prayer. True Christian faith takes people deeper, beyond culture. Centered on relationship with a living God, Christian faith pierces through customs, traditions, and language to divine values and character. This is why Paul told Timothy and the Ephesian church to "pursue righteousness, godliness, faith, love, endurance and gentleness" (1Tim. 6:11).

As the Spirit of Christ infiltrates a life, his truth enlightens that person, clarifying motives, defining values and purpose. In this way the Spirit of God bestows personal responsibility upon the believer—responsibility for spiritual development and responsibility for expressing faith in day-to-day living. This freedom to respond enables the Christian to influence other people and society in purposeful ways.

V. PRAYER

God of both spirit and flesh, guide me so that I may understand the people with whom I work, the neighbors with whom I live, and the values both obvious and subtle that permeate my culture. Fill my mind with wisdom so that I may live fully and creatively, growing in spirit and alive to the world around me. Amen.

VI. DEEPER DISCOVERIES

A. Slaves (vv. 1–2)

Since Christ's birth, people have often been disappointed and angry with what appears to be Christian passivity in the face of social evils. Whether it is slavery, political injustice, the oppression of the poor, racial inequity, or any other social blight, Christians and the church have often been accused of inaction.

Actually, Christian faith has been a leading force in the emancipation of many of the world's tyrannized peoples. But most often the church's participation in social change has been progressive rather than revolutionary.

At the time Paul wrote his letter to Timothy, slaves made up a large portion of the working population in the Roman Empire. One-third of the inhabitants of Rome were slaves, and they were firmly rooted in the economic system. All slaves were owned by masters. Many slaves engaged in hard labor, but others were clerks, draftsmen, teachers, soldiers, craftsmen, and other types of workers. Some were bound with little freedom of movement or choice, while others could travel, buy, and trade, and some actually received an education.

Even so, slavery must not be considered good or acceptable in terms of Christian ethics. Paul encouraged slaves to obtain their freedom if legally possible (1 Cor. 7:21), and he condemned the practice of slave trading (1 Tim. 1:10). Slavery is an oppressive system of subjugating people.

Despite the moral teachings of the Bible, many people would prefer Scripture to be more agitating in its denunciation of slavery and oppression. Despite its ethic of equality and freedom, people have accused Christianity of falling short in the practice of such ideals. But the Christian stance on oppression is actually more radical and revolutionary than insurrection or revolution. The Christian approach is to change people. People changed by God's grace will then bring about changes in society as they live out the teachings of Jesus Christ in their daily lives.

B. Riches (vv. 6–10,17–19)

Even among believers, our view of money is dictated, not by Scripture, but by our own expectations, desires, and the voice of culture. We convince ourselves through intricate reasoning that possessions and money do not have a hold on us but that they are necessary. As Benjamin Franklin observed, "Reason is a wonderful thing because one can always find a reason for whatever it is that one wants to do."

Simply asking ourselves whether we love money will never uncover the truth. The best way to uncover our view of money is to observe our behavior. What drives our decisions? What prompts our buying? What concerns underlie our bank account or investments? What determines our work, promotions, acquisitions, home, and friends?

Paul's command to Timothy was: "flee from all this" (v. 11). He did not allow for moderation. He did not call us to balance materialism with spirituality.

Clearly Paul was not promoting Christian poverty. He was able to live with abundance as well as with little. What Paul called for was a redirection of our energies and affections. Paul did not ask us to turn away from something without directing us toward something better. Giving up possessions or taking a lower-paying job are not, in themselves, virtuous. What clarifies our position on money and the things it will buy is to check our life against what Paul listed as the worthy ambitions of a Christian.

We must ask ourselves, "Am I *pursuing* righteousness, godliness, faith, love, endurance and gentleness?" This is not a question of casual interest or intellectual admiration. This requires an inventory of where our energies, passions, goals, and time are directed.

An honest answer will keep us from "temptation and . . . many foolish and harmful desires that plunge men into ruin and destruction" (v. 9).

VII. TEACHING OUTLINE

A. INTRODUCTION
1. Lead Story: Cadillac Coffins
2. Context: Paul's main emphasis in this chapter was on contentment. He first addressed slaves, encouraging them to focus on the quality of their service rather than on their circumstances. He discussed the issue of money, the responsibilities of the rich, the dangers of wealth. Above all, the Christian is to pursue righteousness, godliness, faith, love, endurance, and gentleness.
3. Transition: Although slavery is not as common today, the ethic Paul presented is equally valid in the employee-employer relationship. Wealth is now more widely distributed in society, making Paul's warnings even more applicable to us.

B. COMMENTARY
1. Slaves and Masters (6:1–2)
2. Understanding Contentment (6:3–10)
3. Christian Character and Life (6:11–16)
4. Instructions for the Rich (6:17–19)
5. The Conclusion and Final Charge (6:20–21)

C. CONCLUSION: THE WORLD TURNED UPSIDE DOWN

VIII. ISSUES FOR DISCUSSION
1. Do you ever feel restless or discontent with what you have? If so, why?
2. What is the proper balance between healthy ambition and godly contentment? Can we be at peace in our spirits and still work to get ahead?
3. Has the love of money ever caused you trouble? Do you find money attractive?

4. Paul tells us to be rich in good works. What can you do to demonstrate generosity in this area?

5. Have you made the "good confession"? How would you summarize the commitment it calls you to keep?

Introduction to

2 Timothy

LETTER PROFILE: SECOND TIMOTHY

- This letter was written by Paul from a Roman prison while he was under a sentence of death.
- Paul sent this very personal letter, with many pastoral instructions and guidelines, to Timothy, his protegé and spiritual son.
- The letter was delivered to Timothy somewhere in Asia Minor, perhaps in the city of Ephesus.
- Paul described the moral degeneration of the last days and issued an impassioned plea for believers to remain faithful, persevering under hardship.
- Paul emphasized the need for pure doctrine, godly living, and preaching the gospel.
- The apostle emphasized the Christian's duty to live faithfully to the end, sobered by the future judgment and encouraged by our future reward.

AUTHOR PROFILE: PAUL

- Paul, a Jew, was born in Tarsus, a city near the Lebanese border in modern Turkey. The citizens of the city zealously studied culture and academic disciplines.
- Paul was a Roman citizen. Whether his citizenship came by birth or payment is uncertain, but he clearly enjoyed the full range of privileges accorded a citizen of Rome.
- He was a prominent Jewish leader, highly educated as a Pharisee and, before his conversion to Christianity, a leading persecutor of the church.
- Paul visited Ephesus on his second and third missionary journeys (Acts 16–20).
- He was known for his tireless pioneer work among the Gentiles.
- Imprisoned by Nero's regime in Rome, Paul was beheaded around A.D. 68.

CITY PROFILE: EPHESUS

- Ephesus was a major trading center and seaport on the Aegean Sea during Paul's day. Today the city lies seven miles inland due to the accumulation of silt from the Cayster River.
- Ephesus was home to one of the seven wonders of the ancient world—the temple of the goddess Artemis. For the Ephesians, the temple and worship of Artemis represented economic opportunity as well as civic pride.
- The city had a reputation as a center for the learning and practice of magical arts.
- Like other major cities in the Roman Empire, Ephesus enjoyed a measure of civic self-rule.

2 Timothy 1

Remaining Faithful
to Christ

I. INTRODUCTION
Last Will and Testament

II. COMMENTARY
A verse-by-verse explanation of the chapter.

III. CONCLUSION
Trivial Pursuit

An overview of the principles and applications from the chapter.

IV. LIFE APPLICATION
Running the Race

Melding the chapter to life.

V. PRAYER
Tying the chapter to life with God.

VI. DEEPER DISCOVERIES
Historical, geographical, and grammatical enrichment of the commentary.

VII. TEACHING OUTLINE
Suggested step-by-step group study of the chapter.

VIII. ISSUES FOR DISCUSSION
Zeroing the chapter in on daily life.

"*L*ife must be given in its wholeness, if life in its

wholeness is to be received."

E v e l y n   U n d e r h i l l

2 Timothy 1

 I N   A   N U T S H E L L

*P*aul gave thanks for the great heritage of faith in his own life as well as in Timothy's. He went on to describe the bold commitment which faith requires, the identification with suffering which must be embraced, and the power and grace which God provides. Paul urged Timothy to respond to God's gifts with faithful obedience.

Remaining Faithful to Christ

I. INTRODUCTION

Last Will and Testament

In times past, people often witnessed the last words of a loved one before he died. Watching at the bedside, the family heard words of advice, or whispers of love, perhaps a few regrets. Of one thing you can be sure, no one talked about their car or business success, or what stocks were on the rise. People who know that the words they speak are possibly their last usually focus on serious matters. They measure their words carefully.

Paul did the same in this, his last letter. His impending execution, by decree of Emperor Nero, stirred within him an urgency to write once again to his dear friend and protegé, Timothy. This impassioned letter, more personal in tone than his first letter to Timothy, depicts a veteran minister eager to bolster the faith of a young pastor. He wanted to ground Timothy firmly in his obligations to Christ and the church.

From his many court trials and his time spent in prison, Paul felt the winds of public and official opinion turning more harshly against Christians. Although the apostle knew it was the Holy Spirit who would guard and preserve the church's message and mission, he seemed to feel the press of love and duty to do all he could to protect its faith and holiness against the future. On the horizon lay some of the most brutal persecutions of the church.

II. COMMENTARY

MAIN IDEA: *Paul knew he had little time before his own execution, so he wrote a very personal letter to Timothy, full of intensity, love, and concern. He encouraged Timothy to be faithful in his trust of Christ, to act with boldness rather than acquiescing to his natural timidity, and to associate confidently with the suffering apostle and Christ. Paul knew Timothy must assume enormous responsibilities in the mission of the church, and he wanted him to be stalwart and obedient in preserving and spreading the gospel of Jesus Christ.*

Greeting (1:1–2)

> **SUPPORTING IDEA:** *Paul opened with a typical greeting, claiming his apostleship and extending the grace of God to Timothy.*

1:1–2. What would you say if asked to describe yourself? Paul always saw himself first as a servant or **an apostle of Christ Jesus.**

Apostle means literally "sent one." The early church recognized as apostles those leaders with a special call who had seen the resurrected Christ. Paul was always eager to establish his apostleship, not because he desired adoration or special privilege, but because he wanted others to recognize that his authority came not from self-appointment, nor from man's selection, but by God's personal choice: **by the will of God.**

It is possible that, with death so imminent, Paul became more cognizant of the eternal life into which he would enter. Certainly he understood this **promise of life that is in Christ Jesus** as experiential to some degree in this present world. But with his approaching execution, he must also have felt the anticipation of seeing Jesus and entering fully into the promise. He must have been aware of standing on the threshold to a blissful existence.

With no expectation that he would be released from prison again, he wrote **to Timothy, [his] dear son.** This attests to more than spiritual kinship; it announces an intimate and emotional bond. Their love for each other increased over time as they stood together in difficulty and worked in ministry. Paul thought about this young man, now separated from him by distance and prison, and considered him with the affection of a father toward a son.

With these emotions, Paul offered to Timothy **grace, mercy and peace from God the Father and Christ Jesus our Lord.**

Ⓑ Christian Heritage (1:3–5)

> **SUPPORTING IDEA:** *Paul looked back upon his own heritage of faith, then reminded Timothy of the rich legacy he possessed as well. Remembering this can impart courage and strengthen commitment to one's duty and calling.*

1:3. Paul began with thanksgiving. It is important, however, to sift through all the clauses of the sentence in order to arrive at the object of his thankfulness. **I thank God . . . as night and day I constantly remember you in my prayers.**

Paul, at the end of life's journey, offered thanks for this young man of faith. Sitting alone in the chill of a Roman prison, perhaps Paul reflected upon the shared struggles and joys of ministry together. As events replayed in his mind, there stirred within him a thankfulness for Timothy's loyalty and commitment to Christ. So with gratitude and concern, even though he knew Timothy's weaknesses, Paul continued in prayer night and day.

In the middle of his thanksgiving, Paul inserted a personal tribute to his heritage of faith. He probably did this to establish a parallel between himself and Timothy. Later he directed Timothy to consider his own upbringing.

Paul thanked God, **whom I serve, as my forefathers did, with a clear conscience**. No one could convict Paul of pandering to public opinion, faddish philosophies, or personal ambition. He served God and no other. The God he served was the same one to whom his ancestors were committed. He drew the line of his faith through previous generations. Paul had not denied his Hebrew heritage by following Jesus Christ; he had fulfilled it (Acts 13:16–33). This he did with a clear conscience, one that was healthy and not diseased by the misinterpretation of Scripture or the hardening of his heart through sin.

1:4. Paul inserted a very personal word to Timothy, one of deep affection. These two men were obviously close companions. They were not afraid to talk about this or to display the emotions of their friendship.

Paul thought back on the last time they saw each other: **recalling your tears, I long to see you.** Why Timothy shed tears, we can only guess. Perhaps it was the frustration of having to deal with difficulties he felt were beyond his ability to manage; perhaps Paul's leaving left Timothy feeling utterly alone; perhaps it was simply the heartache one feels when a dear friend departs. Whatever the cause, it seems Timothy had a sensitive and tender disposition.

This tenderness in Timothy evoked from Paul a greater desire to see the young man. Like a parent for a child, Paul sensed in Timothy a vulnerability, and he wanted to strengthen him through God—he wanted to see him. But Paul also knew that this relationship was not one-sided. Seeing Timothy would benefit him as well: he would **be filled with joy**. This joy is a delight that breaks the bonds of circumstances, centering itself in the person of Christ and his people.

1:5. Paul returned to the subject of spiritual heritage as he thought about Timothy: **I have been reminded of your sincere faith.** He had watched Timothy and worked beside him for years. In Timothy, Paul recognized a genuine faith, one adhering to the teachings of Christ and the apostles, which in turn produced righteous behavior. Proper belief and proper actions are components of sincere faith.

Paul realized that genuine faith had been modeled for Timothy through his family. It was evident **in your grandmother Lois and in your mother Eunice.** Though true faith cannot be inherited, it can be demonstrated in convincing ways within the context of a family. Even so, each person must entrust himself personally to Jesus Christ. True faith is individually claimed.

Timothy's father was Greek. His mother and grandmother, however, were Jewish (Acts 16:1). Apparently they had trained Timothy in reading and memorizing Old Testament texts because Paul later remarked how Timothy had from childhood known the holy Scriptures (2 Tim. 3:15). This had proved a good foundation as he developed into faith in Christ. The genuine faith Paul had noted in Timothy's mother and grandmother, he was convinced **now lives in you [Timothy]**.

Ⓒ God's Empowerment (1:6–7)

> **SUPPORTING IDEA:** *God has equipped every believer to be useful and productive in Christian living. His Spirit enables us in whatever task God gives. But we must fulfill our responsibility by continually granting his Spirit freedom of expression.*

1:6. Having established Timothy's heritage of belief in God and confirmed his conviction that Timothy shared in this genuine faith, Paul issued a command. **For this reason I remind you to fan into flame the gift of God, which is in you.**

The reason Paul could remind Timothy of God's gift was because Timothy was an authentic believer. **The gift of God, which is in you** was probably the Holy Spirit. Every genuine believer receives this gift from God. This is why Paul told Timothy that he was *persuaded* of his sincere faith. Timothy had this powerful gift within him, enabling him to perform all that God required.

Even so, Timothy must **fan into flame** the Spirit's power. This is a present-tense verb. It might better be translated "keep fanning." It was not that the Spirit's flame was weak or needed to be alive by human effort but that the Spirit only works in cooperation with those who desire his enablement. We keep fanning the flame by keeping "in step with the Spirit" (Gal. 5:25), by disciplining ourselves in godliness to produce the fruit which is his nature (Gal. 5:22).

1:7. Having confirmed that Timothy possessed this great gift of God's grace, his own Spirit, Paul pointed Timothy toward the boldness that should belong to every believer: **For God did not give us a spirit of timidity, but a spirit of power, of love and of self-discipline.**

Timothy, many interpreters surmise, was a man of quiet disposition—a retiring, timid individual who had been thrust into a leadership role for which he had no predilection. The battle against the false teachers was strenuous, leaving Timothy weary, perhaps even questioning what he was doing. It is possible that he was overwhelmed by these circumstances.

But Paul countered our natural tendencies and excuses by directing us to consider this great gift which we all possess—the Spirit of God. Our natural abilities can only supplement what God calls us to do. The important consideration in all of life's challenges and duties is to remember that God's Spirit resides within us. He is the giver of power, love, and self-discipline.

Power is simply enablement to do what God requires. We are never asked to do anything beyond what God gives strength and ability to accomplish. **Love** is expressed first to God, then to others. It is the distinguishing quality of Christians, this unnatural love, and it comes only as we allow the life of God's Spirit to live through us.

Self-discipline denotes careful, sensible thinking. It is the ability to think clearly with the wisdom and understanding that God imparts. Fear is a driving force in society today. It is the main subject of the evening news, the underlying premise of advertising and marketing. Fear often spawns confused thinking, irrationalities, and misunderstandings. Thoughts and speculations swirl in our mind when fear enters. This is why Christ calls us to healthy, orderly thought processes.

Perhaps we can look at life and realize our need for God's power (*dunamis*). We need the "dynamite" of God's strength in our daily living, to endure and make wise choices, to live in patience, producing goodness (Col. 1:9–14).

Ⓓ The Confidence and Identity of the Believer (1:8–12)

> **SUPPORTING IDEA:** *Each truth builds on other truths. Paul had described the power that resides within each believer because of the Holy Spirit's life. Paul then called for boldness in identifying with the message and sufferings of Christ. He reviewed the graciousness of God on our behalf and commanded us to be bold witnesses of his goodness.*

1:8. Paul had just rehearsed the power inherent within each believer—power to do whatever God calls us to, power to love God and others, and power to think wisely and clearly. With these in mind, the apostle commanded, **So do not be ashamed to testify about our Lord, or ashamed of me his prisoner.**

The Christian is faced with three basic ways of public identification with Christ. The first is through speech and lifestyle—our affirmation of God's work in us and our agreement with him. Paul's charge for us not to be ashamed to testify is a command to openness. Shame often shows itself through silence. We simply do not say anything about Christ; we keep everything to ourselves. It is not that we live a wicked and self-indulgent life. We simply go along with the way everyone else lives, with no difference in our ethics, moral positions, values, or ambitions.

Another way we identify with Christ is through solidarity with his people, especially those who suffer on his behalf. The people we associate with often reflect on us. If someone is admired, our ties with that person will grant us acceptance by people we do not even know. Everyone enjoys approval, but we must be careful where we seek it. Avoiding those who are controversial because they take a bold stand for Christ or steering clear of helping Christians are signs that we are ashamed of God's people. Our first loyalty and duty is to the household of faith.

The third means of identification is with the message, the proclamation of God's truth and Christ's life. To refrain from speaking about God's truth, to hold back from living it, is to regard the gospel with shame and dishonor. Paul urged all believers to **join with [him] in suffering for the gospel, by the power of God.** Jesus foretold persecution for his disciples (John 15:18–21), and Paul guaranteed it in this letter for all who live for God (2 Tim. 3:12). But enduring suffering for Christ is never accomplished by the force of human will. We gain strength to overcome persecution by the power of God as we depend upon his strength and place confidence in his judgments.

1:9. To endure, we must know the object and purpose in any enterprise. We are not called to witness and suffer just because God thinks it is a good idea. Many Christians, however, have little idea of the overarching goal of Christian living.

God has saved us . . . not because of anything we have done but because of his own purpose and grace. We are delivered out of the worst of disasters because of God's initiative toward us. It is one of the great imperatives of the Christian life that we realize the source of all our goodness and forgiveness—it is God, in Christ.

People throughout the world are consumed in the struggle to find significance and acceptance. All world religions require of their followers some method by which they attain favor with a god or acceptance and good standing in the spiritual hierarchy. Christianity alone puts all the work and effort upon God for salvation. Often, this very grace becomes the stumbling block for some people. It is hard to admit absolute need and powerlessness, yet this is what God requires of us.

But initial trust, the step into salvation, is only the beginning. God has **called us to a holy life.** This is our life purpose, the call which gives structure and substance to all our choices and everything we think, do, or say.

All this stems from God's grace, **given us in Christ Jesus before the beginning of time.** God's purposes and plan existed before creation, intended in Jesus Christ. We cannot limit what God has done or the extremity of his grace just because we do not understand how it works. How can we comprehend it or condense it to a system we can quantify and classify? We must accept with gratitude what Paul declared, keeping in mind that God's grace is undeserved.

1:10. God's grace, though eternally purposed, **has now been revealed through the appearing of our Savior, Christ Jesus.** The appearing of Christ Jesus is the manifestation of God in the flesh (John 1:14).

This incarnation of grace has **destroyed death and has brought life and immortality to light through the gospel.** The Greek word *katargeo,* translated here as "destroyed," means to make something ineffective or powerless. We can see that death has not been obliterated, but for the Christian it has been rendered impotent.

Death is no longer a terror for those who are in Christ. Instead, it is a doorway into a new existence of beauty, joy, and fulfillment. When physical life ceases, we are immediately present with the Lord. Even death's ally, sin, has no power over us in this life because God's Spirit enables us to overcome Satan's trickery. Spiritual death has been overcome by the power of God's life. We have been given true life in this world and immortality in the world to come.

God established his purposes in the beginning, put them into effect in history through Christ's death and resurrection, and extends his life to all through the gospel.

1:11–12. It is this gospel to which Paul was **appointed a herald and an apostle and a teacher.** Once again Paul drew attention to his calling by God. His missionary work was not his idea; he was appointed. As a herald, Paul proclaimed the gospel; as a teacher he instructed others in faith and life; and as an apostle, he spoke with authority.

That is why I am suffering. Paul's appointment resulted in beatings, loneliness, imprisonment, hunger, shipwreck, violent attack, criticism, misunderstanding, and rejection. Even so, he was **not ashamed.** Paul could state, "I am not ashamed of the gospel, because it is the power of God for the salvation of everyone who believes" (Rom. 1:16).

He endured with courage and honor because his trust was in the person of Christ: **I know whom I have believed.** He had no faith in religious systems or in his own personality or ability. His confidence was in God, sovereign of creation, giver of life, conquerer of death.

Paul was able to endure suffering because he was convinced of God's trustworthiness: **he is able to guard what I have entrusted to him for that day.** Paul had an unshakable confidence that God would keep safe whatever he placed in his care. Whether it was his life or ministry, these treasures were safely deposited in God's protection. This does not suggest that God protects us from all harm. But God does protect that which is eternal when it is given without reserve into his keeping: our soul and our work. These are held safe until the day of judgment.

Paul wanted Timothy to follow his example, to be unashamed and to give himself without reserve to the work of Christ in extending the gospel throughout the world. We can stay the course only when we have a sense of design and purpose about what we do—when we understand our past, present, and future.

Why then do we hesitate? Why do we become distracted with building a bigger house or spending our nights in front of the television?

The comprehensive meaning for every Christian is contained in Paul's apologetic: we were called before the creation of the world by God, our present life and work is safeguarded by Christ, and we are destined for an unshakable future with God.

ⓔ Paul's Charge to Timothy (1:13–14)

SUPPORTING IDEA: *Having laid the groundwork of God's purpose and faithfulness, Paul handed to Timothy a solemn charge of ministry.*

1:13–14. A sense of urgency filters through Paul's words as he focused on Timothy and pleaded, **what you heard from me, keep as the pattern of sound teaching.** Once again, Paul pressed home a familiar theme. The true gospel is founded upon the prophets, the words of Jesus, and apostolic teaching. Acutely aware of the damage inflicted by false teachers, Paul returned to the need for orthodoxy as revealed through Christ to Paul. It is this pure doctrine which is the pattern of sound teaching.

The word translated "sound" comes from the Greek *hugies,* used in the Gospels to describe the healing of the sick by Jesus. Paul used the word to distinguish apostolic doctrine from false doctrine. Truth produces health; it results in right thinking and godly behavior.

Paul did not prescribe intellectualism, the building of theological structures for their own sake. Truth is meant for life, and it is to be dispensed **with faith and love in Christ Jesus.** What we proclaim must be matched by our lives. If we are to guide people to Christ, we must hold a sincere trust in our Lord. Equally, our lives must be distinguished by love, divine in strength and giving. Both faith and love should be centered in Jesus.

Paul's words reverberate with his awareness that death was drawing closer. He was anxious that Timothy comprehend the importance and urgency of following through with his instructions. He told him to guard the apostolic revelation: **the good deposit that was entrusted to you.**

Each generation is so charged, for the gospel must be preserved in purity. We must protect it from destructive teachings. It is a serious responsibility, for we handle the very words of God. But we must also admit our inability to fulfill so noble a task. This is why Timothy and all Christians must guard Christ's gospel **with the help of the Holy Spirit who lives in us.** Paul again reminded us of this wonderful gift of God, this person of his Spirit who enables us to perform what God calls us to do.

This is a great picture of the Christian life and responsibility. God grants to us his gifts of grace and his Spirit of life—gifts freely given as we trust

Jesus Christ as Savior. Our responsibility is to respond with obedient trust, not to gain salvation, but to express love, and to fulfill the calling of God upon our lives (Eph. 4:1).

Paul describes this interaction of giftedness and responsibility in Philippians. There he says to "work out your salvation" (Phil. 2:12) with a sense of respect and fear, not to gain salvation, but to flesh it out, to work out in our life the implications of being saved. Then the promise is given, "it is God who works in you to will and to act according to his good purpose" (Phil. 2:13).

Thus, we have personal responsibility before God but the promise of strength and provision by his Spirit as well. We are not alone.

◪ Examples of Faithfulness and Unfaithfulness (1:15–18)

SUPPORTING IDEA: *The battles of faith and the hardships of faithfulness are not theoretical. Paul was involved with real people who chose either to follow Christ or to reject him. This underscores the choice facing any Christian. There is no neutral position in life. We are either for Christ or against him. We are acting either in faithfulness or apostasy.*

1:15. When Paul had lived in Ephesus, so many people had received the gospel that the message of Christ spread throughout Asia (Acts 19:1–20). Since that time, the arrest of Paul and the rise of false teachers had weakened the church and shaken the faith of many. Perhaps, under the circumstances, they supposed Christianity was a failed enterprise. Whatever the cause, a dramatic shift of faith had occurred. Timothy was well aware of this: **you know that everyone in the province of Asia has deserted me, including Phygelus and Hermogenes.** It seems these men had once been faithful, and, although we know nothing about them, they were familiar to Timothy. Perhaps their desertion exemplified the pervasiveness of the apostasy, leading to Timothy's own disheartened outlook.

1:16–18. From the faithless, Paul turned to the faithful. In the midst of widespread defection, one man, **Onesiphorus**, and his family remained committed to Christ. Paul was full of gratitude. He offered a prayer that **the Lord show mercy to the household** (v. 16), and that **he [Onesiphorus] will find mercy from the Lord on that day** (v. 18). God's mercy belongs to those who remain faithful.

Onesiphorus and his family must have shown hospitality to Paul while he stayed in Ephesus. Giving him food and a place to stay, they **refreshed** him. In fact, this man was so devoted to Christ that, despite the general defection in Asia, he **was not ashamed of [Paul's] chains.** At some point, Onesiphorus traveled to Rome and **searched hard** for the apostle. He never gave up but, with determination, hunted for him **until he found [him]**. Visiting Paul in prison could have placed Onesiphorus in a risky situation. Identifying with a condemned man was looked upon with suspicion by the Roman authorities.

In this chapter, Paul set clear choices before each of us. To follow Christ, we must hold to correct doctrine which will produce a healthy spiritual life. A Christian will be characterized by faithfulness and love. A follower must also identify with the suffering Christ and with all believers who suffer for righteousness.

> **MAIN IDEA REVIEW:** *Paul knew he had little time before his own execution, so he wrote a very personal letter to Timothy, full of intensity, love, and concern. He encouraged Timothy to be faithful in his trust of Christ, to act with boldness rather than acquiescing to his natural timidity, and to associate confidently with the suffering apostle and Christ. Paul knew Timothy must assume enormous responsibilities in the mission of the church, and he wanted him to be stalwart and obedient in preserving and spreading the gospel of Jesus Christ.*

III. CONCLUSION

Trivial Pursuit

A student once asked the brilliant and famous Dr. Albert Einstein, "Doctor Einstein, how many feet are there in a mile?"

Einstein astonished his student by replying, "I don't know."

The student felt sure the great teacher was joking. Einstein explained, "I make it a rule not to clutter my mind with simple information which, in a few minutes, I can find in a book."

Most of us are bombarded with data every day. We receive a constant stream of facts, figures, and opinions. All this information "clutters" our minds until we run the risk of ignoring the information we need for creative living.

Second Timothy, and this first chapter in particular, is filled with vital information for Christians and the church. Nothing in this book is trivial. Paul directed us to consider our heritage of faith and the responsibility to faithfulness which this places upon us. He also established the need for all believers to find their identity in Christ Jesus. If we rely on accomplishments, status, wealth, friends, or anything else for our sense of identity, we cannot endure hardship or serve with commitment. Paul always returned to the foundation of our faith and identity—the work of God through Christ Jesus. The risen Lord enables his people; his grace bestows upon us the treasures of the heavens.

PRINCIPLES

- Real life, a life that gives a person fulfillment, purpose, and eternal signficance, is found in Jesus Christ.
- Family heritage models and encourages sincere faith.
- When Christ comes into our lives, we are inhabited by the Holy Spirit. He can free us from our fears and fill us with boldness and love.
- Understanding that God intended grace for us before the world's creation, knowing that we have a glorious future with Christ, and trusting his presence for today can free us from shame and give us courageous faith.
- God's truth rests upon his revelation through the prophets, Jesus, and the apostles. Faithful obedience to this will produce a healthy spiritual life, one that is fruitful in the works of God.

APPLICATIONS

- Every parent and grandparent should think of ways to model Christian faith before their children and grandchildren. We should be open in telling our stories of faith and unashamed in sharing our life in Christ.
- Each Christian should be able to articulate what it means to be saved by God's grace.
- Every believer needs to be a student of Scripture, guarding biblical truth in his or her own life.
- Each person should examine his or her life to see if belief and conduct are in harmony.

IV. LIFE APPLICATION

Running the Race

Perhaps the most elemental sport in the world is the footrace. Unencumbered by equipment, it pits person against person. For thousands of years, the footrace has endured—on playgrounds, in neighborhoods, along mountain paths, in Olympic stadiums. A champion runner must have endurance and desire. All else being equal, the runner who digs deepest into his inner spirit usually triumphs.

But all things are rarely equal, even among trained athletes. Sometimes the person who "loses" but finishes the race displays a nobility of spirit unmatched by the victor.

In 1992, Barcelona, Spain, hosted the summer Olympics. Millions of people watched the world's fastest runners compete in distances from one hundred meters to the twenty-six-mile marathon.

Derek Redmond of Great Britain, a semi-finalist in the 400–meter race, crouched, ready, in his blocks. In the Olympics four years before, one minute before race time, Derek had made the agonizing decision to disqualify himself due to an Achilles tendon problem. Denied the chance to run, he watched from the sidelines. Now, after four years of relentless, focused training and several surgeries, Derek wanted this race more than ever.

An official raised the starting gun, then squeezed the trigger. The sound cracked through the air, and the runners bolted from their blocks. Arms and legs pumping, each runner sprinted down the track. But one hundred meters into the race, Derek's hamstring tore. He stumbled and fell. Paramedics rushed onto the track, but he waved them off. He got up, his face twisted in pain and streaked with tears. He hobbled, then fell again. He crawled. Once more he got to his feet, limping, faltering, yet slowly pressing on. With officials and cameramen crowding, Derek turned the last corner.

Then, from out of the stands rushed a man wearing a cap. "Just Do It" was lettered across its front. Pushing his way through the throng of officials and onlookers, he came alongside Derek. Without hesitation he put his arm around the young runner. No one pushed him away. This time, Derek did not wave off the help. Instead, he put his arm around the man—his dad. Supported by the bonds of affection, strengthened by a relationship of encouragement and care, the two men crossed the finish line together.

Thousands of years earlier, Paul wrote to Timothy, his son in the faith, while sitting in a dark prison cell. Behind them lay years of hard work together, planting churches, teaching, settling disputes, organizing congregations, evangelizing Asia. Paul valued Timothy's devotion to the gospel, his hard work, dependability, and sincere faith. But Paul also understood the frailty of man.

Timothy experienced discouragement during his time in Ephesus. He encountered false teachers, bickering, and opposition. Many people abandoned the faith. With Paul facing death in Rome, Nero rampaging against Christians, public opinion turning hostile toward believers, and those within the church turning away, Timothy may have faltered. So Paul came alongside the young man. By writing this letter, he put his arm around him and directed him back to the object of our faith—the risen Christ. He supported Timothy with expressions of love. He encouraged him to focus on the goal, that day when we will see Christ. He empowered him by reminding Timothy of his responsibility to God and the gospel. Timothy must finish the race.

Today people limp through life feeling the agony of poor choices, relational heartache, and moral breakdown. Weary and discouraged, people stumble in their faith. One of the great privileges of belonging to Christ is our call to break through the crowd of spectators with compassion and encouragement. We are to come alongside, by the power of the Holy Spirit, offering restoration, love, wisdom, and gentleness—so we may finish the race . . . together.

V. PRAYER

Jesus, guide me to those who can instill Christian courage within me, so that I, in turn, can encourage others to persevere in faith. Amen.

VI. DEEPER DISCOVERIES

Suffering (vv. 8,12)

Suffering. We fear it; we run from it; we work hard to ward it off; we turn our eyes away from those whom it engulfs. It is, perhaps, more dreaded than death. Yet, Paul wrote Timothy and, by implication, all believers, to join him in suffering for the gospel.

Paul rejected any suggestion that hardship and affliction are pathways to holiness. But Paul understood the offensive nature of Christian faith. He knew that those who boldly live and proclaim its truth will be subject to hardships. Jesus promised difficulty to those who followed him (John 15:20; 16:33), and the entire Book of Acts presents an almost endless succession of persecution. Paul recounted his own sufferings not to garner pity, but to model patient endurance and to assure every believer that such treatment is to be expected (1 Cor. 11:24–27).

Identification with the suffering Christ compels us to embrace suffering on his behalf. The early Christians discovered in holy suffering a closeness with the risen Christ. When we comprehend our self-identity as resting exclusively in the person of Jesus, we dare not avoid what he willingly endured.

The erroneous expectation that Christianity and our culture's values can be compatible leads us to consternation and surprise when society rejects us. Our faith shudders, and our spirits quiver when Christian faith meets with hostility or cold indifference. Though we rarely say so out loud, we cling to the hope that we will be spared the anguish and torment of earlier generations. Yet this hope is false. It leads to spiritual weakness. We cannot face situations for which we are unprepared.

We would serve the church better by resolutely committing ourselves to suffer for Christ. Perhaps if we entered each day expecting difficulty rather than avoiding it, we could endure it for his sake. Then our faith would grow stronger, and others would find courage.

2 Timothy 1

VII. TEACHING OUTLINE

A. INTRODUCTION

1. Lead Story: Last Will and Testament
2. Context: Paul was facing execution in a Roman prison. He was anxious to bolster the faith of his young friend Timothy. He reminded Timothy of his heritage and the power that God imparts to every believer, urged Timothy to follow his example of perseverance and faithfulness, and issued a solemn charge to guard the gospel.
3. Transition: Leaders of the church must always be diligent in passing on the foundations of the gospel to faithful people who will preserve it through the generations. But all Christians are responsible for maintaining their own spiritual health through study and disciplined living. Everyone is called to pass on to others the message of God's grace.

B. COMMENTARY

1. Greeting (1:1–2)
2. Christian Heritage (1:3–5)
3. God's Empowerment (1: 6–7)
4. The Confidence and Identity of the Believer (1:8–12)
5. Paul's Charge to Timothy (1:13–14)
6. Examples of Faithfulness and Unfaithfulness (1:15–18)

C. CONCLUSION: RUNNING THE RACE

VIII. ISSUES FOR DISCUSSION

1. Give some examples of ways an adult can lead a child to Christ and then nurture his or her faith.
2. All of us have at least one area where we feel timid, unqualified, fearful. Write down what causes you the most fear and insecurity. Consider how you could begin today to apply God's promise of power, love, and balanced thinking.
3. Discuss the ways you might suffer for your faith. What encouragement does Paul give us in these circumstances?
4. Who has refreshed you spiritually? How did they do it? What positive influence could you have on other Christians?

2 Timothy 2

Training and Disciplines of Faith

I. **INTRODUCTION**
Basic Training

II. **COMMENTARY**
A verse-by-verse explanation of the chapter.

III. **CONCLUSION**
So What's the Point?

An overview of the principles and applications from the chapter.

IV. **LIFE APPLICATION**
Apprenticed for Life

Melding the chapter to life.

V. **PRAYER**
Tying the chapter to life with God.

VI. **DEEPER DISCOVERIES**
Historical, geographical, and grammatical enrichment of the commentary.

VII. **TEACHING OUTLINE**
Suggested step-by-step group study of the chapter.

VIII. **ISSUES FOR DISCUSSION**
Zeroing the chapter in on daily life.

2 Timothy 2

 I N   A   N U T S H E L L

*P*aul told Timothy to remain strong in faith despite hardship or opposition. He gave four illustrations from common experience to underscore the need as well as the logic of his instruction. Paul then reminded Timothy of the essence of the gospel and the great security he had in Christ, concluding with instructions for holiness and useful service in Christ's kingdom.

Training and Disciplines of Faith

I. INTRODUCTION

Basic Training

*P*roficiency in any sport requires a person to follow certain rules and disciplines and to develop specific skills. The drive for excellence determines the demands of training. Whether an athlete is in junior high, the pros, or somewhere in between, his inner will to achieve gauges his investment of time and energy in the sport.

Basketball players stay late and shoot extra hoops. A young boy might dribble the ball everywhere he goes just to get a little better. Soccer players hang around after practice, dribbling the ball between obstacles or running sprints in order to outperform the opposition. Baseball enthusiasts stay longer in the batting cages, or they throw balls at a distant target to sharpen skills. Serious sportsmen do whatever is necessary to improve, giving attention not only to the specifics of their sport but also to general fitness—lifting weights, running, getting adequate sleep, eating particular foods, and even practicing meditation.

The same principles of dedicated training, practice, and endurance apply to almost any human effort. Businessmen focused on success drive themselves to keep up with the latest techniques, the newest information. They study business proposals carefully and carry out detailed studies. An artist trains herself in drawing, practicing over and over again until the forms or designs conform to her vision. She studies the masters and the various evolutionary stages of art.

The Christian life demands the same determined spirit, the same focused attention, and the same disciplined practice. This chapter gives one of the strongest calls in the Bible for believers to devote themselves to skillful understanding and practice of the Scriptures. It also calls us to remember who we serve—the risen Christ. "His divine power has given us everything we need for life and godliness" (2 Pet. 1:3). Our commitment determines our progress.

II. COMMENTARY

> **MAIN IDEA:** *Paul called Timothy back to basics—the grace of God and the instructions he had received. The apostle then proceeded to encourage Timothy to remain faithful: enduring hardship, identifying with the crucified Christ, committing to orthodox belief and behavior, disciplining his life for noble use in God's kingdom.*

A The Plan for Perpetuation of the Faith (2:1–2)

> **SUPPORTING IDEA:** *Each generation bears the responsibility of preserving and handing on the basic Christian beliefs to those who follow.*

2:1. Having just shared his disappointment over the growing apostasy spreading through Asia, Paul turned to Timothy and wrote, **You then, my son, be strong**. Difficult circumstances, our own weaknesses and fears, and the negative attitudes or unfaithfulness of others should not determine our course in life. Just as Paul wrote of the power which comes from the Holy Spirit (2 Tim. 1:7), so now he wrote of the strength which comes from Jesus Christ.

No doubt Timothy knew, as Paul did, that he could not find adequate strength within himself to fulfill the responsibilities thrust upon him or to endure the hardships ahead. Our confidence and ability to live successfully as followers of Christ comes when we are **strong in the grace that is in Christ Jesus.** Paul knew that God's grace not only saves us; it enables us to carry out the life of faithful obedience.

2:2. Our own relationship with Christ Jesus must be developing in trust and dependence before we can expect to influence others for his kingdom. The perpetual strength of God's grace would enable Timothy to fulfill his tasks. Timothy must not only guard the gospel; he must take the gospel and the apostolic instructions (**things you have heard me say in the presence of many witnesses**) and **entrust [them] to reliable men.**

Unlike the false teachers who claimed special revelation or secret knowledge, Paul's message stood in accord with all Scripture and in agreement with the apostles. What he received from the Lord he passed on in an open manner (1 Cor. 11:23). Likewise, Timothy received no inside information from Paul. The message was widely known, spoken of freely and before many witnesses.

In his assignment to entrust the gospel to other people, Timothy needed to observe in these believers the quality of adherence to God's truth. Reliability and trustworthiness in remaining true to the gospel were prerequisites.

Timothy must also seek those who evidenced a knowledge and ability to teach others. Paul wanted to establish people of godly character who possessed the aptitude for relating divine truth to everyday life, for clarifying ideas, and for maintaining purity in their instruction.

🅱 Three Metaphors: Devotion, Honesty, and Work (2:3–7)

> **SUPPORTING IDEA:** *The person committed to following Christ must expect difficulty. He must not only expect it but welcome it if he is to receive the reward given to those who remain faithful.*

1. The soldier (2:3–4)

2:3–4. Paul favored military imagery in many of his letters. He understood that Christian living involved warfare. So he told Timothy: **endure hardship with us like a good soldier of Christ Jesus.**

Soldiers on active duty expect hardship. Battling the enemy on the front lines, the soldier lives in harsh conditions—damp weather, poor food, uncomfortable sleep, dirt and filth, inadequate shelter, and exhaustion. The further one retreats from the front lines, however, the more frequent and trivial become the complaints. Those involved in the struggles of survival and the exhaustion of combat rarely complain about the food—they are simply happy to eat.

In the same way, Christians who determine to live holy, obedient lives before God place themselves on the front lines of spiritual warfare. They encounter attacks of Satan, suffer scorn and rejection, and often deny themselves many comforts.

But in serving Christ, no one needs to endure the struggles and difficulties alone. Paul encouraged Timothy to **endure . . . with us.** Even though they were separated geographically, an authentic bond existed between them. Knowing that others join in one's joy or hardship gives courage. In addition, the Holy Spirit creates a connection of love between people.

Enduring hardship requires devotion. Performing as a good soldier requires total commitment: **no one serving as a soldier gets involved in civilian affairs.** The word translated "involved" in the NIV has been translated "entangled" in other versions; it comes from a term used of sheep that get their wool caught in thorns. Such a word picture graphically illustrates what occurs when believers wander off from commitment to Jesus Christ. Unless we keep vigilant watch on our thinking and spirit, we will become snagged on the thorns of popular philosophy and current social values. We must be on constant duty, guarding our commitment and our desires.

In Paul's day, Roman soldiers were not part-time warriors. They were not busy buying real estate or making business plans as they passed through conquered territory. From sunup until they rested at night, every activity involved honing the skills of warfare, ensuring the security of their unit, and gathering the supplies to keep them ready and fit. Nothing was ignored or left to chance. Life and victory depended upon the soldiers' readiness and commitment to the task.

We also must remain unflinching in our devotion to Christ and his kingdom: **to please [our] commanding officer.** Then, when hardship comes, we can endure.

2. The athlete (2:5)

2:5. Paul turned next to athletic competition for his illustration, focusing on the commitment which proceeds from honest and legitimate faith. Sports were probably as popular during the days of the Roman Empire as they are now. The Olympiad and other contests were watched with enthusiasm. Athletes trained rigorously in order to compete.

Before the modern explosion in athletes' salaries, the driving force in most sporting enterprises was attaining the prize—the medal, the ribbon, or the laurel wreath. As important as this prize was, unless the individual trained and practiced and competed according to the rules, there was little possibility of winning. So Paul wrote, **he does not receive the victor's crown unless he competes according to the rules.**

The rules are twofold. One aspect involves training, keeping the body fit, attaining the necessary skills or speed. The second centers on lawful competition. Each game or contest has particular rules which help define the sport and describe proper conduct and etiquette; no athlete makes up the rules as he goes along. If someone breaks these rules or ignores them, the officials disqualify him.

Christian living also requires adherence to certain rules regarding purity, doctrinal orthodoxy, faith, and love. Those who abide by the truth of God's Word will receive their reward on the day of judgment. Those who try to claim the prize without a commitment to faithful obedience will be disqualified.

3. The farmer (2:6)

2:6. People who raise vegetables in their backyard know the hard work involved in nurturing and working a garden. But for those who depend upon the soil for their living, farming demands even greater toil. Planting and harvesting account for only a small portion of the farmer's time and energy. He must also till the soil, battle insects, diseases, drought, flooding, and winds. All this keeps the farmer hard at work through the crucial growing season. If he becomes negligent in his attention to these problems, he will never realize the harvest. But if he labors to the end, he **should be the first to receive a share of the crops.**

The hard-working Christian will also reap a harvest "at the proper time" if he does not give up (Gal. 6:9). But crops do not sprout up overnight. Christian service requires hard work. A person sharing his life in ministry should not demand immediate results.

God has called each of us to ministry. The long haul between our enthusiastic beginning and our anticipated glory requires a great deal of hard work. Each person committed to the life of faith will deal with difficult circumstances, issues of temptation and sin, spiritual struggles, adverse opinions, misunderstandings, exhaustion, and an array of pests which can ruin personal and ministry growth. Once again, commitment must find its home in the heart. Then it will work itself out in enduring service.

4. Reflection (2:7)

2:7. Having set down three examples from common life, Paul told Timothy, **Reflect on what I am saying, for the Lord will give you insight.** These examples required some thinking, not only to understand the truth behind what he had written, but to consider the implications for one's life. Paul had given an unembellished portrait of Christian living and service. It required disciplined living, disassociation from society's comforts and values, suffering, hard work, diligence, patience, and struggle. Paul realized it was far easier to talk about these words than to embrace them. We must also reflect prayerfully on what Paul has written.

Ⓒ Suffering and Blessing (2:8–13)

SUPPORTING IDEA: *Paul wanted Timothy to realize that nothing of value is gained without hard work and suffering, even in the ordinary endeavors of the soldier, the athlete, and the farmer. Now he illustrated this point by focusing on particularly Christian examples—Christ, himself, and all believers.*

2:8–9. Paul had challenged Timothy to stay focused and face harsh conditions like a soldier; to live honestly and endure the difficulties of training like an athlete; and to labor with patience like a farmer. Now he gave the great motivation for all he had written, telling Timothy to **remember Jesus Christ, raised from the dead.**

Thinking on Christ and his resurrection helps in two ways. First, he is our example in times of difficulty. He suffered extreme agony and death for us. Yet he endured. We should be willing to suffer on his behalf. Second, his resurrection provides hope and courage, for we are promised the same resurrection he experienced, if we continue in faith.

Paul also told Timothy to remember Jesus as **descended from David.** Christ, being fully human, understanding and experiencing pain and rejection just as we do, strips away all our excuses. His obedient submission led to his great victory over death, his triumphant resurrection.

This is my gospel, Paul declared, **for which I am suffering even to the point of being chained like a criminal.** Just as Jesus suffered, so will his servants. Like his Lord, Paul's hardships resulted from the natural conditions of human experience—the unspiritual world in opposition to the spiritual. Paul's offense to Rome was that he preached the crucified and risen Jesus. But the apostle also understood that suffering was part of commitment; it is in difficulty that true commitment shows itself.

For Timothy, the possibility of Christianity advancing and the church rooting itself in society must have seemed dim. Discouraged by the general apostasy throughout Asia, abandoned by many in Ephesus, his teacher and friend imprisoned in Rome and facing death, Timothy had little to grasp in hope. Yet, Paul provided it in these words: **But God's word is not chained.** The power of the gospel resides in the living Christ and the ongoing work of his Spirit in the world.

2:10. Because of Paul's identification with Jesus Christ and the confidence he had in the Lord's resurrection power, he was willing to **endure everything for the sake of the elect.**

Election is a difficult theological concept to grasp, but it remains unalterably part of the gospel. Clearly, God has direct involvement in those who consecrate their lives to him. Just as clearly, each individual is responsible for his or her response. To Timothy, Paul emphasized the crucial task of believers to extend the gospel to all people. God has ordained that the dissemination of his message and life will take place through people who are faithful to him. His followers must be willing to do whatever it takes to enlarge his kingdom throughout the earth.

The elect are those who trust Christ Jesus; they are the ones who invest themselves in Christ's saving grace and kingdom. These followers of Jesus affirm God's call upon their life by responding in faith. For these people, some of whom are yet unknown, Paul was willing to suffer any hardship, so **that they too may obtain the salvation that is in Christ Jesus, with eternal glory.**

2:11–12a. Once again Paul shared another **trustworthy saying.** Typically, he used well-known hymns or folk wisdom which the readers recognized. In this instance, he used couplets written as contrasts: *if this . . . then this.* The first two couplets reinforced the theme of suffering as normative to Christian living, contrasting this present life with the eternal future. The second two couplets paired human failings and God's response.

Paul resounded the Christian doctrine of life from death: **If we died with him, we will also live with him** (see also Rom. 6:8). These words are reminiscent of Jesus when he said, "Unless a kernel of wheat falls to the ground and dies, it remains only a single seed. . . . The man who loves his life will lose it, while the man who hates his life in this world will keep it for eternal life" (John 12:24–25).

When we identify with Christ through abiding trust, we die to sin, to the world, and to self. God then raises us to a new kind of life as part of his wonderful work of regeneration (Rom. 6:1–4; Gal. 2:20). But Paul also recognized that the glory of our resurrection comes in the future; we have yet to realize it fully. In this present life we still suffer the effects of a world dominated by death.

The second couplet provides a slightly different slant on the contrast between the difficulties of life now and the rewards to come: **if we endure, we will also reign with him**. Western Christianity has often adopted one of the most damaging values to true Christian faith—the pursuit of comfort and ease. Christ is frequently presented as the answer to *our* problems or the fulfillment of *our* needs. Yet Paul understood the Christian life as one of continual struggle, suffering, and hardship—to bring glory to Christ. Christ brings to the believer the supernatural ability to persist, to endure, and to respond with joy and thanksgiving (Col. 1:10–12).

2:12b-13. Paul's tenor changed in the next set of couplets. Recalling the words of Jesus in Matthew 10:32–33, he wrote, **if we disown him, he will also disown us**. Paul had in mind those who profess Christ and then turn away, denying the faith they formerly claimed. Paul issued a warning that denial of Christ has eternally damning consequences.

But God is gracious when we are feeble. Paul offered this encouragement for the times when we fail: **if we are faithless, he will remain faithful**. If we belong to Christ, we are his completely. In the midst of difficulty, he holds on to us if we stumble. He lives within us, sharing his life with ours as we take from his life—and so **he cannot disown himself**.

ⅅ The Faithful Servant (2:14–26)

SUPPORTING IDEA: *Paul gave practical instructions on how the true servant of Jesus Christ will live. He warned about activities which sabotage our efforts to live a life worthy of God's calling, especially those things which prove divisive. Paul always presented two clear choices without any neutral options. We either choose Christ's way, or we fall into the devices of Satan.*

2:14. As a minister of the gospel, Timothy must remind all those in the church about the instructions and warnings Paul had delivered to him. Pastors are to **keep reminding** their congregations of the truth of Scripture, the nature of God, and the demands of holy living. This task is never complete.

Paul then set up some contrasts. He focused first on the false teachers and those who followed them. Then he turned to the good workman of God.

As for the false teachers, Timothy was to **warn them before God against quarreling about words.** He was to call God as his witness against these troublesome people and their ideas. These teachers argued about words and built enormous theological systems upon them. They fought over small points of interpretation. Not only did they devote themselves to words and esoteric ramblings; they were contentious in their manner. Paul's judgment of such petty obsessions: **it is of no value, and only ruins those who listen.**

Not only the teachers but also those who listened to their foolishness were brought to spiritual ruin. Their debates pulled others into their pointless discussions. People were deluded, thinking it was true spirituality. In fact, their word games came from pride.

2:15. Timothy, by contrast, must do his best to **present [himself] to God as one approved, a workman who does not need to be ashamed.** Timothy, and all who follow Christ, are to consecrate themselves to God, working diligently for his approval. The teacher whom God approves has no need of shame in his presence.

God bestows his approval on the one who exhibits truth, love, and godliness in daily living, and who **correctly handles the word of truth.** The false teachers were mishandling God's words, using them for their own benefit. Timothy was commissioned to handle the words of God correctly. All preaching should present the truth clearly, cutting through erroneous ideas or inaccurate opinions.

The pastor or teacher must acquaint himself thoroughly with Scripture. He should familiarize himself with historical information and the context of the passage, especially when trying to reach back through the centuries to gain an accurate understanding of God's revelation.

2:16. Paul again issued a warning: **Avoid godless chatter.** Paul was not referring to backyard chats or little conversation groups that met over tea. The phrase "godless chatter" describes the empty babbling of false teachers. Their doctrines may have been quite organized and intricate, but Paul labeled them "chatter" because they were without substance.

In addition, their teachings did not promote the life and practices which God approves. Paul declared that those who indulged in such chatter would **become more and more ungodly.** In vivid contrast to God's truth, which results in godliness, the false teachings degenerate into greater ungodliness.

2:17–18. But these false teachers and their philosophies were not pitiful little people to be ignored. They were causing great harm to those whom they influencd: **Their teaching will spread like gangrene.** Just as the teaching they followed was rotten, so its foul and corrupt nature infected more and more people. In contrast, truth is always life producing, creating wholeness and health. Paul gave two examples of leaders who abandoned the faith and whose spurious teachings brought destructive results: **Hymenaeus and Phile-tus, who have wandered away from the truth.**

Other than this mention by Paul, these two men pass unknown in history. But because their names were known to Timothy, they were probably leaders within the Ephesian church. Yet, they wandered away. This describes a slow drifting from the truth. These men did not make a dramatic break from the Christian faith and run after strange philosophies. They slowly shifted their thinking, toyed with new ideas, held to what they liked and discarded what was unappealing. After a time, they had denied the faith.

Paul highlighted one main point of their false teaching: **they say that the resurrection has already taken place.** This supposition, rampant among the false teachers, taught that the fullness of salvation had come. Consequently, there was no future bodily resurrection, for the true resurrection was spiritual. This led to the practice of discounting anything connected with physical life, making daily obligations and concerns for holy living irrelevant. Spiritualizing the resurrection diminished the sacrifice of Christ, removed the necessity of enduring hardship, and promoted immoral living. In this way, **they destroy the faith of some.**

2:19. It would seem gloomy indeed if Paul had stopped with the description of the growing influence of these false teachers. But he sounded a loud note of hope and courage as he wrote, **Nevertheless, God's solid foundation stands firm.**

Despite what people may say or do, God's work of salvation through Christ and his work of the church as established by the apostles and ministers of the gospel continues to stand firm. If the gates of hell will not overcome the church (Matt. 16:18), neither will the apostasy of some, the destructive teaching of others, or the militant arm of Rome. God has established the church, built on Jesus Christ "as the chief cornerstone" (Eph. 2:20). Proof of the church's endurance rests upon the guarantee made by God himself, **sealed with this inscription: "The Lord knows those who are his."**

Paul took this quote from Numbers 16:5. It came out of the story of Korah's rebellion and God's affirmation of Moses' leadership. Paul drew from across the centuries, from the Old Testament to the New Testament, confirming God's changeless character and sovereign rule.

Only God knows the inward working of the heart, but **everyone who confesses the name of the Lord** will evidence increasing godliness—they **must turn away from wickedness.** Both inward and outward change are necessary components of a true believer in Jesus Christ. Timothy and others might have difficulty discerning the faithful from the faithless, but God cannot be fooled. He knows those who belong to him.

2:20–21. Paul drew another word picture to illustrate the distinctions between the true believer and the false follower. He took his imagery from his readers' understanding of an ordinary house. Such a house would have a variety of utensils and wares, some of **gold and silver,** and others of **wood and clay.** Correspondingly, the gold and silver are for **noble purposes,** while the wood and clay are reserved for **ignoble** use. Basically, a person does not use china cups to feed the dog.

Jesus foretold the same truth. The church is a mixed group, some true to their Lord, others impostors (Matt. 13:24–30). Though God knows who belongs to him and though true disciples demonstrate a life reflective of his holiness, scattered among them are unbelievers who deny the truth by their doctrine and their lives. These are the wood and clay within God's earthly house. Their presence should not disturb or discourage those who are faithful.

Paul emphasized that each believer bears the responsibility of service to God: **If a man cleanses himself from the latter** (false teachings and wickedness), he will serve **noble purposes.** God can use only clean or holy vessels. This parallels the Jewish tradition of cleansing vessels for temple use or for religious ceremonies and holidays. God cannot bestow his glory upon anything evil or tainted. The Christian life demands unswerving obedience and allegiance to Christ. It places responsibility upon each believer to maintain a pure, unpolluted life. Such a person is **holy, useful to the Master and prepared to do any good work.**

2:22. The bottom line is that each person chooses whether he will be fit for God's use. This sobering thought brought Paul to this urgent plea: **Flee the evil desires of youth.**

In the first century, the term *youth* was not confined to the teenage years. In fact, only two phases of life were recognized—youth and old age. Many interpreters believe Timothy was in his late thirties or even in his forties when Paul wrote to him. Perhaps "young" people experience greater temptations toward certain sins which diminish with age, such as haughty independence and selfish ambition. Those seriously committed to Christ must flee anything that smacks of evil or anything that would interfere with faithfulness to God.

Fleeing provides only half the equation, however. As we flee from evil, we must **pursue righteousness, faith, love and peace.** Christianity does not consist merely of prohibitions, but of positive and powerful actions.

Righteousness, faith, love, peace—these are common words, easily tossed around in Christian conversation, but they are the essence of the gospel.

Righteousness means to live uprightly, doing good as empowered by God. **Faith** rests on trust in God's revelation and character; it consists of a genuine relationship with God.

Love consists of self-sacrifice, living for the good of others with caring actions. **Peace** demonstrates itself through harmonious relations with God and others.

These qualities are normative for **those who call on the Lord out of a pure heart.** Believers look to God and depend upon him in all of life. People who have authentic faith are cleansed within. Paul encouraged Timothy to join with other true believers in persisting in his commitment to righteousness.

2:23. Paul issued another command: **Don't have anything to do with foolish and stupid arguments.** Paul had the false teachers and their followers in mind. Their dogmas lacked common sense (foolish) and were established upon ignorance (stupid). These bogus leaders and their followers were motivated by selfishness. Such inner drives always degenerate into petty **quarrels** and divisiveness.

2:24. Paul declared, **And the Lord's servant must not quarrel.** Selfish attitudes and manners are inconsistent with the nature of God and the disposition of his followers, especially his leaders. Unfortunately, infighting and positioning for power often characterize churches. Perhaps we have become too accustomed to this blatant disobedience, viewing it as an inevitable component of modern church life.

But pastors and lay leaders who bicker, creating factions within the church, are wrong. Instead, the church leader **must be kind to everyone, able to teach, not resentful.** Kindness presupposes a peaceable attitude. Such a mindset speaks and acts in goodness. This does not mean spineless acquiescence to popular opinion or to those who may oppose us. Kindness must remain firmly rooted in truth.

Paul required that the Christian leader be **able to teach, not resentful.** Though truth can seem harsh, carrying with it conviction or judgment of sin, it must be delivered with compassion and kindness because God always works for the restoration or repentance of the sinner. Pastors and leaders must model this understanding and care.

2:25–26. If a leader's heart is pure, humbled before God's grace, he can then **gently instruct** those who err, **in the hope that God will grant them repentance.** God's earnest desire to draw all people into loving relationship with himself should motivate the pastor to deal kindly with those who oppose him.

Four players participate in this crucial drama for the human soul: the teacher, the unbeliever, God, and Satan.

The Christian teacher not only proclaims truth; he models godliness and kindness as well. As God's representative, he personifies God and his ways. He also recognizes that the battle for human souls takes place on two fronts—the mind and the heart. Unbelievers do not think clearly in matters of the soul or spirit; they need to **come to their senses**. This is why the teacher must feed the minds of unbelievers, leading them to a **knowledge of the truth.**

The unbeliever must remain open and responsive. He must choose to come to his senses. Each person stands responsible before God for his acceptance or rejection of God's truth as found in Jesus Christ.

Beyond the human sphere, God and Satan enter man's spiritual struggle. Those who refuse God's truth come under the influence of **the devil who has taken them captive to do his will.** Satan traps people into his service through clever arguments, fear, and appeals to selfish pride and ambition. Christians should exercise a healthy awareness of the participation of Satan in the thinking of unbelievers. Contending for truth involves contending with spiritual powers; we must not be so naive as to think we confront on purely human terms.

But God remains faithful. He also contends for human souls and minds. As a measure of his grace, he grants repentance. God is sovereign over the universe and all created beings. We should never become overwhelmed at Satan's methods or power. Satan and God are not equals.

As believers, our responsibility is to speak God's truth, live out his nature, and pray earnestly for the salvation of those who continue in Satan's grip. We ask him, by virtue of his authority, to grant a change of heart to those who are estranged from his truth and love.

MAIN IDEA REVIEW: *Paul called Timothy back to basics—the grace of God and the instructions he had received. The apostle then proceeded to encourage Timothy to remain faithful: enduring hardship, identifying with the crucified Christ, committing to orthodox belief and behavior, disciplining his life for noble use in God's kingdom.*

III. CONCLUSION

So What's the Point?

During the days of the Watergate scandal, President Nixon's press secretary testified: "The other interpretation of the problem of the need for money for the purpose that was stated at the time, which was the purpose that was raised several times, as I have testified earlier that I was aware of, and apparently was raised at other times, which I later found out that I was not aware of."

Ever wish the speaker would get to the point? Say it clearly and be done?

Church leaders have been known to engage in the same sort of jabberwockery made popular by politicians. Using inflated language and esoteric mumblings, they form arguments and defend positions. They quarrel over words and dispute issues that rarely make a difference to life and godliness.

In the process, a watching world yawns as the church camouflages the true issues of life and death, forgiveness and grace to which the gospel speaks.

In this chapter of 2 Timothy, Paul gave Timothy some vital commands about priorities and perspective:

- Continue in the foundational truths of the faith and pass them on to others (2:1–2).
- Do not get sidetracked over minor issues (2:3–7).
- Remember the resurrection of Christ; it is central to our faith (2:8).
- Stay away from quarrels; they divide the church and ruin its witness (2:14–19).
- Commit yourself to the eternal purposes of Christ's kingdom (2:20–21).
- When opposed, keep teaching with gentle love and truth and keep on praying. God brings about change in a person's heart (2:22–26).

If Paul's instructions are followed, the church can avoid useless meetings, church splits, and even a few wars. In all we say and do, Christ is the point. Let us get to the point and stick with it.

PRINCIPLES

- Established leaders in the church must train new leaders in orthodox Christian doctrine.
- New leaders must evidence faithful obedience to Christ and an ability to teach others the truths of the faith.
- The Christian life demands a commitment which persists through difficulty and hardship.
- All true Christians can expect persecution.
- God is faithful.
- God knows and rewards the inner heart of all people—the faithful follower with fellowship and eternal life; the unfaithful with judgment.
- God's truth unites people.
- Selfish motives always prove destructive.
- We choose whether our lives honor God and result in noble purposes.
- God empowers his people to display a gentle spirit, even in the midst of controversy or personal attack.

APPLICATIONS

- Churches should have an organized method of training new leaders in the church, establishing them in doctrine and belief. Matters of belief must not be presumed but vigorously taught.
- Classes in teaching methods, or the demonstration of teaching ability, should be required of those who hold teaching positions in the church.
- When believers experience hardship, misunderstanding, or ridicule because of their faith in Christ, encourage them to persist in faithful obedience.
- When people argue over words or form groups in opposition to leaders in the church, stay away from them. God calls us to unity.
- Analyze every opinion or idea by God's Word, the Bible.
- Determine to work for God's kingdom. Put people ahead of projects, reconciliation ahead of personal feelings, and truth ahead of acceptance.

IV. LIFE APPLICATION

Apprenticed for Life

Robert Louis Stevenson knew from childhood what he wanted to be—a writer. But he discovered early on that good writing requires a long and rigorous apprenticeship.

From his youth, Stevenson always carried with him two books—one to read and one to write in. He knew two disciplines were necessary for success: to feed his mind on the works of great writers and to imitate them by constructing his own stories.

Stevenson built on the experience and knowledge of those before him. He understood that as each generation passes on its skill and knowledge to the next, teachers, leaders, and masters emerge—people who edge closer to the ideal. They set the standard for those who follow. Through imitation and practice, Stevenson created such classics as *Kidnapped* and *Treasure Island*.

Apprenticeship has a long history, stretching back to ancient times. Though foundational in the early educational stages of this country, apprenticeships became unpopular with the advent of the industrial revolution. The skill of the craftsman was replaced by the machine.

The fallout has hit us today as business leaders bemoan college graduates who cannot think or solve problems, and industry chiefs worry over the poor quality of American products. We are discovering that manual skill without knowledge and understanding is a poor substitute for old-fashioned competence.

On the flip side, university degrees and theoretical knowledge tend toward uselessness without the creative impulses of real-life experiences. Apprenticeships allow students the personal touch of someone who has mastered their particular art, someone who can give guidance, correction, and encouragement to the emerging craftsman.

In the second chapter of 2 Timothy, Paul urged Timothy to follow the model of apprenticeship. It is a pattern for our own Christian development as well as a standard for development within the church.

Jesus Christ is the Master, the ideal whom we seek to imitate. He also provides mature Christians who serve as flesh-and-bones examples for us. For Timothy, it was Paul. For us there is a long history of exemplary Christians to model as well as those in our daily experience.

Biblical Christianity is not theoretical or bookish. It requires that we fill our minds with truth as well as our everyday living. Christian faith is an apprenticeship by which we progress toward greater mastery of the art of living. This is why Paul told Timothy, "Do your best to present yourself to God as one approved, a workman who does not need to be ashamed" (2 Tim. 2:15).

Robert Louis Stevenson discovered that the art of writing demanded knowledge and practice. So does our personal life of faith and the dynamics of community life within the church. As each person becomes an imitator of Christ, and as we become models and instructors for others, we encourage one another to pursue the standard of Christlikeness.

The church is like a school of apprenticeship—a place where the knowledge of past generations is rediscovered and built upon; a place where eternal truth is kept alive and preserved. It is also a place of interaction, where we "practice" our faith together under the guidance, encouragement, and correction of those who are more mature in the faith.

V. PRAYER

Lord of life, this day I resolve to live fully in your service. By your Spirit's strength I choose to endure any opposition to your truth and love, continuing steadfastly as your child and servant. Amen.

VI. DEEPER DISCOVERIES

A. Correctly Handling the Word of Truth (vv. 14–15)

God uses two means of conveying truth and bringing change. The first is imparting truth by example. This is incarnational. Through the lives of men and women, God displays his power, thoughts, desires, and goals. Prophets, kings, judges, and ordinary individuals fleshed out divine life and thought. This culminated in the appearance of Jesus Christ and continues through his Spirit-indwelled people today.

The second way by which God communicates is through his written Word. The Bible remains the inspired statements of God, written in its original languages without error. These Scriptures were given for our guidance and as a revelation of God's nature and purposes.

Written language, above all other forms of communication, can convey the greatest content. Abstract markings (letters), grouped together in various combinations, create abstract concepts. Even so simple a sentence as "I pulled the red wagon" is open to a multitude of interpretations. How that wagon is visualized, who pulls it, how it is done, where, the setting—all these are dependent upon the reader. A picture, by contrast, can only be understood specifically—as it is. A picture of a red wagon can only be that particular wagon; it can be no other.

While written language allows for broad and complex reasoning, it also has some inherent difficulties. Words appeal to the imagination and are open to interpretation and multiple meanings. All readers filter a written piece through their own assumptions, experiences, and beliefs. This leaves words vulnerable to the mind and disposition of the reader.

God assumed the risks intrinsic to words when he gave us the Bible. Even in the first century, as the apostles wrote God's thoughts, their words were often misunderstood, wrongly applied, and twisted. People mishandled the Old Testament writings in the same manner. They superimposed personal opinion upon revelation, creating a vast network of laws. Ambition led others to neglect certain portions of Scripture. Words became battlegrounds for debates of meaning. Some people devised intricate systems of interpretation through imaginative analogies and hidden messages.

But just as people can misuse God's Word, so they can also handle it properly. Those who desire and pursue the truth of God are assisted by the Holy Spirit so that his truth remains inviolate. In addition, practical and time-honored methods of interpretation safeguard God's words and intentions.

Any student of Scripture must try to discover the intention of the original writers. Normally this is referred to as the historical-grammatical interpretation. Learning about the historical setting, the meaning of words in their original languages, the context of the verses, and the social practices of the time help reveal the writer's meaning.

The Bible is "outbreathed" (inspired) by God, and every word has its place and purpose. Surrounded by false teachers who mutilated God's words for their own purposes, Timothy was told to handle the Scriptures properly, holding to the truth with care. We must do the same.

B. Korah, Dathan, and Abiram (v. 19)

Paul encouraged Timothy by quoting from Numbers 16:5: "The Lord knows those who are his." This Old Testament quote is embedded in a story of rebellion and judgment.

The narrative occurs shortly after the Israelite spies returned from exploring Canaan. The majority report warned against proceeding into the land because of giants and enemies of overwhelming proportions. Filled with fear, the people rejected the divine pledge of the Promised Land, siding instead with human rationality and doubt. God judged the community by barring them from the land of promise and returning them to the desert to wander for another forty years.

In the shadow of this event is the story of Korah, Dathan, and Abiram. All three men were respected leaders. Korah served as a Levite and spiritual leader. Dathan and Abiram led within their tribe of Reuben. Yet, joined by 250 men, "well-known community leaders who had been appointed members of the council" (Num. 16:2), they conspired against Moses and Aaron, questioning their authority and accusing them of arrogance. Their argument sounded egalitarian, reasonable, even appealing as they confronted Moses: "The whole community is holy . . . and the LORD is with them. Why then do you set yourselves above the Lord's assembly?" (Num. 16:3).

Two groups—both respected and holding positions of leadership, both claiming God's blessing and authority. In the end, God decided the dilemma. Korah and his household, Dathan and his household, Abiram and his household, and all their belongings were swallowed up by the earth and buried alive. The 250 men who sided with him were consumed by fire. God knows those who belong to him.

Centuries later, Timothy needed to realize that opposition to spiritual leadership comes from a well-established tendency of the human heart to rebel. Jewish history records time and again the cyclic nature of man's relationship to God—rebellion, followed by judgment and remorse, followed by rebellion. Claims of spirituality do not change the human disposition to challenge authority. This places the church leader in a vulnerable position.

Within God's community the seeds of insurrection are typically sown by respected leaders. It was true of the spies, it was true of Korah and the 250 men who sided with him, and it was true in Ephesus where Timothy battled false teachers within the church. This is why Paul urged the Christian leaders and the church toward vigilance in keeping doctrine pure, character godly, and manner loving. These qualities protect the leader and those who depend upon him from wandering away from the faith or drifting into dangerous ideas.

VII. TEACHING OUTLINE

A. INTRODUCTION

1. Lead Story: Basic Training

2. Context: Knowing Timothy's temperament, the growing persecution of the church, and the defection of many believers, Paul encouraged him to remain steadfast in his faith. He put before him the high calling of God and the responsibility to endure.

3. Transition: Christians in the West are constantly bombarded with attacks upon their faith, whether we recognize them as such. It is imperative that we live with the sense of urgency that leads us to focus exclusively upon Christ and his kingdom. We must decide that godliness is worth any cost, that redemption is worth every effort, that God's honor must surpass our own. Then we will be fit for his service.

B. COMMENTARY

1. The Plan for Perpetuation of the Faith (2:1–2)

2. Three Metaphors: Devotion, Honesty, and Work (2:3–7)

   a. The soldier (2:3–4)

   b. The athlete (2:5)

   c. The farmer (2:6)

   d. Reflection (2:7)

3. Suffering and Blessing (2:8–13)

4. The Faithful Servant (2:14–26)

C. CONCLUSION: APPRENTICED FOR LIFE

VIII. ISSUES FOR DISCUSSION

1. How are you passing your faith on to others? In what practical ways can we "apprentice" other Christians?

2. How might areas of normal daily living (family, work, hobbies, retirement, finances) entangle you and prevent you from serving God?

3. What safeguards enable you to distinguish truth from error?

4. How does remembering who Jesus is and what he has done help you endure hardship?

2 Timothy 3

The Last Days

"*K*eep one thing forever in view—the truth; and if you

do this, though it may seem to lead you away from the

opinion of men, it will assuredly conduct you to

the throne of God."

H o r a c e   M a n n

2 Timothy 3

I N   A   N U T S H E L L

*P*aul began this chapter by describing the moral breakdown occurring in the last days. He gave a very dark portrait of man's spiritual and social position. The Christian, however, must persevere in living by faith, adhering to those characteristics which identify him as belonging to God. Persecutions will come, but those committed to Jesus Christ must prevail in belief.

The Last Days

I. INTRODUCTION

The Race

I was running in one of my first competitive races—ten kilometers, or 6.2 miles, where my main goal was to finish standing up. I did not have to beat anyone, just make it to the end.

Midway, a long sloping hill looked like, or at least felt like, Pike's Peak. An old man, maybe seventy, slid past me on the right. With a squeegee bottle of water in one hand and honey in the other, he was swigging doses of each as he ran.

I did not even have a washrag, and not much will left. Then a woman passed me on the left. Forgive me, but I have just enough male chauvinism in me to feel I was done at this point. Woman is meant to be the glory of man, the Bible says. Surely that does not allow for beating him in footraces!

Another man started around me, and I mentioned in defeat, "It is all yours," meaning the rest of the hill and the rest of the race. The rest of running forever, if he pleased.

But he would not stand for it. Instead he turned to me and said, "No; come on, run with me. You can do it."

I do not know how much was adrenaline and how much was pure ego, but I pulled for something that had not been there up to that point in the race. And it came!

"Lean over," he said, as we ran together. "Always lean forward a little up a hill. Now take shorter strides."

I did.

"That's it," he said. "Shorter steps and lean a little up a hill. Come on, we can do it."

By some kind of shared motion, we ran stride for stride the last few miles, right past the horse farm, up another hill, and onto the college campus where the judges had gone to prepare a finish line for us.

I was even able to stretch it out and finish right beside him with a fabulous kick at the end. We finished strong.

It was a great lesson in spiritual running too, for such is the Christian run. Christ comes alongside when we are tiring or getting down. He has run this way before. He has been tested in every point just as we have. He understands. "Run with me," he says. Or better, "I will help you run and run with you."

It is for us to decide. If we go his way and seek his fellowship and "fix our eyes on Jesus," as Hebrews 12:2 commands, we can do it. There is a spiritual stamina, an invisible grace, but a very felt force, and it gives us character and helps us proceed.

Despite persecutions we might encounter, despite the hardships we come up against, physically, emotionally, or spiritually, Paul encourages each of us to persevere. Life is not easy. Sometimes it is a real struggle—but we are called to endure. It is Christ who gives us strength to finish the race.

II. COMMENTARY

MAIN IDEA: *Paul described for Timothy the downward slide of society and mankind which will proceed with worsening effects during the last days. The moral center of men and women spins out of control. From this portrayal comes a mandate. Believers must reject all false teachers and their ideas, enduring the difficult days in which they live. Scripture stands as the foundation for truth. We must preserve its integrity and submit to its transforming power.*

The Warning: Harsh Times Ahead (3:1–9)

SUPPORTING IDEA: *The days following Jesus' ascension into heaven are marked by progressive selfishness and moral degeneration. Christians must not be alarmed or discouraged by the breakdown of society. God still reigns. Even so, we must steel ourselves against the lure of sin and pessimism, proclaiming and living the nature and purposes of God.*

1. The last days (3:1)

3:1. Paul declared, **Mark this: There will be terrible times in the last days.** The "last days" is not some future event to which we look. It is now. Jesus Christ initiated this epoch, and it will continue uninterrupted until his return. Paul defined this expansive time period as "terrible." God's extravagant grace also characterizes this era, establishing salvation and the church. But these days unleash Satan's wild attempts to destroy and undermine God's redemptive intentions.

In giving us this information, Paul desired that believers maintain a readiness of spirit and life. The battle will rage. What each believer must decide is whether he will prepare for the promised difficulties or give in to personal safety and comfort.

2. Characteristics of ungodliness (3:2–5)

3:2–5. The terribleness of the last days results from the continual decay of man's spiritual nature. As people neglect the spiritual dimension of life, they turn in upon themselves to find meaning and consolation in the face of life's absurdity. Paul penned a list of characteristics of false teachers and all those who turn from truth.

In 2 Corinthians 5:15, Paul wrote: "Those who live should no longer live for themselves but for him who died for them and was raised again." In this era, people refuse the love of God, choosing instead to **be lovers of themselves.**

This sentence offers the key to unlocking the rest of Paul's list of vices. When we fall in love with ourselves, our own appetites consume our souls. We become our own lover, pandering to that solitary "i" which must, of necessity, dismiss all threats and counterclaims to our affections. Everything from thoughts to possessions must be lavished upon the one we love—ourselves.

This leads quite naturally to becoming **lovers of money.** Paul dealt with this rather extensively in 1 Timothy 6. Loving money and all it buys opens the soul to Satan's traps, ensnaring the person in desires which cannot be met and enslaving him to a continual lusting for more money, possessions, or power.

Selfish people are typically **boastful** and **proud.** In stubbornly holding to the view that they are the center of the universe, such people have an exaggerated view of themselves. They actually believe in their own superiority. With this delusion, bragging falls naturally from their lips and pride wraps them in a haughty demeanor. These are the props which support their fantasy.

Pride can then lead to **abusive** speech and behavior. In order for arrogance to survive, it must view others as lesser individuals, as unworthy or unfit. This degraded view dehumanizes others, stripping away all respect and allowing the proud to slash with words or hurt by actions. When someone fails to see another person as wholly human, it becomes easy to destroy them. This is the antithesis of Christian teaching. Christ left us an example of servanthood, submission, and sacrifice (Phil. 2:6–11). Paul wrote: "Consider others better than yourselves" (Phil. 2:3).

Children **disobedient to their parents** also characterize the last days. In the Jewish mind, this equaled rebellion. Rebellion against authority always implies revolt against God. The stability of the home and society, and even the church, rested upon the harmonious functioning of family members. Disobedience represented a destructive force in all three spheres, and it struck at the heart of God's authority over mankind.

The next few words—**ungrateful, unholy, without love, unforgiving—** need little analysis except to highlight that these terms describe people totally given to selfishness. Unthankful people refuse to acknowledge their need or appreciation of anyone but themselves. Such persons are unloving. They see no need to offer the grace of forgiveness to others.

Slanderous refers to an unbridled tongue, a mouth that spreads rumors, gossip, or lies to the harm of others. The ungodly, who proliferate during the last days, also evidence a lack of self-discipline or **self-control**. They are brutal, or savage. They degenerate to wildness and are **not lovers of the good**. These people possess an appetite for evil, for all that opposes good. As such, they are **treacherous**, or traitorous, lacking in faithfulness. The ungodly are **rash**, thoughtless in their actions and speech.

Paul closed his list much as he began it, calling such people **conceited**. Pride surrounds all these sins and vices. He then concluded with the statement: **lovers of pleasure rather than lovers of God**. Those who elevate themselves above others will eventually elevate themselves above God. Their own appetites and desires become their passion.

Paul's words pile up into a negative portrait. Yet we need only look around us, or within our own hearts, to discover the seeds of selfishness. These phrases describe the unbelieving world as well as those within the church. The last days in which we live feature a mixed church, with wheat and weeds growing together.

Paul summarizes these days: **having a form of godliness but denying its power**. The essence of ungodliness comes from within, and then it comes out in behavior. Those who profess God, who claim spiritual or religious knowledge, do not necessarily possess a relationship with God or his righteousness. True spirituality issues from right thinking in concert with God's power within the spirit of a person which transforms outward behavior. True Christianity cannot be hidden, nor is it a private religion without public effect. This was the erroneous view of the false teachers of Paul's day. This theory still finds acceptance in modern thinking.

In these last days in which we live, there exists a decreasing belief in the Holy Spirit's regenerating power for forgiveness and eternal life. People go through the motions of religion, refusing to depend upon Christ. Self-focus then supersedes everything else, and the spiral of immorality sweeps people into its vortex.

As we seek God's power for patience and godly character, Colossians 1:9–14 is a wonderful prayer for believers. We often think of God's might as applying only to momentous occasions. But his strength finds expression as he supplies power for daily endurance, courage to choose what is right, the ability to love and forgive, and the commitment to follow Christ.

3. The false teachers (3:6–9)

3:6. Paul had kept the false teachers in mind, even in his general description of ungodliness. In this verse, he returned more specifically to these teachers.

The false teachers carried out a "standard operating procedure"—they would **worm their way into homes and gain control**. This description implies sneaking or creeping into homes. These false teachers would hold home Bible studies, perhaps, or lead discussion groups with the intent of gaining control over the household.

They found greatest success in the homes of **weak-willed women.** I do not believe Paul targeted women as inherently weak-willed or prone to deception. Instead, he recognized and pointed out a pattern he observed. Women offered easier access into homes, and those women whom the false teachers could most easily exploit were vulnerable: **loaded down with sins and . . . swayed by all kinds of evil desires.**

This suggests that these women, perhaps the teachers as well, possessed a history of sin which remained unconfessed. Loaded down with a past they could not relinquish, or which they refused to conclude through confession, they became easy prey to faddish doctrines. Not only did their past remain unresolved; it left them susceptible to sins in the present. The weight of guilt reduces a person's ability to make proper decisions. It also leaves the conscience scarred so that temptations overcome the will more easily.

3:7. These women were mirror images of the false teachers they followed. They masked the disarray of their inner spirit through religious practices, especially Scripture studies. They were probably familiar with the Old Testament and could discuss the intricate doctrinal strategies of their teachers. But because their souls had not been cleansed of sin, they were blind to the truth. It is also possible that they did not want to discover truth but sought in Christianity a salve for their bruised lives. Despite the hours they invested in studying, they were **always learning but never able to acknowledge the truth.**

3:8. Paul compared the false teachers to **Jannes and Jambres** who **opposed Moses.** These men do not appear in the Old Testament records, but they remained familiar names in Jewish tradition as sorcerers who opposed God's authority through Moses in Egypt.

So also these men oppose the truth. This phrase summarizes Paul's indictment against the false teachers: they contended with God's truth as given through Paul. This exposed the false teachers' **depraved minds.** These people were incapable of comprehending God's truth because their minds were irrational and devoted to lies. Consequently, they could not acknowledge God's truth. So, Paul declared, **as far as the faith is concerned, [they] are rejected.** A good workman is approved by God through adherence to correct doctrine and the evidences of a holy life (2 Tim. 2:15,21). Conversely, these false teachers were unacceptable because they opposed the apostolic teachings, and their lives reflected a progressive degeneration.

3:9. Just as Pharaoh's court enchanters succeeded against Moses only to a point, so the false teachers would flourish for a limited time. Eventually, however, the false cannot match the truth. Truth exists, not as an option, but as testimony to what actually is. The counterfeit exists by delusion and cannot withstand reality's judgment.

Timothy probably felt that truth was losing to the spread of false doctrines and philosophies as well as to the brutality of persecution. But Paul affirmed that these apparent successes were temporary: **they will not get very far** (cf. Ps. 73). When people peddling bogus philosophies or theologies encounter the truth of God and his power, **their folly will be clear to everyone**. Lies and deceptions must crumble, dissolving to dust. Among the ruins of these elaborate but false beliefs are the men who devised them, exposed in their foolishness.

Ⓑ Paul's Charge to Timothy (3:10–17)

SUPPORTING IDEA: *In turbulent and stressful times, it becomes easy to lose heart, to feel weary and hopeless. Paul, wanting Timothy to refocus, offered Timothy a reflection on his own life of godliness in the midst of persecution. Paul referred to Timothy's heritage and reminded him of the unshakable source of truth for life and holiness—the Scriptures.*

3:10–11. Our lives exhibit the reality of our inner character. The manner in which we live, the decisions we make, the circumstances with which we must contend—all these reveal the beliefs we hold and the priorities we maintain. Paul concluded the last paragraph by assuring Timothy that the false teachers and their ideas would come to ruin. Their folly would be revealed through the disparity of their lives against the truth. Now Paul boldly offered himself as a counter argument to these false teachers.

The evidence against the false teachers resided in their theology and behavior. Paul asked Timothy to evaluate him on these issues: **You . . . know all about my teaching, my way of life, my purpose**. He was certain that upon examination he would be found blameless—his teaching founded in truth, his life expressed in purity, and his purpose driven by God's glory.

In addition, he wanted Timothy to reminisce a little and recount Paul's **faith, patience, love, endurance, persecutions, sufferings**. These stand as hallmarks of the Christian life. Faith defines our trust, patience acknowledges God's sovereignty, love expresses to others the sacrificial grace which we receive, endurance keeps our focus on God's kingdom, while persecutions and sufferings represent our fellowship with Christ. Timothy had shared some of Paul's difficulties as they traveled together through **Antioch, Iconium and Lystra**. He had witnessed the way Paul lived and the constancy with which he taught. He had also witnessed how **the Lord rescued** Paul.

3:12. But persecutions are not reserved for super saints and apostles. **In fact, everyone who wants to live a godly life in Christ Jesus will be**

persecuted. Timothy had experienced it before, was suffering under it now, and would undoubtedly continue in the sufferings of Christ after Paul's execution. Distress belongs to the believer who commits himself to loyal obedience and growth in godliness. But it remains in the hands of each believer whether he will choose the life of godly obedience or shy away into the shadows of compromise.

3:13. Paul typically discussed issues by placing arguments in opposition, creating a clarifying tension. The fate of godly men and women is persecution; the fate of **evil men and impostors** was ongoing corruption as they **go from bad to worse.** But the deceptions to which these people were prey, and the deceiving teachings which they promoted, explain why followers of Christ face continual persecution. Godliness elicits a strong reaction from unbelievers. The reaction becomes all the more intense and violent when Christians live out their godliness because it convicts others of their sin.

Those who neglect the truth of God become enmeshed in a confusing web of deception. Their consciences and reasoning capabilities suffer damage through sin, and they become incapable of extricating themselves from Satan's delusions. Only God's truth possesses the power to free such persons.

3:14–15. Each of us is susceptible to this dangerous trap of deception unless we obey Scripture vigilantly. Following Christ is more than a one-time decision or an occasional church service or kind act. True Christianity involves continual dependence and obedience to Christ the king. Paul told Timothy to **continue in what you have learned and have become convinced of.** Our faith is proved by its endurance.

Two elements are necessary for faithful living. First, we must possess knowledge of the truth. Truth enlightens a person about what is right and wrong, what constitutes purpose and happiness. We cannot trust or love what we do not know. The second element is conviction or belief. We express our belief system in the daily decisions we make and the behaviors in which we engage. No one acts contrary to belief (though we may act contrary to our professions of belief).

Paul also wanted Timothy to consider **those from whom you learned [truth], and how from infancy you have known the holy Scriptures.** Once again he had Timothy's mother and grandmother in mind (see 2 Tim. 1:5). Timothy was schooled in the Old Testament writings and had learned the need for forgiveness, the provision of God, and the necessity of faith. He had also been discipled by Paul, learning Christ and the church. In each case, Timothy had not only been given knowledge; he had been witness to godly lives.

These people served as examples to Timothy about the truth of God, the need for endurance, and the reward of faithfulness. Each person had staked his or her life on the revelation of the Scriptures which, according to Paul, **are able to make you wise for salvation through faith in Christ Jesus.**

3:16. The power of the Bible to affect change and demand obedience resides in the fact that **all Scripture is God-breathed.** The Bible originates with God. Claims of origins carry great significance because authority lives in the Creator. This is why people invest such Herculean efforts in trying to disprove God as the earth's Creator and in questioning the authenticity of the Bible. Admitting to God's authorship is an acceptance of his authority over every aspect of life. By stating that Scriptures are God breathed, Paul established the Bible's claim as God's authoritative Word over all people.

The Scriptures were written by men "as they were carried along by the Holy Spirit" (2 Pet. 1:21). The picture is that of a sailboat being moved along by the wind. Indeed, men wrote the Bible, but the words and substance of what they wrote came from God. This makes the Bible **useful.** Paul listed four main uses of Scripture, all of which intertwine with one another.

Teaching involves instruction. Since Timothy was feeling the attacks of false teachers, Paul encouraged the young pastor to continue in teaching correct doctrine and correct living. The Scriptures must be known so people will grasp their need of salvation and so the confessing community will adhere to its instructions on proper Christian conduct.

Rebuking and **correcting** are the disciplinary authority of Scripture. Because the Bible is God's Word and because it reveals truth, it exercises authority over those who deviate from its standard. "Rebuking" points out sin and confronts disobedience. "Correcting" recognizes that a person has strayed from the truth. Graciously, lovingly, yet firmly, we should try to guide the errant individual back into obedience.

Many times the Old Testament relates Israel's disobedience to God, how the people suffered God's chastisement for their rebellion, and how God corrected their sinful habits. The New Testament continues with stories and instructions, warnings regarding disobedience, disciplinary actions for those who fail to heed God's revelation, and teachings on proper conduct.

Training in righteousness is the counterpoint to correction. The Scriptures give us positive guidance for maturing in faith and acceptable conduct.

3:17. The goal of all this instruction, discipline, and training is not to keep us busy. God intends **that the man of God may be thoroughly equipped for every good work.** We study the Bible, we rely upon God's Spirit, his revelation, and the community of the faithful to keep us on track—obedient and maturing in faith. Continuing in this commitment will enable us to do whatever God calls us to do. Timothy could withstand the attacks of false teachers, the abandonment of professing believers, and the persecution that surrounded him because God had equipped him for the task. God never calls us to do something without first enabling us through his Spirit and the power of his truth to accomplish the task.

We neglect the Scriptures at our own peril. Through them we gain the ability to serve God and others. The Scriptures not only point the way; through the mysterious union of God's Word and faith, they give us the ability to serve.

> **MAIN IDEA REVIEW:** *Paul described for Timothy the downward slide of society and mankind which will proceed with worsening effects during the last days. The moral center of men and women spins out of control. From this portrayal comes a mandate. Believers must reject all false teachers and their ideas, enduring the difficult days in which they live. Scripture stands as the foundation for truth. We must preserve its integrity and submit to its transforming power.*

III. CONCLUSION

How Should We Then Live?

It happens regularly. A group of people sells their belongings or gives them away. They gather on a hill to await the Lord's return. Through an intricate system of biblical interpretation and political analysis, they have pinpointed the date of the coming of the Lord.

Others, alarmed at the chaotic conditions within society and disturbed at governmental policies and practices, band together in seclusion. Like frightened pioneers in the old west, they circle the wagons to keep the enemy outside. Some form theological cliques, and others gather into survivalist camps to wait for the coming of the Lord.

A great many others, not quite so organized, simply wait. They work, make money, and wait. Desperately wishing things were different, they long to escape the moral and social madness. Yet, deep within, they believe nothing can be done to change the conditions around them. There is nothing to do, but wait . . . for the coming of the Lord.

Although they are correct in their assessment of evil, these groups remain wrong in their conclusions about living. Nowhere does Christ call his followers to figure out dates, hide from the unbelieving world, or give up. In this third chapter of 2 Timothy, Paul directed us to stay at it. He urged us to keep living godly lives, keep sharing the faith, keep teaching about righteous living and the future hope of all who believe in Christ.

After giving a catalog of sins which characterize the last days (days in which we currently live), Paul issued a challenge to the faithful: persevere in hardship, do not retreat, cling to the Scriptures as the power of God to affect change and give direction in a godless time. Despite the raging spiritual battles, the moral disintegration, and the anarchy, Christ and his church cannot be overwhelmed. God's truth and Word will triumph, both now and in the future.

The days will become progressively more evil. Christians must be realists, not blind to the truth of suffering, opposition, and persecution. People increasingly hate the truth, despise God, and cling to evil. Our focus, however, looks beyond the moral confusion to the victorious Christ and the goodness of his Word. Through the Holy Spirit and the Scriptures, he has given us everything we need for living successfully in this fallen world.

Many good things continue to occur all over the world in the name of Christ because people believe in him, are confident of his return, and remain faithful to his teachings. Christ referred to his followers as lights in a dark world. Lights of love and redemption shine brightest where it is darkest. In these dark places even the smallest light penetrates with an undeniable presence. In these days of social gloom and moral collapse, believers can pierce and diminish the gloom. We should not give up.

PRINCIPLES

- We are living in what the Bible calls "the last days." These days began when Christ ascended into heaven, and they will conclude when he returns to earth.
- The last days are characterized by increasing ungodliness.
- Truth will always be opposed. A spiritual war rages, and those who commit themselves to living obediently to Christ will suffer; often the persecution will be harsh.
- God requires spiritual knowledge and godly conduct from those who claim his salvation.
- The Bible remains the supreme authority for life. It has the power to convict and transform and the authority to correct and discipline.

APPLICATIONS

- Believers can protect themselves from disillusionment or unfaithfulness by embracing the reality that obedience to Christ results in persecution. False expectations of "the good life" lead to discouragement.
- Christians must continue to study the Scriptures, prayerfully seeking its discipline and guidance.
- Churches need to instruct their people in the fundamental doctrines of the Christian faith.

- Each Christian should understand the points of doctrine that are nonnegotiable.
- As followers of Christ, our behavior should be in agreement with our professed beliefs.
- Church discipline should issue from scriptural truth and its revelation of godliness.

IV. LIFE APPLICATION

Purifying Fire

Stories about Christians suffering persecution often produce more guilt than inspiration among Christians in the West. We may admire those imprisoned, beaten, or martyred for their faith, but compared to our experiences and circumstances, they seem a bit otherworldly.

Jesus said, "In this world you will have trouble" (John 16:33); Peter wrote, "Dear friends, do not be surprised at the painful trial you are suffering, as though something strange were happening to you" (1 Pet. 4:12); and Paul reminded Timothy, "everyone who wants to live a godly life in Christ Jesus will be persecuted" (2 Tim. 3:12). These statements assure us that Christians will experience hardships and difficulties as a direct result of their lifestyle and faith—it is guaranteed.

We need to understand, however, that suffering takes many forms. The root word which Paul used for persecution, *dioko,* carries the meaning of "pursuit," or "chasing after." In other words, those who commit themselves to godly living will be hounded by those who are intent on evil, ungodliness, and deception; the righteous will not be left alone. Though inwardly they rest in the peace of God, outwardly they encounter the relentless antagonism of Satan through those who are opposed to God.

This pressure may evidence itself through torture, beatings, imprisonment, or death. But the godly may also experience persecution in the form of betrayal, hatred, scorn, slander, and contempt. These express the hostility of those who are opposed to Christ and his followers.

V. PRAYER

Suffering Christ, help my resolve to follow you. Strengthen me so that I do not shrink from the discomforts or difficulties that result from my love of you. I give myself to serve you in this spiritual war, confident that you will preserve my soul until your appearing. Amen.

VI. DEEPER DISCOVERIES

A. The Last Days (vv. 1–5)

The phrase "the last days" generally elicits visions of apocalyptic catastrophe—doom, judgment, fire, and suffering—the end of the world. Though the last days do, in fact, involve Christ's imminent return in judgment, they qualify an epoch, not an event. Tying the term to a narrow band of time in the future keeps people off balance in regard to living in the present. Indeed, right now we live in earth's final time period, as Paul did. The last days constitute a real and historical epoch. The last days began with the ascension of Jesus, continue to this day, and extend into the future until Christ's return.

Though a great deal of speculation and uncertainty surround the end times, Paul supplied a list of last-day characteristics. He presented a composite of fallen humanity acting out its estrangement from God, mastered by selfishness, greed, ingratitude, disobedience, and brutality. He also described an empty religiosity infiltrating the church, pandering to human desires while excluding truth, righteousness, and God's power. Many who at one time identified with Christ will abandon the faith in sweeping movements of apostasy.

Yet all of Paul's descriptions also summarize life at any moment during the last two thousand years. The ebb and flow of history testifies to fierce societal wickedness and human depravity. Though the chaos and corruption of these final days continues with multiplied intensity, basically life continues as it always has.

This barbarism coupled with a sense of normalcy keeps even believers anesthetized to the impending closure of human history. Christ is patient, yet poised to return. This insight was handed to the church to inspire faithfulness, devotion, endurance, and joyful expectancy. Instead, Christians in the West often respond with a yawn.

Though Jesus, Paul, and Peter gave portraits of the last days, the actual culmination of history cannot be pinpointed. It is a divine mystery which we cannot unravel by biblical interpretation, political scrutiny, or social analysis of our disintegrating culture. God's revelation about the time of his judgment and Christ's return was given in ambiguous terms so we would continue to live by faith in confident hope.

Peter put it well when, after writing of the last days, he concluded: "What kind of people ought you to be?" (2 Pet. 3:11). The purpose of disclosing the conditions surrounding Christ's return is not to titillate our curiosity, send us into esoteric speculations, or relieve us from the hard work of living in this present moment. Instead, the revelations about earth's final days are intended to motivate Christians to "live holy and godly lives" (2 Pet. 3:11), to focus upon the task of serving Christ (Matt. 24:36–46), and to persevere through hardship and opposition and so remain faithful (1 Thess. 1:3).

B. Trouble in the Cities (v. 11)

In this chapter, Paul mentioned three cities in which he suffered: Antioch, Iconium, and Lystra. Acts 13:42–14:22 details Paul's persecutions and the troubles he encountered in these towns as well as his return to these cities to encourage the believers to endure hardships.

Antioch. The Book of Acts mentions two Antiochs, one in Syria, the other known as Antioch of Pisidia—the city to which Paul refers here. Antioch of Pisidia was situated 3,600 feet high in rugged mountains. Only one route led into the city, making it a bit isolated. Even so, it was the capital of Galatia, and the Romans intended that their influence should spread from this city and infiltrate the remainder of the province. The citizens of the city were primarily native Phrygians and Jews. The remainder of the population was composed of Roman army veterans, making it a military center for the surrounding area.

It was in Antioch of Pisidia that Paul and Barnabas preached so boldly of Christ that many Gentiles heard the word of the Lord and believed. "But the Jews incited the God-fearing women of high standing and the leading men of the city. They stirred up persecution against Paul and Barnabas, and expelled them from their region" (Acts 13:50). So they set off for Iconium.

Iconium. This city lay ninety miles from Antioch. It was known as "the last city of Phrygia," located in the interior regions on a high plateau. It was ringed by plains and forests, and beyond that to the north and east, mountains. The people of Iconium did not welcome the Romanization process and remained essentially Greek.

Upon arrival in Iconium, Paul and Barnabas went to the synagogue as usual. They preached with such power that a great number of Jews and Gentiles believed. Despite the opposition of the Jews, and their efforts to incite the Gentiles, Paul and Barnabas remained in Iconium longer than at Antioch. They continued to preach and perform miracles. In time, however, a plot developed to stone the missionaries. Finding out about the plan, Paul and Barnabas fled to Lystra and Derbe.

Lystra. Lystra was about twenty miles from Iconium. Like Antioch, it was a Roman colony, made so by the emperor Augustus. The two cities were linked by a military road, since Lystra's ruling class was also comprised of army veterans. Beyond the Roman military and the Jewish community, however, the indigenous population of Lycaonians spoke their own tribal language and was considered uneducated.

Lystra was Timothy's hometown. When Paul and Barnabas began evangelizing in the city, it is likely that they met Timothy and his mother and grandmother. From this association came Timothy's conversion and the enduring friendship with the great apostle.

It was also at Lystra that Paul suffered some of his most brutal persecution. At first, the townspeople were overwhelmed by Paul and Barnabas, especially after witnessing a miraculous healing of a cripple. They began worshiping the two missionaries, bringing wreaths and sacrifices for them. The Lycaonians considered Barnabas to be Zeus, and Paul, Hermes (because Paul was the principal speaker). Paul had a difficult time convincing the people that these missionaries were ordinary men.

Some interpreters have suggested that the Lycaonians were insulted by Paul's rejection of their gifts and worship. Thus, when Jews came from Iconium and Antioch, the crowd turned against Paul and Barnabas. The attitude of the people changed from adoration to violence: "They stoned Paul and dragged him outside the city, thinking he was dead. But after the disciples had gathered around him, he got up and went back into the city" (Acts 14:19–20).

VII. TEACHING OUTLINE

A. INTRODUCTION

1. Lead Story: The Race
2. Context: Paul discussed at length the manners and actions of people during the last days before Christ's return. Rather than sketching events, he detailed the moral decay within the hearts of men and women. Paul also warned about those who feign religion, who mask their sins with public propriety. In the midst of this, Timothy was to remain faithful, enduring to the end. To encourage Timothy, Paul offered himself as an example of loyal obedience. He concluded by giving Timothy a solemn charge to continue in righteousness, biblical truth, and diligent ministry.
3. Transition: We also live in the last days before Christ's return. The world is in a perpetual downward spin toward rebellion and anarchy. Even the community of faith experiences an apathetic, selfish turning away from God. Just like ancient times, the present is treacherous to those who are committed to godliness and devotion. Though the experiences of persecution vary from continent to continent, there appears to be a growing antipathy toward Christians. Believers must remain constant in their faith, alert to the dangerous and heretical notions which are proclaimed under the banner of religion. All Christians must take seriously the critical need for personal study of the Scriptures, using God's Word to guide and discipline life.

B. COMMENTARY

1. The Warning: Harsh Times Ahead (3:1–9)
   a. The last days (3:1)
   b. Characteristics of ungodliness (3:2–5)
   c. The false teachers (3:6–9)
2. Paul's Charge to Timothy (3:10–17)

C. CONCLUSION: PURIFYING FIRE

VIII. ISSUES FOR DISCUSSION

1. How are you preparing for "the last days"? Do you recognize any of Paul's descriptive phrases as occurring within your own heart?
2. Have you experienced a Christian heritage through relatives who taught and modeled God's truth? If so, describe what you learned from these people and how they influenced you.
3. Do you ever find yourself tired of the Christian life? If so, what do you suspect causes this? How can we maintain a positive, enduring, continually maturing life in Christ?

2 Timothy 4

The Charge to
Faithful Ministry

"Belief is a truth held in the mind;

faith is a fire in the heart."

Joseph   Fort   Newton

2 Timothy 4

 IN A NUTSHELL

Paul gave his final charge to Timothy about faithfulness and ministry. Then, as he looked toward his own impending death, he summarized his life goal and purpose, concluding with thanks to others who partnered with him in his ministry and a personal request for Timothy.

The Charge to Faithful Ministry

I. INTRODUCTION

Finishing the Race

*E*veryone knows about the agony of defeat. But there is also agony in victory. The winner sometimes has worked the hardest and agonized the longest. And he feels the best. There is the agony of running, but there is also the joy of the race.

What could be more thrilling than to stand at the end of life and say, "I have agonized the good agony. I have fought the good fight. I have finished the course. I have kept the faith."

That is quite a way to go. And it is a prize available to all who wish. That gives me hope.

Maybe you have heard the story of the most lopsided football game ever played, when mighty Georgia Tech beat tiny Cumberland College, 222–0.

I think that was the game where the Cumberland quarterback tossed a short but errant lateral to the halfback. The quarterback yelled, "Pick it up, pick it up!"

But the halfback had other ideas. "*You* pick it up," he shouted. "You dropped it."

It is easy to lose drive in life. Many Christians are sitting on the sidelines counting splinters in their backsides. Or sitting on pews counting mistakes in the pastor's sermons. Or thinking back about how they used to experience real joy in the Christian life and wondering what went wrong. Such is the dropout way.

You have probably heard that man's greatest ability is not his ability to think but to rationalize. To excuse himself for going to the sidelines, at times.

Paul's life was often one of agony. Hard work. But I imagine that at the end of the day he felt good. At least, he felt good in the inward sense—that he had done God's will in the twenty-four hours just ended.

We are not called to win the world. Messianic complex or not, we are not responsible for everyone. I am to finish *my* course. You, yours. That is it.

What we really need—and what God really wants—is endurance. Enduring means you do not think anything is more important than your faith, and no one more significant than Christ. Fix your eyes on him. Keep running. To the end.

II. COMMENTARY

MAIN IDEA: *Paul had little time left. He gave Timothy one final charge to preach God's Word, and to do so with integrity and purity. Not everyone will listen. In fact, many will not. Apostasy always lurks at the edges of faith. But the pastor must remain faithful to his calling to honor God's Word. Paul offered himself as an example of ardent devotion, closing with personal remarks about some of his friends and ministry associates.*

The Charge (4:1–8)

SUPPORTING IDEA: *Paul gave Timothy the solemn command to preach the truth of God's Word. He did not inspire Timothy through empty positivisms, but warned him that people will listen less and less to the truth. Even so, he must remain faithful, applying God's Word to his own life and those within the church.*

1. Pastoral responsibilities (4:1–2)

4:1. The solemnity of Paul's charge to Timothy became apparent as he issued it **in the presence of God and of Christ Jesus.** Paul was giving Timothy a binding oath to ministry. Besides the magnitude of the trust, sealed by God, Paul provided motivation for Timothy, and all Christians, to follow through.

First, God through Christ Jesus **will judge the living and the dead.** There ought to exist in all of us a healthy fear of the future. God's judgment reaches into the hearts of all people—Christians and unbelievers alike. No one escapes his penetrating gaze. All will tremble in his presence; the inevitability of confronting the Holy One with a review of one's life should cause serious and careful living in the present moment. All Christians have received a charge to remain faithful in serving him, and we are bound to this by the covenant of Christ's blood.

The second motivation derives from **his appearing and his kingdom.** His coming again has yet to occur; it is the event to which Christians look with anticipation. He can come at any moment, and we must be ready. Jesus provided plenty of warnings in his parables about lazy servants unprepared for the master's return (Matt. 24:45), or virgins ill-equipped for the bridal party (Matt. 25:1–13). Though outposts of his kingdom are established whenever God's will is carried out by the power of his Spirit, the fullness of his kingdom remains in the future. Just as salvation has come in part to each believer, still we await the fullness of our salvation when Christ appears. Paul intended these coming realizations, though partially experienced now, as encouragement for faithful service.

4:2. Paul's charge to Timothy was: **Preach the Word**. Through the course of his two letters to Timothy, Paul had referred often to God's revelation, his Word. Timothy understood that **the Word** was the same as Paul's teachings (2 Tim. 2:2), "sound doctrine" (1 Tim. 1:10; 2 Tim. 1:13), the "glorious gospel" (1 Tim. 1:11; 2 Tim. 1:11), the "true faith" (1 Tim. 2:7; 4:1; 2 Tim. 1:5), and the "Scriptures" (1 Tim. 4:13). All pastors are bound by their duties as ministers of the gospel, to herald, or proclaim, the words of God. Whether on Sunday mornings or throughout the week, as they teach and instruct, their duty is to pass on what God has revealed.

Personal opinions and theories provide interesting discussions, but conviction about the essential truths of God remain necessary. The mandate for the church and its leadership remains: Preach the Word.

The subject of ministry is God's Word. The duty of ministry is preparedness and accessibility: **in season and out of season**. The pastor, the Christian, is to view ministry as full-time, all the time, because faith involves all of life. There is no moment of the day that Christ cannot redeem if his people are prepared to seize the opportunities as they come. Those who remain ready and alert in their faith participate willingly in proclaiming the gospel, whether it is convenient or not.

The manner of ministry is to **correct, rebuke and encourage—with great patience and careful instruction**. God's Word is extremely practical for every encounter and situation in life.

To **correct** means to convince or reprove. The pastor works to guide a person along the proper path of obedience and faith. To **rebuke** means to chide or censure, even blame. The pastor seeks to put a stop to wrong behavior or belief. To **encourage** means to exhort, give courage, or come alongside. The pastor walks with his people, living the example of faith and urging others to follow.

All these duties are to be carried out with kindness. Our battle is not against the weak, the errant, the sinful, but against Satan, who enslaves people to do his will. We are commissioned to offer peace in the name of Christ, and we must extend it in love and care as we proclaim the truth. It is the Word that confronts and convicts, not our spirits. We are to tell the truth in love (Eph. 4:15), allowing God's Word and Spirit to work in people's minds and hearts.

2. The majority response (4:3–4)

4:3–4. Despite patience, kindness, and truth, **the time will come when men will not put up with sound doctrine**. Timothy's duty to continue preaching God's Word finds its imperative in the spiritual decadence that surrounded him. People will not care to hear the truth.

All truth, whether spiritual or scientific, resides in the nature of God. As such, truth commands either change or sacrifice; it removes excuses and opinions, allowing only for obedience or defiance. Confrontation with truth can produce a great deal of discomfort, especially for those unwilling to submit to its authority. This is why people have always tended to gather "yes" men about themselves, those who say what we like to hear.

The prophet Isaiah wrote, "These are rebellious people, deceitful children, children unwilling to listen to the LORD's instruction. They say to the seers, 'See no more visions!' and to the prophets, 'Give us no more visions of what is right! Tell us pleasant things, prophesy illusions. Leave this way, get off this path, and stop confronting us with the Holy One of Israel!'" (Isa. 30:9–11).

Nothing has changed. People still like to hear only pleasant things, teachings that correspond to their **own desires**. This allows them to continue in the lifestyles and practices with which they are comfortable. The human heart works hard to fortify itself against truth, creating rationalizations and systems of thought to justify selfishness. Unfortunately, there are teachers and leaders who give people what they want to hear, tickling their **itching ears** with curiosities that allow them to remain untouched by God's transforming power. They **turn their ears away from the truth and turn aside to myths**—things devised by man.

God's truth, in addition to pointing out error and sin, leads to reality, grace, and freedom. Truth becomes a burden only when we try to reach the beauty of its perfection without the enabling strength of our Creator. Truth, as delivered by God through his ministers and people, becomes the power for living in the fullness for which God created us. But human beings fear exposure, and so we pretend we can hide from the truth. In reality, we only deceive ourselves and lead others astray.

3. The command for constancy (4:5)

4:5. Once again, Paul called Timothy to live in contrast to the prevailing practice of the time. Christians must not take their cues for living or thinking from the attitudes of society—religious or otherwise. Instead, God's Word must be central to the life of every believer; it must dictate all yearnings and actions, thoughts and dreams.

Despite the prevalent distaste for truth and the unsettling atmosphere of multiple doctrines and philosophies, Paul declared, **But [Timothy], keep your head in all situations.** Do not panic. Keep your head "screwed on straight," as the common expression has it. Muddled and noncritical thinking leads many people to wander off after false teachers. Timothy, and all Christians, must think correctly, holding firm to the unshakable truth of God's Word and the apostolic teachings.

Paul reminded Timothy again to **endure hardship.** Suffering and hardship are a recurring theme in this letter. Paul continued to emphasize the need for endurance as a sign of faithfulness.

Timothy's commission revolved around doing **the work of an evangelist.** Godly living, holiness, perseverance, and adherence to truth were never intended as private practices to ensure personal well-being. All these form the platform from which the gospel can be delivered. Timothy was to **discharge all the duties of . . . ministry,** to preach and spread the knowledge of God among those who had not heard. Paul, in his final days, turned over to Timothy the mission to the Gentiles and care of the churches.

4. Paul's example (4:6–8)

4:6. Paul had already provided Timothy with sound reasons to stay faithful to the ministry: God's certain return, the increase of falsehood and wickedness, and his own commissioning. Now Paul gave Timothy another compelling reason to stay with the hard work of ministry: **the time has come for my departure.** Paul would die soon, and Timothy must carry on the work.

Paul referred to his coming death in terms of a willing sacrifice to God, reminiscent of Romans 12:1. He stated, **I am already being poured out like a drink offering.** His imagery came from his Jewish heritage and the biblical rites of devotion given to the sanctified community of faith. In Numbers 15, God defines for Israel some of the burnt offerings "made by fire . . . as an aroma pleasing to the LORD" (Num. 15:3). A drink offering of wine was to accompany the sacrifice of animals or grain. Just as Christ, the Lamb, was sacrificed to remove our sin guilt, so we are called to offer our lives in service as expressions of worship. Paul's offering was a literal offering of blood (often symbolized as wine) as he gave himself to the executioner's sword.

4:7–8. Paul offered three statements as a short review of his life. He meant to inspire Timothy, and all Christians, to continued faithfulness.

First, Paul declared, **I have fought the good fight.** Athletic competitions were as popular in the ancient world as in our own. Most people were familiar with the training and discipline necessary to succeed in athletic contests. Paul described his life in similar terms, except that the focus and discipline he employed were for the good fight of faith. He gave his life to the only cause worthy of devotion. He stayed with the rigors, the sacrifices, and the deprivations in order to receive the victor's reward.

Then Paul stated, **I have finished the race.** He viewed the successful completion of his life before God; he endured to the end. He remained true to the gospel despite terrible opposition. It was the very thing he asked of Timothy. Jesus gave a similar sentiment in John 17:4: "I have brought you glory on earth by completing the work you gave me to do."

There were still lepers to heal and blind people who could not see. There were many who did not believe. But both Jesus and Paul had submitted their wills to the will of God and had done what God called them to do.

This is all any of us can do. We can finish our own race. God's call upon each life is different in details and specifics, but he desires faithful endurance from all of us. We finish the race one step at a time, choosing to testify of God's goodness and grace and living rightly every day.

Paul concluded, **I have kept the faith**. This summarized what all the other phrases had described. In life and in doctrine, he had stayed the course with integrity.

4:8. As Paul awaited death, he stood on the threshold of a more glorious life to come. He knew what was ahead: **the crown of righteousness**. He knew who would confer it: **the Lord, the righteous Judge**. He knew when he would receive it: **on that day**.

Biblical writers often used the metaphor of a crown to describe the conferring of honor or reward. Paul used this metaphor in reference to the reward of righteousness that believers will receive when Christ returns. Though an individual receives the righteousness of Christ when he trusts in him as Savior, this righteousness is not fully realized until the day of his appearing. Legally, before the holy God, we are righteous. Practically, we await Christ's return when we will experience the reward of his total righteousness.

This great future urged Paul on through the persecutions, the loneliness, the disappointments. He looked ahead to the sweep of eternity, the bliss of living in God's presence, and wrote, "Though outwardly we are wasting away, yet inwardly we are being renewed day by day. For our light and momentary troubles are achieving for us an eternal glory that far outweighs them all" (2 Cor. 4:16–17).

This future exists, not for Paul alone, **but also to all who have longed for his appearing**. To set our hopes on Christ's appearing qualifies us as children of God. The unbeliever cannot look forward to the day of Christ's return. It means nothing to him. But to those who have staked their lives upon his coming, that day promises a uniting with the Lord. There is joy in anticipation of seeing him.

Ⓑ Personal Remarks (4:9–22)

SUPPORTING IDEA: *We are used to hero worship, to admiring people of accomplishment. It would be easy to set Paul upon a saintly pedestal. But serving Christ always takes place in community, as a team effort. In the final verses of this chapter Paul wrote of his love, appreciation, and need of others who served with him. Some had deserted Paul, while others had remained faithful. He expressed personal concern and thanks in these final words.*

1. Friends (4:9–13)

4:9. Paul embraced his humanity in this and the following verses. Though the cold breath of death was upon him, he did not know how many days he had left. He longed to see Timothy one last time, so he urged, **Do your best to come to me quickly.**

4:10. Here, at the end of his life, Paul felt lonely. This was probably the main reason he wanted desperately to see Timothy. We can learn from Paul, and find encouragement. Although we still struggle within the frame of our emotions and difficulties, our future remains secure. We should never expect Christians to exhibit perpetual happiness, as though the harsh realities of life do not affect them. This life seethes with difficulties, and all the more so for those who faithfully live and proclaim God's truth. Weariness, discouragement, and loneliness visit the faithful Christian.

In order to provide background and impetus for Timothy's visit, Paul reviewed his solitary condition.

Demas . . . has deserted me. Being alone does not always create a sense of loneliness, but being deserted almost certainly will. Desertion has betrayal as its root. Nothing strikes at the heart of a person more than violated trust.

Demas was one of the apostle's friends and associates; Paul mentioned him in Colossians 4:14 and Philemon 24, describing him as a "fellow worker." He seems to have served faithfully with Paul, Luke, and others in the missionary endeavor. Yet, at the end, he abandoned Paul and the work **because he loved this world.** In a few words, Paul penned a double tragedy: not only was Paul abandoned, but Demas had forsaken the goodness of the gospel. Two men suffered loss, though Demas's was more lasting.

Demas probably did not deny Christ and march off to Thessalonica in defiant arrogance. He does not appear as a heretic, signing on with the false teachers. Instead, Demas seems to exhibit the human tendency to seek personal safety. He probably traded in the values of God for the values of this world—the values of immediacy. He probably still believed in Christ, but he was unwilling to endure hardship, to identify with the imprisoned apostle and his unpopular teachings. His heartstrings were attached to personal protection and comfort. This can easily happen to us who live in the affluent Western cultures.

One more thing about Demas: he began well. Faithful service and zealous work do not guarantee the future. Our lives must be lived faithfully each day, each week, year upon year. Here was a man who had served Christ well, who had belonged to an intimate circle of workers with the apostle Paul, and yet he abandoned it in the end. Demas serves as a warning to each of us that we cannot rest on our past or assume the future. We must maintain a steady diligence in the present moment.

In addition to Demas's desertion, **Crescens** had gone to **Galatia**, and **Titus** to **Dalmatia**. These were fellow workers who had proceeded to other locations to continue work in established churches, perhaps even to plant new congregations. Paul found nothing wrong in their travels, but their departure magnified his loneliness.

4:11. Paul stated, **Only Luke is with me.** Luke always seemed to be there, quietly serving, Paul's faithful physician and friend.

Paul then gave Timothy a "wish list" of sorts. First, he said, **Get Mark and bring him with you.** Behind this request lies a story of grace and restoration. Mark, along with Barnabas, had accompanied Paul on his early missionary travels. But at a certain point Mark left them and returned to Jerusalem. His reason for leaving is omitted, but his parting was viewed negatively by Paul. Later, Barnabas wanted Mark to travel with them again, "but Paul did not think it wise to take him, because he had deserted them in Pamphylia and had not continued with them in the work" (Acts 15:38). A sharp division occurred, and Paul split company with Barnabas and Mark.

In time, however, Mark must have demonstrated maturity and enduring commitment. Paul may have had occasion to work beside him again, for now Paul viewed him as **helpful to me in my ministry.**

4:12. Paul continued to review his close associates. **Tychicus** he sent **to Ephesus,** to work in the church there. In Colossians 4:7, Paul described him as a "dear brother, a faithful minister and fellow servant." Tychicus had previously delivered the Colossian and Ephesian letters.

4:13. Paul then turned to a few personal needs. When Timothy came, he wanted him to arrange his journey so as to pass through **Troas.** There he was to visit **Carpus,** probably a Christian in that city, and collect Paul's **cloak . . . and . . . scrolls, especially the parchments.**

The cloak was a woolen outer garment. Paul suspected he would remain in prison into the winter months and so would need the warmth of his cloak.

The scrolls and parchments were probably the Scriptures. Paul still wanted to study, to learn. Filling his mind with the Word of God was important to him, even at the end of his life. The parchments were apparently of special value, written on vellum rather than the common papyrus.

Paul's desires were simple at the close of his life. He wanted to be in the presence of friends, to stay warm, and to refresh himself by the Scriptures.

2. An enemy (4:14–15)

4:14–15. Perhaps as Paul thought about Timothy's journey to Rome, he realized that the young pastor could possibly encounter **Alexander the metalworker.** Evidently this man had created difficulty for Paul and was an outright opponent of the gospel. Though we cannot be certain, it is possible that this Alexander is the same person whom Paul "handed over to Satan to be taught not to blaspheme" (1 Tim. 1:20). We can conjecture that he rose to leadership, then wandered from the true faith to become a leader among the false teachers who plagued the Ephesian church.

Paul's choice of words suggests that this Alexander may have played a leading role in having him arrested. Whatever the specifics of the situation, Alexander caused **great . . . harm.** Nevertheless, the final outcome rested not with Paul or Timothy but with God. Paul was certain that **the Lord will repay him for what he has done.** Alexander's fate remained in the hands of a just God.

In the meantime, Paul warned Timothy: **Be on your guard against him, because he strongly opposed our message.** Paul exhibited balance in his approach. On the one hand, he refused personal revenge or plots of retaliation. "'It is mine to avenge; I will repay,' says the Lord" (Rom. 12:19). On the other hand, he rejected naiveté and stupidity and warned Timothy to be careful.

3. The Lord's sufficiency (4:16–18)

4:16. Reminded that God's sovereignty overcomes all human efforts, Paul exalted in God as his strength and defender. He turned to another personal example: his preliminary trial.

Paul probably had a pretrial hearing to determine the grounds of the accusations against him. At that time, no one offered a word in his defense: **no one came to my support.** Not only was the hearing void of testimony on his behalf, but his friends **deserted** him. Perhaps Demas was in mind here along with others. Luke probably had not arrived in Rome by the time of Paul's initial trial. The event, however, brought back painful memories for Paul. Still, he viewed it through the goodness of God, choosing gratitude and forgiveness rather than bitterness: **May it not be held against them.**

4:17. Paul's purpose in telling the story was not to elicit sympathy or pity but to focus upon the goodness and sufficiency of God: **But the Lord stood at my side and gave me strength.** We need never limit ourselves to our own resources.

Note that God supplied strength, and not just as a personal favor to Paul. God strengthened him **so that through me the message might be fully proclaimed and all the Gentiles might hear it.** Preaching the gospel was Paul's goal. He needed power not simply to remain on his feet, but to speak clearly so salvation might come to all mankind through Jesus Christ.

Paul's passion was to preach the gospel to the Gentiles. Not even his arrest interfered with this. Indeed, it enlarged his audience as he was brought before the cosmopolitan gathering of Roman officials. A little Jewish man, chained, defenseless and alone, friendless and humiliated, now stood before the imperial Roman court with all its pomp and regalia—and preached the full gospel of Jesus Christ. He fulfilled by his own example the words he had passed on to the Corinthian church: "But God chose the foolish things of the world to shame the wise; God chose the weak things of the world to shame the strong . . . 'Let him who boasts boast in the Lord'" (1 Cor. 1:27,31).

Paul also declared that he was **delivered from the lion's mouth.** Some interpreters believe Paul was referring to Nero, whose ferocity had increased toward Christians. Others believe the "lion" was Satan, who lies behind all schemes against the gospel and God's followers. Perhaps Paul was speaking of those accusers who stood before him in the court or even death itself that was cheated one more time. Whatever the "lion" represents, the point Paul made was that God delivered him.

4:18. Not only was Paul rescued on this occasion, but he shared a confidence that **the Lord will rescue me from every evil attack and will bring me safely to his heavenly kingdom.** He knew God would not rescue him from the death that awaited him in the immediate future. But Paul remained firm in his conviction that God protects those who are his, guarding their souls until the time when he brings them into his kingdom. No evil plot of man or Satan can snatch God's children from his loving care. Thus, Paul declared, **to him be glory for ever and ever. Amen.**

4. Final words (4:19–22)

4:19–20. Paul's final words were common and personal, the closing words of a man deeply bound to friends in Christ.

Paul instructed Timothy to greet **Priscilla and Aquila.** Paul met this couple in Corinth where they had moved after being driven from Rome by Claudius's expulsion of the Jews. Since they were fellow tentmakers, the apostle enjoyed their friendship and hospitality while in the city (Acts 18:1–2). They seemed to have moved about also. While living in Ephesus, they were instrumental in instructing Apollos in the gospel (Acts 18:24–26). Eventually this couple moved back to Rome. Paul greeted them in his Roman letter as his "fellow workers in Christ Jesus" (Rom. 16:3). He further explained, "They risked their lives for me" (Rom. 16: 4). To this committed and godly couple, Paul gave final greetings of affection.

Paul mentioned once again **the household of Onesiphorus** (see 2 Tim. 1:16–18). There is reason to believe from Paul's wording that Onesiphorus died, possibly in service to Christ. At the beginning of the letter, Paul was moved by his devotion as Onesiphorus searched hard for Paul while in Rome. Now, in view of those who deserted him, this man and his household remained as dear reminders to Paul of brotherly love and loyalty.

Erastus, an associate of Timothy, stayed at Corinth in the Macedonian region. **Trophimus,** another fellow worker, was left sick by Paul in Miletus. We know little about these men other than that they were valued workers in ministry, men in whom Timothy would have an interest.

4:21. Paul returned to immediate needs. He pressed Timothy to hurry, to try and get to Rome **before winter.** Travel was difficult in those days, and the sea passage across the Adriatic Sea to Italy would prove impossible during the stormy winter months. Paul needed the warmth of Timothy's companionship.

Paul then extended greetings from four men, **Eubulus, Pudens, Linus,** and **Claudia,** as well as **all the brothers.** Since all bear Latin names, it may be supposed that these Gentile believers were part of the church in Rome. They evidently were known to Timothy, though nothing about them is known to us except as their names appear here in Paul's concluding thoughts. We may surmise that they worked faithfully and quietly for Christ and his cause.

4:22. Paul closed with the hopes that had echoed throughout the letter: **the Lord be with your spirit.** He prayed God's continual ministry in and through Timothy's life. He desired that this young man, to whom he was passing the torch of ministry, would remain faithful until the end, kept by God's Spirit.

And then, **Grace be with you.** The "you" is plural, and it includes all who would read the letter. Paul prayed for God's full goodness and concern, his unrelenting kindness and strength for all who seek to please him and who claim Christ as Lord.

Fittingly, these were probably Paul's final words. His ministry began in the blaze of God's grace on the road to Damascus, and he ended his life bestowing that same grace on all who remain faithful.

> **MAIN IDEA REVIEW:** *Paul had little time left. He gave Timothy one final charge to preach God's Word, and to do so with integrity and purity. Not everyone will listen. In fact, many will not. Apostasy always lurks at the edges of faith. But the pastor must remain faithful to his calling to honor God's Word. Paul offered himself as an example of ardent devotion, closing with personal remarks about some of his friends and ministry associates.*

III. CONCLUSION

The Omaha 10,000

When Bill Broadhurst was eighteen, an aneurysm occurred on the right side of his brain, leaving the left side of his body partially paralyzed. By the time he was twenty-eight, he was able to walk without the use of a cane. Although still hampered by a stiff-legged limp, it no longer prevented him from pursuing his interest in running.

The marathon in Omaha, Nebraska, like races all over the country, began predictably—the gun sounded and the runners flooded through the streets. As in most contests, the leaders become apparent early on. Bill Rogers, lean and practiced, was among the front-runners. Bill Broadhurst, among the throng at the beginning, was now running considerably behind.

Rogers won the race, covering the distance in less than thirty minutes. Fast by any standards. Other runners were not far behind, bringing in competitive times as they sprinted across the finish line. Joggers and weekend marathoners clocked in at an hour or more. The stragglers and the weary finished after about two hours.

After two hours and twenty minutes, Bill Broadhurst continued to run. There was no one in sight. His left side felt numb. A child, seeing him struggling along by himself, yelled, "Hey, mister, you missed the race."

Broadhurst's body screamed with pain, but he kept going. He wanted to finish. As a believer, he thought of 1 Corinthians 9:27 where Paul, speaking of running a race with endurance, said, "I beat my body and make it my slave." Broadhurst wanted to finish his race.

Two hours and thirty minutes after the starting gun, the sky was darkening. The police were gone. No crowds pressed along the streets to catch glimpses of the runners; tables cluttered with water cups no longer dotted the route. Broadhurst's limp worsened, his left leg almost dragging as he pushed himself on. He began to wonder if it was worth all the effort. Everything hurt.

Finally, he caught sight of the end point. As he hobbled along, he saw that the finish banner no longer fluttered over the street; it was already packed away for next year's race. The place was deserted. His heart sank as he realized how far behind he had run, how long ago the race had ended. On the dark street, with no one watching, what difference would it make if he crossed an imaginary finish line?

But he did.

As he did, from out of the alleyway stepped Bill Rogers and a small group of people. Stumbling across the finish line, Broadhurst was welcomed by the outstretched arms of the champion, his hero. Taking the gold medal from around his own neck, Rogers put it on Broadhurst's, declaring him the winner.

It was a moment of victory more electric, perhaps, than two hours earlier when the crowds had cheered Bill Rogers across the line.

Soon, after the struggles and weariness of this life, we will also cross the finish line to meet our hero and Savior, Jesus Christ.

As we step across the finish line, he will step out, not from the shadows, but from the blaze of his own glory. He will give us the gold—the crown of his own righteousness—for he has run the race before us . . . perfectly. "Well done, good and faithful servant" (Matt. 25:21), he will say to those who endure to the end.

PRINCIPLES

- Everyone will face Christ the judge.
- The Word of God provides guiding principles and mandates for the church and its people.
- Faithfulness and endurance are hallmarks of the true follower of Christ Jesus.
- Godliness results in persecution.
- Every person contributes either to the strengthening of the church and the spread of the gospel, or to the weakening of the church and the curtailment of the kingdom. There is no neutral position.

APPLICATIONS

- As believers, we need to speak up for the truth of God not only when the situation seems convenient or when we are "on duty," but when it is inconvenient. We must live the faith and be available as witnesses to the truth all the time.
- Each of us has a ministry in the world, and God desires that we "discharge our duties" fully and competently. We must determine in what ways we can serve Christ in our communities and the church.
- Hardships for the sake of righteousness is a reality for Christians. We need not be discouraged or surprised, nor should we consider ourselves in unusual circumstances. We share good company with the apostle Paul, Timothy, and a host of Christians through the ages.
- God calls believers to live and think in a balanced, thoughtful, and wise manner. We need to guard against quick reactions, rash decisions, and theological curiosities.
- God strengthens us to endure the tests of faith, hardships, and pain that come our way. We must depend on God's power through his Holy Spirit, relinquishing our control to him.

IV. LIFE APPLICATION

Tornado Alley

"Compromise" is a very slippery word. Sometimes wisdom dictates finding a middle course for the sake of peace, granting concessions in areas of lesser importance for the sake of a higher, more noble purpose. But compromise can also demonstrate an insidious willingness to jeopardize standards, slowly eroding personal character and goodness. Each situation demands a careful examination of the costs of compromise. What often appears as a small matter at first may develop into the loss of a crucial principle.

Paul and Timothy faced people who constantly compromised the gospel in order to accommodate their own ideas. Paul referred to them as false teachers. These were the ring leaders. But there were many ordinary people who trivialized the gospel by following human reason and pop theology. It was not that these people rejected God's Word outright; they added to it or reconfigured its message. Therein lay the danger. This had the appearance of reasonableness and truth.

The description Paul gave reminds us of Jesus' story about two men who constructed houses—one beachside, the other "rockside." The modern version might feature two men living in Tornado Alley, that fickle expanse of prairie in America's midsection. Whether these men are in Oklahoma or Kansas does not change the vital elements: Mr. A moves into a house trailer, while Mr. B settles into a modest home with a basement.

The inevitable occurs. One spring day, moist hot air speeds inland from the Gulf, while cold, dry air rushes south from Canada. This unstable condition creates faster air currents high in the atmosphere which rotate horizontally over slower air swirls beneath, like pencils rolling over a table top. Suddenly there is an updraft and the horizontal spirals are tipped on their heads—a twister is born.

House trailers are highly vulnerable in storms, especially tornadoes. Mr. A finds himself sucked into the whirling disaster. But Mr. B finds refuge and safety in his basement.

Their choice of homes, where they chose to dwell, determined their outcome. The laws of nature remained intact, unaltered by their desires or beliefs.

God's Word remains an unwavering reality. It simply is. People argue against it, try to disprove it, dismiss it, and compromise its message. People think they can cut corners with God's revelation as given in the Bible. They reconstruct its message to fit their own liking. This was popular in Paul's day, and it is no less so in our own. We bump up against the demands of discipleship, or the probability of hardship. We squirm under our guilt, or succumb to selfishness. Rather than change ourselves, we try to change the message. We fiddle around with the words, or reinterpret the passage, and soon we feel safe and comfortable. But the tornado inevitably comes.

Truth and falsehood collide, resulting in a violent swirl of conflicting propositions. Those who choose the fabrications of modern philosophy or current opinion, who dwell in the flimsy constructions of personal desire, will get pulled into destruction—if not in this life, most certainly in the life to come.

Paul urged Timothy to remain grounded in God's truth—during the calm or the storm, whether convenient or not. God's Word provides the only stability and refuge in this life and the only hope for eternity.

V. PRAYER

Lord, against the onslaught of society's values and beliefs, keep my mind and heart established in your truths as I study and apply your Word to my life. Amen.

VI. DEEPER DISCOVERIES

A. The Drink Offering (v. 6)

Paul's declaration that he was **already being poured out like a drink offering**, comes from the Mosaic Law of sacrifices. Numbers 15:5,7,10 provide the background for Paul's statement.

The system of sacrifices in the Old Testament symbolized the consecration of man to God. There were two basic classifications of sacrifices: those that reestablished fellowship with God (sin offerings), and those that expressed an ongoing fellowship with God (thank offerings, freewill offerings). The drink offering, freely given to God as an act of adoration and worship, belongs to this second classification.

The drink offering always consisted of wine. There was no substitute. It represented the fruit of the earth, or a product of a person's labor. The drink offering recognized God as Creator and Lord over all the earth. On a deeper level, wine also represents blood, the essence of human life. Pouring wine upon the altar in sacrifice to God depicted a person's total dedication—soul, spirit, and body.

Paul knew that atonement for his sins had been achieved through Jesus Christ. But as he languished in prison, perhaps he reflected on the meaning of his approaching death. He knew that his death was a freewill offering to God, an oblation of his life upon the altar. He sacrificed himself in the service of Christ, recognizing him as sovereign over all creation. As a drink offering, Paul poured out the fruit of his labors and the essence of his life.

B. The Time for Departure (v. 6)

Speculations, myths, and traditions generally surround famous people. So it is about Paul's martyrdom. Various speculations have been given about the time and place of his death and burial, but they are just that—speculations.

It is believed that Paul's imprisonment approximated the time of Nero's great persecution of Christians in A.D. 64. In July of that year a fire broke out in a section of Rome's Circus Maximus. The area was full of volatile materials and the flames quickly spread. Added to this was a wind which fanned the fire throughout adjacent areas of the city. The inferno raged five days, destroying three of Rome's fourteen sectors and damaging seven others.

Nero was away at the time, and he rushed back to attend to the catastrophe. A rumor circulated among the people that Nero had purposely set the blaze so he could rebuild the imperial city after his own designs. In order to squelch the gossip, Nero plucked from the populace some scapegoats—the Christians of Rome.

The Christians were already a suspect and misunderstood group. They worshiped and served Christ beneath a cloud of accusations: traitorous activities (because they rejected emperor worship), antisocial behavior, and cannibalism (associated with the Lord's Supper). Unpopular and held in contempt, the Christians were deemed dispensable.

As a Roman citizen, Paul escaped these particular tortures, but not Nero's fury. By imperial decree, he was probably beheaded on the Ostian Way near the town of Aquae Salviae, around A.D. 68.

VII. TEACHING OUTLINE

A. INTRODUCTION

1. Lead Story: Finishing the Race
2. Context: These are some of Paul's last recorded words. They offer a mix of passion, concern, theological truth, ordinary remarks, and personal greetings. He charged Timothy to endure, preaching and ministering as God's chosen spokesman. He warned that many would defect because they preferred comfort and falsehood to the rigors and discipline of Christian faith. In the end, Paul confessed his loneliness and asked Timothy to visit him in Rome, giving thanks for many of his friends.
3. Transition: Some basic issues stand out in this closing chapter of 2 Timothy. First, Paul referred to the need for Christians to endure hardship. As people of the living Christ, we must not hesitate or shrink from difficulty. Second, it is imperative for believers to guard and proclaim God's truth without reserve or embarrassment. Third, people remain the priority of the gospel and Christian witness. We must love, encourage, and guide people into relationship with God and holiness of life.

B. COMMENTARY

1. The Charge (4:1–8)
   a. Pastoral responsibilities (4:1–2)

b. The majority response (4:3–4)
c. The command for constancy (4:5)
d. Paul's example (4:6–8)
2. Personal Remarks (4:9–22)
a. Friends (4:9–13)
b. An enemy (4:14–15)
c. The Lord's sufficiency (4:16–18)
d. Final words (4:19–22)

C. CONCLUSION: TORNADO ALLEY

VIII. ISSUES FOR DISCUSSION

1. Paul says we are to be prepared to preach God's Word at all times. When are you most likely to hesitate in sharing the gospel? How could you prepare beforehand to overcome your timidity or fear in such situations?

2. Identify some popular ideas which could be attractive to Christians and yet lead us away from God's truth—environmental issues, tolerance, promises of wealth. What are you most susceptible to?

3. It is always good to examine our lives, to recognize the patterns, habits, and influences that determine who we are and how we live. As Paul faced death, he summarized his own life. Write a summary or eulogy of your life. Are there changes that you should make?

Introduction to

Titus

LETTER PROFILE: TITUS

- Letter written by Paul, sometime between A.D. 63 and 65.
- It is postulated that Paul embarked on a missionary journey after a time of imprisonment in Rome, perhaps journeying west into Spain. On his return east he may have received news of problems in Ephesus and Crete and so penned his letters to Timothy (1 Timothy) and Titus.
- Titus was a minister of the gospel who previously had been of great help to Paul in the missionary enterprise.
- Though written specifically to Titus, the letter was intended to be read before the gathered church. The church probably consisted of several house churches throughout the major cities of Crete.
- The Cretan church was young and the members inexperienced. Most were Gentiles, though there were Jewish communities on the island.
- Paul appointed Titus to establish a sound and healthy church on Crete. He gave Titus instructions on appointing church leaders; he provided a model of teaching, the older instructing the younger, which ensured the ongoing strengthening of the church and its people; Paul emphasized order, good behavior, and trustworthy character as fitting for Christians; he warned of the false teachers and their destructive influence; he closed with personal remarks.

AUTHOR PROFILE: PAUL

- Jewish-born in Tarsus, near the Lebanese border in modern Turkey.
- Roman citizen.
- Prominent Jewish religious leader, highly educated as a Pharisee.
- Persecuted Christians before his own dramatic conversion in A.D. 35.

- Though it remains uncertain whether Paul ever visited Crete as part of his missionary work, he did stop there on his way to Rome when the ship harbored for a short time at Fair Havens.
- Known for his tireless pioneer work to Gentiles.
- Imprisoned by Nero's regime in A.D. 67 in Rome, where he was executed the next year (2 Tim. 4).

GEOGRAPHIC PROFILE: CRETE

- Crete is a fertile, agricultural island located south of Greece in the southern Aegean Sea.
- Most Cretan cities developed along the northern coast to benefit shipping and trading with the mainland.
- Ethnically, Cretans were linked to ancient Minoan and Mycenaean civilizations.

Titus 1

Establishing the Church

Titus 1

IN A NUTSHELL

*P*aul began by establishing his authority as an apostle—one to whom God had entrusted the message of salvation and eternal hope. He then proceeded to outline for Titus the qualifications for officers of the church. Much of what he said is similar to his instructions in 1 Timothy, including a warning about the false teachers.

Establishing the Church

I. INTRODUCTION

Good Ol' What's His Name

A man and his wife came hurrying up to me one Sunday after morning worship. "We have just been to a terrific course on memory. The seminar showed us how to use word associations and other methods for recalling information. It was terrific!" he enthused.

I listened as he told me the details. His wife nodded excitedly as he described the workshops they attended.

"So, who was the teacher of the seminar?" I asked.

The man looked down, put his finger to his lips, looking rather pensive. I could tell his mind was grinding through the techniques. Finally, he looked at me and asked, "What's the name of the flower that has red and pink petals, and thorns?"

"Rose," I said.

He looked toward his wife and asked, "Rose, what was the name of that teacher at the memory course?"

Our methods often fail, even those for living the Christian life. We set up rules and devise systems of belief or practice, only to discover that nothing is working out as we had planned. Some people spend a lifetime working and planning on how to get to heaven. But when the test of truth comes, all strategies and schemes fail. We need the truth and designs of God.

Just as he wrote to Timothy, Paul wrote to another pastor, Titus, outlining the necessity for truth, the need to establish strong leadership, the Christian's call to godliness, and the essential nature of the church in the life of believers.

Paul called us to remain faithful to the fundamentals of the faith—to focus on truth and godliness as prescribed by God through Jesus Christ. If we do not, we will become entangled in false ideas and systems that will fail us.

II. COMMENTARY

MAIN IDEA: *Paul handed instructions to Titus on how to establish and secure the new churches in Crete, describing the qualifications for leadership. He also encouraged Titus to confront those who spread false doctrines and brought division to God's community. Above all, Paul emphasized the need for truth and godliness— orthodoxy of belief and a changed life that validates the power and truth of God.*

A Greeting (1:1–4)

SUPPORTING IDEA: *As in most letters, Paul began with a claim to his apostleship, thereby confirming the authority with which he delivered the following commands and instructions. His opening paragraph also briefly described the hope to which he looked. He then named the recipient of the letter—Titus.*

1. The apostle's authority and purpose (1:1–3)

1:1. Paul described himself as a **servant of God.** In this phrase he established the master-servant relationship between God and himself, viewing his life and work as dictated by the Father. Further, he was **an apostle of Jesus Christ.**

Apostleship was conferred on only a few people. It required, among other things, that the person had seen the risen Christ and had been commissioned by him to service. Paul's encounter with Jesus on the Damascus road qualified him in both respects. With his apostleship came the delivery, through revelation, of the message of God's grace to the Gentiles: **faith of God's elect.**

Spiritual election is a mystery to the human mind. In a phrase, Paul displayed the two sides of God's sovereignty. On the one hand, God had chosen, electing those who will belong to him forever. Paul described the Colossians as "God's chosen people" (Col. 3:12), and Peter wrote "to God's elect, strangers in the world" (1 Pet. 1:1). Under his sovereign rule, he has rescued particular people. As Jesus stated, "No one can come to me unless the Father has enabled him" (John 6:65). On the other hand, Paul understood the responsibility of proclaiming the message to all people and that those who respond must do so based upon a rational, personal decision. Personal faith remains the requisite for life in Christ. God chooses, but we must respond in trust.

God's particular assignment for Paul was to bring the understanding of salvation to the elect, those who would believe. His life mission also involved guiding the elect into mature and developing faith: **the knowledge of the truth that leads to godliness.**

Truth involves rational understanding, but God's truth is also transforming (cf. John 8:32). Once again, Paul established the dividing line between the true gospel and the doctrines of the false teachers. The necessity of any theology or philosophy is that it must work; it must apply to the world in which we live. Because only truth is consistent with life and reality, there is always some point at which all other approaches to life and spirituality fail. When Christians fail or life appears contradictory to biblical revelation, it is because we have departed from the truth either in belief or practice. God's truth, Paul declared, leads to godliness—to a different and complete manner of life.

1:2. This **faith and knowledge**, life and understanding, were **resting on the hope of eternal life**. It takes some rethinking for English-speaking people to think of hope as anything other than wishing. For instance, we hope it will snow on Christmas, or we hope a friend will call—desires that may or may not occur. But hope in the New Testament is an established certainty because it issues from the promise of God.

Our hope is eternal life, **which God, who does not lie, promised before the beginning of time**. Unlike the promises we make, many of which are broken or forgotten, God's promises remain immutable. God does not lie. Just as God brought forth the world by the spoken word, so he confirms the future by a word of promise. Whatever God says, must happen, since he designs reality. His spoken word cannot be contradicted in actuality. If it could, he would be dethroned. But that is impossible. God by his very nature remains reliable and trustworthy. What he says, must be.

1:3. Paul's phrasing in this verse shows the reader the parallel course between Christ and the apostle, using matching terminology to describe their missions. Christ came at the "fullness of time." He was the living Word who brought light to the world. Similarly, the timing of Paul's ministry to the Gentiles was determined by God for a precise moment in history: **at his appointed season he brought his word to light through the preaching entrusted to me** (Paul) **by the command of God our Savior**.

This does not diminish the work of Christ and his fulfillment of God's promise to all people. Instead, it marks Christ as the beginning point of the promise's attainment. The work which Jesus began extends to the present and to all those entrusted to preach the gospel. Christ Jesus accomplished salvation for those who believe. Preaching continues the offering of the promise to all people until his return.

2. The recipient of the letter (1:4)

1:4. Paul wrote to **Titus, my true son in our common faith**. Little is known of Titus, but most agree that, like Timothy, Paul considered him reliable and mature enough in faith to handle difficult situations. Titus had probably worked alongside Paul at different times, affirming in the apostle's mind his capabilities in leadership. It is also probable that Paul led Titus to faith.

Typical of Paul's greetings, he offered Titus **grace and peace from God the Father and Christ Jesus our Savior.** Grace is the unearned blessing or favor of God toward mankind. It springs from the eternal well of God's goodness. Peace, for the believer, is tranquility of the soul, a spirit at rest in God despite the turbulence of circumstances. Grace and peace can be known only in relationship with God, only as we develop intimacy with God and his Christ. Paul desired that Titus experience these treasures.

B Establishing the Churches (1:5–9)

> **SUPPORTING IDEA:** *Paul reminded Titus of his mission on Crete. From this he established the qualifications for church leadership that are essential to a healthy church and a maturing Christian community.*

1. Titus's job description (1:5)

1:5. Paul got to the purpose of the letter by reaffirming Titus's purpose for staying on the island of Crete. There is no mystery here: **I left you in Crete . . . that you might straighten out what was left unfinished.** The churches there were young, fledgling congregations without proper organization, leadership, or strong teaching. Titus was assigned the task of forming these gatherings into balanced, functioning churches.

Paul told Titus to **appoint elders in every town, as I directed you.** Perhaps he had told him the necessity of this before. But, for whatever reason, Titus had not done it yet, so Paul mentioned it again. Without sound leadership, the church would flounder and become susceptible to perverted doctrines.

2. Qualifications for church leadership (1:6–9)

1:6. Paul told Titus the characteristics a person should have in order to assume leadership within the church. The standards for church leadership are consistently high; they do not change based on location or time. Paul wrote almost identical instructions to Timothy. (For a more detailed explanation, see the Commentary for 1 Timothy 3.) The same basic principles hold true in any circumstance. The inner spirit and outward life must be consistent, ethically pure, and morally innocent.

Though Paul did not insist on perfection, he did require that the leader live above blame, or beyond accusation. The **elder must be blameless.** The Greek word here, *presbuteros*, is translated variously as "bishop" or "elder." These words point to those men within the church with official leadership roles. Such a person keeps his accounts settled with God and others. He confesses his sin, makes restitution when needed, and commits to purity in all areas of life.

He must also be **the husband of but one wife**. Literally, he must be a "one-woman man." In addition, he must be **a man whose children believe and are not open to the charge of being wild and disobedient.** In other words, the church leader must exhibit a dedication to family life. More of a person's character and inner qualities are revealed at home than at work or in public. Paul implied that those who do a good job at home possess the ability to do well in other arenas of leadership as well. The parent's ability to secure the obedience of his children reflects his own faithfulness, commitment, and leadership capability.

1:7. The standard for leadership remains high, because the **overseer** (leader, pastor, elder, bishop) **is entrusted with God's work.** Paul understood that church leadership is a position of trust given from God to those official guides of his church. Such a trust required faithfulness in every corner of a person's life: **he must be blameless.**

As has been noted before (1 Thess. 3:13; 5:23), blamelessness refers not to perfection but to a pattern of life against which no charge of wrong can be brought. Such a person, having committed a sin, immediately seeks forgiveness and enacts restitution, if needed. Sinful behavior in a blameless person is recognized as an aberration, not a normalcy.

Paul refined his definition of blamelessness by first highlighting five negative characteristics, none of which can reside in the qualified church leader. The presence of any of these traits betray a person as lacking self-control and, more seriously, lacking the strength of God's Spirit upon his life.

Not overbearing. An overbearing disposition comes from arrogance or insecurity, resulting in a domineering, despotic manner of leadership which crushes the spirit and extinguishes the gifts and abilities of others. Leadership by control quickly divides a group into factions and arguments, taking away the spirit of unity and cooperation.

Not quick-tempered. Anger typically finds its root in pride. A person's temper flares when, set upon a certain course or determined in his opinions, he is thwarted or interrupted. Such a person "knows" he is right and disallows any other opinions. In those who do not get their own way, anger spits its fire quickly. They demonstrate emotional immaturity, lack of Spirit-control, and an inflated view of their own agenda. In any case, such behavior in a leader will not prove a good model for others, nor will it promote unity, love, and the development of spiritual life in others.

Not given to drunkenness. This is another reference to control. People who abdicate the control of their actions to substances such as alcohol or drugs cannot be considered fit for exercising guidance or authority over others.

Not pursuing dishonest gain. Financial integrity, or its lack, exposes a great deal about a person's inner character. The pursuit of money, and the fascination and absorption which it generates, pulls a person's affections away from legitimate loves and service. Add to that a person whose greed pushes him into dishonesty, and you have a leader controlled by money. Such a person will make decisions not from wisdom but for personal advantage. He will barter away his faith for gain. Obviously, such a person is unqualified as God's representative in the community of faith.

1:8. Having given the negatives, Paul now turned to the positive qualities for which a church leader should be known.

He must be hospitable. This became a hallmark of Christian life. First-century hospitality involved vulnerability and sacrificial giving, in contrast to modern hospitality, which centers around entertainment, parties, and pot-luck suppers. The church leader was to have a reputation for welcoming others into his home, especially believers in need. This meant identifying openly with the cause of Christ and his oppressed people. In addition, it typically meant giving from one's poverty, rather than from wealth. Most Christians lived in humble homes, with food adequate to meet only their own needs. Hospitality required them to open their personal belongings and supplies for the welfare of others.

One who loves what is good. There is no need to dissect the word *good*. Suffice it to say that a leader must bear the quality not only of doing good but of devotion to any moral and ethical acts that result in good and benefit others.

Who is self-controlled. Here again is the flip side of those unqualified to lead. Self-control reveals itself in a myriad of ways—through patience, gentleness, sobriety, faithfulness, financial integrity. It is through God's Holy Spirit within a life that the self can be harnessed and brought under control. Such a person is proof of God's divine life within. He is qualified to lead others into spiritual growth.

Upright. This refers to pure conduct before other people.

Holy. Holiness refers to a cleansed heart and relationship with God.

Disciplined. This covers the entirety of life—a person exercising control in his thoughts, attitudes, actions, and speech.

1:9. Having described the personal qualities of a person fit for church leadership, Paul finished with one more necessity. The leader **must hold firmly to the trustworthy message as it has been taught.** Those who presume to lead must embrace the traditional teachings which came through Christ and the apostles. Leaders must not come from among those who flirt with new doctrines. Not only must their behavior be open to observable goodness; they must also remain unwavering in their commitment to the faithful message of truth.

Paul offered two reasons for this requirement in leaders. First, dedication to the true gospel message would qualify them to **encourage others by sound doctrine**. Only truth brings change, encouragement, and actual spiritual development. False teachings can offer only temporary gratification or intrigue. They can never satisfy. Secondly, knowledge and adherence to sound doctrine will equip a person to **refute those who oppose it**. False teachings, human inventions and philosophies create confusion and bring destruction upon the thinking and faith of many.

Ideas are not idle games of philosophers. They are the fundamental structures of our behavior and responses. Paul knew that anything not springing from the truth must be shown for its fallacy. "We demolish arguments and every pretension that sets itself up against the knowledge of God, and we take captive every thought to make it obedient to Christ" (2 Cor. 10:5).

The False Teachers (1:10–16)

> **SUPPORTING IDEA:** *Paul next turned his attention to the false teachers who were plaguing the Cretan churches. He spared no words in describing their behavior and destructive influence.*

1:10. Paul transitioned easily from the false doctrine that must be opposed to the nature of those who were promoting such error. He began by categorizing them as **rebellious**. People of rebellion do not wander from the path so much as they willfully strike off on a different route. The false teachers were defiant in their opposition to the gospel message.

In addition, they were **mere talkers and deceivers**. Paul used the same tone in 1 Timothy 1:6, when he described these people as participating in "meaningless talk." These teachers dealt in empty discussions and pointless ideas. Since anything false is ultimately ineffective and worthless, it only stands to reason that it is deceptive. So the false teachers worked by sleight of hand, using the trickery of words and the enchantment of novelty to entice the ignorant or weak to follow them.

Paul then offered a clue about who these false teachers were. The harm sprang primarily from the **circumcision group**. These were probably people who had turned to Christianity from Judaism.

1:11. Paul was adamant. **They must be silenced**. They were **ruining whole households by teaching things they ought not to teach**. We cannot be certain what these people were teaching. Some interpreters suggest they promoted a liberationist view that created unrest among women and slaves, disrupting traditional community values. But whatever the particulars of their message, it is clear that its damaging effects penetrated deeply into social and relational structures.

As if this were not enough, the spiritual damage from these teachers came out of a depraved desire for **dishonest gain.** Selfishness lay at the heart of the false teachers and their religious system. Nothing is more antithetical to the Christian faith.

1:12–14. Paul next refuted the false teachers by calling forth the testimony of **one of their own prophets** who said, **"Cretans are always liars, evil brutes, lazy gluttons."** The apostle used a familiar saying of the day against the ones who bandied it about.

Cretans were stereotyped as liars because they claimed the tomb of Zeus was located on Crete. This was an unfounded claim that everyone recognized as a deception. Reference to their base and uncontrolled behavior may trace back to religious or cultural practices which were less refined than their Jewish counterparts.

By restating the slanderous words of one of the false teachers' own prophets, Paul intended the slander to work back upon itself. The false teachers were guilty of the very wrongs for which they chastised others. Therefore, **this testimony is true,** for the Cretan false teachers practiced deception, uncontrolled behavior, and greed. The whole system which they advanced was designed for the benefit of the leaders.

Paul's response to the duplicity of the false teachers and their followers is clear in the directive he gave Titus: **rebuke them sharply.** Sometimes the pastor or church leader must boldly confront those who wander from the truth. Though exhibiting gentleness and care, the leader must not shrink from using strong words. He needs to speak to the issue and clarify the wrong and evil into which the individual or group has fallen.

The motive comes not from an enjoyment of confrontation, or from the heady position of pointing out faults, but from an earnest desire that people **will be sound in the faith.** Encouraging and promoting healthy faith—correct belief and righteous behavior—should remain the goal of all who lead within the church.

Those who exhibit a sound faith will **pay no attention to Jewish myths.** Paul and the other missionaries often found that the false teachings which festered within the new churches arose from Jewish traditions and fables. These were the stories woven between the lines of the Old Testament. Similarities may have existed between the teachings on Crete and those in Ephesus because Paul also warned that church against those who dealt in myths and genealogies (1 Tim. 1:4). Paul wanted those within the churches to understand the truth of the gospel. They should devote themselves to holiness so they would not pay attention to spiritual fables **or to the commands of those who reject the truth.**

Not only did the false teachers propagate spiritualizing stories and tales, they also created a system of rules and rituals. These man-made commands became the measuring stick of spirituality for the heretical. In fact, these regulations became barometers of their spiritual decline and hollowness. This is often the situation for those who grope about for spiritual direction yet refuse to turn to Christ. In an effort to attain religious distinction, they refuse God's revelation, then masquerade behind strict customs, rules, and traditions.

1:15. In Matthew 23:25–26, Jesus said, "Woe to you, teachers of the law and Pharisees, you hypocrites! You clean the outside of the cup and dish, but inside they are full of greed and self-indulgence. . . . First clean the inside of the cup and dish, and then the outside also will be clean." In essence, Paul said the same thing: **To the pure, all things are pure, but to those who are corrupted and do not believe, nothing is pure.**

True purity resides not in the practice of ritual or in devotion to rules and regulations. Purity that God recognizes and commends comes from within, and a person can attain this only through faith in Jesus Christ. Cleansed from within, that person becomes free to live in purity, washed of all selfishness. The mind, transformed by the truth, ignites the conscience to obey God willingly in all manner of living.

Those who refuse the truth—who stubbornly exalt themselves, who believe they can attain righteousness through self effort—are impure. Their minds continue in enslavement to false ideas, self-deceptions, and empty philosophies. In such a condition, their consciences remain damaged and dysfunctional. **Both their minds and consciences are corrupted.** For such individuals, nothing will ever be pure, right, or righteous because they remain defiled within.

1:16. The marks of a Christian are genuine relationship with God and conduct that grows in holiness. But the marks of the false teachers and their followers are the absence of these qualities: **They claim to know God** (have a relationship with him), **but by their actions they deny him** (their conduct remains selfish and worldly).

Because false teachers devise their own systems of spirituality and rules of religious practice—because they teach what opposes orthodox belief—they disqualify themselves in all aspects of Christian life. These people do not just irritate church life; they threaten it. Dangerous men, they divide what God seeks to unify. They destroy grace through laws and commands. They confuse what Christ clarified through the gospel message.

Therefore, Paul declared, **they are detestable, disobedient and unfit for doing anything good.** While they appear to seek God, following rituals of outward purity, before the Almighty they are disgusting. While they demand strict obedience to rules and regulations, before God they remain defiant. Though they trumpet their actions, Christ declares them unfit and useless.

MAIN IDEA REVIEW: *Paul handed instructions to Titus on how to establish and secure the new churches in Crete, describing the qualifications for leadership. He also encouraged Titus to confront those who spread false doctrines and brought division to God's community. Above all, Paul emphasized the need for truth and godliness—orthodoxy of belief and a changed life which validates the power and truth of God.*

III. CONCLUSION

Follow the Leader

"You are a minister, so I know you will not understand this kind of temptation."

"Pastors are paid to be good."

"What a privilege for me to introduce to you the Right Reverend Joseph Logan."

There are many misconceptions, jokes, and formalities related to pastors and spiritual leaders, none of which have anything to do with the gospel of Christ's kingdom. While their position places them under great responsibility before God, pastors and church leaders are normal, regular sorts of people. They experience temptations common to all people and even some related specifically to their job and position. They struggle like other believers, they sleep at night, brush their teeth, have to pay bills, and navigate through a variety of relationships . . . just as we all do.

In his letter to Titus, Paul outlined some specific guidelines and character qualities that pastors and church leaders must exhibit. But these standards are not intended only for the superspiritual or the official leaders of the congregation. The pastor is not held to a different standard than other Christians. Every believer should determine to live a life of progressive holiness. These characteristics should be normative for every follower of Christ.

James recognized that teachers, or pastors, bear a responsibility for which they will be held accountable. They "will be judged more strictly" (Jas. 3:1). Those who handle God's words, who instruct others in divine matters, will undergo a more exacting examination. But this does not relieve all other Christians from the responsibility of ordering their lives in accordance with righteousness. Jesus Christ is our model, our example of how we must live. Pastors may be judged more strictly, but they will be examined by the same standard of holiness.

Anyone who rejects the principles which Paul handed on to Titus is guilty of rebellion and disobedience. Leaders must exemplify a life of godliness, but those who comprise the congregation must then follow their lead.

PRINCIPLES

- Eternal life and godliness are part of an eternal plan that God has entrusted to his followers and the church so they in turn can reveal it to the world.
- The church should have multiple leaders to assure accountability and a sharing of duties and responsibilities.
- Those who assume positions of leadership within the church must meet specific standards of belief and conduct.
- Disqualification in either orthodoxy or lifestyle eliminates a person from a position of church leadership.
- All believers are to adopt a pure lifestyle.
- False teachers and their teachings must be eradicated from the church.

APPLICATIONS

- If we claim eternal life and the Spirit's indwelling, we must help share the news of God's truth and power.
- We must apply ourselves to purity and righteousness.
- Divisive and disobedient teachers must be silenced. Speculations, strange ideas, and unfounded doctrines must not be allowed within the church.
- We must always correct people with a view to restoration and redemption.
- Church leaders and pastors should help keep one another accountable so they will develop spiritual strength and health.

IV. LIFE APPLICATION

The Verdict

In Western cultures, a curious phenomenon has developed over the years. Sometimes we call it privatization, the process by which we take something which should belong in the public domain and confine or reduce it to personal use. This outlook concludes that almost everything of importance belongs to the personal control of the individual. This approach divorces private and public life. This privatization has shoved religion, morality, community responsibility, and relational commitments to the margins of life.

Such an approach not only confines religion and ethics to individual taste; it also drives a wedge in people's thinking. Most people do not recognize when a dichotomy exists between their professed beliefs and their behavior. They can espouse belief in God, fidelity, and honesty, while at the same time neglecting prayer, giving, and the authority of Scripture. Without a sense of accountability, they participate in adultery, cheating, and lying as long as it serves personal advantage.

Christians hover on the same precipice, in danger of advocating a divine message while neglecting the necessity of its transforming power. As the divide between professed belief and lifestyle widens, we enter the danger zone of self-delusion, concluding that mere statements of belief are the essence of faith, that declarations of orthodoxy release God's grace upon us, liberating us from the necessity of biblical conduct.

But the Christian faith rests on Jesus Christ. He penetrates the mind with the knowledge of God and invades our spirit, changing the believer into a different person. No longer does the Christian appease his conscience by duty; he expresses his love and commitment to God by a changed lifestyle. To sever our beliefs from our behavior is a denial of the faith we profess.

Belief *and* conduct define the individual. This is why Paul, in speaking of false teachers or those who had wandered from the faith, easily transitioned between their faulty belief system and their discredited behavior. This is also why, when defining the qualifications for Christian service and leadership, he addressed both doctrinal purity and ethical behavior.

The unbelieving world longs to see authentic Christianity. Christians are expected to witness to the power and saving goodness of God, to testify to Christ's ability to transform this present life. But the gulf between what *is* and what *should be* is sometimes very wide.

Paul urged, "Do not be ashamed to testify about our Lord" (2 Tim. 1:8). What we must recapture is the sum and substance of authentic witness. A witness validates a claim. He affirms or denies a particular position. As Christians, we either confirm or refute God's revelation. While we cannot achieve the salvation of our soul through hard work, we do verify our salvation by the way we act, the purity of our life, the lifestyle we follow.

In a court of law, when a person is called to bear witness, his testimony is validated by his character. If words and conduct do not agree, behavior always takes precedence over statements. What we do is far more convincing than what we say.

V. PRAYER

Lord, judge of my heart, purify me and keep me sensitive to your Holy Spirit so that I may live consistent with your truth and your power. Amen.

VI. DEEPER DISCOVERIES

A. God's Elect (v. 1)

At the beginning of Paul's letter to Titus, he prefaced his instructions by proclaiming his apostleship. His authority for what followed came from the fact that he was "a servant of God and an apostle of Jesus Christ for the faith of God's elect."

The "elect" encompasses those who trust in Christ to restore the relationship between themselves and God. These are people who depend upon Jesus' death as a substitute for their own deserved punishment for sin. They rely on his resurrection for their hope for life now and into eternity.

Even so, election is not a strictly New Testament concept. Election refers to the sovereign choice of God, especially in selecting people for a particular purpose. What seems to be the underlying necessity of God's election is that his choice remains hidden in the depths of his own wisdom. None of his selections depend upon the actions of the individual or group elected. God chooses. We are not told why or how. But the election of God issues from his love. In addition, it places unique responsibility upon the chosen.

Israel is called God's chosen (or elect) in Isaiah 45:4. As a nation, they were expected to represent God's holiness, his goodness and his love among the nations. Israel, though unimpressive in itself, was picked by God to transmit his nature and salvation.

Paul writes about the election of Jacob over Esau: "Yet, before the twins were born or had done anything good or bad—in order that God's purpose in election might stand: not by works but by him who calls—she was told, 'The older will serve the younger'" (Rom. 9:11). Jacob was selected as the minister of God's promises, in spite of his personal failures.

Looking ahead, Isaiah wrote, "Here is my servant, whom I uphold, my chosen one in whom I delight; I will put my Spirit on him and he will bring justice to the nations" (Isa. 42:1). This is a reference to God's election of Jesus for the work of salvation. God's selection in this case depended on the perfect holiness of Jesus and his ability to carry out the work chosen for him to do. Even so, God chose him, the perfect image of God, the untainted Servant, before the earth was created, before his incarnation. The election of God occurs as the first action—the initiating movement in the transaction between himself and Man.

How election meshes with free will is a mystery the human mind cannot unravel. What the human mind must come to grips with, however, is that God's call goes forth to all mankind to believe in his Son, Jesus Christ. For those who respond in faith, the issue becomes not "*how* did God elect me?"

but *"why* did God elect me? The "why" question must be answered by discovering God's purpose in his selection.

Paul wrote to the Ephesians, "For he chose us in him before the creation of the world *to be holy and blameless in his sight* . . . in accordance with his pleasure and will—to the praise of his glorious grace" (Eph. 1:4–6, emphasis added). The intention of God has been to create a people who would belong to him, worshiping him freely, loving him intentionally, obeying him joyously. He desires to "purify for himself a people that are his very own, eager to do what is good" (Titus 2:14).

B. The Circumcision Group (v. 10)

In each of Paul's pastoral letters, he warned against false teachers. These were people, often from among church leadership, who promoted heresy in some form. In writing to Titus, he portrayed them as "rebellious people, mere talkers and deceivers." He went on to point out a particularly troublesome faction: "the circumcision group" (v. 10).

The circumcision group consisted of Jewish converts. Although they had accepted the gospel of Jesus Christ, they continued to hold to their Jewish traditions. As a group, they caused continual trouble, especially for Paul in his ministry to the Gentiles.

To the Jew, circumcision was a sign of covenant relationship with God. Instituted by God, it represented an agreement between the divine and man. In this act an individual was marked and identified with the God of Israel; he was set apart for service to Jehovah. As part of the covenant, God conferred upon the individual all the privileges of belonging to his family. Circumcision remained a sign of God's ongoing relationship and promises to the Jewish people.

At the time of the church's birth, Jesus' disciples had not understood that God was bestowing a universal gift. Christianity was viewed as a strictly Jewish concern. Having been raised with a sectarian understanding of God and his activity among mankind, the apostles initially confined Christ's offer of salvation to Jews. Peter was given a vision in which the prohibitions of Jewish law were lifted. Then he participated in the baptizing of Cornelius, a Gentile believer. Finally he understood the greatness of God's gift: "I now realize how true it is that God does not show favoritism but accepts men from every nation who fear him and do what is right" (Acts 10:34–35).

Even so, there were still believers who could not comprehend that God had begun something new. Later, in defending his interaction with Cornelius, Peter came under sharp attack by circumcised believers for associating with non-Jews (Acts 11:2–3). These rancorous people belonged to the circumcision group.

The influence of this group, especially among Jews, was powerful. Paul recounted an incident in which Peter, having acted in solidarity with Gentile believers by eating with them, reversed himself and withdrew from their company. The reason was because Peter "was afraid of those who belonged to the circumcision group" (Gal. 2:12). These Jewish converts exerted a tremendous amount of power and intimidation.

Paul's experience with these Jewish believers had taught him about their damaging effect on other Christians. This is why he warned Titus against their manipulative power that enslaved believers to Jewish legalism and undercut God's grace.

VII. TEACHING OUTLINE

A. INTRODUCTION

1. Lead Story: Good Ol' What's His Name
2. Context: Paul assigned Titus to establish the churches on the island of Crete. Although the believers were new, leadership was essential, so Paul outlined the qualifications necessary for those whom Titus must select to help guide the church. The fledgling congregations were also experiencing infiltration and confusions caused by false teachers who were steeped in Jewish traditions and myths. Paul wanted Titus to oppose and refute these people and their followers in order to safeguard the gospel and the Cretan believers.
3. Transition: Paul's message in this first chapter of Titus targets the qualifications required for church pastors and leaders, but he actually addressed all believers. The criteria for leadership has not changed over the centuries. Neither has the demand for a growing righteousness in all believers. The church must carefully guard the fundamentals of the gospel, oppose all ideas and philosophies which violate the truth, and determine to live in godliness. The Christian life penetrates both the privacy of the heart and the public arena of personal lifestyle.

B. COMMENTARY

1. Greeting (1:1–4)
   a. The apostle's authority and purpose (1:1–3)
   b. The recipient of the letter (1:4)
2. Establishing the Churches (1:5–9)
   a. Titus's job description (1:5)
   b. Qualifications for church leadership (1:6–9)
3. The False Teachers (1:10–16)

C. CONCLUSION: THE VERDICT

VIII. ISSUES FOR DISCUSSION

1. Give examples of ways in which Christian belief is demonstrated in daily living. How is your Christian faith evident?
2. Paul limited the position of elder to those men whose children are believers and who are not wild and disobedient. In Western cultures, however, it is expected that teenagers will go through a period of willfulness and rebellion. Is this inevitable? How can individuals and the Christian community assure social and spiritual stability in our youth?
3. If hospitality is more than "entertainment," what are some ways Christians can demonstrate the sacrificial giving that characterized first-century hospitality?

Titus 2

Establishing Order and Godliness

I. INTRODUCTION
Control Tower

II. COMMENTARY
A verse-by-verse explanation of the chapter.

III. CONCLUSION
The Copernicus Solution

An overview of the principles and applications from the chapter.

IV. LIFE APPLICATION
Methods and Madness

Melding the chapter to life.

V. PRAYER
Tying the chapter to life with God.

VI. DEEPER DISCOVERIES
Historical, geographical, and grammatical enrichment of the commentary.

VII. TEACHING OUTLINE
Suggested step-by-step group study of the chapter.

VIII. ISSUES FOR DISCUSSION
Zeroing the chapter in on daily life.

Titus 2

> ## Quote
>
> "*It* is the great work of nature to transmute sunlight into life. So it is the great end of Christian living to transmute the light of truth into the fruits of holy living."
>
> A d o n i r a m   J .   G o r d o n

IN A NUTSHELL

Paul worked within the existing social structures of his time, addressing common groups such as young and old, men and women, and slaves. The intention of the gospel is not to overthrow particular cultural establishments, but to transform them by a new ethic. Paul was eager that the gospel not be attacked or refused for peripheral reasons, but that the gospel be attractive to those outside the church, drawing them in by the goodness of Christ's people and the grace of God.

Establishing Order and Godliness

I. INTRODUCTION

Control Tower

My wife and I were headed west, flying across the country toward California. I had plugged a set of earphones into the airline's sound system and for some time had been listening to an engaging story told by Bill Cosby. Now we were approaching Los Angeles International Airport.

Cosby's story was building, carefully preparing me, the listener, for the ending. It was what all the descriptions and dialogue had been for—the final few lines. I knew the conclusion would be funny.

Then, someone switched all the stations. No more Beethoven, jazz, country . . . or Cosby. We were now all listening to the conversation between our pilot and the control tower at L.A.'s airport.

I was a bit disappointed. I found myself wishing they would hurry up and get done with all their information on altitude, winds, and runways so I could get back to Cosby's story. Then it occurred to me how grateful I should be that the pilot and air traffic controller were not hurrying and that the pilot was not listening to Cosby. I was thankful our pilot had not dismissed the tower with, "Yah, we have done all this before." He had landed that jet many times, but every landing demanded communication, care, and his undivided attention.

In our own lives, we decide who we will listen to. We select which messages gain our attention, which words influence our thoughts and actions.

Just as the control tower sends out messages about direction, guiding the aircraft through clouds and weather to a safe landing, so Christ sends out the message of truth to pilot and direct our living. His message of godliness and grace determines our journey in life now and our safe conduct into eternity. Still, it is our choice whether we tune him in.

Paul sent out the message of divine guidance in his letter to Titus. In this particular chapter he sounded forth the need for personal godliness, church order and repute, and the basis of all this—Jesus Christ.

II. COMMENTARY

> **MAIN IDEA:** *Paul always maintained a great concern for the reputation of the church within society. In writing to Titus, he outlined an orderly approach for establishing godliness among the members of each congregation, thereby reinforcing the positive character and work of the church. In this way, people progress in righteousness, and the church attracts unbelievers to investigate the message of God.*

A Sound Doctrine (2:1)

> **SUPPORTING IDEA:** *Paul's original letter had no chapter breaks. This first verse follows logically and necessarily upon the denunciation of false teachers in chapter 1. Sound doctrine produces health in the individual, making him fit for service and spiritual development.*

2:1. If Paul had been talking with Titus in person, he would have looked him straight in the eye to emphasize his strong directive: **You must teach what is in accord with sound doctrine.**

Titus, and all believers, must stand in stark contrast to the false teachers. Correct belief produces health and wholeness, while erroneous teachings result in disobedience and worthlessness (Titus 1:16). Paul was not advocating the "health and wealth" doctrine of modern triumphalists but a spiritual health which proceeds from faith in God. Doctrine which remains undistorted, free from the infections of human opinion or philosophies, will bring healing to the soul and stability to life.

The church must be aware of cultural shifts, adjusting to the peculiar needs of society. I enjoy studying new methods for presenting the message of Scripture and developing different strategies for reaching people with the gospel. But we must not tinker with doctrine. Biblical revelation is complete, founded upon the prophets, Christ, and the apostles. It is God's unadulterated Word which carries the power to turn hearts toward him. Scripture remains the inviolate Word of God. Christ remains the incarnate Truth. In him, spiritual wholeness is fleshed out in a person. Through him we can experience the transformation of the whole person, awakening our spirit, mind, and soul to our Creator.

B How Godliness Looks (2:2–10)

SUPPORTING IDEA: *Paul did not rearrange or demolish cultural groupings. He recognized that society needs structures in order to operate coherently. He took the existing groupings of gender, age, and slavery, and addressed each group in order to ensure the process of godliness and the health of the church.*

1. Older men (2:2)

In the Greco-Roman world in which Paul lived, only two age categories were recognized: young and old. This is quite unlike our own culture which has a myriad of generational divisions. The issue here is not to establish some "biblical" age divisions by which we can measure one another. Paul set forth responsibilities and assigned them to groups which were already recognized and in place. In his time, older men were probably those over about forty, while "young" encompassed everything else.

Older men, by virtue of their age, were called on to model certain qualities of godliness. Note that these characteristics were not for them alone, leaving the young free to ignore the instruction. However, the older men were recognized as examples for younger men. These men were to live carefully, manifesting a respectable lifestyle. They were to be:

Temperate. The older men were to exercise sound judgment in every area of life. They were to be known as clearheaded and self-possessed.

Worthy of respect. Their lives were to evoke respect and honor. This deference by others was not to be gained by age alone, but by the grace, goodness, and purity of their lives.

Self-controlled. An older man must be in charge of himself. He will subject his body, mind, and will to the higher order of godliness. This covers a wide range of thoughts, attitudes, and behaviors.

These three qualities were admired by the unbelieving citizens of Paul's day, and they were considered a positive attribute in any man. But Paul moved on to areas outside the realm of pagan society. Even self-control was not wholly within the grasp of the unbeliever. True control is a divine ability, gifted by the Holy Spirit (Gal. 5:22–23). But the older Christian man must excel beyond his contemporaries, and the following characteristics must find their source in God.

Faith. This forms one of the pillars of Christianity, representing an individual's relationship with God. Health, in our interactions with and obedience to our Lord, is foundational to soundness in any other endeavor. Faith encompasses correct doctrine, correct relationship, correct living.

Love. This is the other pillar of Christian faith, without which all else crumbles. It envisions a harmonious relationship with God which issues in self-giving to other people. Love seeks the welfare of others, even at personal loss.

Endurance. A person who models steadfastness in life and godliness commands respect, and it deserves to be heard, to be followed. Those who falter over time, who cave in to apathy or human philosophies, or simply follow their own petty desires, have wandered from the faith. "Sticking with it" remains a requisite of Christian belief. This is the very definition of faith.

2. Older women and younger women (2:3–5)

2:3. Although the goals of respectability and dignity are the same, men and women face differing temptations and attacks upon character. Paul instructed Titus to teach the older women on issues specific to their situation within society.

The umbrella term which Paul used regarding older women is **reverent**. These women were to be suitable for what was sacred. The tenor of their lives was to display a consecrated holiness to God. The Christian is to exceed the ethical and moral standards of surrounding society. The call upon a Christian's life comes not from the neighborhood or nation, the mores of consensus, but from the divine personality and nature of God.

Paul highlighted two vices which older women were prone to follow: malicious talk and alcoholism.

In accordance with holiness, Titus must teach the older Christian women **not to be slanderers**. Christian women were to rise above the status quo. By the Lord's strength, they were to live in love. One of the ways this would be evident would be by their speech. They were not to participate with the over-the-fence crowd who gossiped, judged, or passed on the latest bit of babble. The inference is that older women were to model propriety and respect for others.

In addition, older women were not to be **addicted to much wine**. This is the parallel to self-control about which the men were instructed. Drinking seems to have prevailed among older women within society, but the Christian was to follow a higher standard. She was to be controlled by God's Spirit, not by wine. She was to break ranks with common habits and values and exceed them by living a life of restraint, honor, and usefulness.

Not only were the older women to refrain from certain behaviors; they were to **teach what is good**. This refers not to formal classroom education but to teaching by example. Rather than following the degenerative tendencies within the secular community, these Christian women were to model the redemptive capacities of the community of faith.

2:4. Jesus once remarked to his disciples, "A student is not above his teacher, nor a servant above his master. It is enough for the student to be like his teacher, and the servant like his master" (Matt. 10:24–25). The teacher or master sets the tone, defines the curriculum, and exemplifies what the student aspires toward. This is why the older women must be sound in their inner spirit, their outward lifestyle, because these women were to **train the younger women.** By living in a godly manner, they would be qualified to pass on the life of faith and godliness to younger women.

Paul wanted Titus to be specific. He was to outline the agenda these older women must follow in their lives and teachings. Rather than speaking to the younger women directly, Paul addressed them through the older women. Imbedded in his instructions were Paul's directives for godliness in younger Christian women.

Most young women in the first century were married. Thus, the social sphere of women was typically within the home. Here she exerted her greatest influence. Here her life was most observable. Paul wanted the young Christian women to **love their husbands and children.**

The word *love* in this instance comes from the root word *phileo,* or "brotherly love." It emphasizes the strength of companionship, of pulling together toward a goal, of devotion measured by kindness and mutual friendship. This forms the basis of a secure and solid marriage and home. At times spouses and parents must exhibit *agape,* or "sacrificial love." But the fundamental strength of home life is the intertwining strands of kindness, companionship, and friendship. There exists among the household shared values, shared interests, and, among Christians, a shared Lord and vision of life.

2:5. Women, both young and old, were to be **self-controlled and pure.** In this context these terms probably refer to sexual control and purity.

Paul also wanted the younger women to be **busy at home.** To modern readers this statement may conjure visions of a young woman chained to the kitchen sink with six crying children at her feet. Paul has been accused by some interpreters of male chauvinistic tendencies. The context, however, does not support such notions. In first-century cultures, the home was the domain of the woman. This instruction by Paul would not have sounded foreign or oppressive to anyone in the Greco-Roman culture. He was not defining or limiting a woman's place; he was addressing women where they were. This is not a picture of enslavement but of useful enterprise.

Whether a woman works outside the home or not, she is to bring special graces and beauty to her home. More than any other member of the family, the woman tends to set the tone for the household. Paul is commending women who understand the importance and high priority which God has designed into the roles of mother, wife, and homemaker. Society rests not only on politics and commerce, but more critically upon the home where each member of society learns respect for authority, values, relational skills, and duty to neighbor and nation.

Women, both young and old, are **to be kind.** This provides the balance which busy women need. Not only must they devote themselves to the management of their home; they must not ignore their neighbors or those with whom they do business. Kindness toward others must characterize Christian women. To those within their family they should exhibit a gentle benevolence; to those in the community they must act with grace and patience. To all people she extends goodness.

Finally, the young women must be taught **to be subject to their husbands.** Though Paul omits any corresponding instructions to husbands in this letter to Titus, it is always best to interpret a passage in light of other biblical sections which relate to the same subject. In Ephesians 5:21–33 and Colossians 3:18–19, Paul gave a more expansive teaching on marriage. In these passages mutual submission is emphasized as well as the necessity of binding love. It is unlikely that Paul disregarded these imperatives in writing to Titus.

It should also be noted that Paul's directive for submission was given in the middle voice. This means that the woman was to submit herself. The husband must not take it upon himself to make his wife submissive. This is her responsibility, just as it is the husband's responsiblity to love his wife just as Christ loves the church (Eph. 5:24–25).

Two strong purposes compel the Christian to exhibit self-control, to guard purity in his or her life.

First, a person's claim to the name "Christian" results from an intimate relationship with God. We bear the very name, nature, and Spirit of Christ. Every principle and command which God extends to the believer comes from his character. We do not follow rules; we respond to a compelling reality, the power of truth, and the motion of life from within and without. As God is, so we should be.

Second, the mission of the church is to extend God's rule and grace throughout the earth. This demands a people who live blamelessly. Paul was anxious that Christians live above the finger-pointing crowd. He wanted the church and its people to be respected and admired citizens of the community so God would not be associated with rebellion, questionable behaviors, or civil contempt: **so that no one will malign the word of God.** All the behaviors that Paul commended to both men and women in this chapter would find acceptance in secular society. These are not practices of which others would disapprove. They represent an orderly and dignified lifestyle in anyone's eyes.

3. Younger men (2:6–8)

2:6. Titus was to **encourage the young men to be self-controlled.** Paul still had the evangelistic mission and reputation of the church in view. He wanted the young Christian men to exercise sober judgment in everything. This refers to sexual purity and restraint, to discretion in personal relationships so that anger does not replace grace, to self-mastery regarding alcohol and food. Self-control was a manifestation of God's Spirit which touched many aspects of daily living.

2:7–8. Paul turned directly to Titus and wrote, **In everything set them an example by doing what is good.** Just as Paul's instructions to older and younger women blended together, so his instructions to younger men mingled with this charge to Titus. While Titus must lead the way in his behavior, the clear implication is that all the younger men should be characterized by acts of goodness. Once again Paul had in mind outward, observable actions. Followers of Christ are to demonstrate a changed lifestyle marked by goodness in everything they do. This stands in contrast to the false teachers, who were "disobedient and unfit for doing anything good" (Titus 1:16).

Paul emphasized two fundamental structures of true Christianity—behavior and belief. In contrast to the false teachers, the proclaimer of the gospel must live a life typified by goodness. Such a proclaimer must deliver the message with **integrity, seriousness, and soundness of speech that cannot be condemned.**

Integrity denotes purity of motives as well as content. Corruption of the message or the inner life of the bearer of the message was intolerable. By contrast, Paul declared the false teachers' minds and consciences to be "corrupted" (Titus 1:15).

Seriousness speaks to the manner in which the message is given. Titus, and all pastors, are to teach God's Word with the dignity it deserves. The Christian teacher must deliver God's truth in a way that conveys the importance of the message; he must offer the truth with humility.

Soundness of speech includes the method as well as the effect. The pastor must speak words of "health." His teaching must be doctrinally pure, full of grace, and effective for producing spiritual health in others. Unlike the false teachers whose message led to quarrels, rebellion, greed, and irresponsible living, the true Christian offers a message of health, or "soundness"—unity, obedience, generosity, goodness, and responsible actions.

Paul longed for the church, its pastors, and all followers of Christ to be blameless. He desired that no one find fault in what we say, how we say it, or in the manner of our lives. Though people may hate us, we must conduct ourselves and speak after the manner of our Lord **so that those who oppose [us] may be ashamed because they have nothing bad to say about us.**

Paul wanted nothing to detract from Christ and the salvation he offers to all people. He wanted nothing to stand in the way of the missionary enterprise. The apostle wanted the church united, speaking the unadulterated truth of God's goodness and grace, living an unblemished life as exemplified by Jesus the Christ.

4. The slaves (2:9–10)

2:9. Paul's charge to slaves underscored his intention to work within the social structures and expectations of the day. Slaves were foundational to Roman economic stability. They comprised the lowest rung of the social ladder, but they could be anything from ship oarsmen to craftsmen to teachers. Many slaves served within the Roman households in various duties, some rising to managerial positions over other slaves. It is possible that the false teachings which stirred the women into defiant attitudes may have produced the same effect upon the slaves.

Paul addressed the slaves of Crete with the same instructions he had delivered to slaves everywhere: they were to **be subject to their masters in everything.** Paul's concern was not to address civil arrangements or conventions, with which he may have disagreed, but to assure that the Christian behaved in a decent and orderly manner.

The gospel does not advocate revolt but submission to the sovereignty of God. Outside of insurrection or escape, the slave was rarely in the position to overturn civil injustices (see Philemon for Paul's view on this). As difficult as it is to submit to such a position, the Christian must be convinced of God's lordship in all human affairs.

The slave must not only submit to his masters (even Roman culture would have applauded this), but the slave must also work to **please them.** The Christian ethic always transcends human reason and practice. Christianity penetrates to the inner spirit. The hope may be freedom, but the impetus is pleasing God.

The slave was also **not to talk back to them.** Those who have little freedom of choice often express a measure of independence through verbal strikes. The student in the classroom may mutter sarcastic remarks at the teacher; the secretary may whisper defiance as she carries out a request she dislikes; the wife may degrade her husband while obeying his decision. In each case, rebellion bubbles beneath the surface and leaks out through caustic remarks or challenging words. In contrast, the Christian slave must obey in action as well as in heart.

2:10. The next command may be easy to gloss over. Slaves were **not to steal** from their masters. The slave worked for others, whether as a craftsman or by carrying out duties within a household. Because of this, it was easy for slaves to indulge in petty theft.

Little has changed over the centuries. Although we do not classify ourselves as slaves today, most of us do work for someone else. It becomes easy to see the boss or the corporation as impersonal and wealthy. Taking home extra pens or paper, logging on to the company's Internet account for private use, driving the company car for personal errands—there are a great many ways we can steal. Such abuses are out of bounds for the Christian. In every aspect of our behavior we are to demonstrate that we can be **fully trusted.**

Another person's trust is invaluable. It reflects an investment between two people on the deepest levels of human interaction. Whether between employer and employee, husband and wife, or between friends, trust is earned by honorable behavior performed consistently and dependably. Trust comes not only from actions but from our demeanor, our constancy of soul.

Paul's instructions were not driven by a desire for personal advancement or praise, but by the desire to **make the teaching about God our Savior attractive.** Religious systems hold little appeal if those who follow the teachings live unchanged lives. Spirituality holds little interest if its doctrines are nullified by the lives of its followers.

The Strength for Godliness (2:11–14)

SUPPORTING IDEA: *Instructions are fine, but spiritual mandates often stem beyond our ability. Yet, we are never expected to live righteously in our own strength. The power of the risen Christ enables the believer to obey, living worthy of his high calling.*

2:11. Paul did not leave the Christian with a list of duties to perform. He called us to a noble purpose, a higher life. He showed us that it is God's grace—past, present, future—which strengthens and motivates us to live beyond the call of society, embracing obedience to God.

Paul followed up his instructions by proclaiming that **the grace of God that brings salvation has appeared to all men.** Grace has appeared, "epiphanied." It is the same word used in 2 Timothy 1:10 when Paul wrote of the "appearing of our Savior, Christ Jesus." The word connects us to Christ's incarnation, his unveiling. The grace of God did not evolve in history; it came forth from concealment, became visible, made its appearance.

Grace breaks upon our moral darkness like the rising sun. This is the incarnation and atonement, the birth, death, and resurrection of Jesus Christ our Lord, "full of grace and truth" (John 1:14). This grace brings salvation that God offers to everyone, though not every person responds to his goodness.

Salvation refers to deliverance or preservation. Salvation brings deliverance from our enslavement to our natural, selfish desires. It frees us from the process of degeneration which leads to the death of the body and soul. In salvation we enter into the redemption of God. The process begins immediately and finds fulfillment in eternity when our soul finds completion in Christ's righteousness and our body changes from decay to wholeness. Christ saves us from the destruction that estrangement from God brings. He restores us to our Creator and recreates a new person and existence for those who believe.

2:12. Grace instructs us. Through Christ's appearing and the Holy Spirit's tutoring, graces **teaches us to say "No" to ungodliness and worldly passions.**

God wants us to learn how to live to the full. When we believe in Christ as our salvation, we become enrolled in his school of living. In turning to God, we agree that we must turn away from ungodly living and turn toward godly living. We do not just wish for this change to occur; we do not simply hope it might happen. We must take ourselves in hand and say "no" to all those behaviors, attitudes, and desires that are opposed to God. Then we can learn **to live self-controlled, upright and godly lives.**

We have encountered the word **self-control** before. It designates mastery of the self, personal authority over natural impulses. **Upright** living involves all that is respectable and good. But Paul's inclusion of **godly** takes these qualities beyond the philosopher's jargon and connects behavior with faith in God. A Christian's life should point toward God.

Many are the voices today which argue against such "narrow" terms of right and wrong. Postmodern people claim a liberation from religion's inhibitions. The popular response to life today is not Paul's "no" or "yes" but a faddish "whatever." Most of the people who deny a standard of righteousness leave the philosophical reasoning on the shelf when their own children confront them, reject their ideas, and live rebellious lifestyles. Man's denials and rationalistic fabrications do not survive reality. Only God's truth and revelation do.

Paul focused on now. *This* salvation, *this* godly living, is for today: **this present age.** Christians often speak of salvation as though it applied only to a far-off eternity. But salvation begins in this present life, in this present age. God intended redemption to infiltrate the current state of affairs, to penetrate the human heart in the entanglements of this life.

2:13. While salvation digs deeply into the difficulties of our todays, we recognize that our experience of God's rescue is incomplete. We are not left with the partial successes and recurrent failures which even faith encounters in this world. Instead, **we wait for the blessed hope—the glorious appearing of our great God and Savior, Jesus Christ.**

This "hope" is not a wish. It is the certainty of blessing which will occur when Christ appears again. In this epiphany, the splendor of God's glory will be seen. This is the brilliance of his beauty that was witnessed at the transfiguration and the dazzle of his holiness before the world began. Christ's Second Coming will not be hidden. It will blaze in fulfillment of his authority over all the universe. It is what all creation groans and waits expectantly for (Rom. 8) and what all believers anticipate.

2:14. Paul illustrated the glory of God's grace in Christ Jesus, **who gave himself for us.** Christ was not the victim of Roman authority and Jewish malevolence. He gave himself willingly in obedience to the Father. In addition, he gave himself **for us.** His death was suffered on our behalf. We deserved the punishment of our sins, the wrath of God upon us for our rebellion and evil. But Christ stepped in and suffered and died on our behalf.

The reason he did this was **to redeem us from all wickedness.** To redeem is to release at a price, or to buy back. This was a term used for slaves who were purchased out of slavery. Their freedom was bought at a price. This pictures Christ's purchase of our freedom from slavery to sin. At the cost of his life, we were released from our bondage to evil which resides by nature within all human beings.

But God never quits halfway. He redeems us for a purpose, and this is **to purify for himself a people that are his very own.** Not only were we paid for; we were released into the freedom of belonging to God, of fulfilling our original design and purpose for which he created us.

God's plan can be traced throughout the entire Bible. From the very beginning, God chose particular people to belong to him—people who would bear his image and establish his righteousness on the earth. Whether we speak of Noah, Enoch, Abraham, or his selection of Israel as a special nation, God has always worked to establish a community of faith that honors him and lives in obedience to his laws.

In Christ God flung wide the doors of admission into his family, accepting anyone who would trust in Christ's saving death and resurrection. In the act of faith, we transfer our obedience from wickedness to righteousness, from Satan and self to God. "You are not your own; you were bought at a price. Therefore honor God with your body" (1 Cor. 6:19–20).

Belonging to God carries responsibilities. We should live with the sole objective of pleasing our Lord. Paul told us how we can delight our Savior— by being people who are **eager to do what is good.**

The Book of Ephesians has great theme verses of salvation by grace: "For it is by grace you have been saved, through faith—and this not from yourselves, it is the gift of God—not by works, so that no one can boast" (Eph. 2:8–9). But we should keep reading, for the next verse completes God's purpose for his creation: "For we are God's workmanship, *created in Christ Jesus to do good* works, which God prepared in advance for us to do" (2:10, emphasis added). Christians are the creative work of Christ. We are new creations, formed and shaped by Christ's death and resurrection.

Good works, deeds born from the goodness of God's Spirit, characterize those who belong to God. Christians should never have to be cajoled into service, nor should they follow God's commands as a duty. We should be zealous, eager, passionate to please the Father by extending his goodness to others.

D Instructions to Titus (2:15)

SUPPORTING IDEA: *Paul concluded this section as he began, with a strong reminder to Titus to teach what is right and proper.*

2:15. Having gone through Titus's responsibilities for teaching the various social groups within the church, Paul punctuated his thoughts with another reminder to Titus: **These, then, are the things you should teach.** He did not want Titus's duty to get lost in the details of his instructions.

Titus must not only teach, but **encourage and rebuke with all authority.** Most members of the Cretan churches were young in the faith, untried in the difficulties of obedience and piety. Titus needed to instill courage in these new converts, by words as well as example. But fledgling churches and new believers also need **rebuke** at times. They must be called back from error, corrected in their thinking, and restrained in their actions. This Titus was to do **with all authority.**

Titus, as Paul's representative and as a spokesman of God's truth, exercised the full authority of divine command. He was not to hesitate in using it nor forget to whom he was accountable. These teachings, delivered by Paul, were God's holy words and commands. The believers must understand this solemn trust and authority as well.

Finally, Paul encouraged Titus: **Do not let anyone despise you.** Literally, this means not to allow others to "think around" or "out think" you. He was not to allow others, even those opposed to him, to circumvent his authority. Titus was not to be ignored or dismissed. He was to stand his ground, speak the truth, model the message, and not permit others to "go over his head" in matters pertaining to the church.

MAIN IDEA REVIEW: *Paul always maintained a great concern for the reputation of the church within society. In writing to Titus, he outlined an orderly approach for establishing godliness among the members of each congregation, thereby reinforcing the positive character and work of the church. In this way, people progress in righteousness, and the church attracts unbelievers to investigate the message of God.*

III. CONCLUSION

The Copernicus Solution

Science and theology often reinterpret each other. A discovery in one field of study often elicits from the other a readjustment or denunciation. But typically, once the theories and postulates are set aside and thorough examination is completed, people can come to an enlightened understanding of God, one's self, the world, and the universe.

Since the time of the philosopher-scientists, particularly Aristotle and Ptolemy, Western civilization has held to an anthropocentric view of life. This is a long word which places man at the center of the universe. This outlook interprets all of life in terms of human values, benefits, and experiences. The human race becomes the driving purpose and central force behind the vast universe.

At first glance, this may seem logical, reasonable, even Christian. Man, after all, is the central figure in God's redemptive work. God talked to man, visited him, became like him in Jesus Christ. The Scriptures interpret history from God's perspective as he pursued the human race with his grace. With this understanding, scientists and theologians concluded that man was the center of creation, that the earth was the center of the universe, and that all the planets rotated around them. It was only logical.

Early in the sixteenth century, Nicolaus Copernicus's claim that the earth rotates around the sun rather than vice versa shook the foundations of science and Christianity. Time has proved Copernicus correct in his theory. Science has built upon this discovery, allowing us to explore space and detect new components of our universe. But mankind resists being placed on the periphery. Our history confirms a stubborn refusal to allow anything to displace our self-importance . . . even God. Locating man on the edges of the planetary system made him feel tossed aside, diminished in importance. This caused a growing suspicion of science among theologians.

Just as the earth rotates around the sun, so God is the center of everything he has created. He is the fixed center around which everything revolves. Mankind may be the centerpiece of God's redemptive work, but his purpose is to proclaim his goodness, grace, love, sovereignty, and might. That is why Paul urged Titus to say "No" to the world, its egocentric notions, and its self-indulgent practices. Christians are called to live in the reality of God's truth. This places upon us the responsibility to live in the manner of Jesus Christ—self-controlled, pure, good, diligent, and obedient.

The unchanging God must stand as the immovable center of the Christian life if we are to live in a godly manner. God is our enabling power, the master of our spirit, the light that casts upon us a measure of his glory.

PRINCIPLES

- Church teaching must be in agreement with the revealed Scriptures, the "sound doctrine."
- Self-control and faithfulness should characterize all believers.
- Church leaders and pastors must be exemplary in their conduct, serving as an example of godly living to those whom they lead.

- As God's representatives, Christians make the gospel message of God's salvation and love either attractive or disreputable.
- The grace of God undergirds all his wonderful gifts to us, including the glorious return of Christ for his church.

APPLICATIONS

- Pastors and church leaders should develop a plan for teaching all ages the truths of Scripture. The goal should be to develop whole, healthy Christians whose lives exhibit God's grace, goodness, and holiness.
- Churches should have a system in place whereby older women can teach younger women in daily living of faith, and older men can instruct younger men how to discipline themselves in righteousness.
- Christians who work for others, or volunteer in service, should excel in their work, trustworthiness, courtesy, and dedication.
- Christians should give thanks and set aside times of worship, focusing on God and his grace through Jesus Christ. We should make it a consistent practice to acknowledge God as our Lord and Savior.
- In church and out, we should teach and talk more about Christ's return. By encouraging one another and discussing our future, our anticipation of his appearing will fill our hearts, urging us on to greater service and righteous living.

IV. LIFE APPLICATION

Methods and Madness

The word *relevant* is often thrown about when speaking of biblical teaching or church mission. We want the sermon to be relevant, the programs to be relevant . . . and on and on it goes. But we can only be relevant *to* something. A topic or action must be under discussion. Then we can proceed to see if one thing relates to another, to see if this is relevant to that.

Consequently, the question that comes begging is, What is the church trying to be relevant to? The answer, most likely, is that it is trying to be pertinent to many things at once—to culture, life, people, subgroups, and issues. In short, the church wants to matter to society.

It is a good and worthy ambition. Christians should never isolate themselves through style or behavior. We must know what is going on, identify with the people around us, and participate in the life of society. But since we find ourselves in a culture that is predictable only in its changeableness, let us not be swept along in the breathless pursuit of trying to shape meaning out of all the disparate pieces of the culture around us. Our central concern is God's eternal rule, a dominion that overshadows all cultures and time.

We must persistently ask ourselves, "How am I, and how is the church, relevant to *God's kingdom?*" The truly contemporary issues are eternal. The most fitting concerns for the church are truth, love, sacrifice, purpose, peace, kindness, and dependence on Christ. We must take these eternal matters and, like Paul, apply them to the particulars of our own settings.

In writing to Titus, Paul insisted that the noble principles of godliness, love, and truth should be practiced in the daily living of Cretan Christians. This involved how women should respond to their husbands, work in the home, and live among their neighbors. Similarly, it involved the character of men and how they should respond to the pressures of business and temptations. This was the relevance of God's truth, that it determined daily existence. It was not intended as an aside, a religious nicety reserved for Sundays or particular occasions. In Christ, and through the indwelling Spirit, God's power infiltrates the most mundane corners of living.

The modern church cannot afford to think that by adopting certain cultural habits—by singing, playing, and working like everyone else, with Jesus thrown in—we have become necessary in the public conscience. In fact, we need to remind ourselves that in keeping pace with our culture we run the risk of sanctifying the status quo. The danger is that there will be no prophetic voice sounded, no alternative offered that transcends the cultural milieu.

Does this mean we should abandon Christian videos and drama, contemporary music and sports outreach? Not a bit. But we need to keep our perspective, realizing that society is always trying to catch up with itself. We need to remember that most people's opinions and practices are adopted without forethought, based on false views of what is meaningful and important. Each day another fascination will vie for attention. The church must be more than just another variation on culture's changing themes.

People are in desperate need of seeing a true demonstration of God's nature. This is why Paul advocated an agressive morality. This was not one that simply restrained from certain activities but an ethic that refuted common opinion and practice through changed behavior. The gospel is forever incarnational. This is its attraction and power.

Paul recognized that the greatest methods for evangelizing the unbelieving world were proclamation and life. People long to see those who live according to their creeds, people who rise above common failures and demonstrate that life need not be abandoned to futility and self-gratification. Deep in their souls, the unbelieving world watches Christians, hoping to find someone whose life and message match.

Meanwhile, we diagnose the world and its needs based upon psychology, marketing, statistics, programming, and parking spaces . . . all the while ignoring the real problem of our ineffectiveness—our unbelievable lives.

The answer lies in our being a people unashamed of truth, pure in behavior, and thoroughly consumed with love for others. Society needs to witness a community made up of rich and poor, old and young, minorities and whites, liberals and conservatives—people who form a community as diverse as society, yet who are not threatened by their differences because they are united by something larger than themselves—Jesus Christ.

V. PRAYER

Lord of my heart, it is so easy to become distracted by secondary issues, to fool myself into thinking that my profession of faith is the same as faithful living. But it is not. May your Spirit convict me of my waywardness, of my compromise with society. Stir within me the creativity and courage to live the truth of your love, purity, and integrity with boldness. Amen.

VI. DEEPER DISCOVERIES

A. Making the Gospel Attractive (v. 10)

Paul wrote that slaves should live in a diligent, trustworthy manner so that "they will make the teaching about God our Savior attractive." The word *attractive,* as the NIV translates it, comes from the Greek word *kosmeo,* a verb form of the word *kosmos.*

Kosmos designated a harmonious arrangement of something. It spoke of order. Consequently, it came to refer to the universe, with its pattern and organization. The world and everything in it contains observable unity, purpose, and balance.

The verb form, *kosmeo,* retains the ideal of order, while adding to it ornament and enhancement. In Luke 11:25, Jesus used the word in speaking of the inner state of a person. He stated that when an evil spirit goes out of a person and, finding no place to rest, returns to the individual, he finds that person "swept clean and put in order." Life has become properly arranged. The word is used again in Luke 21:5 as the disciples look around the temple and remark "how the temple was adorned with beautiful stones and with gifts dedicated to God."

In whatever way the word is translated, it speaks of adding to something that already exists for the purpose of beautifying it, or returning it to its proper harmony. In the Book of Titus, Paul used the word in relation to our manner of living and how this can adorn or beautify the gospel, making it more attractive to people outside the faith.

The message of grace retains an inherent beauty of God's goodness, design, and love. But, as in Christ the beauty of God was incarnated, so in Christians the splendor of his salvation must be demonstrated. It seems peculiar, perhaps, that mere mortals can add loveliness to what God has made. But it is true. Righteous living, faithfulness, courtesy, and integrity embellish God's message of love and hope.

Our lives adorn the doctrinal truth with the jewels of holy conduct. We enhance its appeal, its inherent beauty.

B. Grace Teaches Us (vv. 11–12)

Paul awarded grace a teacher's certificate, stating that "it teaches us to say "No" to ungodliness and worldly passions, and to live self-controlled, upright and godly lives in this present age." Grace has a specific curriculum—to restrain certain behaviors and to promote others.

Grace. Divine grace is the favor, kindness, and goodwill of God directed toward his creation. It is free and spontaneous, totally unmerited. It cannot be coerced, though it can be sought. God's grace is exercised universally, but not everyone experiences it. God's grace is exemplified by salvation, where his goodness and kindness meet in Christ Jesus, allowing people to know the greater depths of grace as they experience his joy, love, goodness, and mercy. All these are extended to the believer in Jesus—the bounty of the heavens.

God's goodwill and kindness "teach" us. Earlier in the chapter, Paul told Titus to **teach what is in accord with sound doctrine** (Titus 2:1). The word *didasko* is used in this passage. It carries the common meaning of "instruction" and parallels our Western understanding of the teacher in the classroom. But when Paul wrote of God's grace teaching us (2:12), he used the word *paideuo*, a term employed in the training of children. It suggests education in a broad sense, not restricted to formal teaching, classrooms, or books.

Grace teaches us throughout the practicalities of our days as God uses whatever means necessary to lead us to maturity. Paul clearly understood this teaching of God to be gracious and kind, but he also recognized that at times God uses difficulties and calamities to affect our training in righteousness. Kindness is not saccharine passivity. Kindness seeks the best for someone else, seeing beyond the moment to the ultimate welfare of the person. This is the approach of parents as they train their children to be competent, skillful adults.

In fact, *paideuo* carried the overtones of chastisement. It is the word used in 1 Corinthians 11:32: "When we are judged by the Lord, we are being *disciplined* so that we will not be condemned with the world" (emphasis added). It is used again in Hebrews 12:7: "Endure hardship as *discipline*; God is treating you as sons. for what son is not *disciplined* by his father?" (emphasis added). It is also used in Hebrews 12:11: "No *discipline* seems pleasant at the time, but painful. Later on, however, it produces a harvest of righteousness and peace for those who have have been trained by it" (emphasis added).

This passage from Hebrews agrees with the intent of Titus 2:11–12. The favor of God may discipline us through the reprimand of a friend, injustice, gossip, death of loved ones, sickness, or inner anguish. Whatever the particulars, God uses difficulties, rebukes, and hardships to exercise our spiritual dependence on him and to strengthen us in righteousness. The intention is to create holy, godly people who live on the basis of God's grace and nature in the midst of a world opposed to him.

VII. TEACHING OUTLINE

A. INTRODUCTION

1. Lead Story: Control Tower
2. Context: This is a chapter about teaching. Paul told Titus what he must teach to those in his congregation—sound doctrine. He then outlined a teaching curriculum for church members, instructing older men to teach young men and older women to teach younger women. Each group was to pass on an example of godly living so the gospel would be blameless in the community and believers would mature in the practical outworking of their faith. He concluded by pointing to God, who instructs and disciplines us so we can experience the depths of his kindness and grace.
3. Transition: The gospel of Christ is enhanced, and its message is preserved when each generation trains those who will follow in the moral expectations that God has of his people. The principles of love, mercy, purity, and trustworthiness must be translated into the specifics that each age group confronts. In this way, God's people will develop and strengthen spiritually and demonstrate the power and relevance of God's truth.

B. COMMENTARY

1. Sound Doctrine (2:1)
2. How Godliness Looks (2:2–10)
   a. Older men (2:2)
   b. Older women and younger women (2:3–5)
   c. Younger men (2:6–8)
   d. The slaves (2:9–10)
3. The Strength for Godliness (2:11–14)
4. Instructions to Titus (2:15)

C. CONCLUSION: METHODS AND MADNESS

VIII. ISSUES FOR DISCUSSION

1. Are you involved in mentoring people younger than you, helping them learn how to form Christian relationships, how to develop a Christian witness in the community, and how to mature in their spiritual walk?
2. What do you think is the role of women in today's society? Does it parallel Paul's description in Titus 2? If not, what should be changed?
3. How does grace teach you to say "no"? Give some practical examples.
4. Discuss the "blessed hope" and what it means to you. What can we do to develop a sense of expectancy about Christ's return?

Titus 3

The Church and the World

"The true Christian is the true citizen, lofty of purpose, resolute in endeavor, ready for a hero's deeds, but never looking down on his task because it is cast in the day of small things; scornful of baseness, awake to his own duties as well as to his rights, following the higher law with reverence, and in this world doing all that in his power lies, so that when death comes he may feel that mankind is in some degree better because he lived."

Theodore Roosevelt

Titus 3

IN A NUTSHELL

Though distinctly different from unbelievers, Christians are not to create enclaves from which they emerge only to buy groceries or take piano lessons. Christians are to interact with neighbors, society, the world at large. This creates a tension, so Paul outlined the behaviors and attitudes which believers should maintain. He then formed a theological basis for his instructions, closing with personal greetings and remarks.

The Church and the World

I. INTRODUCTION

The Way We Were

*T*hroughout his writings, Paul demonstrated an aversion to legalism and a distaste for those who promoted it. He viewed laws and regulations as antithetical to the grace and freedom that God bestowed through Christ. Yet, Paul constantly handed us behavioral to-do lists. He did it in chapter 2 of Titus, and he continued in the same manner in chapter 3. What is the difference between Paul and the legalist?

Their differences are most striking in three areas: the reason for one's conduct, the depth of one's behavior, and the results of personal actions.

A simple example might be the interaction between a father and his daughter. Speaking of her mother, she yells, "I hate her!"

The father returns, "Don't ever say that again!" He should not shrug his shoulders and say, "Well, if that is how you feel." But his censure has created damage on three fronts—he has not penetrated to the source of the daughter's hatred, he has advocated a dishonest and masked response, and he has taught her that image and rules matter most.

This, in essence, is the approach of the legalist.

It is easy to approach life this way, to pretend in our actions while neglecting the true state of affairs within our hearts. It is easy to believe that if everything appears all right on the outside, then there is nothing to be concerned about. From there we are one step away from self-deception, arrogance, and unproductive living.

In this chapter of Titus, Paul began by commending particular behaviors which reflect the goodness and nature of God. But rather than suppose that these actions gain God's favor, they reflect instead a recognition of his goodness toward us in granting mercy and salvation. Good actions never achieve relationship with God; they express a kinship that already exists.

Paul also draws our attention to our life before Christ, our depravity and rebellion, our wayward lifestyle. The legalist cannot tolerate such memories. But for Paul, this remembrance is necessary. It opens up the heart of thanksgiving, humility, and understanding. As we remember how we were, we easily see that what we have become results not from our goodness but from Christ's. This prepares the way for gratitude and loving service to others.

Christians cannot ignore their nation, their community, or their neighbors. This chapter leads us through our responsibilities to each, illuminating the basis for our engagement in society, our service to others, and our love for all people—the grace of God in Christ.

II. COMMENTARY

> **MAIN IDEA:** *Paul wanted Titus to remind the Cretan Christians to behave with propriety and to be gracious, kind citizens. Followers of Christ are to remember their associations and sinful past in order to live humbly among their neighbors and to exhibit gratitude to God for his mercy. Paul warned against becoming enmeshed in legalistic controversies and esoteric speculations. Christianity is meant to influence others for Christ and his kingdom, resulting in goodness to all people.*

A Proper Conduct (3:1–2)

> **SUPPORTING IDEA:** *We need to be reminded over and over again about what constitutes proper conduct and thinking. It is not only the outer behaviors which require training but our inner attitudes as well. Without encouragement, we fall into old and damaging habits that do not serve the purposes of God.*

3:1. Over time, certain "household tables" or "household codes" were circulated among Christians. These codes delineated Christian response and relationship, especially to authority—the individual to government, one believer to another, the wife to the husband, child to parent, slave to master. These codes were treated most extensively in the books of Colossians and Ephesians, but Paul touched on them in his letter to Titus. His remarks on the behavior of women, men, and slaves in chapter 2 reflect these codes of submission and personal integrity. These codes were in mind as Paul wrote, **Remind the people.**

The first reminder calls for the Christian **to be subject to rulers and authorities.** Christian submission is always voluntary. Recognizing God's sovereign rule, the individual is to submit willingly to those recognized leaders of the social order. The phrase "rulers and authorities" refers to government officials and law.

The Christian teaching of God's coming judgment of the nations, coupled with the doctrine of freedom, may have led many believers to disregard civil authority. Besides, Roman rule was not always appreciated, especially by conquered groups and tribes. Polybius and Plutarch wrote that the Cretans fumed under Roman rule. So it is possible that Titus had to deal with antigovernment sentiment even in the churches.

Paul's directives to Titus are consistent with his writings elsewhere as well as other biblical texts. Submission to government involves being obedient, as long as civil law does not conflict with divine command (Acts 5:29). In the Book of Romans, Paul gave not only the command but the rationale and theological basis for obedience (Rom. 13:1–7). But, as usual, Christian ethics goes beyond the obvious.

Not only must the Christian willingly obey those in authority; he must also be ready to do whatever is good. The Christian should comply with the rules and obligations of government, and then work for the benefit of the community and his fellow citizens. Doing good encompasses anything that benefits others, including praying for those in leadership (1 Tim. 2:1–2) while seeking the nation's welfare and peace.

3:2. The sphere of Christian behavior expands beyond one's formal relationship to the government. Paul wrote, slander no one. Any speech that harms another qualifies as slander—insults, abusive speech, defamatory remarks, rumors. Slander desires to elevate self at another person's expense.

As usual, Paul created a contrast. It is never enough to refrain from a behavior; Christians must engage life properly. So Paul instructed believers to be peaceable and considerate, and to show true humility toward all men. The opposite of slander, these qualities seek to elevate others, even at one's own expense.

A peaceable person maintains a congenial attitude, ready to defer to someone else. Such a person rejects aggressive or violent methods of attaining personal advantage. Regarding unbelievers, a Christian is to remain focused on the individual, guarding the relationship. Believers sometimes get mixed up in the war with sin, regarding others as enemies rather than people in need. Our fight is not against flesh and blood, Paul wrote (Eph. 6:10–18), but against authorities and powers.

A peaceable person is considerate, setting aside personal concerns for the welfare of others. This person is careful in thought, speech, and action, weighing the ramifications of each.

In summary, we are to show true humility. Once again, the scope of Paul's instructions is wide—including all people. True humility retains a proper understanding of one's self. A person need not debase and malign himself in order to be humble; this is self-absorption of another sort. True humility thinks sensibly, refusing the lure of competition and comparison.

Ⓑ The Basis for Right Living (3:3–7)

SUPPORTING IDEA: *Having described the proper conduct expected of Christians toward government and all people, Paul formed the basis for our behavior. He urged us to recall our past alienation from God and our disobedience and then to remember that our righteousness comes from God's mercy and grace. Our goodness is not self-generated. Purchased by Christ, it is empowered by the Holy Spirit.*

1. Natural man (3:3)

3:3. At one time we were not anything like the person described in verses 1 and 2. Paul made two points in remembering our past: it forms a basis for humility and compassion in the present, and it emphasizes the change that Christ has brought.

In the past **we too were foolish, disobedient, deceived.** Paul included himself in this description. Without Christ all people follow this type of lifestyle and thinking. Like all people everywhere, we belonged to the fallen system and lived according to our fallen nature. Being **foolish** is obstinacy, a dig-in-your-heels refusal to admit the truth. The fool willfully goes his own, headstrong way. Being **disobedient** involves choice. It refers to a decision to reject God's ways. As a person becomes seduced either by twisted Christian doctrines or man-made philosophies, he becomes **deceived** regarding the truth. This fuels both foolishness and disobedience, resulting in a life marked by sin: **enslaved by all kinds of passions and pleasures.**

Paul painted a picture of bondage. Having succumbed to the illusions of this world, unbelievers participate in unrestrained passions and pleasures. This leads to a loss of will. People eventually become prisoner to their urges and cannot break away. These may even be socially acceptable pursuits, like materialism, or they may involve the lowest sorts of degradation. Either way, the heart is captivated and cannot free itself.

Our relationships with others proved no better in the past as **we lived in malice and envy, being hated and hating one another.** It is common practice to destroy others in order to preserve one's self. Without Christ we cannot understand ourselves, nor can we comprehend our place in the world. In an effort to make sense in a violent, threatening environment, people often protect themselves by striking out at others. **Malice** seeks to harm others; **envy** betrays our discontent and restlessness. Our self-protection results in **hatred** toward others, and they return the favor. It is a vicious cycle from which we need to be freed, but we remain enslaved, unable to cast off the shackles.

2. The work of salvation (3:4–6)

3:4. "At one time" we were enslaved to depravity (v. 3). Then Paul wrote **But when** and introduced a seismic shift. Something crucial happened through a dramatic, historical event that challenges our imprisonment to sin: **the kindness and love of God our Savior appeared.** This is the incarnation, the appearance (epiphany) of Christ among men. God's kindness and love compelled Christ's appearance at Bethlehem, his exemplary life, and his substitutionary death and resurrection.

3:5–6. Jesus, in these actual events, gained salvation for all people who believe. Rescuing us from the grip of corruption, **he saved us.**

The work of salvation comes solely from God's mercy, **not because of righteous things we had done.** As Isaiah 64:6 states, "All our righteous acts are like filthy rags." We can contrive no goodness by which to attain the favor or forgiveness of God. Salvation comes independent of human effort or desire. God initiates, acts, and pursues **because of his mercy.**

Salvation comes **through the washing of rebirth and renewal by the Holy Spirit.** These terms explain, in part, the complex activities which faith in Christ generates. The **washing of rebirth** refers to the cleansing from sin which results from trust in Jesus Christ. This purification of the soul and spirit brings life. No longer living on a purely natural or physical level, believers are transformed from spirit-death to spirit-life. They count themselves "dead to sin but alive to God in Christ Jesus" (Rom. 6:11). **Renewal** carries the same idea, that a person has come into a new existence, both in this life and for eternity. The Holy Spirit participates in salvation, establishing his presence in the soul and enabling each person to act in true righteousness.

God has **poured out** this Holy Spirit **on us generously.** God always acts in extravagance, and his gift of the Spirit to those who believe demonstrates his greatest liberality. Not only has he rescued us from the frustrations and enslavements of sin; he has assured a spiritual power and development that would lie beyond us without his personal interaction. The Spirit enables us to follow in the ways of Christ.

3. Salvation's result (3:7–8)

3:7. Paul told us God's purpose in providing salvation: **so that, having been justified by his grace, we might become heirs.** Some people claim that *justification* means "just as if I'd never sinned." That may be cute, or clever, but it does not do salvation justice. Actually, "salvation" is a legal term describing a guilty person before the bar who is then pronounced blameless by the judge. This does not mean the individual has been found guiltless. Instead, it means that the person has been released from guilt, his offense paid for. All of this is by God's grace, apart from human merit.

Christ purchased our soul's freedom through his death and resurrection. In this way, God pardons those who trust in Jesus, bestowing upon them Christ's righteousness. Romans 3:22–26 states, "This righteousness from God comes through faith in Jesus Christ to all who believe . . . God presented him as a sacrifice of atonement, through faith in his blood . . . he did it to demonstrate his justice at the present time, so as to be just and the one who justifies those who have faith in Jesus."

God cannot tolerate or excuse sin, but he can give his own Son as the substitute payment that justice must extract. Personal trust identifies us with the life, death, and resurrection of Jesus. In the same way that we share in his death, we share in his victory *over* death. He grants us his righteousness through faith.

Having received pardon and been given his righteousness, we share in his glory. We become **heirs having the hope of eternal life.** Those who rely upon the salvation work of Jesus are adopted by God into his family. He extends to us an inheritance. Each family member receives equally from the goodness of the Father. There is no favoritism with God. The riches of God become our inheritance—eternal life, full righteousness and holiness, uninterrupted fellowship, and unhindered fulfillment of our creative intent. "Now if we are children, then we are heirs—heirs of God and co-heirs with Christ, if indeed we share in his sufferings in order that we may also share in his glory" (Rom. 8:17).

The historical appearance, life, death, and resurrection of Christ and the gift of his Holy Spirit are guarantees of our future inheritance. God has acted, and his promises stand.

3:8. All that Paul has written is **trustworthy**; it is unfailing because it was given by God. Salvation, righteousness, faith, and hope are indisputable facts of Christian belief. Paul wanted Titus to teach these truths to the Cretan believers.

If we can agree that Paul's statements are true, we conclude that:

- Christians are called to a high standard of thinking, attitudes, and conduct.
- Every believer comes with a background of disobedience toward God and with selfish drives which alienate him from God and others.
- God has provided a way for people to reestablish a pure and honest relationship with him through Jesus Christ.
- Faith in Christ's death and resurrection results in God's pardoning our corrupted lives and spirits.
- Our future holds a glorious existence with God in eternity.

If we can hold to these conclusions, then we must also reason that the life which Paul commended to Titus is an attainable and worthy pursuit. But Christian growth does not occur automatically: we must **be careful to devote [ourselves] to doing what is good.**

New life in Christ comes to those who determine to act upon their professions of belief. They do not "give it a shot" now and again; they resolve to obey constantly and continuously.

In *Systematic Theology,* Louis Berkhof wrote, "Sanctification is that gracious and continuous operation of the Holy Spirit, by which he delivers the justified sinner from the foolishness of sin, renews his whole nature in the image of God, and enables him to perform good works." God does enable us. But we must partner with his Spirit to produce the goodness he intends, putting faith into practice through the commitment of our wills.

Committing to God's truth and to righteous behavior through God's enablement proves **excellent and profitable for everyone**. Good deeds always bring good results. Paul's reference to "everyone" probably referred primarily to unbelievers (as "all men" of Titus 3:2). Good actions by Christians spread positive benefits to those outside the faith by drawing them toward the truth of God in Christ. Certainly this is profitable. More people will enter into a trusting relationship with the Lord.

C Detriments to the Church (3:9–11)

SUPPORTING IDEA: *Even with orthodox teaching, reminders of God's goodness, and the spiritual development and good works of people committed to Jesus Christ, the church remains a "mixed bag" of genuine and false Christians. Paul warned that theological abstractions and arguing cause great harm to the church and must be avoided.*

3:9. Paul wrote to Titus with the same energy and purpose with which he wrote Timothy (1 Tim. 1:4–7) about false teachers and their message. He warned Titus and the church to **avoid foolish controversies and genealogies and arguments and quarrels about the law**. The false teachers appear to have had a standard operating procedure with standard results. They created intricate systems of interpretation based upon Old Testament Jewish law. These systems involved genealogies, legends, and fables of Hebrew tradition and invention which pulled the new convert and others into a tangle of speculation. The genealogy fascination probably stemmed from a desire to establish Hebrew tribal identity. These obsessions probably came from the circumcision group that held tightly to Jewish privilege and tradition. Claims of tribal legitimacy or accusations of illegitimacy, debates about ancestral purity, Jewish blessing, and positions of authority must have pulled the church into a storm of controversy.

People wasted their time running down theological "rabbit trails," becoming lost in futile discussions and ideas, contending with one another and destroying the community of believers. Paul pronounced such activity as **unprofitable and useless**—the opposite of the true gospel of grace that is "excellent and profitable for everyone" (Titus 3:8). As they argued and quarreled with one another, a climate of anger and bitterness developed, and the church was derailed from its mission.

The modern church falls prey to the same mentality, arguing and dividing itself over opinions, political views, parenting styles, worship styles, secondary theological issues, and a vast assortment of opinions and personal preferences that we elevate to spiritual law. Where this occurs, the result is the same today as in the first century. The church is distracted from its mission to bring salvation, love, and hope to a dying world. Rather than attracting the unbeliever to something new and good—a community of faith and the grace of God—the church repels the outside world because of its judgmental attitude and political bickering.

3:10. Paul was gentle with unbelievers because they lived in ignorance of God's goodness and power. With Christians, however, he was often forceful. Christians have little excuse for unloving, selfish behavior. They know God's goodness, have experienced his grace and love, and are indwelt by his Holy Spirit. Paul recognized that arguing with false teachers pulled a person into their convoluted dialogues, accomplishing nothing. Therefore, he told Titus: **Warn a divisive person once, and then warn him a second time.**

Even the divisive person is offered hope. The purpose of warning people who disrupt the church or mislead others is to bring about repentance in the erring believer. A warning must be clear, not couched in vague references or surrounded by excuses. Rebuke must be loving but not timid. The goal is to bring the disobedient back into the fellowship of obedience. Warning or rebuking seeks this with humility.

But if these warnings fail after a second attempt, then **have nothing to do with him.** This procedure complements the instructions given by Jesus in Matthew 18:15–17, where the Christian who sins against another believer is to be confronted. If he refuses to acknowledge his sin and repent, a second rebuke in front of witnesses is called for. If he persists in his stubbornness, he is taken before the church. With continued willfulness, he is to be treated "as you would a pagan or a tax collector" (Matt. 18:17)—he is cut off from Christian fellowship, benefit, service, and worship.

Church discipline is still necessary. Unfortunately, few churches take it seriously enough to act with courage and boldness when necessary. The pervasive philosophy of tolerance, along with the desire to be inoffensive, drives the church to compromise. To ignore the harm of false teaching or to overlook continued sin is to render a disservice to the church and the offending believer. Allowing sin to continue will never rescue a person from disobedience.

3:11. Cutting such a person off from Christian association has the individual's repentance at heart. Once the person feels the isolation, perhaps he will consider his error and change. But a person who refuses the terms of grace and continues in error is **warped and sinful.** His thinking, perspective, and conscience are twisted. His hardness of heart makes his judgment unreliable so that he cannot recognize the truth. In such a condition, he continues to sin.

Here is a warning for everyone. Those who dabble in false ideas and theological oddities or those who sin and refuse to come to terms with their disobedience follow a dangerous path that leads to self-deception. It happens slowly as a person permits himself self-apportioned leniency, ignoring the warning signs, the rebukes, the sinful habits that engulf him. Through negligence and unbelief, these Christians become **self-condemned**. By willfully rejecting the truth, they pronounce judgment on themselves.

DFinal Remarks (3:12–15)

> **SUPPORTING IDEA:** *As he did in other letters, Paul ended with very personal remarks. Some of these remarks were about the missionary enterprise, some were directed toward individuals, and some were related to his own plans and desires.*

3:12. Paul conveyed to Titus his plans regarding the future ministry on Crete. He planned to send either **Artemas or Tychicus** to the island to assume Titus's responsibilities. At the time of writing, Paul had yet to determine which of these men would assume leadership from Titus. Nothing else is known of Artemas. Tychicus, however, had worked with Paul before, traveling with him through Macedonia and Greece (Acts 20:4). Although it cannot be proved, it is likely that Artemas sailed for Crete to relieve Titus of his duties. In his letter to Timothy, Paul mentioned sending Tychicus to Ephesus (2 Tim. 4:12).

Titus carried on with Paul's instructions and the development of the Cretan church until his replacement arrived. Then Titus left Crete and went to **Nicopolis**, a seaport in western Greece where Paul had **decided to winter**. Why Paul decided to spend the winter in this particular city remains unknown, for Nicopolis was known for its harsh winters. Paul probably had in mind the advancement of the church, not a winter holiday, when he developed his itinerary.

3:13–14. Paul then asked Titus to **do everything you can to help Zenas the lawyer and Apollos on their way**. These two men were probably Paul's messengers in delivering his letter. Titus was to extend hospitality to them. He was to **see that they have everything they need**. Titus was to be exemplary in demonstrating Christian hospitality, generosity, and good works—the things Paul had instructed the church to practice as evidence of their faith in Christ.

Paul clearly had the entire church in view as he asked Titus to show kindness to Zenas and Apollos. He followed the request by stating, **Our people must learn to devote themselves to doing what is good**. This was the same phrase Paul used in Titus 3:8.

By taking care of Zenas and Apollos, Titus would show the congregation in practical terms what "doing good" meant. They would see that goodness was not something lofty but pragmatic, not a contemplative exercise but an activity. As they provided **for daily necessities**, they would **not live unproductive lives**. Good deeds, as Paul noted in Titus 3:8, "were profitable for everyone." Now here is an example of this very thought. By extending goodness to these traveling missionaries, doing what was to their benefit, the Cretans would participate in something profitable or useful for all concerned.

3:15. Paul closed with greetings from himself and all those with him: **Everyone with me sends you greetings.** Titus must have found encouragement in these words, knowing that others were praying for him and the Cretan Christians and that the fellowship of Christ bound them all together despite the miles between them. In turn, Paul wanted Titus to pass along his greeting and affection to those in Crete who genuinely loved Christ and his people: **Greet those who love us in the faith.**

Paul ended his letter with **Grace be with you all.** As always, Paul longed that all people would experience the grace of God not only in salvation but in continued blessing. As they came to know him better, they would serve him from a deeper devotion.

> **MAIN IDEA REVIEW:** *Paul wanted Titus to remind the Cretan Christians to behave with propriety and to be gracious, kind citizens. Followers of Christ are to remember their associations and sinful past in order to live humbly among their neighbors and to exhibit gratitude to God for his mercy. Paul warned against becoming enmeshed in legalistic controversies and esoteric speculations. Christianity is meant to influence others for Christ and his kingdom, resulting in goodness to all people.*

III. CONCLUSION

Engine Repair Made Simple

On a scale from one to ten, my mechanical skills hover around the zero mark.

Back when gas stations offered repair services, there were occasions when I had to have my car repaired. I would pull in the garage and be greeted by the auto mechanic. He would listen as I tried to describe the buzz, whistle, or rattle (this was in the days before computer diagnostics). Then the mechanic would stick his head under the hood, or, rolling away beneath the car's bumper, disappear entirely.

Eventually he would emerge, the automotive disease diagnosed. Smiling, he would wipe his hands on one of those purple rags that smelled of motor oil and begin to explain what he had found. Sometimes he would have me lean over the engine with him while he pointed at hoses and wires. Or he would put the car on a lift and wave his finger at one thing or another, always emphasizing the importance of oil, water, and gasoline in maintaining a well-running engine.

Misreading my boredom as confusion, he would sigh, then try again. He spoke to me in the same way many Americans speak to non-English visitors—loudly, with painful slowness, exaggerated enunciation, and contemplative silence punctuating each sentence. He would do all this as if looking me in the eye and distorting his mouth would bring instant comprehension or interest on my part. But it never did.

The truth is, I never wanted to understand. It simply did not matter to me. Either the engine worked or it did not. I was not going to tinker with it. He could take care of the details.

In the same way, some people simply do not care about their final destiny, their purpose, the true issues of life. They may look around and agree that life can become a mess, that emptiness tugs at them on occasion, and that deep within something seems amiss. But when you point out God's mercy and grace or ask them to lean over and inspect the Bible with you, they stare, yawn, or smile politely. Even people in the church react this way at times.

God generously pours out his grace, goodness, and kindness on those who want it. He responds to those who seek him, to those who want to know him.

While we do not deserve God's salvation and blessing, nor can we earn it, we must respond to his Spirit's enlightenment. God pursues us, demonstrates his love toward us, opens our understanding—but it still remains for us to listen and respond. If we are to know God and participate in the life of faith, we must heed what he says, follow through on what he commands.

As Paul wrote to Titus, he diagnosed some serious problems in the Cretan church. He instructed Titus and the congregation on the steps they needed to take to ensure that the church would function properly, fulfilling its mission and purpose. The apostle pointed to the salvation that God had brought to them through Jesus Christ. He explained the transformation that had occurred when the Holy Spirit was given to these believers, enabling them to live after the righteousness of Christ. But the Christians still needed to listen, to pay attention and comprehend the truth if they were to live godly lives that produced goodness for God's kingdom.

PRINCIPLES

- Christians are to be good citizens of their country, being obedient to government leaders, as conscience allows, and doing good in the community.
- All people have a common heritage and background of selfishness, disobedience, and enslavement to sin.

- Salvation comes from the goodness, kindness, and grace of God.
- We cannot merit God's favor or salvation.
- A changed life and the indwelling Holy Spirit are validation of God's saving goodness as well as evidences of our future bliss.
- Christians should eagerly do good.
- Believers and churches must avoid wrangling over opinions or theological positions that undermine the goodness and grace of God and divide the church.
- In cases of false teaching or unrepentant sin, church discipline should be exercised carefully but courageously.

APPLICATIONS

- Christians must obey their government's laws and leaders, paying taxes, working for the good of the community, and praying for leaders.
- We should examine our lives so that we do not drift into false beliefs or laziness regarding our mission to extend God's kingdom and to live at peace with all people.
- Christians should be characterized by gratitude and thanksgiving as they live with the daily blessings of God's salvation, grace, and mercy.
- Christians should search for ways to use their abilities for the welfare of others.
- Each church should have a procedure in place for dealing with false teachers, unrepentant members, and church discipline problems.
- Through loving and humble correction, believers can help those who err, restoring them to fellowship and righteousness.

IV. LIFE APPLICATION

The Prince and the Pauper, Revisited

Diminutive and frugal, Anne Scheiber lived in a tiny Manhattan apartment with peeling paint and thick dust. She reportedly "never bought a stick of furniture" and "rarely bought a newspaper." Though in her younger years she graduated from law school and passed the bar exam, she spent her working days as an auditor for the IRS. When she retired at age fifty, she invested five thousand dollars in various stocks and bonds. Over the years she devoted her life to increasing her profits. By the time she died at age 101, her moderate investment had grown to a net worth of twenty-two million dollars.

Although she bequeathed most of her money to Yeshiva University, one must wonder at what personal cost she purchased this gift.

She lived most of her life unhappy and friendless. During her last five years, she never received one phone call, not even from relatives. Wearing an old black coat and hat, she attended shareholder meetings religiously. If food was served at these meetings, she would fill a bag and take it home to live on for days. She spent her days reading the *Wall Street Journal* or visiting her brokerage firm's vault to gaze at her stock certificates.

While few of us participate in such eccentricities, a person such as Anne Scheiber can provoke us to reassess our own passions and how we invest our lives. Four times in close succession, Paul urged the Christian to do good. He defined the believer as one who was eager, ready, and devoted to goodness.

Goodness is not a complicated concept. We need not dig through our dictionaries to come to terms with the word. If we feel compelled to decipher the word, perhaps we are not seeking clarity but chasing excuses. Goodness encompasses anything morally honorable that results in positive effect, especially for others. Deeds of goodness come from a good heart, and we achieve a good heart by transforming our thinking (Luke 6:45; Rom. 12:2). "Whatever is true, whatever is noble, whatever is right, whatever is pure, whatever is lovely, whatever is admirable—if anything is excellent or praiseworthy—think about such things" (Phil. 4:8). A mind preoccupied with good thinking will result in a life devoted to goodness.

Opportunities for good deeds present themselves every day, but we see them only if we look for them. If our focus is trained elsewhere, we will miss them entirely. We should take inventory of our enjoyments, our objectives, and how we spend our time. Even if our pursuits do not rank as obsessions, forcing out all other interests or obligations, we may belong to that great crowd of "moderate fanatics" who pursue the lesser gods of comfort, material security, or fun.

Some may argue that Anne Scheiber's life was useful. Certainly her endowment will prove beneficial to others. But I imagine few of us would want to be remembered with the words, "No one paid her much mind when she was alive." It is far better to order our thinking, our hearts, and our lives to pursue the good that comes from God. If we do, we will "not live unproductive lives" (Titus 3:14).

V. PRAYER

Lord, I can only repeat what David sang, "You are good, and what you do is good; teach me your decrees." Amen.

VI. DEEPER DISCOVERIES

The Christian's Obligation to Government (v. 1)

From Augustine to Luther to the present day, people have developed various interpretations concerning the Christian's obligation to government. Much of the difficulty lies in our inability to reconcile the command for submission with the truth that many governments throughout history have been cruel, even diabolical. Should a Christian disobey the law by holding secret meetings or smuggling Bibles? Should a Christian participate in the military, endorse national expansionism, support nuclear buildup, protest governmental positions through marches and sit-ins, help illegal aliens? Do we have a responsibility as believers to confront the government or resist its policies?

Paul wrote to Titus, "Remind the people to be subject to rulers and authorities, to be obedient, to be ready to do whatever is good." In isolation, this phrase seems to endorse unquestioning loyalty to government. But we must examine the context, the word meanings, and other Scriptures to come to a more balanced conclusion.

The English phrase "be subject to" (or "submit") is translated from the Greek military word, *hupotasso*. Paul used this term in reference to the believer's relationship to other believers (Eph. 5:21), to government (Rom. 13), to a husband (Col. 3:18), to slave-masters (Titus 2:9), and to rulers (Titus 3:1). If we divide the word into its parts we have *hupo* ("under") and *tasso* ("arrange"). The thrust of the word is that each person must put himself under the existing order or hierarchy in which he finds himself.

Throughout history, governments have sprung up to provide security among people living together. Various means are employed to this end—religion, laws, military, rulers, and police. God permits bureaucratic states to exist in order to restrain evil and promote order. This does not mean that God approves all that government does. In fact, his judgment will eventually fall on every social institution and political system. Nevertheless, God has permitted the human agency of government to continue for his purposes.

Typically, Christian duty acts in a fluid rather than rigid manner, working within a framework of principles which are nonspecific and timeless. Certain acts and attitudes are categorically wrong, but there are far more activities and dispositions which require our thought, analysis, and choice. Once we discover the standards of God, the next crucial element in our moral responsibility is our conscience.

The word Paul used for "obedient" in Titus comes from the Greek word, *peitho*. Literally, it means "to listen, pay attention, or be persuaded." Children are to obey (listen to) their parents (Eph. 6:1). More generally, Paul reminded us that we are a slave to whatever persuades us or what we obey (Rom. 6:16).

In reference to government, the type of Christian obedience which Paul desired grows out of our persuasion that this is proper: "because of conscience" (Rom. 13:5). Submission and obedience are not an endorsement of thoughtless compliance. We are never to suppose we have no alternatives, no options, no choices. Obedience must issue from a conviction that we act under God's sovereign purposes and that we remain morally innocent before our Lord. In every relationship the Christian retains his moral obligation and responsibility before God.

Paul sandwiched his command for Christian submission between two distinct calls to practice acts of goodness (Titus 2:14; 3:1). The same construction is found in Romans 13 where Paul treated our relationship to governmental powers more extensively. The command to submit to governing authorities in Romans is preceded by the injunction, "Do not be overcome by evil, but overcome evil with good" (Rom. 12:21). This injunction is followed by the precept, "Let no debt remain outstanding, except the continuing debt to love one another. . . . Love does no harm to its neighbor" (Rom. 13:8,10). In both passages, these appeals to charity define the central theme and principle for Christian behavior, even in reference to government. Love and deeds of goodness stand as the Christian's fundamental purpose in society.

In essence, the Christian must follow the existing social and political order under which he lives, rejecting rebellion or disorder. He must obey his government while retaining the responsibility to act according to conscience. With Christ as his guide, the Christian must carefully weigh the choices, acting in love and goodness for the benefit of society. But our ultimate submission and obedience is to God and his laws.

VII. TEACHING OUTLINE

A. INTRODUCTION

1. Lead Story: The Way We Were
2. Context: After telling Titus to teach with authority, not allowing church members to disregard what he said (Titus 2:15), Paul expanded this thought to include respect for all authority, including government. He listed several characteristic behaviors that Christians should model. Then, he reminded the church of God's unmerited goodness as found in salvation through Jesus Christ. This jewel of God's mercy did not come because people deserved it. Quite the contrary! They were rescued while foolish and disobedient. From gratitude for what God has done, Paul wanted the Cretans to devote themselves to doing good. He ended with personal greetings and instructions.

3. Transition: We live in a time of disrespect for authority. Leaders are constantly paraded through the newspapers or televisions and subjected to ridicule. Paul wanted Christians to exhibit a higher ethic of respect for authority. We must remember our roots, the moral decadence from which God rescued us, and the glory for which we are destined. In this way we can live a life of goodness toward all people. The church must avoid entangling itself in arguments, controversies, and divisions over minor issues and opinions. These hinder the appeal of Christ and his message to those outside the faith. People who create disharmony or spread false doctrine must be disciplined so they may come to repentance.

B. COMMENTARY
1. Proper Conduct (3:1–2)
2. The Basis for Right Living (3:3–7)
   a. Natural man (3:3)
   b. The work of salvation (3:4–6)
   c. Salvation's result (3:7–8)
3. Detriments to the Church (3:9–11)
4. Final Remarks (3:12–15)

C. CONCLUSION: THE PRINCE AND THE PAUPER, REVISITED

VIII. ISSUES FOR DISCUSSION

1. Can you think of current issues that might call for your disobedience, while still maintaining submission to government?
2. Does your church have a process for disciplining members? Do you know what it involves?
3. Paul gave a strong warning about divisive people. Examine yourself and your actions to be sure you are not harming the church.
4. List some acts of goodness that you can do, starting with your neighborhood and extending into the greater community.

Introduction to

Philemon

LETTER PROFILE: PHILEMON

- Letter written by Paul, between A.D. 60 and 62, during Paul's first imprisonment in Rome.
- Written to Philemon, a Christian living in Colosse. Probably a man of some wealth, his home was used as a gathering place for the church.
- This is a personal letter concerning Philemon's runaway slave, Onesimus, who had come to Christian faith through Paul.
- Paul's main purpose in writing was to restore Onesimus to Philemon, not as a slave, but as a brother in Christ. He asked Philemon to extend forgiveness and love to this former slave.
- Paul also seemed to hint that he would like Philemon to release Onesimus back to Paul to provide his help in the missionary ministry.
- The letter was probably carried by Tychicus, who was also carrying letters to the Ephesian and Colossian churches.

AUTHOR PROFILE: PAUL

- Jewish-born in Tarsus, near the Lebanese border in modern Turkey.
- Roman citizen.
- Prominent Jewish religious leader, highly educated as a Pharisee.
- Persecuted Christians before his own dramatic conversion in A.D. 35.
- Paul probably never visited Colosse. The churches in this region, including Laodicea and Hierapolis, were probably established by Epaphras.
- Known for his tireless pioneer work to Gentiles.
- Imprisoned by Nero's regime in A.D. 67 in Rome, where he was executed the next year (2 Tim. 4).

GEOGRAPHIC PROFILE: COLOSSE

- Colosse, Philemon's home city, was a small town on the Lycos River in the southwest interior of modern Turkey.
- Though at one time located on an important trade route, at the time of the Roman Empire the roads had changed, and Colosse's significance had declined.
- An independent city, it was known for its fine wool.

Philemon 1–25

Grace and Forgiveness

I. **INTRODUCTION**
Dragnet, A.D. 62

II. **COMMENTARY**
A verse-by-verse explanation of the chapter.

III. **CONCLUSION**
We Are Family
An overview of the principles and applications from the chapter.

IV. **LIFE APPLICATION**
Free to Forgive
Melding the chapter to life.

V. **PRAYER**
Tying the chapter to life with God.

VI. **DEEPER DISCOVERIES**
Historical, geographical, and grammatical enrichment of the commentary.

VII. **TEACHING OUTLINE**
Suggested step-by-step group study of the chapter.

VIII. **ISSUES FOR DISCUSSION**
Zeroing the chapter in on daily life.

"*Every happening, great and small, is a parable whereby God speaks to us, and the art of life is to get the message.*"

Malcolm Muggeridge

Philemon

IN A NUTSHELL

Paul wrote a very personal letter to his friend, Philemon. The purpose of his writing was to ease the way for Onesimus, Philemon's runaway slave, to return to his master. Since fleeing from Philemon, Onesimus came to Christian faith through Paul's ministry. Paul asked Philemon to receive his slave back not as property, but as a Christian brother. It is a letter urging grace and forgiveness, reconciliation and renewed relationship based upon Christ.

Grace and Forgiveness

I. INTRODUCTION

Dragnet, A.D. 62

*B*ack in the 1950s and early 1960s a police drama known as *Dragnet* aired on television. Captain Joe Friday and Sergeant Bill Gannon tracked down criminals in methodical, deadpan precision, sticking to "just the facts." Of course, justice always triumphed, and the lawbreakers were put behind bars. Since then, crime stories have remained a popular television genre. Now we take rides in police cars and witness live-action arrests via video camera. We have nationwide criminal searches for the country's most wanted. The goal is always to catch the thug, the delinquent, and put him in prison. Back around A.D. 62, a crime occurred in Colosse, an unimportant corner of the Roman Empire. It probably would have remained unsolved and historically unknown, except that the fugitive went to Rome, eventually meeting the apostle Paul.

As a runaway slave, Onesimus could have been executed, tortured, or sold again. Whether he sought out Paul for refuge or met him through other acquaintances is unknown. Though Paul was under house arrest at the time, the two men became friends. Through continued fellowship, Onesimus became a Christian, helping Paul in his ministry. Somewhere along the line, Onesimus must have confessed his background, his relationship to his former master, Philemon, and his flight to freedom. Despite Onesimus's new-found life in Christ, Paul knew his past actions needed resolution so his present life could be lived honorably before his Savior.

Paul, therefore, wrote to Philemon. This little book is a very personal letter, surrounded by a true story of crime, faith, confession, grace, and forgiveness. These people lived out a picture of redemption, as Onesimus, guilty of a crime, sought reconciliation with Philemon. It must be assumed that Philemon responded as Paul had hoped, extending forgiveness and, perhaps, freedom to his slave.

Like Onesimus, we stand guilty of crimes before God. Typically, we run away, seeking freedom in all the wrong places, unable to contend with our past or find true freedom in the present. Yet through Christ we can find true release from slavery to sin and imprisonment to our past. As we confess our inability to save ourselves and seek the forgiveness of God, we receive the joyous liberty of reconciliation.

II. COMMENTARY

> **MAIN IDEA:** *From house arrest in Rome, Paul wrote a personal letter to his friend, Philemon, a leader in the Colossian church. He praised Philemon's faith and his love of other Christians. Paul then presented a challenge. Would Philemon take back Onesimus, his runaway slave, who had become a Christian? Paul appealed to Philemon to extend forgiveness and to welcome Onesimus as a brother in Christ.*

A Greeting (vv. 1–3)

> **SUPPORTING IDEA:** *Paul greeted Philemon and the church which met in his home. He offered grace and peace to those in Christ Jesus.*

vv. 1–2. Paul began his letters with his name, followed by a word or phrase describing his position in relation to those to whom he wrote. He referred to himself as a servant (Romans, Philippians, Titus), and, most frequently, an apostle (1 and 2 Corinthians, Galatians, Ephesians, Colossians, 1 and 2 Timothy). In writing to Philemon, however, he chose to call himself **a prisoner of Christ Jesus.**

The reasons are practical and diplomatic. Paul truly was in prison at the time, under house arrest in Rome because of his work as a missionary for the gospel of Christ. But he wrote other letters from prison without referring to himself as a prisoner. In fact, Tychicus—who probably carried this letter to Philemon—also carried a letter for the Colossian church. In the Colossian letter he addressed the church as an apostle. But the message he intended for Philemon required care. Paul set out to restore a runaway slave to his master. Rather than confront Philemon with heavy authority, Paul preferred to entreat him as a fellow sufferer. With this purpose, Paul identified with Onesimus the slave and appealed to Philemon's compassion rather than his sense of duty.

The letter came also from **Timothy our brother.** Evidently, Timothy was in Rome with Paul at this time. He seemed always to help and refresh Paul throughout his travels and difficulties. It is possible that Philemon knew Timothy, and sending his greetings also added to the compelling nature of Paul's letter. Designating Timothy as **our brother** also bound the three men in a relationship of friendship and devotion.

The letter was written **to Philemon our dear friend and fellow worker.** We know nothing more of Philemon than what this letter contains. From it we can deduce that Philemon was moderately wealthy. He owned a home large enough to accommodate the congregation of Colossian believers. Paul and Timothy considered him a dear friend, a man expressive of Christ's love, committed to the missionary work, and devoted to other believers. Paul recognized in Philemon a dedication to the cause of Christ, a colaborer in ministry.

Paul also greeted **Apphia our sister.** Most scholars believe Apphia was Philemon's wife. Beyond that, she also was a Christian; she cared for the Christian fellowship, extended hospitality and love, and responded to God's mission to extend the gospel. In addition, Paul also recognized that Onesimus would return not only to Philemon, but to the household, including Apphia. She also needed to understand the necessity of Christian forgiveness and love.

Paul mentioned one more name: **Archippus our fellow soldier.** Archippus was probably Philemon's son. Paul described him as a soldier, a fighter in the cause of Christ, one who endures difficulty. Many interpreters believe Archippus served at the church in Laodicea which was close to the city of Colosse. Both he and the church are mentioned in Colossians 4, with Paul asking the church to remind Archippus to "complete the work you have received in the Lord" (Col. 4:17). Philemon's son may have been discouraged. So Paul, identifying Archippus as a fellow soldier, chose to encourage him as one who shared the difficult work of Christian ministry.

Paul also mentioned **the church that meets in your home.** Christians met not in church buildings, but in homes throughout the cities of the Roman Empire. Paul addressed this letter to this group of believers because when Onesimus returned, they would need to welcome him into their fellowship. They must receive this slave as a Christian brother.

v. 3. Paul extended to this family and this church the blessing of **grace** and **peace from God our Father and the Lord Jesus Christ.** Paul wanted these believers to experience the fullness of God's good gifts, his undeserved but rich favor toward those who trust in Christ.

Paul began to build his case for Onesimus by reminding all these Christians that no one deserves the forgiveness and grace of God. No person gains merit before the Lord. Everyone stands equally sinful and equally guilty.

Peace exists on two fronts—reconciliation and personal tranquility of soul. Paul wanted Philemon to recall that peace with God results from a judicial settlement purchased by God through Christ's death. Paul later asked Philemon to reconcile with his former slave, to settle all accounts. In this way, they would experience the other side of peace, inner quietness which flows from righteousness.

🅑 Gratitude for Philemon and His Family (vv. 4–7)

> **SUPPORTING IDEA:** *Paul expressed his love and appreciation for Philemon's faith in God and his demonstration of love toward other believers. He then offered a prayer for Philemon to develop a richer relationship to Christ and a more expansive ministry. Paul included personal thanks for the joy that Philemon brought to him.*

vv. 4–5. Paul told Philemon, **I always thank my God as I remember you in my prayers.** Prayer with God was Paul's place of utter abandon, a place where he could fully express his anxieties, concerns, struggles, hopes, and joys. Prayer provided the stable center as well as the surrounding calm in every relationship and every endeavor.

Paul did not suddenly put Philemon on his prayer list because he was sending Onesimus back. For Paul it was the relationship, not simply the occasion, which determined his prayers. Writing to Philemon elicited an expression of the thanks he continually felt toward God because of this Christian brother.

Paul mentioned two sterling qualities in Philemon: **faith in the Lord Jesus** and **love for all the saints.** Philemon's salvation rested in Jesus Christ and the cross. But his faith was continuous. Philemon demonstrated an abiding faith in Christ through his life. His trust was placed firmly in Christ.

This faith resulted in love—*agape*—self-sacrificing love which sought the welfare and benefit of others. Philemon's conduct was marked by giving, kindness, and generosity. Philemon's love was inclusive: **for all the saints.** In commending him for this indiscriminate love, Paul continued to lay the groundwork for Onesimus's inclusion in Philemon's household and in the Colossian church. Onesimus would return not as a slave, but as a saint, a person deserving of the same affection as all the other believers.

v. 6. Paul then divulged the content of his prayer for Philemon: **that you may be active in sharing your faith.** This does not infer that Philemon was negligent. Rather, it asserts a continual desire by Paul that all believers would grow more and more in their spiritual life and understanding. Paul prayed that Philemon's expressions of faith would continue unbroken, that he would integrate life and belief. Christian faith should not exist as a private possession, passive and assumed. Instead, it must energetically manifest itself through daily living and human relationships.

In this way, Philemon would draw on the strength and wisdom of Christ. He would have **a full understanding of every good thing we have in Christ.** Those who neglect Christian development, who never do good acts on behalf of others, who never exercise their spiritual muscles will experience spiritual atrophy. They waste away, incapable of knowing the riches of Christ or the power of his Spirit through life's daily encounters. A full understanding of

God's goodness refers not to book knowledge but to experiential comprehension. It happens when, appropriating God's truth into life, we see its good results and power. This deepens our faith and trust.

Paul's prayer was general—one that all believers can pray on behalf of one another. Even so, Paul's concern for Onesimus shadows these lines. He understood that theology is empty unless it is connected to real life. We can speak the Christian jargon and go through the motions of worship, but true faith must intersect life's choices. Philemon needed to recognize that true faith is constant, uninterrupted, and unbiased in its application. What he had shown toward the Colossian fellowship must now encompass a runaway slave turned Christian.

v. 7. Although he was a thousand miles away in Rome, confined to house arrest, Paul's friends kept him informed of the various churches and their members. Epaphras, who began the Colossian church, was with Paul in Rome "wrestling in prayer" for the Christians of Colosse and "working hard" for them (Col. 4:12–13). Undoubtedly, Epaphras told Paul about Philemon and his love for the fellowship. The news of a believer engaged in Christian love and works of service brought Paul **great joy and encouragement.**

Philemon's goodness and love **refreshed the hearts of the saints.** Other believers were encouraged in their faith, compelled to progress in love and goodness because of Philemon's life and example.

Paul's acknowledgment of Philemon's devotion to Christian brotherhood, as well as his deepening love and expressions of faith, would undoubtedly stir within Philemon's heart a receptiveness to Onesimus's return. Paul did not give hollow praise or flattery to Philemon. His compliments were declarations of true gratefulness and joy. But Paul did lay a solid and compelling groundwork for what he was about to ask of Philemon.

Ⓒ Paul's Great Request (vv. 8–21)

> **SUPPORTING IDEA:** Having affirmed the strength of Philemon's Christian love and devotion for all believers and the personal joy he brought Paul, the apostle asked Philemon to receive back his runaway slave. Paul wanted Philemon not only to permit his return but to welcome him as a fellow-believer, a brother in Christ, extending to him the same love, goodness, and friendship that all Christians deserve.

vv. 8–9. This verse begins with **Therefore,** connecting it to the preceding verses in which Paul expressed great joy because of Philemon's love and encouragement of the believers. Philemon's past and continuing faithfulness and love are connected to Paul's coming request.

Paul knew, as Philemon did, that Paul could have approached the whole situation from a position of authority, appealing to his apostleship: **I could be**

bold and order you to do what you ought to do. Paul had every right to issue commands in situations requiring the enactment of Christian ethic. In spiritual battle, as in all warfare, authority lines must be strong, respected, and quickly obeyed. He had often used this prerogative in disciplining churches and individuals. He knew that Onesimus's return and reception hinged on Christian principle, not merely personal desire; that it would serve as a precedent for Christian community, love, and forgiveness. Philemon's refusal would be a rejection of Christian morality and a dismissal of Christian truth.

Even so, Paul chose a different course in this situation. He appealed to Philemon **on the basis of love**. He did not refer to Philemon's love for Paul but to his love of God and God's people. Paul appealed to *agape* love, that force and power from God which sets aside personal rights and safeguards, acting instead for Christ's glory and the welfare of others. Paul always pointed people to Christ's higher ethic, a morality which superseded the morality of culture. A respectable person might well respond to duty, carrying out his obligation, but the higher standard of Christian virtue springs from love.

Paul made one more appeal—for Philemon to remember that he was **an old man and now also a prisoner of Christ Jesus.** We live in a far too cynical age if we take Paul's plea as manipulation or an emotional dig to elicit guilt in Philemon. It is none of that. Paul's reference to his age and predicament issued from deep emotion, but it was heartfelt and not deceptive. Paul opened his heart. He was old, perhaps tired, and he felt the loneliness and isolation of prison; he appealed to Philemon's sensitivities, friend to friend.

v. 10. Paul then put forth the object of his concern: **I appeal to you for my son Onesimus, who became my son while I was in chains.** We cannot imagine Philemon's response in seeing that name in the letter. Suddenly the face of Onesimus came to his mind and with it the slave's treachery, even theft. Yet, Paul called him **my son.**

However the two met, in time Onesimus responded to Paul's friendship and teaching about the crucified and risen Christ; Onesimus became a Christian. From that moment, everything changed between them. Paul understood the creative act of God in salvation, the newness which infiltrates every act and relationship. He believed in the goodness of God's grace where "there is neither Jew nor Greek, slave nor free, male nor female, for [we] are all one in Christ Jesus" (Gal. 3:28).

In response, Paul lifted the slave into the intimacy of kinship, just as Christ lifts the sinner into the loving fellowship and inheritance of his family. Paul demonstrated true Christian faith and love. He did not pity the slave or patronize him through condescending kindness. He embraced the captive and identified with him, just as Christ did in his incarnation and saving death.

v. 11. Paul was not ignorant of Onesimus's history—his lawlessness, his lowly position, his poverty. Paul indulged in a little word play as he acknowledged to Philemon, **Formerly he was useless to you.** The name Onesimus actually means "helpful" or "profitable." Paul admitted in his letter what Philemon was probably thinking: Onesimus is worthless—look at his past.

But Paul asserted that a transformation had already occurred. Admittedly, this slave used to be "useless," but he had changed—**he has become useful both to you and to me.** Now his name reflected his character.

Paul never dismissed Onesimus's former conduct (the letter proves this), but he also did not restrict Onesimus to his past. Based on Onesimus's confession of faith, Paul freed him from the constriction of categories and judgments. Paul welcomed him into the joy and camaraderie of his ministry in Rome. The slave had proved beneficial both personally and in the work of Christ. Paul looked ahead and stated with confidence that, due to his spiritual rebirth, Onesimus would prove equally helpful to Philemon.

Perhaps Paul recalled his own conversion when he was smitten by Christ's glory, then for three days sat in a little house on Straight Street in Damascus. Blind, unable to eat, and suspect because of his past, Paul was visited by Ananias, a Christian, who placed his hands on Paul and called him "brother" (Acts 9:17). As the disciples in Damascus accepted him into their fellowship and as Paul demonstrated the transformation that Christ had accomplished, Paul was also released from his past into the freedom of God's service.

vv. 12–13. Fresh beginnings come through confession, repentance, change, and right choices. Onesimus had proved himself in every respect, joining in ministry with Paul while in Rome. But the evidence of his transformation did not erase former obligations and relationships.

Paul and Onesimus must have talked long into the night about Onesimus's responsibilities and his role within society as a Christian slave. Paul had written often about submission to authority, and they had probably discussed God's view of work, goodness, obedience, and personal worth. Both apostle and slave agreed: Onesimus must fulfill his duty, however difficult, and return to his master. Unlike the common perception that Christianity is an escape from life's difficulties, true faith confronts the harsh realities of this world. Onesimus's faith led to action as he submitted to the necessity of Christian responsibility, returning willingly to his master. This strained the emotions of both men. Paul wrote, **I am sending him—who is my very heart—back to you.**

Onesimus had not only proved a benefit to ministry, but he had become a personal friend, a companion who touched the heart and affections of Paul. Sending Onesimus back was no stoic response to duty; it was a heart-wrenching affair. Paul felt he was tearing his own heart out, as though a piece of himself would be gone once Onesimus departed. In fact, he admitted, **I would have liked to keep him with me.**

Paul stood between these two men, both friends and brothers in Christ. Onesimus had become an invaluable friend and helper; Philemon was a loving friend and faithful minister to the church. Paul assessed the hearts of both and found them the same—devoted friends and servants of Christ. So Paul mused to Philemon that, if Onesimus should stay in Rome, he **could take your place in helping me while I am in chains for the gospel.**

It is unclear whether Paul referred to some obligation that Philemon owed him (hinted at in v. 19), or whether he recognized a similar giving spirit in both men. But Paul was certain that if Philemon had been in Rome, he would have demonstrated the same faith and love for which he was known in Colosse.

v. 14. Despite Paul's longings, he **did not want to do anything without [Philemon's] consent.** Though Onesimus and Philemon were brothers in Christ, Paul acknowledged the social situation in which Onesimus belonged to Philemon as a slave. That relationship, as yet, had not changed.

Slavery mocks Christian compassion and brotherhood; it assaults the biblical principle of equity before God. Through forced subjection and inhumane practices, slavery tramples on God's creation: "He who oppresses the poor shows contempt for their Maker" (Prov. 14:31). But rather than attacking social structures and relationships, Christianity works within the human conscience. In this way, a more thorough and lasting change occurs. When Christian ethics and cultural practices conflict, the Christian response is reformation of the heart and mind rather than revolution over social institutions.

Tychicus carried another letter besides this one to Philemon. This letter was addressed to the church of Colosse. In it, Paul wrote to slaves (was he thinking of Onesimus?): "Slaves, obey your earthly masters in everything; and do it, not only when their eye is on you and to win their favor, but with sincerity of heart and reverence for the Lord . . . since you know that you will receive an inheritance from the Lord as a reward. It is the Lord Christ you are serving" (Col. 3:22–24). He then turned to slave owners (was he thinking of Philemon?) and wrote, "Masters, provide your slaves with what is right and fair, because you know that you also have a Master in heaven" (Col. 4:1).

When the hearts of people become captured by truth and compassion, social evils disappear. In our own day, abortion, pornography, abuse, prostitution, and unfair labor practices will diminish only when people uphold the value and preciousness of life, when they agree with God that each person reflects God's glory and deserves our mercy and grace, brother to brother.

It was this matter of the heart that Paul did not want to violate. Rather than presume upon Philemon's friendship, he returned the slave **so that any** favor Philemon extended would **be spontaneous and not forced.** Paul refused manipulation or false guilt—both common means of achieving our own ends. If Philemon returned Onesimus to Rome, he must do so from a generous spirit. So Paul released both men to act according to conscience, prayerful and expectant that they would respond according to God's truth and goodness.

vv. 15–16. Paul then offered something for Philemon to think about: **Perhaps the reason he was separated from you for a little while was that you might have him back for good**—*no longer as a slave, but better than a slave, as a dear brother* (emphasis added). God's sovereign grace works through all human affairs.

The lawless acts of Onesimus were used of God to bring about his salvation and the maturity of Philemon, just as the natural viciousness of the Assyrians in the Old Testament was used of God to exact his punishment and accomplish his will. The treachery of Joseph's brothers was refashioned by God's providence: "You intended to harm me, but God intended it for good to accomplish what is now being done, the saving of many lives" (Gen. 50:20). The treachery of Onesimus was taken by the regenerative hand of God and shaped into blessing—for Onesimus, Philemon, Paul, and the countless numbers who benefited from their ministries.

Onesimus may have run away, but God's grace ran with him; Philemon may have lost a possession, but God's grace further enriched him, proving "that in all things God works for the good of those who love him, who have been called according to his purpose" (Rom. 8:28).

Once again Paul expressed his appreciation and love for Onesimus: **He is very dear to me.** But however affectionately Paul viewed Onesimus, this slave was **dearer to [Philemon], both as a man and as a brother in the Lord.**

The word *dear* derives from *agape,* and it can be translated as "beloved." It is the same word used of the love that the Father has for Jesus, the Son. Paul emphasized to Philemon the possible relationship that could exist between these two men. Even if Onesimus remained a slave, nothing would ever be the same. Onesimus was changed, and Philemon would find him valuable as a man, as a worker, as a friend—but also as a spiritual brother, a man with whom he found the deeper communion of soul to soul before the Lord.

v. 17. Throughout his letter, Paul had united Philemon and Onesimus through the brotherhood of Christ, through the commonality of their friendship with Paul, and also through their mutual passion for ministry. Now he joined both men to himself: **if you consider me a partner, welcome him as you would welcome me.**

Partners form a bond that survives distance and difficulty. This partnership deepens through service and flourishes amid shared goals, ideas, and purposes. Paul put forth the strong but tender plea for Philemon to act on the basis of kingdom partnership.

Those who partner for God's glory will develop a camaraderie in which personal identity rests upon identification with Jesus Christ. Few people experience this closeness. Yet Paul appealed to it. In essence, he told Philemon, "If we are joined in Christ and in ministry, then we will respond the same way."

Paul then told Philemon to **welcome him as you would welcome me.** There can be no difference between the apostle and the slave, between Paul and Onesimus, for both belong to Christ. Jesus said, "I tell you the truth, whatever you did for one of the least of these brothers of mine, you did for me" (Matt. 25:40). The Father accepts us as he accepts the Son, because we are partnered with Christ through faith,

vv. 18–19. Love, brotherhood, and forgiveness sound very nice, but their implications often cause these ideals to disintegrate under the pressure of practical application. But Paul's identification with Onesimus was not theoretical. Nor did he intend to minimize Onesimus's past wrongs with a wave of the hand and a glib statement, "Treat him as you would treat me." Paul acknowledged Onesimus's theft—the debt he owed Philemon: **If he has done you any wrong or owes you anything.**

Paul went on to say, **Charge it to me.** Paul did not neglect obligations and relationships. Instead, he worked to rectify problems and resolve difficulties. Paul must have known the full story. Onesimus would have confided and confessed to Paul during the course of their friendship and work. The sin confessed, Paul assumed the debt.

Pictures of Christ's redemption present themselves in the ordinary occurrences of life. Here Paul acted the Christ-figure, identifying with the accused so strongly that his debt became his own. But, like all of us before God, Onesimus cannot pay his debt. So Paul accepted it as his own—just as Christ did for all humankind upon the cross.

Paul wanted Philemon to understand that he was not throwing out clichés or flowery phrases. He meant what he wrote. To prove it, he wrote, **I, Paul, am writing this with my own hand.** Then, as an exclamation—**I will pay it back.**

Even though Paul intended to repay Philemon whatever Onesimus owed him, the apostle wanted his friend to understand the true nature of indebtedness and forgiveness. He wanted Philemon to look beyond the specific case to the broader principle. Like the background in a painting, Jesus' parable of the ungrateful steward illuminates Paul's words to Philemon. In the parable, a servant who was granted forgiveness for an enormous debt refused to release others from smaller debts. In this way he treated his own master's mercy with contempt. Paul told Philemon, "I will pay back Onesimus's debt," but then added the words: **you owe me your very self.**

Philemon had the right, as slave master, to have Onesimus flogged, imprisoned, even executed. But Paul did not dabble in rights; he reached for divine grace. He wanted Philemon to recall the great debt that Christ paid on his behalf and the new life to which Paul had introduced him when Philemon trusted the Savior. "Onesimus may owe you a lot," Paul was saying, "but it cannot compare to what you owe me—your very self." All that God offers, the eternal riches of the heavens, fullness of life at this moment—all these came to Philemon because Paul had faithfully preached the gospel.

v. 20. Though the return of Onesimus to Philemon is the heart of the letter, that object was not Paul's sole intent. Around his compassionate request he attended to Philemon's needs, expressing gratitude for his family, his good reputation and service to Christ, and his love and encouragement of the believers. Paul appealed to him once more as brother to brother: **I do wish, brother, that I may have some benefit from you in the Lord.** Paul may have been using another play on words. The word *benefit* is a derivative of *Onesimus.*

We do not know the specific nature of this benefit, though perhaps it referred to this new request: **refresh my heart in Christ.** Paul did not want Philemon to obey "just because Paul said so." He desired that Philemon follow through based on all Paul had written—understanding the full implications of God's grace within the community of believers, their partnership in Christ's kingdom, and the transformation that Onesimus had experienced. If Onesimus was welcomed back as a Christian brother, Paul would find refreshment. Just as the Colossian believers experienced Philemon's refreshment through his life and encouragement, Paul would experience relief by Philemon's act of love and faith.

v. 21. Paul did not waste time with wishful thinking but wrote expectantly: **Confident of your obedience . . . knowing that you will do even more than I ask.** He knew Philemon, his character and love for Christ, and Paul felt justified in anticipating Onesimus's warm welcome by this Christian brother and the church that met in his home. All of us have built a reputation for ourselves based on our patterns of action. Paul's confidence speaks a great deal of Philemon's reputation for love, reasonableness, obedience, and generosity.

Paul also expressed the conviction that Philemon would go beyond his basic request to take Onesimus back as a Christian brother. This may be a veiled request, or at least a subtle hope, that Philemon would free Onesimus. Still, Paul was not out to abolish slavery as an institution (his letter to the Colossian church has clear instructions for slave submission). If he had commanded Philemon to release Onesimus, this would have spread through all the churches as apostolic command, causing social upheaval and a disintegration of the core gospel message. Rather than command, Paul appealed to the heart of Philemon.

D Closing Remarks (vv. 22–25)

SUPPORTING IDEA: *Paul's letter was intensely personal, going beyond the request for Philemon to welcome Onesimus back. He expressed love for Philemon and appreciation for the joy he brought the apostle through his devoted life. Then he closed his letter by encouraging Philemon and his household, and perhaps the entire church, that their prayers on his behalf might result in his release from prison. He also sent greetings from other friends who were with him in Rome.*

v. 22. Paul had one final request: **Prepare a guest room for me.** The word he used for "guest room" is the same word used in Acts 28:30 for "rented house." We may suppose that Paul wanted Philemon to locate a place for him to stay within Colosse which would allow him to receive visitors, to teach, and to minister to the church of that city. Once again, Paul's humility and tact are evident. Rather than commanding Philemon to get one of his own rooms ready, presuming upon his hospitality, he asked for a rented room to be located. Philemon remained free to follow the request or to go beyond it and offer the apostle lodging in his own home.

Paul wrote all this while under house arrest in Rome. But through this request for a room, he demonstrated confidence in God's goodness and grace as well as in the effectual power of prayer. Paul outlined plans to visit Colosse because **I hope to be restored to you in answer to your prayers.**

To Paul, prayer was not ritual performance of religious duty. He experienced prayer as a dialogue between man and God in which the aspirations and longings of the human heart were exposed to the divine will and purpose. He placed confidence in God's design to work through this channel of summons, in which God listened to his children, then acted on their behalf. Paul's hope for release came not because of political maneuverings in Rome, but because his friends a thousand miles away were praying.

In addition, he viewed his release not as personal victory, but as beneficial for God's people. His restoration to the believers in Colosse was for their good, their further spiritual development. In all issues of life, Paul exhibited that same quality of Christ which sought not his own advantage, but that of the Father. Paul's life in Christ was consumed by extending God's kingdom and ministering to God's people.

It should also be noted that the "you" in this verse is plural in the Greek, whereas the "you" in the preceding verses is singular. Up until this point, Paul directed his comments to Philemon, but now he included everyone in his household and, we may presume, the Colossian church. Paul's desire to be **restored to you** meant everyone in that group of believers, and we may be sure he envisioned Onesimus among them.

vv. 23–24. Paul then turned to others with him in Rome whom Philemon and those in Colosse would know.

Epaphras, my fellow prisoner in Christ Jesus, sends you greetings. Epaphras founded the Colossian church and was well-known by Philemon and all who gathered in his home. He had probably traveled to Rome seeking Paul's counsel regarding difficulties at Colosse. Paul's Colossian letter sheds light on the problems with which Epaphras struggled—the theology of Christ's supremacy, the battle against legalism, proper conduct for believers, and correct relationships among households and Christians.

Epaphras struggled in prayer for this church and its people, longing that they would "stand firm in all the will of God, mature and fully assured" (Col. 4:12). Paul also described him as **my fellow prisoner in Christ Jesus.** Though Paul called him a "fellow prisoner" in this instance, in the Colossian letter he referred to him as "a servant of Christ Jesus" (Col. 4:12) and called Aristarchus "my fellow prisoner" (Col. 4:10). This difference has led scholars to believe that both Epaphras and Aristarchus underwent voluntary house arrest, living under the same conditions and restrictions as Paul, in order to minister to him. This devotion reveals the greatness of their dedication to Christ and the deep friendship that the gospel inspired.

Greetings came also from **Mark, Aristarchus, Demas and Luke,** Paul's **fellow workers.**

Mark was involved in the early church at Jerusalem, and he was acquainted with Peter and other disciples. Because of these friendships, Mark carried the distinction of writing the first of the Gospel accounts of Jesus' life and ministry. He met Paul and Barnabas while in Jerusalem and accompanied them into Judea to deliver a gift of help to the churches there (Acts 11:30; 12:25). He also traveled with them on Paul's first missionary journey, although he returned home without completing the trip. This caused a serious disagreement between Paul and Barnabas. For some time Paul considered Mark unreliable, but eventually the hurt was resolved and they again joined in ministry, as noted here. In time, Mark became invaluable to Paul. At the end of his life the apostle wrote Timothy of his eagerness to have Mark with him in Rome, "because he is helpful to me in my ministry" (2 Tim. 4:11).

We know less of **Aristarchus,** although Paul mentioned him as a "fellow prisoner in Christ Jesus" (Col. 4:10) and here as a "fellow worker." These facts alone attest to Aristarchus's devotion to the gospel and its minister, Paul. He is also mentioned in Acts 19. When the Ephesians rioted because they feared Christianity threatened their worship of Artemis, they seized "Gaius and Aristarchus, Paul's traveling companions from Macedonia, and rushed as one man into the theater" (Acts 19:29). We may presume that Aristarchus's life was in danger during this violent and irrational reaction of the mob. For hours these men were held in the public theater while the mob shouted and threatened. Aristarchus also accompanied Paul to Jerusalem and Rome.

The life of **Demas** is tinged with sadness. Paul counted him a "fellow worker." He was also mentioned in the Colossian letter. No doubt he served with strength and dedication. But something happened. At the end of Paul's life, perhaps when the excitement had faded from the ministry and the apostle awaited the executioner's sword, Demas deserted "because he loved this world" (2 Tim. 4:10).

We cannot construct details from this phrase or decipher precisely what Demas did. Whether the pull of security or the temptation for safety caused Demas's defection can only be surmised. We do find certainty in this—Demas began well, and his life progressed admirably in the cause of Christ and in service toward his Lord and his church. But a poor conclusion in life can negate a good beginning and a commendable advance. We can nullify all progress if we give up and retreat at the end.

Luke rounded out Paul's list of fellow workers. Trained as a physician, he was a prolific writer and tireless worker. He wrote one of the Gospel accounts of Christ's life and traced the history of the apostles' acts and the growth of the early church. He traveled with Paul from place to place, laboring for Christ and his church and supporting the apostle. When everyone else deserted Paul during his last Roman trials, Paul wrote, "Only Luke is with me" (2 Tim. 4:11). A dear friend of reliable and trustworthy character, Luke stayed with Paul to the bitter end when Nero's diabolical judgment hung over his head. And he was probably there when the sword fell at that lonely spot along the Ostian Way.

v. 25. Paul closed as he began, bringing the reader full circle. He prayed for God's grace and peace upon Philemon and his household at the start (v. 3), and he concludeed with the same prayer for all those gathered in this Colossian house: **The grace of the Lord Jesus Christ be with your spirit.** Jesus Christ the Lord is the source of all our blessings. From God flows the unending goodness of his kindness toward us.

MAIN IDEA REVIEW: *From house arrest in Rome, Paul wrote a personal letter to his friend, Philemon, a leader in the Colossian church. He praised Philemon's faith and his love of other Christians. Paul then presented a challenge. Would Philemon take back Onesimus, his runaway slave, who had become a Christian? Paul appealed to Philemon to extend forgiveness and to welcome Onesimus as a brother in Christ.*

III. CONCLUSION

We Are Family

During one of their greatest years, the Pittsburgh Pirates built their baseball team around the theme, "We Are Family." While they had some superstars and well-known players, the attraction to most who watched them play was their unity. They treated one another with honor and kindness. No one belittled anyone else, mistakes were forgiven, praise was liberal. They knew that success depended on the entire team and that teamwork depended on individual respect.

Unfortunately, such camaraderie is notable by its absence. Athletes today have enormous personal egos and bank accounts to match. But occasionally a team establishes relationships that bring them together in such a way that the team becomes more than the sum of its parts.

The church also retains the noble and beautiful model of family life. Philemon is a book that demonstrates these relationships in the practical matters of everyday living as well as in the greater principles of Christian ethic. In this personal letter, Paul made a request for Philemon to receive his runaway slave, Onesimus, back into his household. But Paul drew from the Christian code of righteousness—reconciliation, forgiveness, love, trust, and service. He tied these together with the strong bonds of Christian brotherhood that we obtain through Jesus Christ.

PRINCIPLES

- All Christians are to model faith in Christ and love for fellow Christians.
- Although certain situations require leaders to exercise authority, a great deal can be accomplished through the appeal of love and expressions of confidence.
- God views all believers equally and without partiality.
- Forgiveness is a hallmark of Christian faith.
- All lasting changes and reformations result from inner transformation.
- In dealing with his people, God's sovereign authority converts bad situations into good situations.
- Christ has paid our debt in full, freeing us to serve in his kingdom with love, grace, and gratitude.
- Christian faith requires an enduring obedience from beginning to end.

APPLICATIONS

- Believers should assess their lives, determining what their reputation is among Christians as well as unbelievers.
- Each person should try to build a life of good repute, serving others from love, honesty, and God's grace.
- We should work for change by appealing to love, bringing out the nobility and goodness in others.
- Jesus called peacemakers "blessed." All Christians should help in efforts of reconciliation, working to restore broken relationships.
- Understanding God's authority over all creation, Christians should live above the swirl of circumstances.
- We should commit to a life of enduring trust, serving and obeying Christ Jesus our Lord.

IV. LIFE APPLICATION

Free to Forgive

Forgiveness is the center around which our faith revolves. But when we are the ones who need to forgive, forgiveness becomes more difficult. To believe that God forgave me, pardoning me in a broad theological sweep with billions of others, seems more reasonable than my granting forgiveness to someone who has wronged me.

In Colossians 3:13, Paul wrote, "Bear with each other and forgive whatever grievances you may have against one another. Forgive as the Lord forgave you." Forgiveness is intensely personal. It affects the way I relate to God and interact with others. We can begin to understand forgiveness by looking at what it is not.

Forgiveness is not a cover-up, or a game of "let's pretend." It is not a performance in which we shrug our shoulders and pretend the offense was "no big deal."

Forgiveness is not teeth-gritting determination to keep going, no matter what. Sheer willpower to overlook or minimize an offense will never achieve forgiveness. Such an approach often creates bitterness instead, especially when the other person fails to respond as desired.

Forgiveness is not passive resolve to wait the problem out, hoping that time will heal all wounds. Forgiveness is not excusing people who offend our personal preferences or who annoy us by their selfish choices. These may test our tolerance levels, but not our willingness to forgive. While tolerance makes allowances, forgiveness releases a legitimate debt.

When Christ tells us to forgive, he is speaking to those who are most vulnerable—those who have been violated. He knows that he speaks to people whose trust has been betrayed or who face humiliation. His words are intended for those whose character has been unjustly damaged, for the one whose life has been marred by the sin of others. And that is the difficulty of forgiveness: the offended person is affected by someone else's moral failure. Quite plainly, it is not fair. Yet, in the midst of pain and disillusionment, Christ says, "Forgive."

We must understand that God is not minimizing the violation that maims lives. He is not questioning the authenticity of the offense and its harm. But at the point of trampled innocence, we are still told to forgive. We are told to release a legitimate debt. When we forgive, we guarantee that the offending person's violation will not be held against him.

Jesus did not qualify his statement. Whatever the failed obligation, whatever the violation, from first to last he says, "Forgive." And, to make his point clear and to silence all exceptions, he added, "as I have forgiven you."

Here there can be no argument. There is no debt of love and honor greater than what we owe Christ. There is no moral violation more profound than our disobedience to God. Yet, he releases us. We are forgiven. And, as always, he says, "Follow me."

Personal definitions of fairness are set aside. In fact, self is set aside altogether. The focus becomes Christ. However real the offenses or injustices against us, however justified our hurt, we must view it from Calvary. True forgiveness rises from a deep-rooted trust in Jesus Christ and in the values of his kingdom.

V. PRAYER

Lord, help me to release all personal hurts and grievances to your care. May I nail the offenses of others to your cross, just as I have nailed mine there. Guide me along the path of forgiveness, transforming and blessing all my relationships so that I may be useful in your kingdom. Amen.

VI. DEEPER DISCOVERIES

A. The Colossian Church (v. 2)

Philemon, his family, and Epaphras were members of the Colossian church. Tychicus and Onesimus carried several letters from Paul—one to Philemon, and others to the churches in Colosse and Laodicea.

Like so many churches, the one in Colosse experienced problems. These probably prompted Epaphras to seek Paul in Rome and gain his help and wisdom on various matters.

The believers were becoming confused about the authority and position of angels, supernatural beings, and of Christ himself. The whole cosmos was reconstructed by the false teachers. They advocated a higher wisdom and spiritual knowledge which only the elite understood, leaving many Christians vulnerable to deceptive theology.

Jewish false teachers had probably infiltrated the Christian gatherings, bringing with them legalisms and traditions of no consequence to Christian truth. Regulations, ordinances, adherence to new moon celebrations and other Jewish customs were binding these believers to rules and preventing them from experiencing Christ's freedom. The grace of God was being exchanged for legalistic bondage.

So when Paul wrote to the Colossian church, of which Philemon was a member, he emphasized the supremacy of Christ. He is the "image of the invisible God . . . by him all things were created: things in heaven and on earth, visible and invisible, whether thrones or powers or rulers or authorities; all things were created by him and for him" (Col. 1:15–16). He recounted the grace of God through Jesus: "He has reconciled you by Christ's physical body through death to present you holy in his sight, without blemish and free from accusation—if you continue in your faith, established and firm, not moved from the hope held out in the gospel" (Col. 1:22–23).

Paul also opposed the legalistic burden that the false teachers had placed upon the people. He came down hard on their insistence that God needed to be placated through observing rituals and astrological celebrations. He warned them, "See to it that no one takes you captive through hollow and deceptive philosophy, which depends on human tradition and basic principles of this world rather than on Christ" (Col. 2:8).

Spiritual maturity did not depend on what a person ate or drank, but on the character of Christ modeled in outward behavior, on holy living: "Therefore, as God's chosen people, holy and dearly loved, clothe yourselves with compassion, kindness, humility, gentleness and patience. Bear with each other and forgive whatever grievances you may have against one another. Forgive as the Lord forgave you" (Col. 3:12–13).

Paul then addressed possible disruptions of social etiquette, laying down the principles of Christian relationships: "Wives, submit to your husbands . . . Husbands, love your wives . . . Children, obey your parents . . . Fathers, do not embitter your children . . . Slaves, obey your earthly masters . . . Masters, provide your slaves with what is right and fair" (Col. 3:18–22; 4:1).

B. Onesimus (v. 10)

Regarding the slave, Onesimus, it is possible only to reconstruct what scholars have proposed after much research and conjecture. Onesimus was a slave in the household of Philemon, although his actual duties remain unknown. Because he had easy access to items throughout the house, Onesimus used his job to personal advantage and stole an item or more from his master. Then he fled.

From Colosse he ran west, eventually arriving in the great metropolis of Rome, over one thousand miles from his crime. Eventually he met Paul. Some interpreters believe Onesimus sought the apostle, having heard and perhaps met Paul in Philemon's home. In whatever way it came about, Onesimus became friends with Paul, visiting and talking with him, learning of Christ Jesus and God's grace and forgiveness. Within the confines of the apostle's imprisonment, under the watch of Roman guards, Onesimus was introduced to spiritual freedom and became a Christian.

Most scholars believe the letter of Philemon made it into the canon of Scripture for two reasons. First, because Philemon did exactly as Paul anticipated, doing even more than the apostle asked (Phlm. 21). Onesimus was probably welcomed back into the Colossian church and into Philemon's household not as a slave but as a Christian brother. With the loving and generous character that Philemon had demonstrated before, Onesimus gained personal freedom.

The second reason for this letter's inclusion in the Bible stems from the tradition that Onesimus went on to become bishop of Ephesus. Having demonstrated a zeal for Christ and a tireless devotion to Christian ministry, Onesimus progressed in spiritual maturity to the point of church leadership. During his lifetime the church made an effort to collect and publish Paul's letters for distribution among the believers. Onesimus might have used his influence as a church leader to make sure this letter was included in this collection.

VII. TEACHING OUTLINE

A. INTRODUCTION

1. Lead Story: Dragnet, A.D. 62.

2. Context: Paul wrote a very personal letter to his friend Philemon. He thanked God for this Christian leader in the Colossian church, expressing appreciation for his faith and love toward other Christians. Paul's main purpose in writing the letter was to request that Philemon receive back his runaway slave, Onesimus. Paul had led this slave to faith in Christ. Onesimus then worked tirelessly with Paul on behalf of the gospel. Paul appealed to Philemon's friendship and to the bond of Christian brotherhood. Paul closed with a personal request that Philemon find him a room so that he might visit

when released from prison. He closed the letter by extending greetings from other friends who were with him in Rome.

3. Transition: Paul's letter to Philemon is a model for all believers in approaching sensitive issues. Rather than charging in with commands and authority in delicate situations, it is well to proceed with caution, love, and tenderness. If we desire lasting change to occur, we must remember that truth must penetrate to the heart before it becomes revealed in action. We cannot make our case on personal preferences or emotion alone. Prayer, love, and kindness are essential to the process of reformation.

B. COMMENTARY
1. Greeting (vv. 1–3)
2. Gratitude for Philemon and His Family (vv. 4–7)
3. Paul's Great Request (vv. 8–21)
4. Closing Remarks (vv. 22–25)

C. CONCLUSION: FREE TO FORGIVE

VIII. ISSUES FOR DISCUSSION

1. How do you resolve confrontational situations? Discuss a current problem you are facing and how Paul's model of Christianity could help you.
2. How could you prepare to be a mediator between people in need of reconciliation? Discuss the characteristics and attitudes which Christians should exemplify.
3. As you examine your heart, are there people you need to forgive, regardless of the wrong they have done to you? What steps could you take today, in Christ, toward forgiveness and healing?

Glossary

angel—A messenger from God, either heavenly or human, who delivers God's message of instruction, warning, or hope

Antichrist—Anyone who opposes God or Christ, but especially the evil leader at the end of the age that Christ will defeat at his Second Coming

church—The community of those who believe in and follow Jesus Christ. Used to designate a congregation, a denomination, or all Christians

conversion—God's act of changing a person's life in response to the person's turning to Christ in repentance and faith from some other belief or from no belief

day of the Lord—God's time of decisive intervention in history and the final day of judgment in the end time

deacon—An office in the church that involves ministry and service

discipline—Instruction or training used by God to train his children in righteous living

doctrine—Statements of an individual's or a group's beliefs about the Christian gospel based on the teachings of the Bible

elder—In the New Testament, a leader in the early church

election—God's gracious action in choosing people to follow him and obey his commandments

eternal life—The quality of life that Jesus gives his disciples and unending life with God given to those who believe in Jesus Christ as Savior and Lord

evil—Anyone or anything that opposes the plan of God

faith—Belief in and personal commitment to Jesus Christ for eternal salvation

fall—The result of the first human sin which marred the image of God in humans and created an environment for and a tendency toward sin for all people

fellowship—Shared encouragement and support among Christians

forgiveness—Pardon and release from penalty for wrongdoing; God's delivery from sin's wages for those who repent and express faith in Christ; the Christian act of freeing from guilt and blame those by whom one has suffered wrong

free will—The freedom God gives people to make decisions without the decisions being predetermined; the human freedom to reject God's will or to choose to obey God

Gentiles—People who are not part of God's chosen family at birth and thus can be considered "pagans"

glorification—God's action in the lives of believers, making them able to share the glory and reward of heaven

gospel—The good news of the redeeming work of God through the life, death, and resurrection of Jesus Christ

grace—Undeserved acceptance and love received from another, especially the characteristic attitude of God in providing salvation for sinners

heaven—The eternal dwelling place of God and the redeemed

hell—The place of everlasting punishment for the lost

holy—God's distinguishing characteristic that separates him from all creation; the moral ideal for Christians as they seek to reflect the character of God as known in Christ Jesus

Holy Spirit—The third person of the Trinity; the presence of God promised by Christ and sent to his disciples at Pentecost representing God's active presence in the believer, the church, and the world

Glossary

hope—The assurance that God grants eternal life to those who have trusted Jesus Christ as Lord and Savior

intercession—A prayer presenting one person's needs to another as Christians presenting the needs of others to God or as Christ or the Holy Spirit representing believers before God

Jesus Christ—The eternal Son of God; the Lord and Savior; the second person of the Trinity

joy—The inner attitude of rejoicing in one's salvation regardless of outward circumstances

judgment—God's work at the end time involving condemnation for unbelievers and assignment of rewards for believers

justification—The act or event by which God credits a sinner who has faith as being right with him through the blood of Jesus

kingdom of God—God's sovereign rule in the universe and in the hearts of Christians

koinonia—Greek word for fellowship

law—God's instruction to his people about how to love him and others. When used with the definite article "the," *law* may refer to the Old Testament as a whole but usually to the Pentateuch (Genesis through Deuteronomy)

laying on of hands—Setting apart or consecrating a person to God's service through placing hands on the head of the person being dedicated

Lord's Day—The first day of the week (Sunday) on which most Christians have worshiped since Christ's resurrection on the first day of the week

love—God's essential quality that seeks the best interests of others regardless of the others' actions; love is commanded of believers

mediator—One who seeks to settle disputes between other persons; Jesus as the one who brought together God and believers through his death and resurrection

mercy—A personal characteristic of care for the needs of others. The biblical concept of mercy always involves help to those who are in need or distress

miracle—An act of God beyond human understanding that inspires wonder, displays God's greatness, and leads people to recognize God at work in the world

parousia—Greek word meaning "coming" or "presence" used to refer to Christ's coming, especially the Second Coming

perseverance—The response of enduring even in the face of difficulty. Christians develop this trait by facing and overcoming hardship and adversity

prayer—Communication with God

reconciliation—The bringing together of alienated persons; the saving work of Christ and a ministry given believers

redemption—The act of releasing a captive by the payment of a price. Jesus' death provided our redemption from sin's power and penalty (Heb. 9:12)

repentance—A change of heart and mind resulting in a turning from sin to God that allows conversion and is expressed through faith

resurrection—The raising of Jesus from the dead to eternal life; the raising of believers for eternal life with Christ; the raising of unbelievers to eternal punishment

righteousness—The quality or condition of being in right relationship with God; living out the relationship with God in right relationships with other persons

saints—Those holy or set apart to God; any person in Christ

salvation—Deliverance from trouble or evil; the process by which God redeems his creation, completed through the life, death, and resurrection of his Son Jesus Christ

sanctification—The process in salvation by which God conforms the believer's life and character to the life and character of Jesus Christ through the Holy Spirit

Satan—The personalized evil one who leads forces opposed to God and tempts people

Second Coming—Christ's return in power and glory to consummate his work of redemption *shalom*—Hebrew word for peace and wholeness meaning fullness of life through God-given harmony with God, the world, others, and oneself

sin—Actions by which humans rebel against God, miss his purpose for their life, and surrender to the power of evil rather than to God

trials—Afflictions and hardships permitted in our lives by God to develop stamina and endurance in believers (Jas. 1:2–4)

Trinity—God's revelation of Himself as Father, Son, and Holy Spirit unified as one in the Godhead and yet distinct in person and function

Word of God—The Bible, God's inspired written revelation; God's message in oral form revealed through prophetic or angelic speakers; Jesus Christ, God's eternal Word in human flesh

wrath of God—God's consistent response opposing and punishing sin

Bibliography

1, 2 Thessalonians

Bruce, F. F. *1–2 Thessalonians*. Word Biblical Commentary. Waco, Tex.: Word, 1982.

Hiebert, D. Edmond. *The Thessalonians Epistles: A Call to Readiness—A Commentary.* Chicago: Moody Press, 1971.

Marshall, I Howard. *1 and 2 Thessalonians*. New Century Bible Commentary. Grand Rapids: Wm. B. Eerdmans, 1983.

Martin, D. Michael. *1, 2 Thessalonians*. New American Commentary. Nashville: Broadman & Holman Publishers, 1995.

Morris, Leon. *The First and Second Epistles to the Thessalonians*. New International Commentary on the New Testament, rev. ed. Grand Rapids: Wm. B. Eerdmans, 1991.

Wanamaker, C. A. *Commentary on 1 and 2 Thessalonians*. Grand Rapids: Wm. B. Eerdmans, 1990.

1, 2 Timothy

Griffin, Hayne, and Thomas Lea. *1 and 2 Timothy and Titus*. New American Commentary. Nashville: Broadman & Holman Publishers, 1993.

King, Guy. *A Leader Led: A Devotional Study of 1 Timothy*. London: Marshall, Morgan, and Scott, 1951.

King, Guy. *To My Son: An Expositional Study of 2 Timothy*. London: Marshall, Morgan, and Scott, 1944.

Stott, John R. W. *The Message of 2 Timothy*. The Bible Speaks Today. Grand Rapids: Zondervan, 1973.

The Pastoral Epistles and Philemon

Guthrie, Donald. *The Pastoral Epistles*. Tyndale New Testament Commentaries. Grand Rapids: Wm. B. Eerdmans, 1957.

Kelly, J. N. D. *The Pastoral Epistles*. Grand Rapids: Baker Book House, 1981.

Lenski, R. C. H. *The Interpretation of St. Paul's Epistles to the Colossians, to the Thessalonians, to Timothy, to Titus, and to Philemon*. Minneapolis: Augsburg, 1961.